STREET

Co Tyrone
Co Fermanagh

Cookstown, Dungannon, Enniskillen, Omagh, Strabane

www.philips-maps.co.uk

First published 2006 by

Philip's, a division of
Octopus Publishing Group Ltd
www.octopusbooks.co.uk
2-4 Heron Quays, London E14 4JP
An Hachette Livre UK Company
www.hachettelivre.co.uk

First edition 2006
Second impression with revisions 2008
TYRAB

ISBN 978-0-540-09495-0 (spiral)

© Philip's 2008

is a registered Trade Mark of the Department of Finance and Personnel

This material is based upon Crown Copyright and is reproduced with the permission of Land and Property Services under delegated authority from the Controller of Her Majesty's Stationery Office, © Crown copyright and database rights Licence No 100, 370

© Crown copyright and database rights 2008.

Includes Ordnance Survey of Ireland data reproduced by permission of OSi. Unauthorised reproduction infringes Ordnance Survey Ireland and Government of Ireland Copyright.
© Ordnance Survey Ireland 2005

Contents

III   **Key to map symbols**

IV   **Key to map pages**

VI   **Route planning**

VIII   **Administrative and Postcode boundaries**

1   **Street maps** at 1¾ inches to 1 mile

134   **Street maps** at 3½ inches to 1 mile

139   **Index** of towns, villages, townlands, streets, hospitals, industrial estates, railway stations, schools, shopping centres, universities and places of interest

Digital Data

The exceptionally high-quality mapping found in this atlas is available as digital data in TIFF format, which is easily convertible to other bitmapped (raster) image formats.

The index is also available in digital form as a standard database table. It contains all the details found in the printed index together with the Irish Grid reference for the map square in which each entry is named.

For further information and to discuss your requirements, please contact victoria.dawbarn@philips-maps.co.uk

Key to map symbols

III

Motorway with junction number

Primary route – dual/single carriageway

A road – dual/single carriageway

B road – dual/single carriageway

Minor road – dual/single carriageway

Other minor road – dual/single carriageway

Road under construction

Tunnel, covered road

Track, private road or narrow road in urban area

Gate or obstruction to traffic (restrictions may not apply at all times or to all vehicles)

Path, or track

Pedestrianised area

BT23 Postcode boundaries

International boundary

County and county borough boundaries

Railway, tunnel, railway under construction

Miniature railway

Lisburn Railway station

Private railway station

Bus, coach station

Ambulance station

Coastguard station

Fire station

Police station

Accident and Emergency entrance to hospital

H Hospital

+ Place of worship

i Information Centre (open all year)

Shopping Centre

P Parking

PO Post Office

Camping site

Caravan site

Golf course

Picnic site

Prim Sch Important buildings, schools, colleges, universities and hospitals

Built up area

Woods

River Bann Tidal water, water name

Non-tidal water – lake, river, canal or stream

Lock, weir, tunnel

Church Antiquity

51 Adjoining page indicators and overlap bands

136 The colour of the arrow and the band indicates the scale of the adjoining or overlapping page (see scales below)

Acad	Academy	Ct	Law Court	Resr	Reservoir
Cemy	Cemetery	L Ctr	Leisure Centre	Ret Pk	Retail Park
C Ctr	Civic Centre	LC	Level Crossing	Sch	School
CH	Club House	Liby	Library	Sh Ctr	Shopping Centre
Coll	College	Mkt	Market	TH	Town Hall/House
Crem	Crematorium	Meml	Memorial	Trad Est	Trading Estate
CC	Cricket Club	Mon	Monument	Univ	University
Ent	Enterprise	Mus	Museum	W Twr	Water Tower
Ex H	Exhibition Hall	Obsy	Observatory	Wks	Works
Ind Est	Industrial Estate	Pal	Royal Palace	YC	Yacht Club
IRB Sta	Inshore Rescue Boat Station	PH	Public House	YH	Youth Hostel
Inst	Institute	Recn Gd	Recreation Ground		

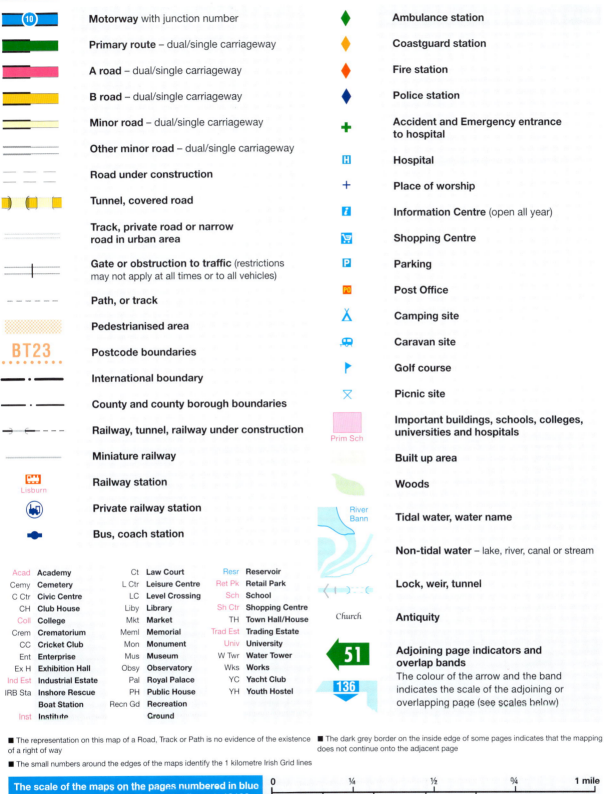

■ The representation on this map of a Road, Track or Path is no evidence of the existence of a right of way

■ The dark grey border on the inside edge of some pages indicates that the mapping does not continue onto the adjacent page

■ The small numbers around the edges of the maps identify the 1 kilometre Irish Grid lines

The scale of the maps on the pages numbered in blue is 5.52 cm to 1 km • 3½ inches to 1 mile • 1: 18103

0   ¼   ½   ¾   1 mile
0   250 m   500 m   750 m   1 kilometre

The scale of the maps on pages numbered in green is 2.76 cm to 1 km • 1¾ inches to 1 mile • 1: 36206

0   ¼   ½   ¾   1 mile
0   250m 500m 750m 1 kilometre

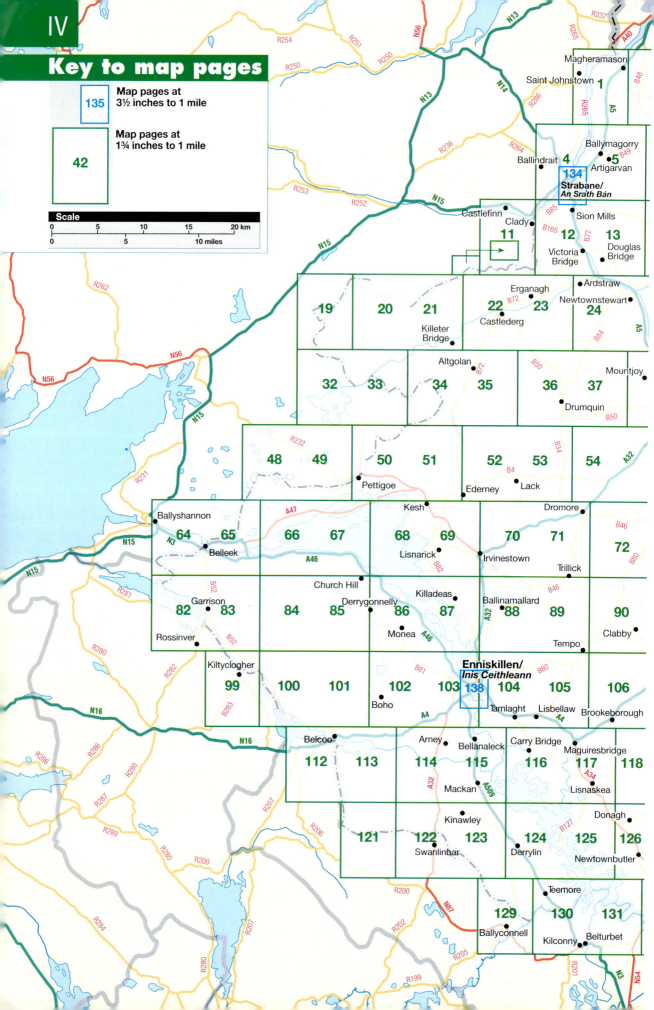

IV

Key to map pages

	Map pages at 3½ inches to 1 mile
135	

	Map pages at 1¾ inches to 1 mile
42	

Scale

0 — 5 — 10 — 15 — 20 km

0 — 5 — 10 miles

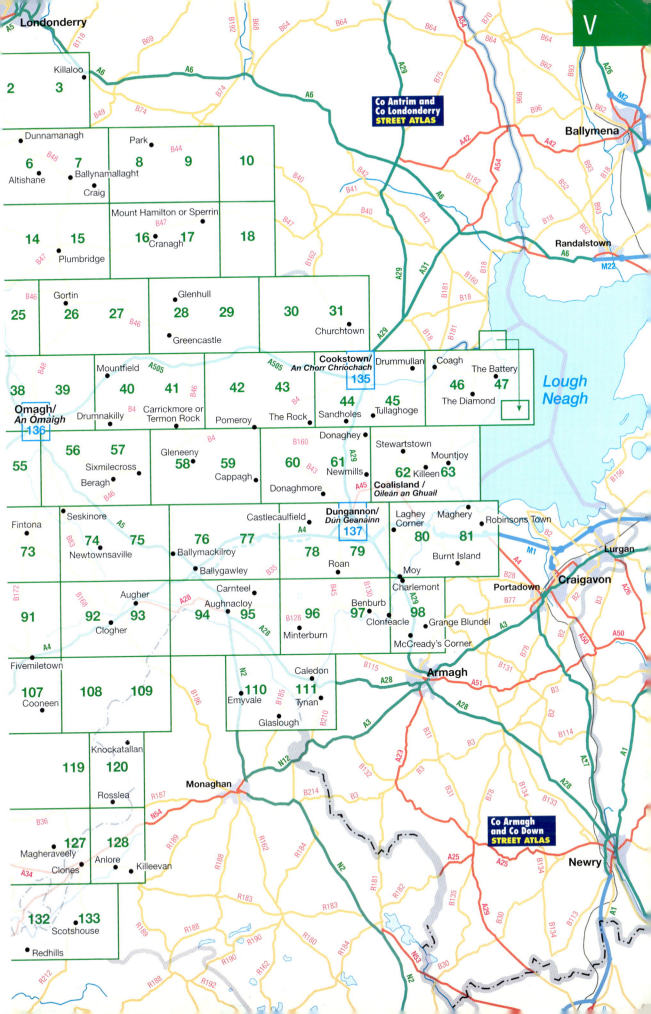

Londonderry

Killaloo

2   **3**

Ballymena

Co Antrim and Co Londonderry STREET ATLAS

Dunnamanagh   Park

Altishane   **6**   **7**   **8**   **9**   **10**

Ballynamallaght
Craig

Randalstown

Mount Hamilton or Sperrin

14   **15**   **16**   **17**   **18**

Plumbridge   Cranagh

Gortin   Glenhull

25   **26**   **27**   **28**   **29**   **30**   **31**

Greencastle   Churchtown

Lough Neagh

Mountfield   Cookstown/ An Chorr Chríochach   Drummullan   Coagh

135

The Battery

38   **39**   **40**   **41**   **42**   **43**   **44**   **45**   **46**   **47**

Omagh/ An Ómaigh

136

Drumnakilly   Carrickmore or Termon Rock   Pomeroy   The Rock   Sandholes   Tullaghoge   The Diamond

Donaghey

Stewartstown   Mountjoy

55   **56**   **57**   **58**   **59**   **60**   **61**   **62**   **63**

Gleneeny   Cappagh   Newmills   Killeen

Sixmilecross   Coalisland / Oileán an Ghuail

Beragh   Donaghmore

Castlecaulfield   Dungannon/ Dún Geanainn   Laghey Corner   Maghery

Fintona   Seskinore   **137**   Robinsons Town

73   **74**   **75**   **76**   **77**   **78**   **79**   **80**   **81**

Newtownsaville   Ballymackilroy   Roan   Burnt Island

Ballygawley   Moy

Lurgan

Carnteel   Charlemont   Craigavon

Augher   Aughnacloy   Benburb   Portadown

91   **92**   **93**   **94**   **95**   **96**   **97**   **98**

Clogher   Minterburn   Clonfeacle   Grange Blundel

McCready's Corner

Caledon

Fivemiletown   Armagh

107   **108**   **109**   **110**   **111**

Cooneen   Emyvale   Tynan

Glaslough

Knockatallan

119   **120**

Monaghan

Rosslea

Co Armagh and Co Down STREET ATLAS

Magheraveely   **127**   **128**

Clones   Anlore   Killeevan

Newry

132   **133**

Scotshouse

Redhills

Route Planning

Scale

0	5	10	15	20	25 km
0		5		10	15 miles

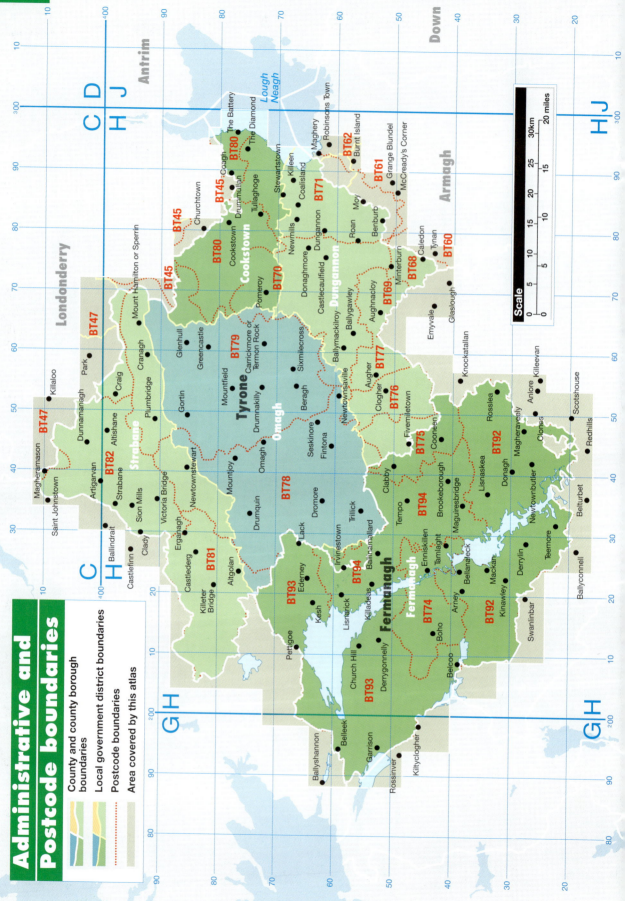

Administrative and Postcode boundaries

County and county borough boundaries

Local government district boundaries

Postcode boundaries

Area covered by this atlas

Scale

0   5   10   15   20   25   30km
0   5   10   15   20 miles

Londonderry

Antrim

Down

Armagh

Lough Neagh

BT47

BT47

BT82

BT81

BT45

BT45

BT45

BT80

BT80

BT79

BT70

BT78

BT93

BT93

BT94

BT94

BT74

BT92

BT92

BT75

BT76

BT77

BT69

BT68

BT60

BT71

BT61

BT62

Strabane

Tyrone

Omagh

Cookstown

Dungannon

Fermanagh

Killaloo

Park

Magheramason

Saint Johnstown

Castlefinn

Ballindrait

Clady

Sion Mills

Strabane

Artigarvan

Dunnamanagh

Craig

Attishane

Plumbridge

Cranagh

Mount Hamilton or Sperrin

Glenhull

Greencastle

Churchtown

Coagh

The Battery

The Diamond

Drummullan

Tullaghoge

Stewartstown

Killeen

Coalisland

Maghery

Robinsons Town

Burnt Island

Grange Blundel

McCready's Corner

Caledon

Tynan

Glaslough

Emyvale

Knockatallan

Killeevan

Scotshouse

Anlore

Clones

Redhills

Belturbet

Ballyconnell

Swanlinbar

Teemore

Newtownbutler

Derrylin

Kinawley

Mackan

Bellanaleck

Arney

Boho

Belcoo

Derrygonnelly

Church Hill

Lisnarick

Killadeas

Ballinamallard

Kesh

Ederney

Lisnaskea

Maguiresbridge

Brookeborough

Donagh

Rosslea

Magheraveely

Lisbellaw

Tempo

Tamlaght

Enniskillen

Tamlaght

Coonen

Fivemiletown

Clogher

Augher

Newtownsaville

Ballygawley

Aughnacloy

Minterburn

Benburb

Roan

Moy

Dungannon

Castlecaulfield

Donaghmore

Newmills

Pomeroy

Sixmilecross

Carrickmore or Termon Rock

Beragh

Seskinore

Fintona

Dromore

Omagh

Mountjoy

Drummakilly

Mountfield

Gortin

Newtownstewart

Victoria Bridge

Erganagh

Castlederg

Killeter Bridge

Altgolan

Petigoe

Belleek

Garrison

Ballyshannon

Rossinver

Kittyclogher

Ballymackilroy

Seskinore

Trillick

Drumquin

Lack

Irvinestown

Clabby

Ballymackilroy

Cookstown

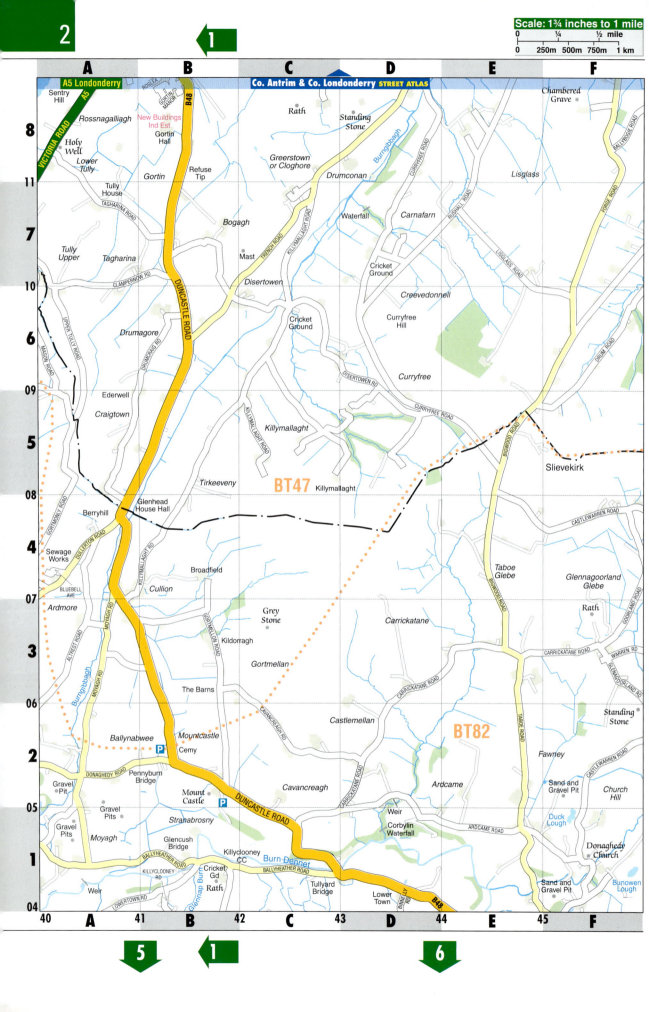

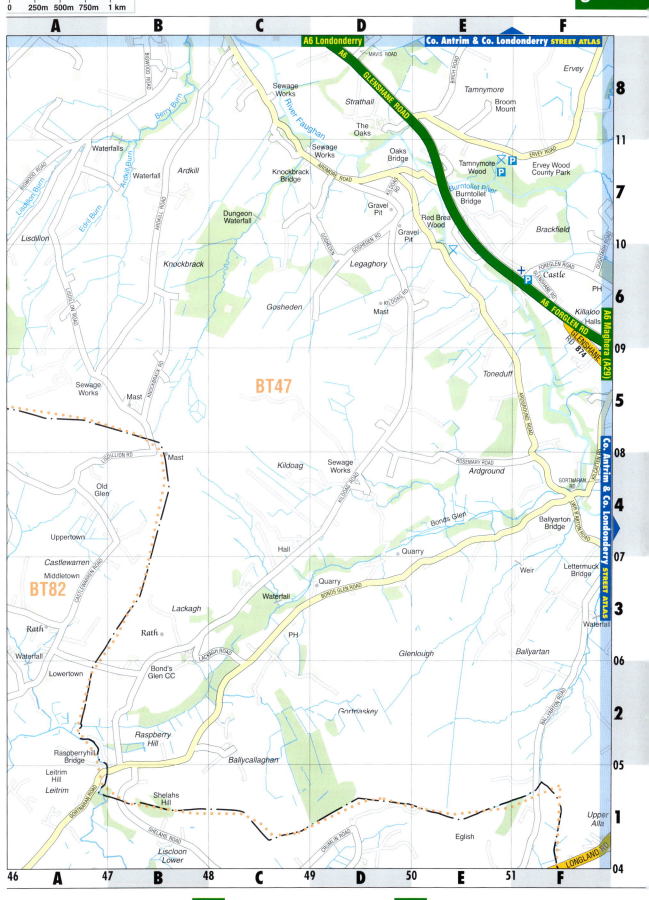

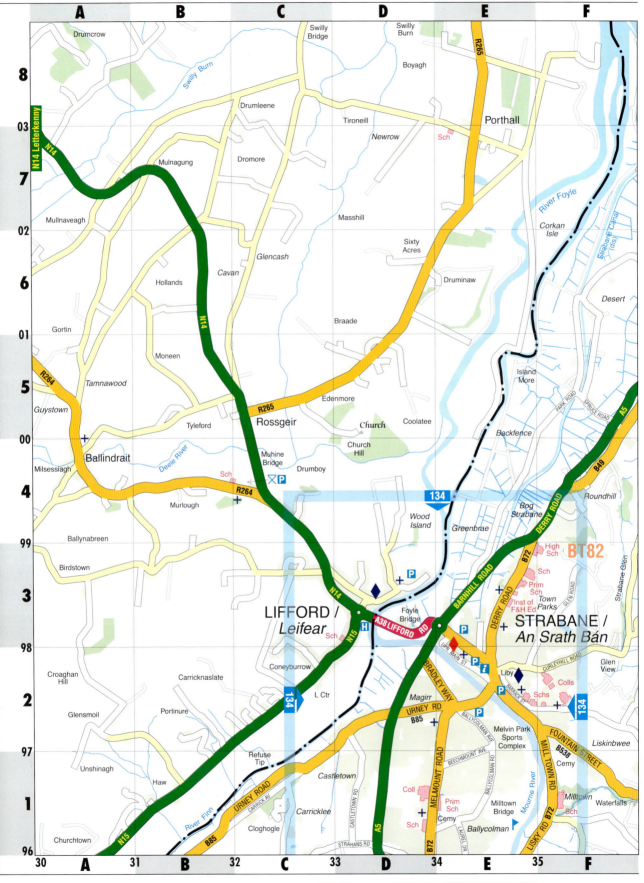

1

For full street detail of the highlighted area see page 134.

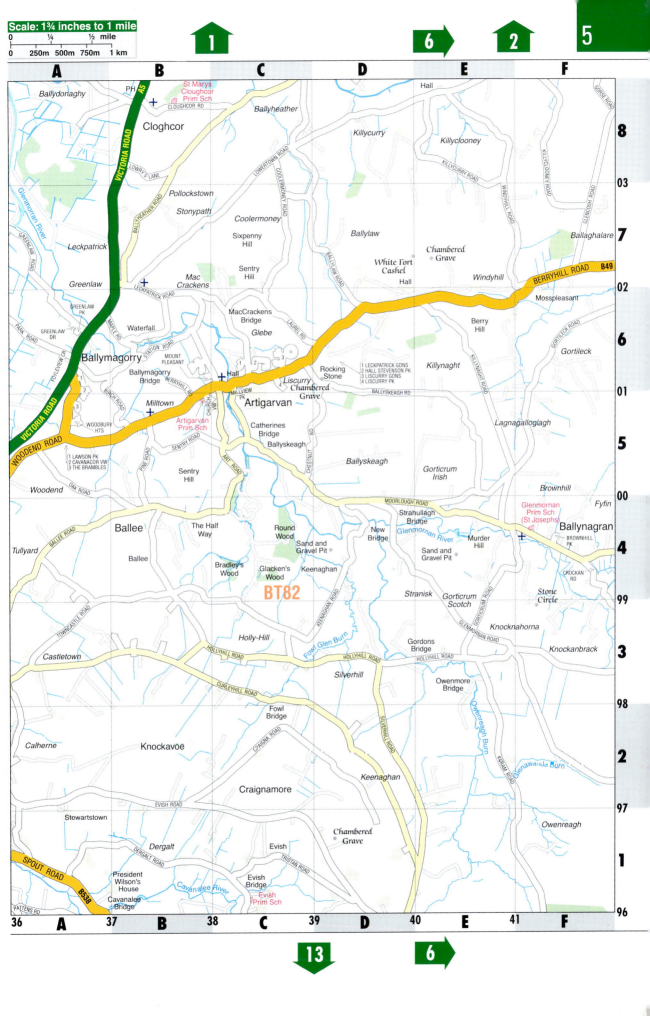

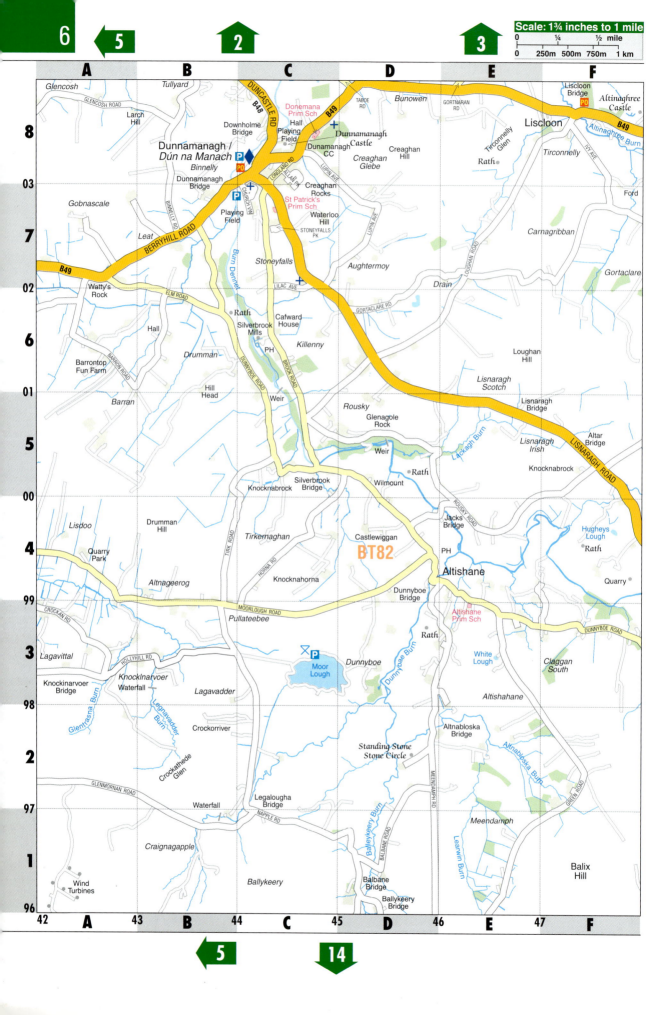

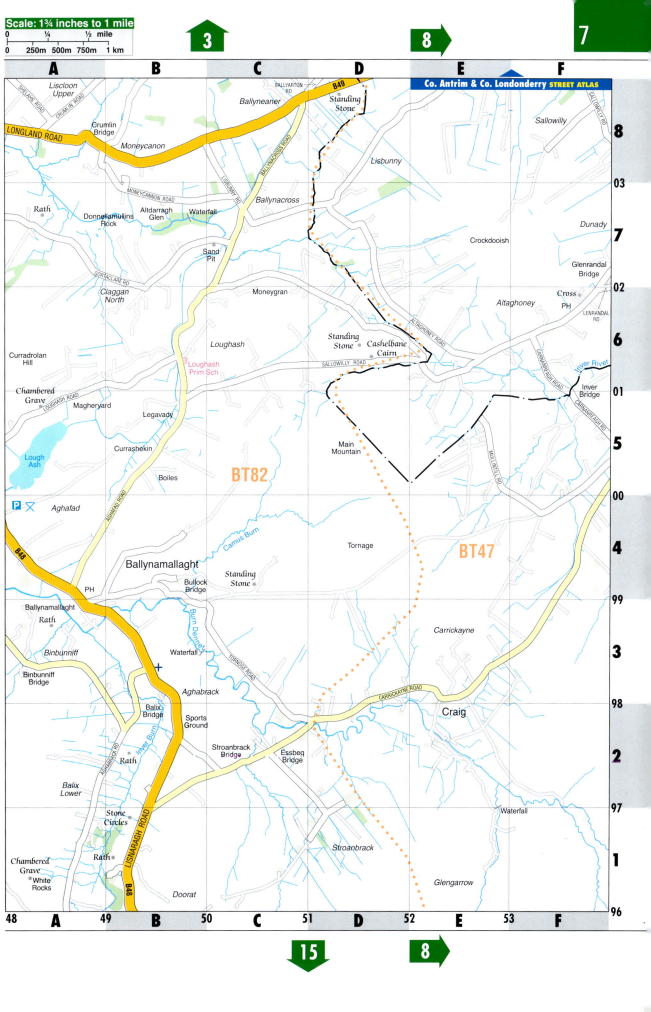

E7
1 MILLSIDE CRES
2 GLENGRAINNE PK
3 SYCAMORE HTS
4 BUSHFIELD MILL

Co. Antrim & Co. Londonderry STREET ATLAS

A   B   C   D   E   F

Straid
Hill

Ballyrory

Loughtilube
Standing
Stone

Weir

Slieveboy

SLIEVEBOY PK

Rath

Altinure
Upper

UMRYCAM RD

Caranbane

River Faughan

Rath

Gortscreagan

Altinure
Bridge

ALTINURE PK

MONADORE ROAD

Altinure
Lower

Rath

SLIEVEBUOY ROAD

Turrasaglin
Well

Park
FC

Playing
Field

Park

St Mary's Altinure
Prim Sch

EDEN ROAD

Playing
Field

GLENRANDAL ROAD

Hall

St Joseph's
Craigbane GFC

Fish
Pond Hill

Kilgort
Bridge

Rath

YH

Learmount
Wood

TIREIGHTER
CTS

Com
Ctr

Weir PH

B44

GORTSCREAGAN ROAD

Crockmore

Standing
Stone

Laurel
Hill

Chambered
Grave

Playing
Field

Crockjack

Gortin

Gortnashammer
Bridge

Ford

Lower
Dreen

TAMNAGH RD

Tamnagh
Bridge

CARNANREAGH ROAD

Tireighter

CROCKMORE ROAD

Carnreagh

KILGORT ROAD

Kilgort

PLANTATION ROAD

TIREIGHTER ROAD

Tireighter
Bridge

TIREIGHTER RD

Tireighter Burn

CARNANREAGH RD

Stranagalwilly
Bridge

Meeny
Hill

Lear

BT47

Legnarainy

Glenrandal River

Stranagalwilly

Drumbog

Oughtavaddy Burn

Learmount
Mountain

Pollandoo Burn

Tamnagh

Altacapple Glen

Sluggada

Pollanore

Oughtnashancullion Glen

Legnagappoge

Mullaghdou

Cornakilly

BT49

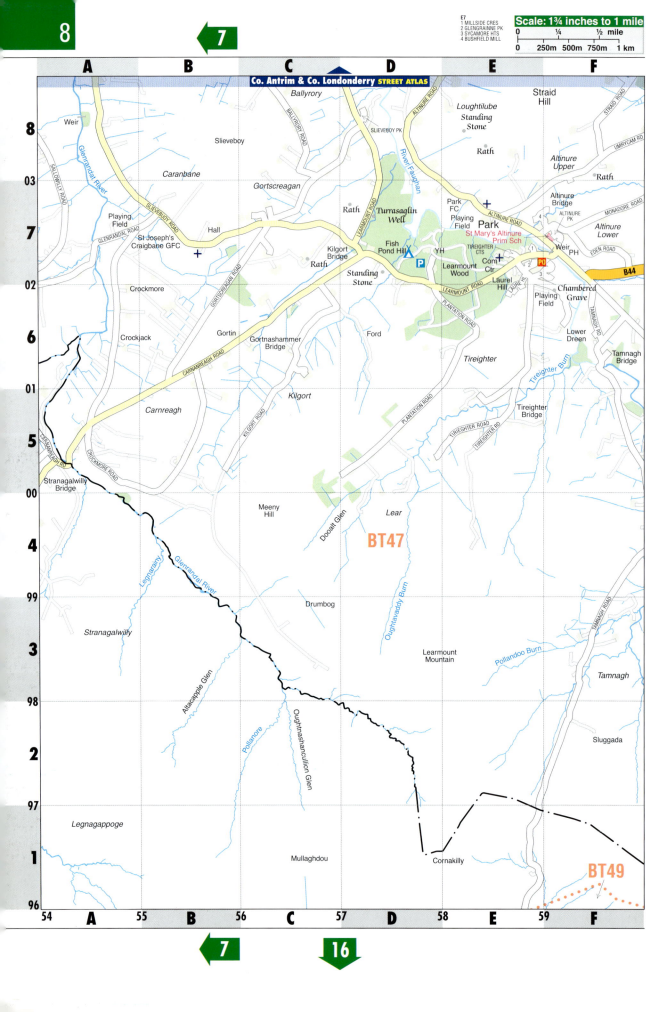

A   B   C   D   E   F

Co. Antrim & Co. Londonderry **STREET ATLAS**

Standing
Stone

Umrycam
Hill

Coolnamonan

Fincarn

Aughlish
Bridge

B40

GLENEDRA ROAD

8

03

Rath

Rath

MACHERABRICK RD

Standing
Stone

Tamnyagan

Monadore
Bridge

Moneyhoghan

Gallogh
Bridge

PH

B44 ALTINURE ROAD

7

Eden

Raths

Aughlish

Sruhan Meenard

02

Fairmount
House

Ford

KILCREEN ROAD

Mullaghash

Owenbeg River

6

Middle
Dreen

Kilcreen

Ford

Ballydonegan

Kerlan Burn

01

Dromore

Toberid
Mountain

5

BARNES ROAD

Upper Dreen

The Crooked
Bridge

Knockanbane
Mountain

Kerlans Burn

00

Sluggada Burn

CROCKAHILLY RD

Curraghanarwar

BT47

Barns
Top

4

Dreen

Glashagh
Bridge

Glashagh Burn

99

River Faughan

SPERRIN ROAD

S p e r r i n

M o u n t a i n s

3

Glenfore

98

Eagle
Rock

County
Rock

2

Sawel
Mountain

Cloghornagh

Binleana Burn

Glenerin

97

Oughtvabeg

BT79

1

Dart
Mountain

96

60   A   61   B   62   C   63   D   64   E   65   F   96

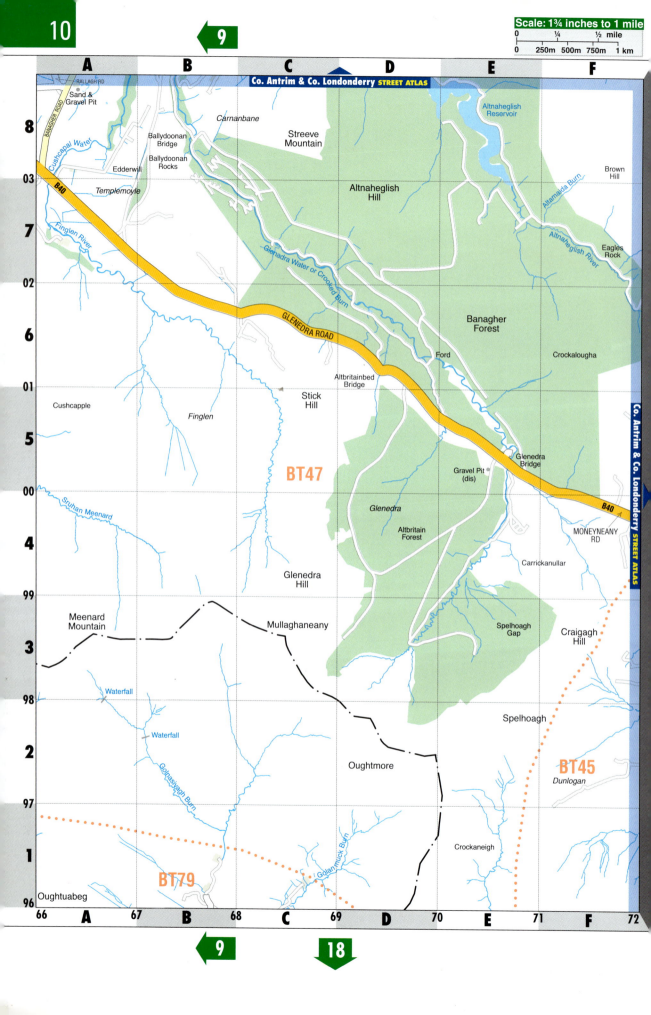

9

Scale: 1¾ inches to 1 mile

0 ¼ ½ mile
0 250m 500m 750m 1 km

A B C D E F

Co. Antrim & Co. Londonderry **STREET ATLAS**

RALLAGH RD

Sand & Gravel Pit

8

BANAGHER ROAD

Cushcapal Water

Carnanbane

Ballydoonan Bridge

Streeve Mountain

Altnaheglish Reservoir

03

Edderwill

B40

Ballydoonan Rocks

Altnaheglish Hill

Brown Hill

Templemoyle

7

Finglen River

Glenedra Water or Crooked Burn

Altamacla Burn

Altnaheglish River

Eagles Rock

02

6

GLENEDRA ROAD

Banagher Forest

Ford

Crockalougha

01

Cushcapple

Finglen

Altbritainbed Bridge

Stick Hill

5

BT47

Gravel Pit (dis)

Glenedra Bridge

00

Sruhan Meenard

Glenedra

MONEYNEANY RD

B40

4

Altbritain Forest

Carrickanullar

99

Meenard Mountain

Glenedra Hill

Mullaghaneany

Spelhoagh Gap

Craigagh Hill

98

Waterfall

Spelhoagh

2

Waterfall

Oughtmore

BT45

Golnasiagh Burn

Dunlogan

97

BT79

Golanmuck Burn

Crockaneigh

1

96

Oughtuabeg

66 A 67 B 68 C 69 D 70 E 71 F 72

Co. Antrim & Co. Londonderry STREET ATLAS

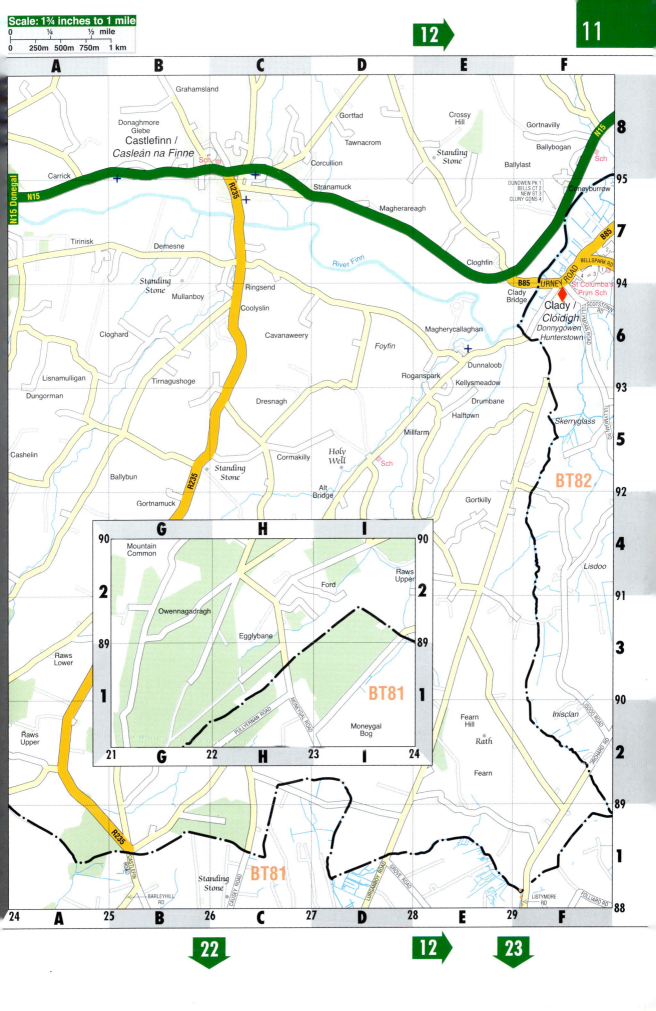

A   B   C   D   E   F

8
95
7
94
6
93
5
92
4
91
3
2
89
1
88

Grahamsland
Donaghmore Glebe
Castlefinn / *Caslean na Finne*
Sch
Gortfad
Tawnacrom
Crossy Hill
Standing Stone
Gortnavilly
Ballybogan
Ballylast
Sch
N15

N15 Donegal

Carrick
Corcullion
Stranamuck
Magherareagh
Cloghfin
DUNOWEN PK 1
BELLS CT 2
NEW ST 3
CLUNY GDNS 4
Coneyburrow
B85
BELLSPARK RD

Tirinisk
Demesne
River Finn
URNEY
B85
St Columba's Prim Sch
SCOTSTOWN RD
TULLYMOAL RD

R235

Standing Stone
Mullanboy
Ringsend
Coolyslin
Clady Bridge
Clady / *Cloidigh*
Donnygowen Hunterstown

Cloghard
Cavanaweery
Foyfin
Magherycallaghan
Dunnaloob

Lisnamulligan
Dungorman
Tirnagushoge
Dresnagh
Roganspark
Kellysmeadow
Drumbane
Halftown
Skerryglass

BT82

Cashelin
Ballybun
Standing Stone
Cormakilly
Holy Well
Millfarm
Gortkilly
Lisdoo

R235
Gortnamuck
Alt Bridge
Sch

G   H   I

90
2
89
1
2

Mountain Common
Owennagadragh
Egglybane
Ford
Raws Upper

Raws Lower
BT81
PULVERNAN ROAD
MONEYGAL ROAD
Moneygal Bog

Raws Upper
R235
CASTLEFIN ROAD
21   G   22   H   23   I   24

Fearn Hill
Rath
Inisclan
LISDOO ROAD
ORCHARD RD
Fearn

90
2
89
1

R235
CASTLEFIN ROAD
BARLEYHILL RD
Standing Stone
CAUSEY ROAD
BT81
LURGANBOY RD
GROVE ROAD
Listymore RD
FOLLIARD RD

24 A 25 B 26 C 27 D 28 E 29 F 88

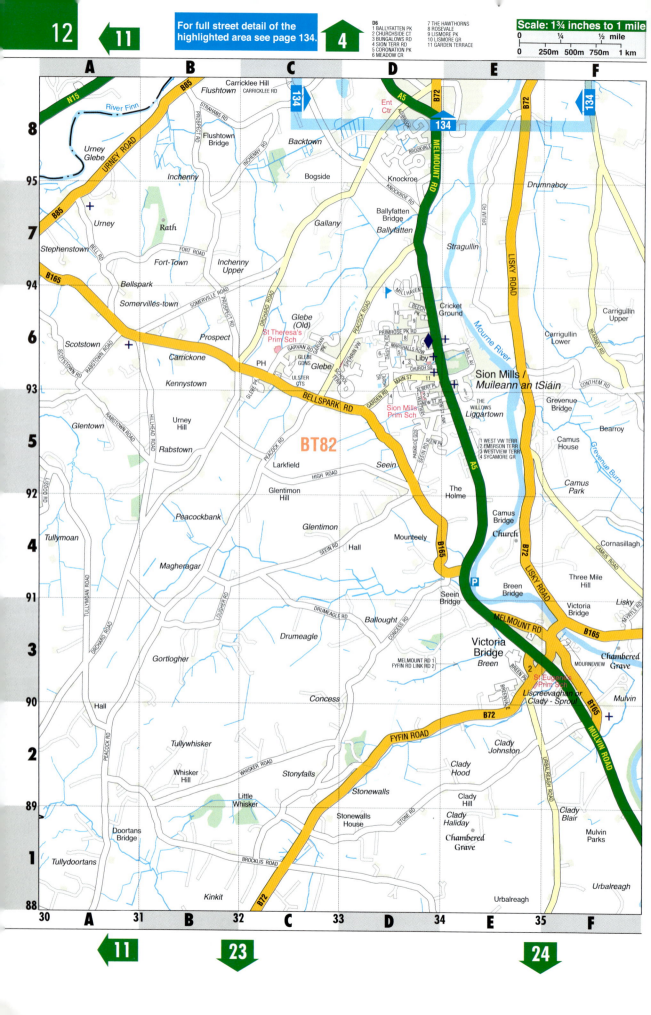

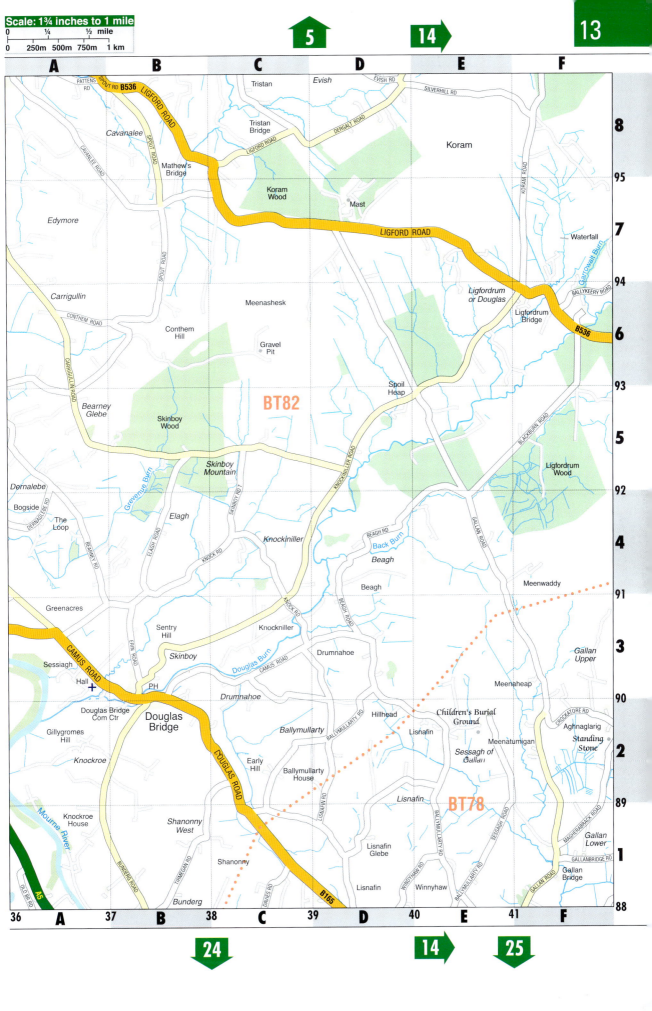

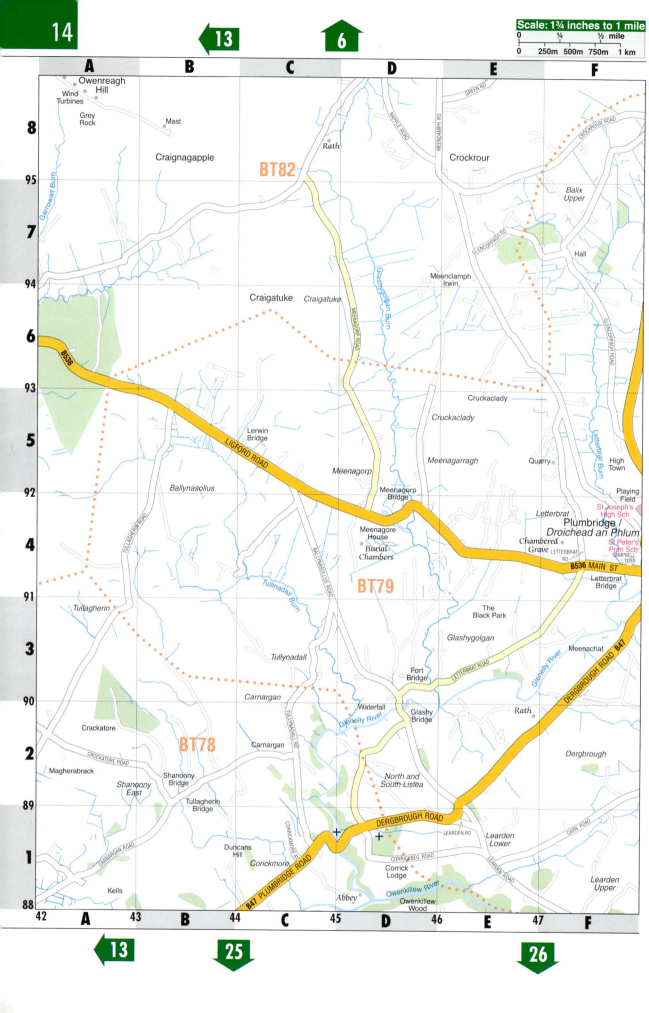

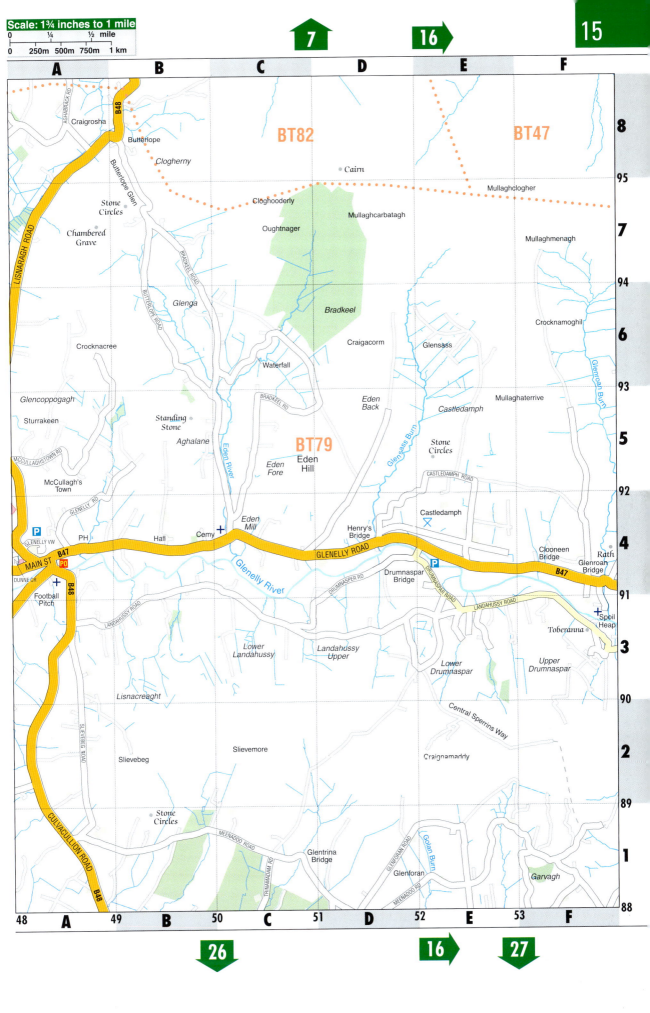

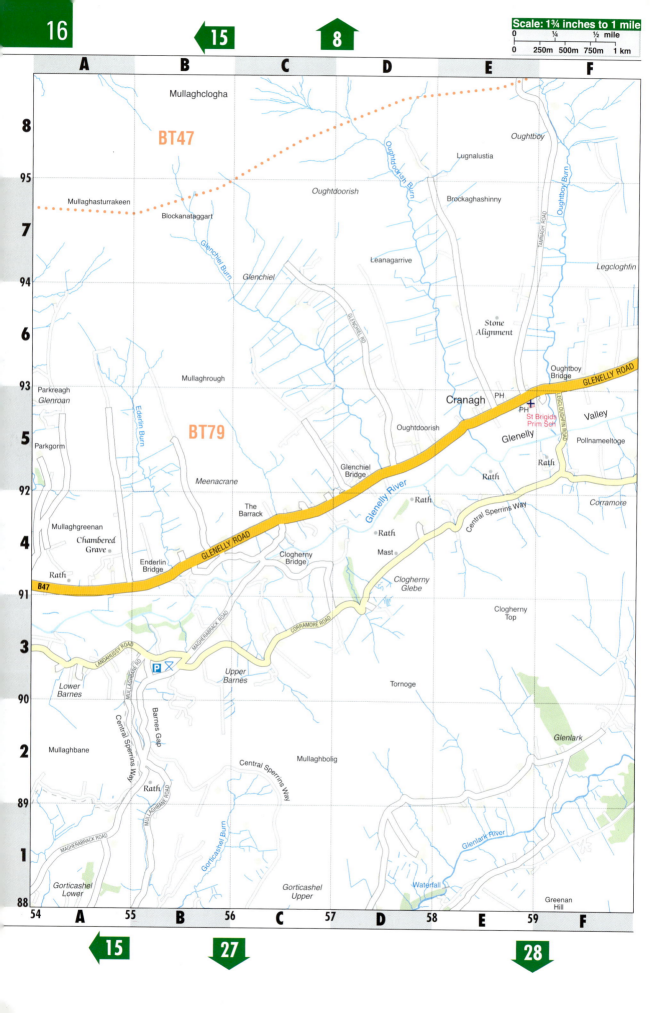

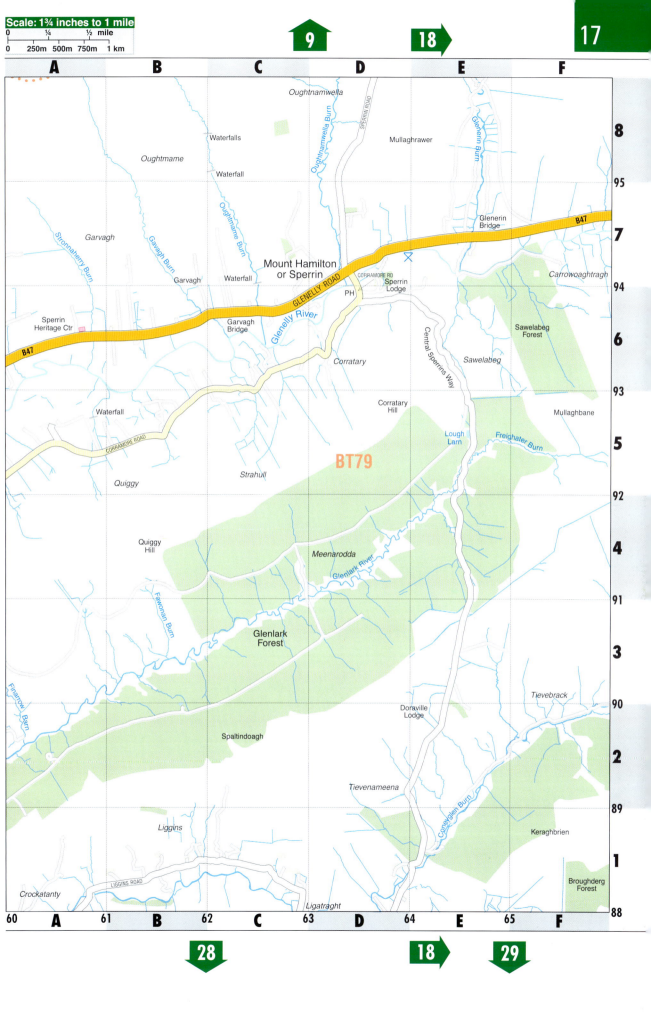

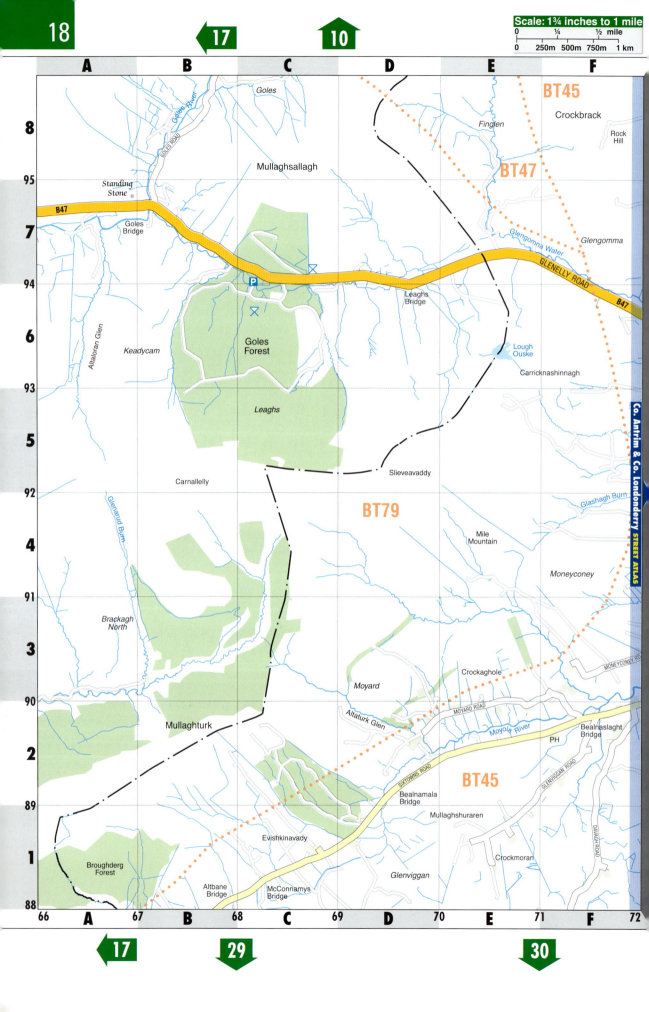

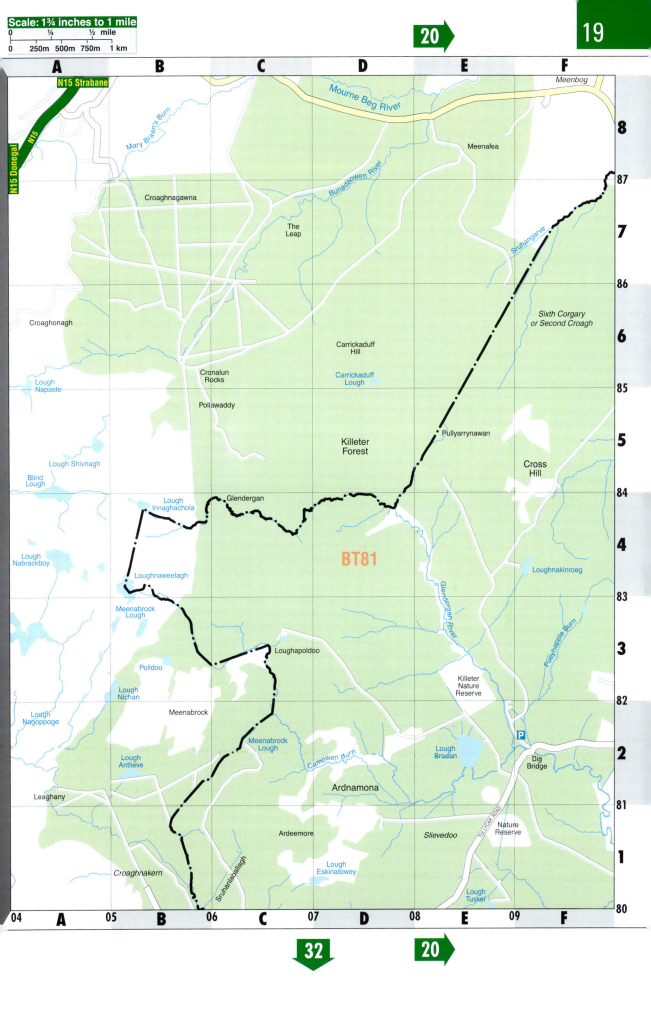

19

Scale: 1¾ inches to 1 mile

0   ¼   ½   mile
0   250m 500m 750m 1 km

A   **B**   **C**   **D**   **E**   **F**

8

87

7

86

6

85

5

84

4

83

3

82

2

81

1

80

Sruhangarve

Sruhangarre Bridge

Mourne Beg River

Croagh Plantation

Tievecloghoge

Rath

Croagh

Croagh Bridge

Deevog Bridge

CORGARY ROAD

Meenreagh Bridge

Croagh Burn

Fifth Corgary or First Croagh

Meenablagh or Fourth Corgary

Third Corgary

THIRD CORGARY RD

Second Corgary

First Corgary

MEENABLAGH ROAD

Meenbog Hill

Rushy Burn

Ardnabrandy

Golan

Sruhanbrack

BT81

Meenakeeran

Attyowen

Tullycar

Sturrin

Altamullan

Rampart Bridge

Sruhananess Bridge

TULLYCAR ROAD

Middle Town

Glendergan River

Ballyeitragh

MULLYFAMORE ROAD

Meenagrogan

Sheskinawaddy

Sruhanaloughra Burn

Lough Sallagh

Mullyfa

Waterfall

ESSAN ROAD

Mullyfarmore

Mullyfabeg

Clagernagh

10   **A**   11   **B**   12   **C**   13   **D**   14   **E**   15   **F**

19   33

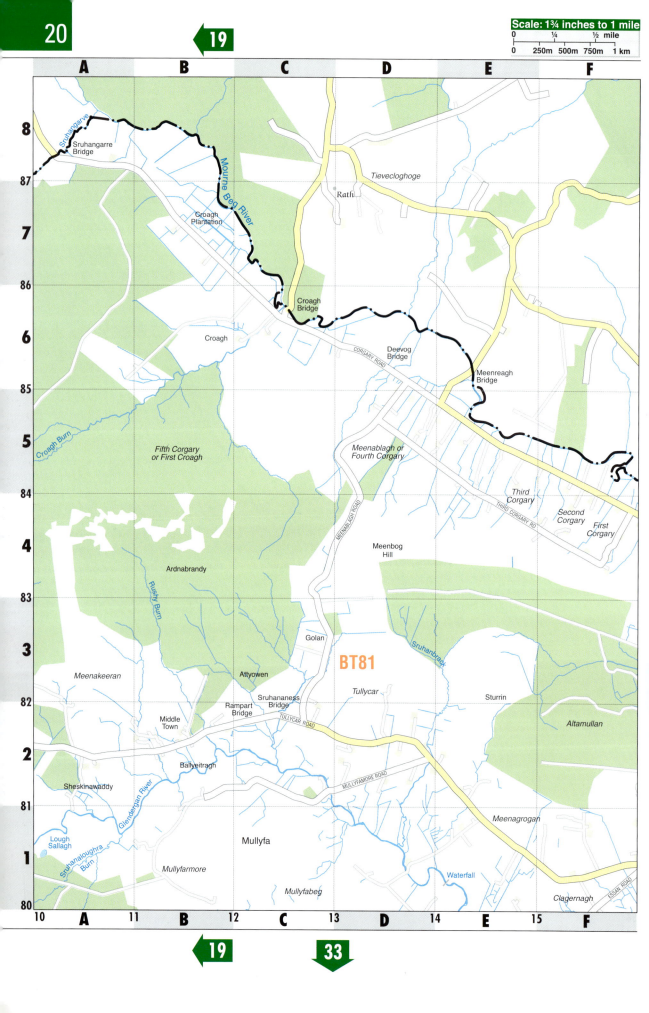

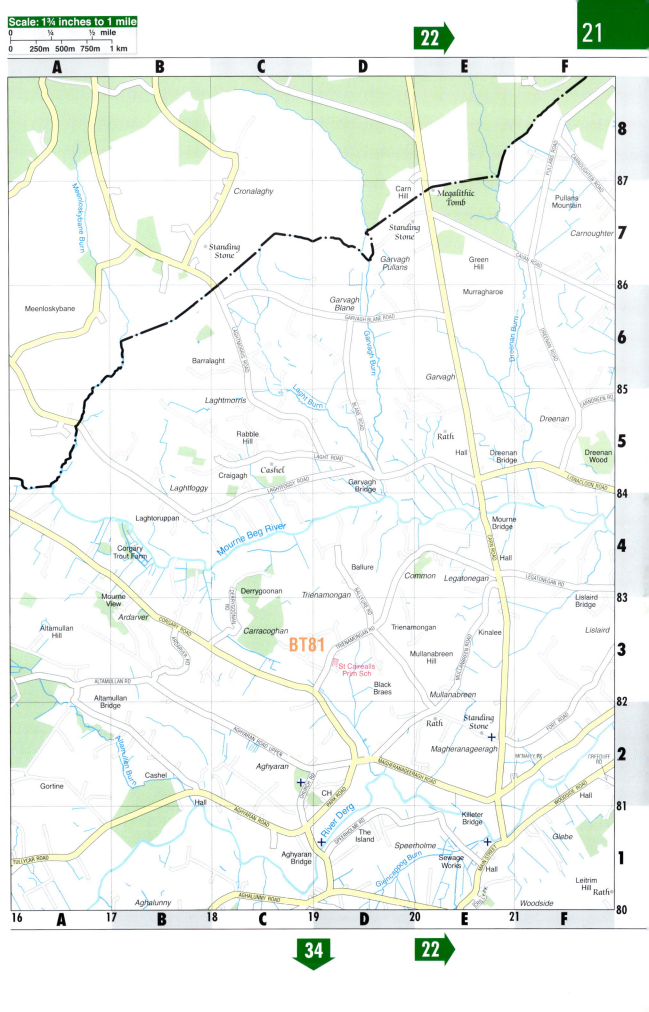

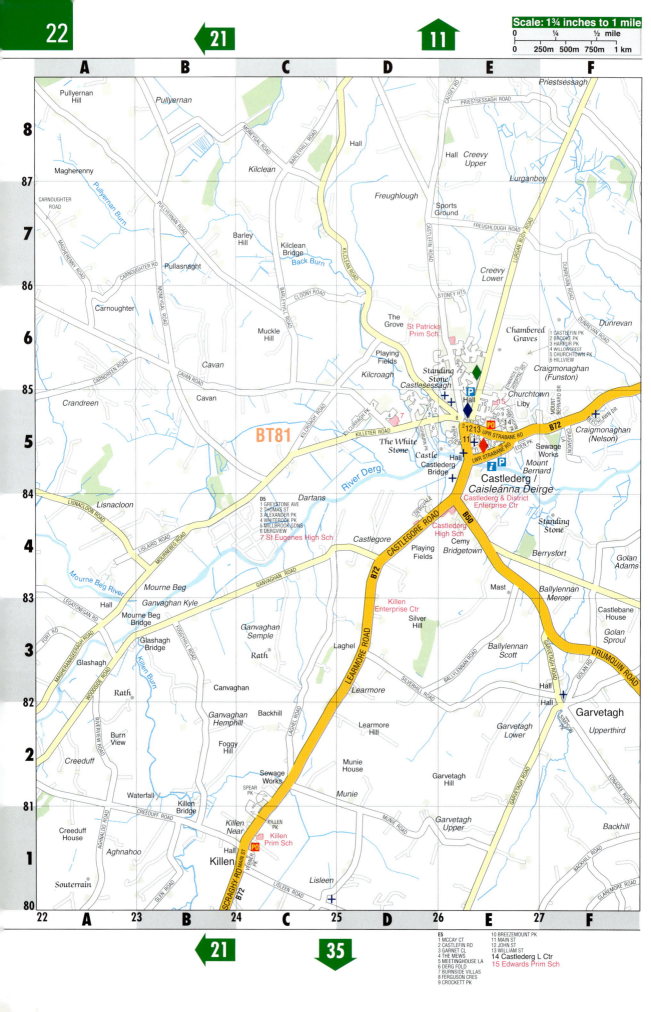

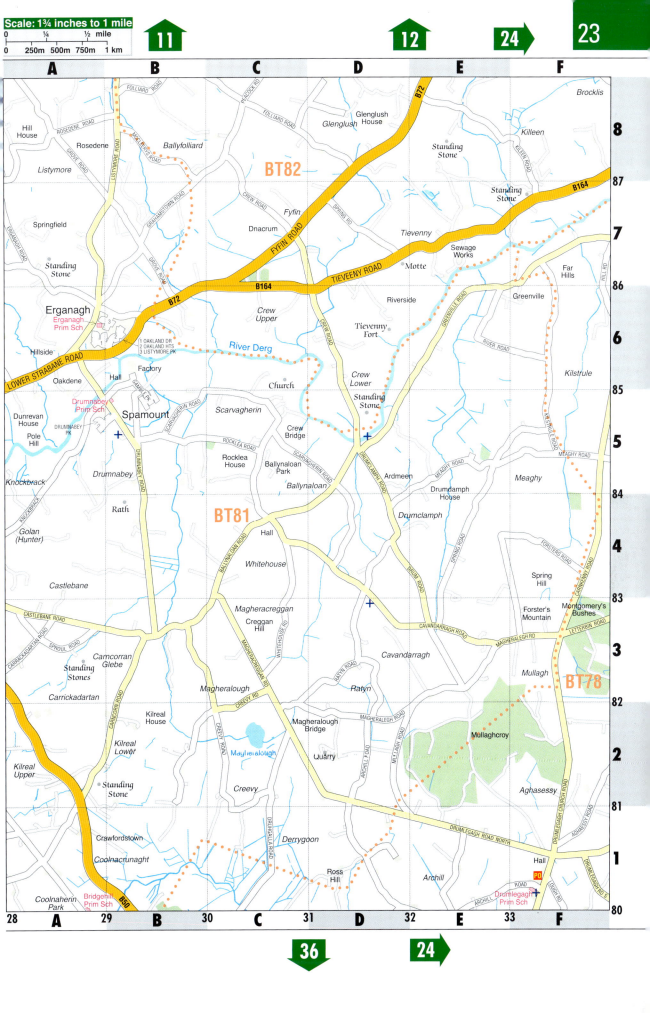

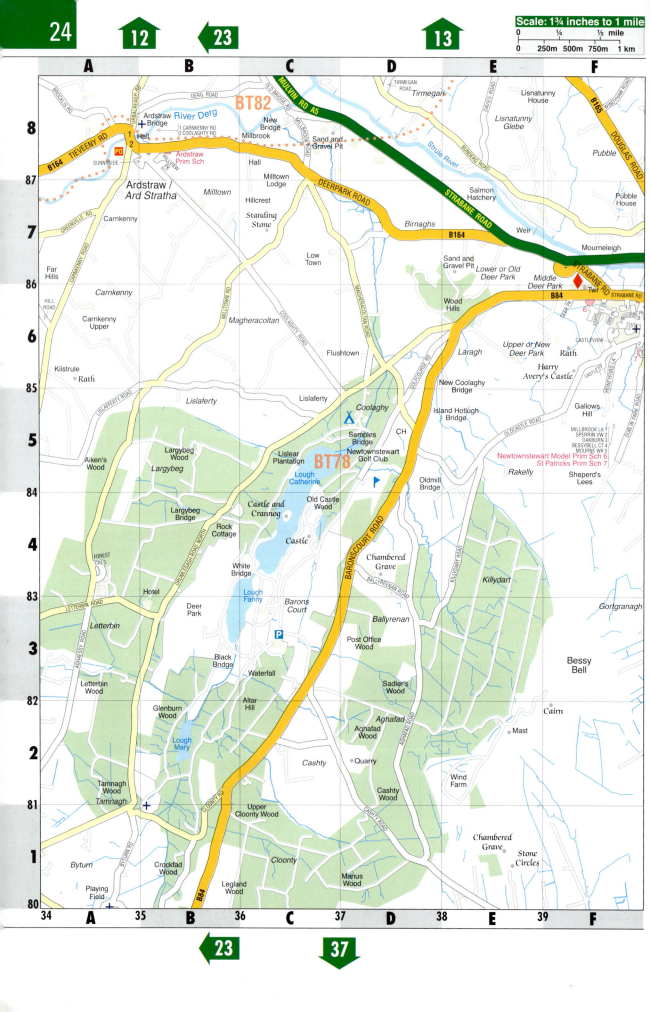

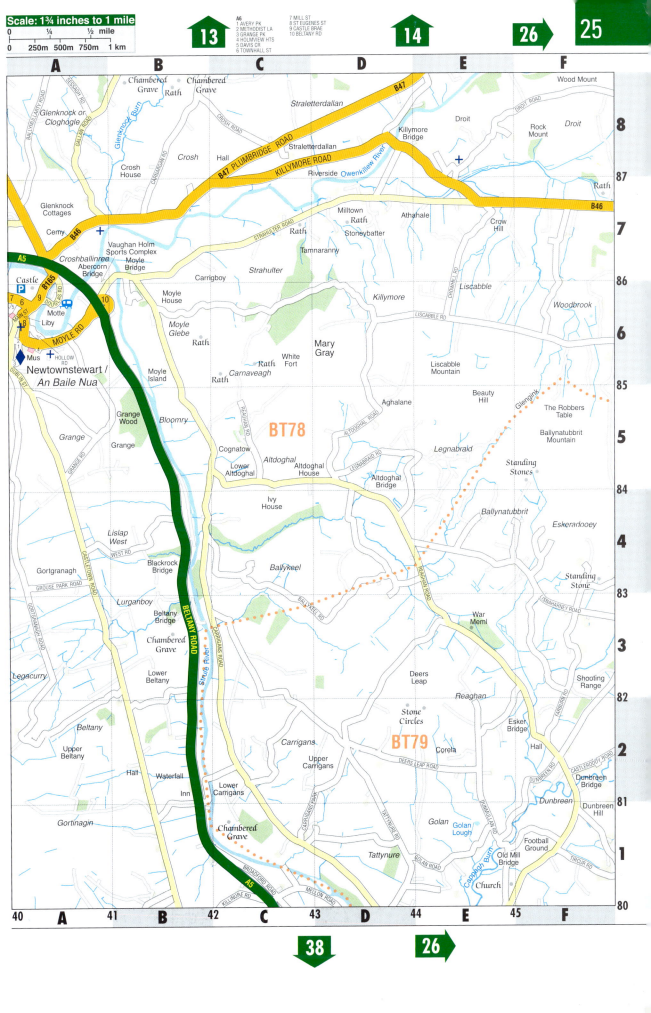

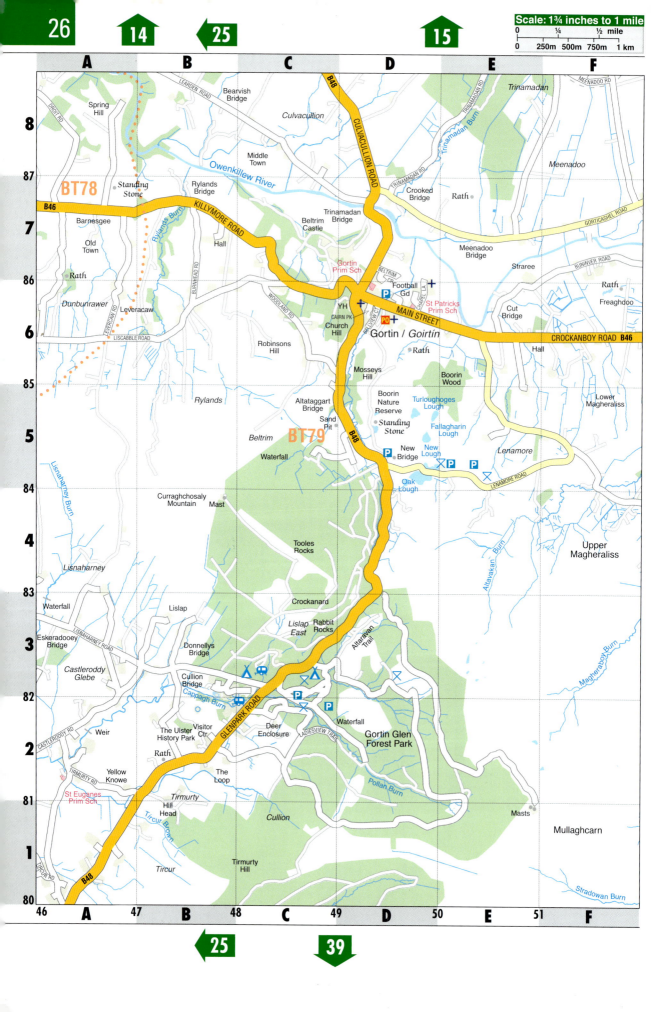

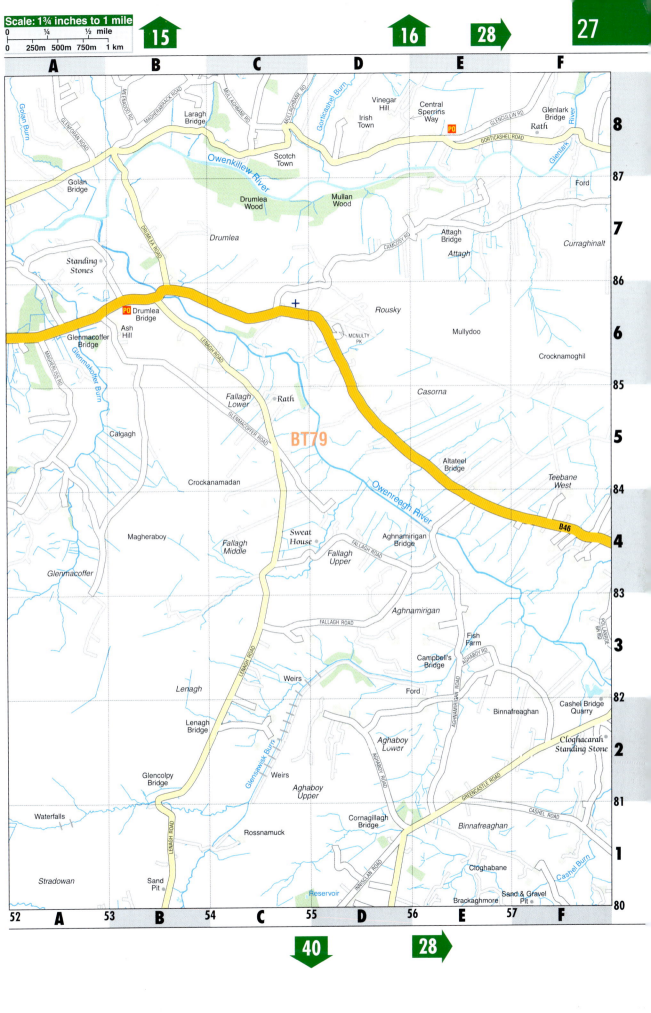

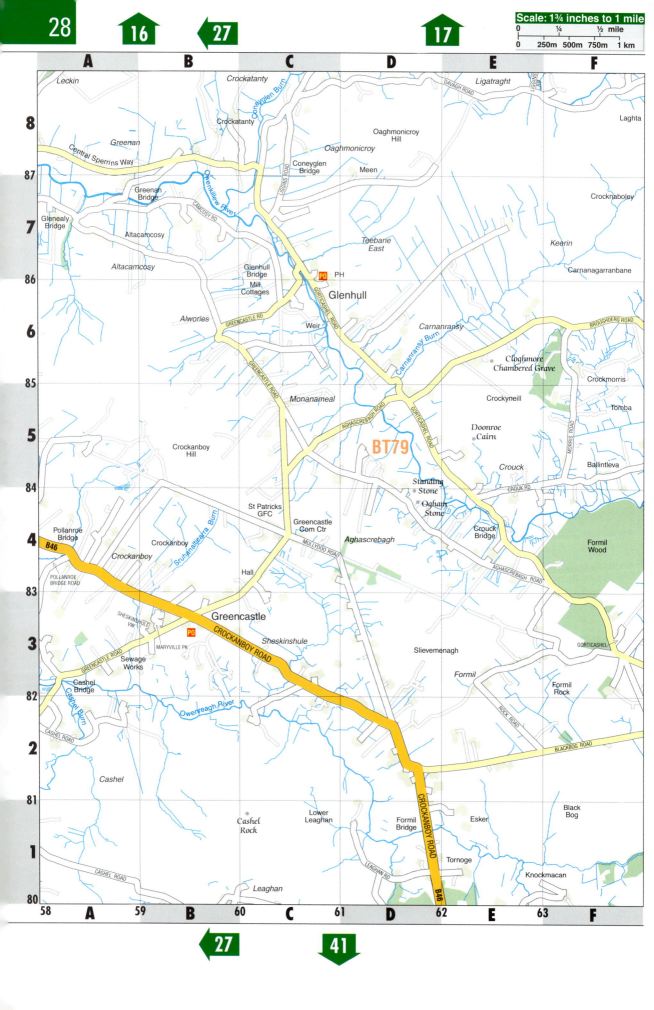

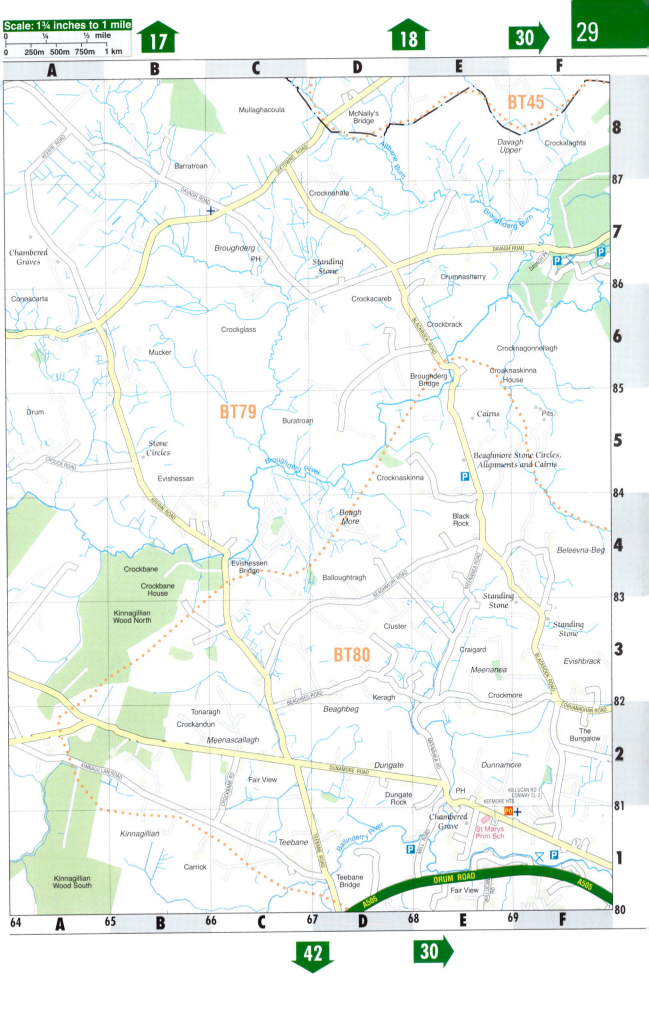

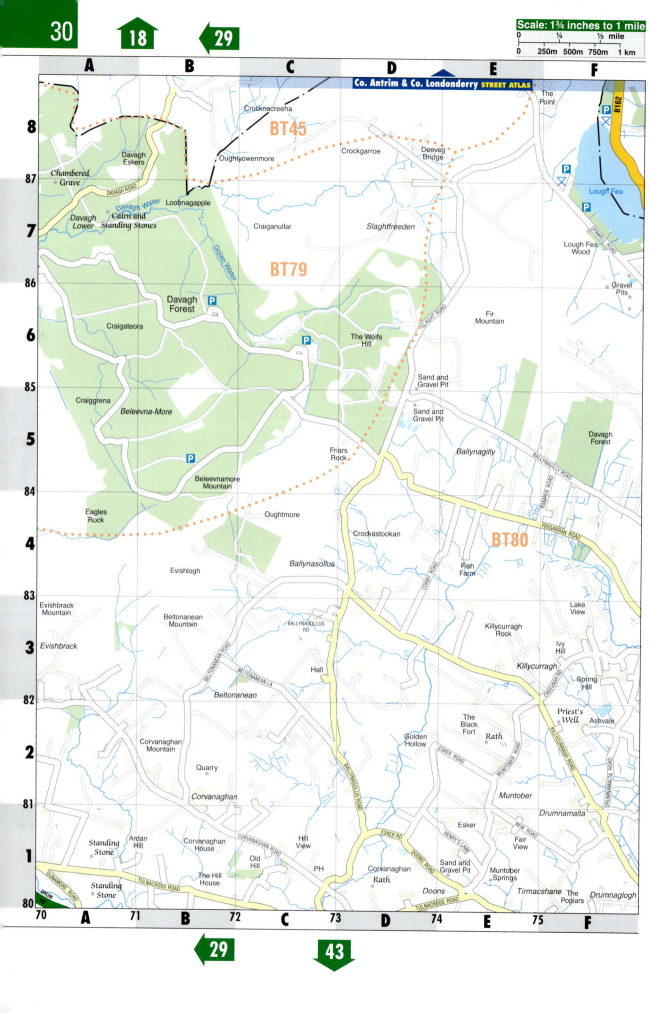

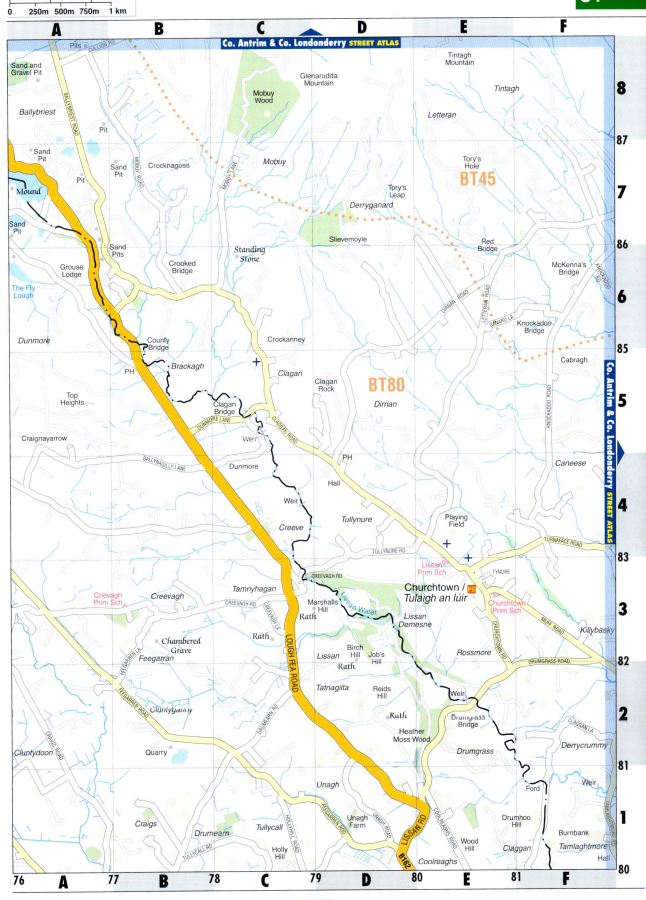

Scale: 1¾ inches to 1 mile

Co. Antrim & Co. Londonderry STREET ATLAS

Co. Antrim & Co. Londonderry STREET ATLAS

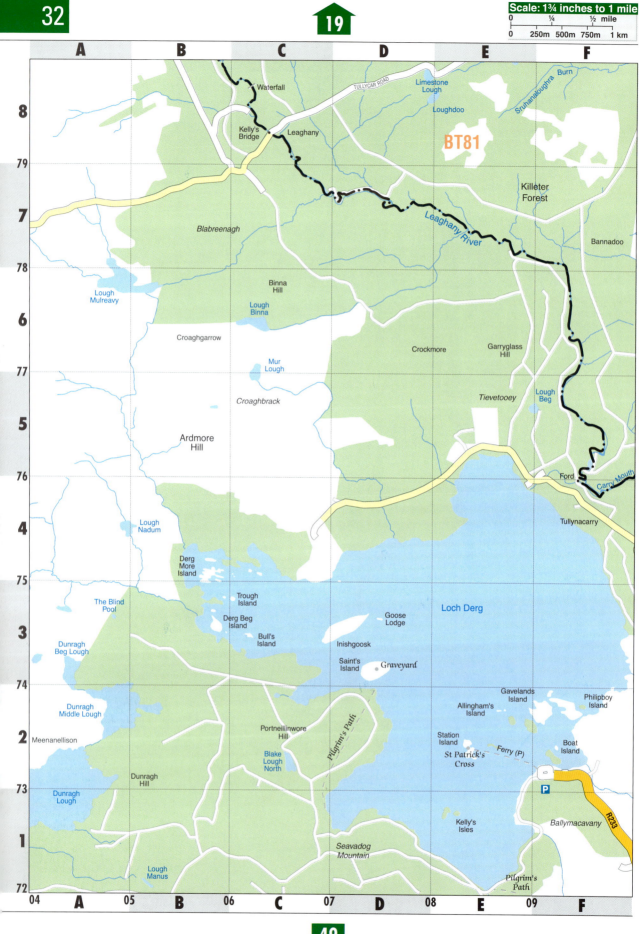

A   B   C   D   E   F

8

79

7

78

6

77

5

76

4

75

3

74

2

73

1

72

Waterfall
Kelly's Bridge
Leaghany
Tullycar Road
Limestone Lough
Loughdoo
Sruhanaloughra Burn
BT81
Killeter Forest
Bannadoo
Blabreenagh
Leaghany River
Binna Hill
Lough Binna
Crockmore
Garryglass Hill
Lough Mulreavy
Croaghgarrow
Mur Lough
Tievetooey
Lough Beg
Croaghbrack
Ardmore Hill
Ford
Carry Mouth
Lough Nadum
Tullynacarry
Derg More Island
The Blind Pool
Trough Island
Loch Derg
Dunragh Beg Lough
Derg Beg Island
Bull's Island
Goose Lodge
Inishgoosk
Saint's Island
Graveyard
Gavelands Island
Philipboy Island
Dunragh Middle Lough
Allingham's Island
Meenanellison
Portneillinwore Hill
Pilgrim's Path
Station Island
Ferry (P)
Boat Island
Blake Lough North
St Patrick's Cross
Dunragh Hill
Dunragh Lough
Ballymacavany
R233
Kelly's Isles
Lough Manus
Seavadog Mountain
Pilgrim's Path

04   A   05   B   06   C   07   D   08   E   09   F

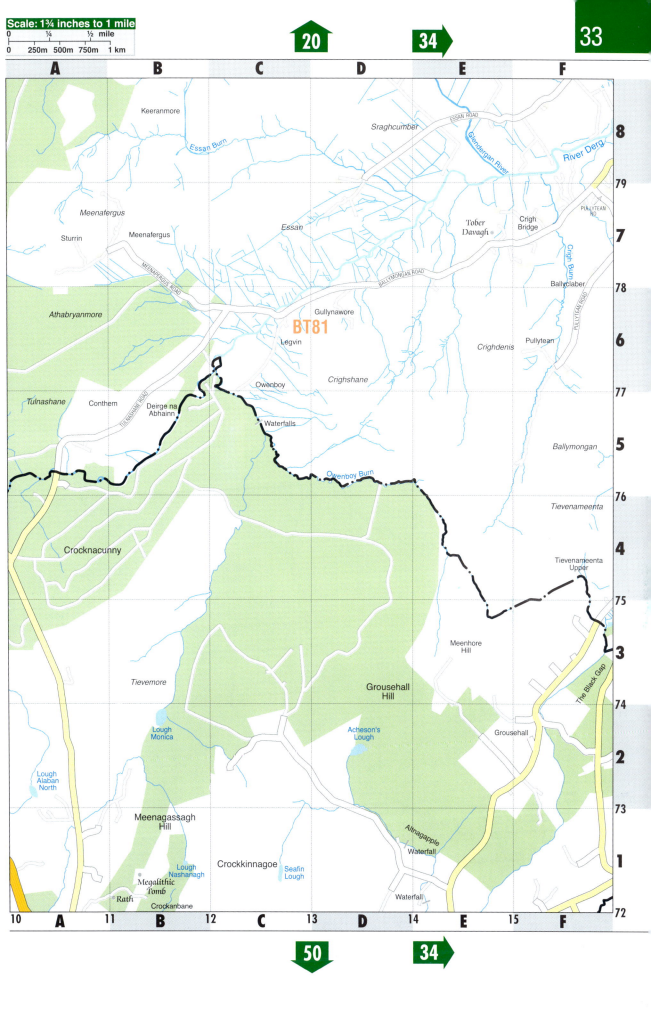

A B C D E F

8

79

7

78

6

77

5

76

4

75

3

74

2

73

1

72

Keeranmore

Sraghcumber

Essan Burn

ESSAN ROAD

Glendergan River

River Derg

Meenafergus

Sturrin

Meenafergus

Essan

Tober Davagh

Crigh Bridge

Crigh Burn

PULLYTEAN RD

MEENAFERGUS ROAD

BALLYMONGAN ROAD

Ballyclaber

Athabryanmore

Gullynawore

BT81

Legvin

Crighdenis

Pullytean

PULLYTEAN ROAD

Tulnashane

Conthem

Deirge na Abhainn

Owenboy

Crighshane

TULNASHANE ROAD

Waterfalls

Owenboy Burn

Ballymongan

Tievenameenta

Crocknacunny

Tievenameenta Upper

Tievemore

Meenhore Hill

Grousehall Hill

The Black Gap

Lough Monica

Acheson's Lough

Grousehall

Lough Alaban North

Meenagassagh Hill

Altnagapple Waterfall

Lough Nashanagh

Seafin Lough

Crockkinnagoe

Megalithic Tomb

Rath

Crockanbane

Waterfall

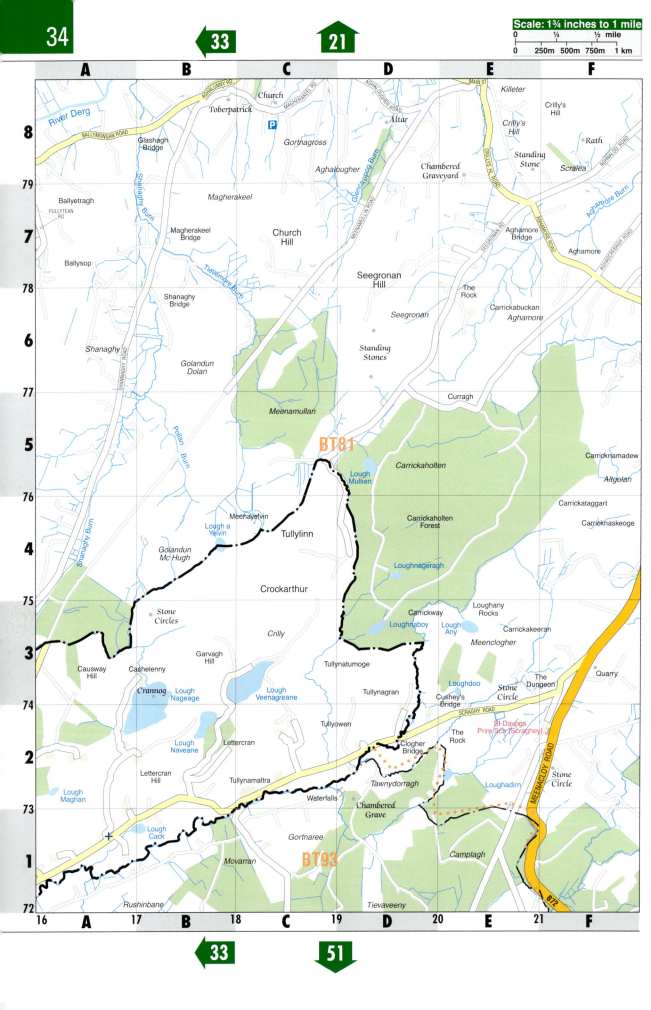

River Derg

BALLYMONGAN ROAD

AGHALUNNY RD

Church

Toberpatrick

MAGHERAKEEL RD

Altar

AGHA CLOGHER ROAD

MAIN ST

Killeter

Crilly's Hill

Crilly's Hill

Glashagh Bridge

Gorthagross

Standing Stone

Rath

Ballyetragh

PULLYTEAN RD

Magherakeel

Aghalougher

Chambered Graveyard

CRILLYS HI ROAD

Scralea

AGHNALOO ROAD

Ballysop

Magherakeel Bridge

Church Hill

Tievemore Burn

SHANAGHY BURN

Seegronan Hill

Seegronan Rd

Aghamore Bridge

Aghamore

AGHMORE ROAD

Aghamore Burn

AGHASCREBAGH ROAD

Shanaghy Bridge

The Rock

Carrickabuckan

Aghamore

Shanaghy

SHANAGHY ROAD

Golandun Dolan

Standing Stones

Curragh

Pollan Burn

Meenamullan

BT81

Carrickaholten

Carricknamadew

Altgolan

Shanaghy Burn

Lough a Yelvin

Meenayelvin

Tullylinn

Lough Mulken

Carrickaholten Forest

Carrickataggart

Carricknaskeoge

Golandun Mc Hugh

Crockarthur

Loughnageragh

Causway Hill

Stone Circles

Crilly

Carrickway

Loughnaboy

Lough Any

Loughany Rocks

Carrickakeeran

Meenclogher

Cashelenny

Garvagh Hill

Tullynatumoge

The Dungeon

Quarry

Crannog

Lough Nageage

Lough Veenagreane

Tullynagran

Loughdoo

Stone Circle

MEENACLOY ROAD

Lough Maghan

Lettercran

Tullyowen

Cushey's Bridge

SCRAGHY ROAD

St Davogs Prim Sch (Scraghey)

Lettercran Hill

Tullynamaltra

Clogher Bridge

The Rock

Lough Naveane

Waterfalls

Tawnydorragh

Loughadirn

Stone Circle

Lough Cack

Gortnaree

Chambered Grave

Camplagh

BT93

Movarran

Rushinbane

Tievaveeny

B72

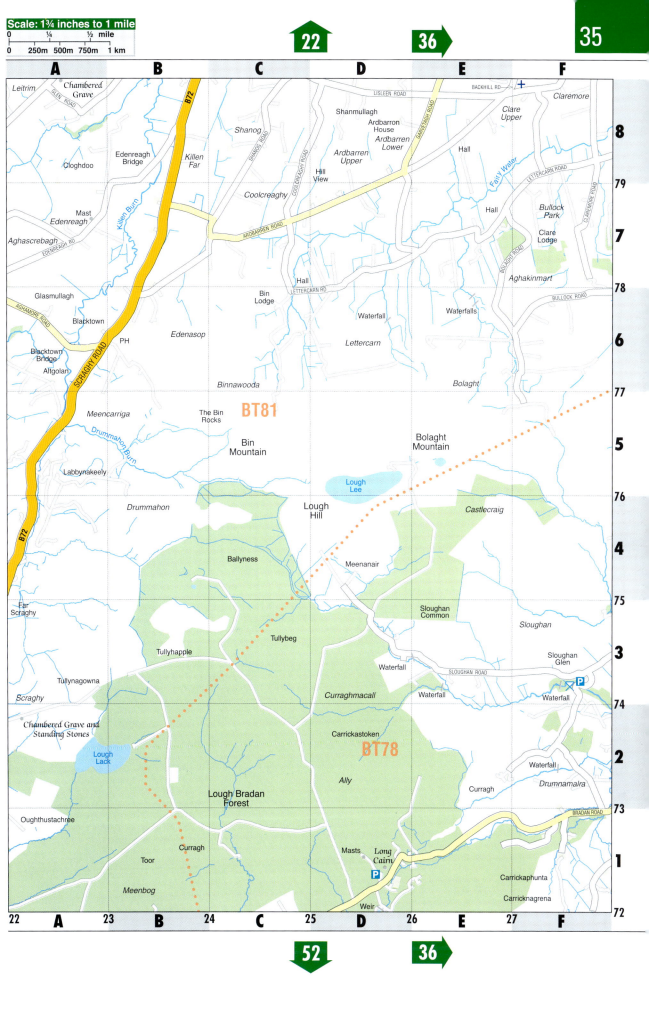

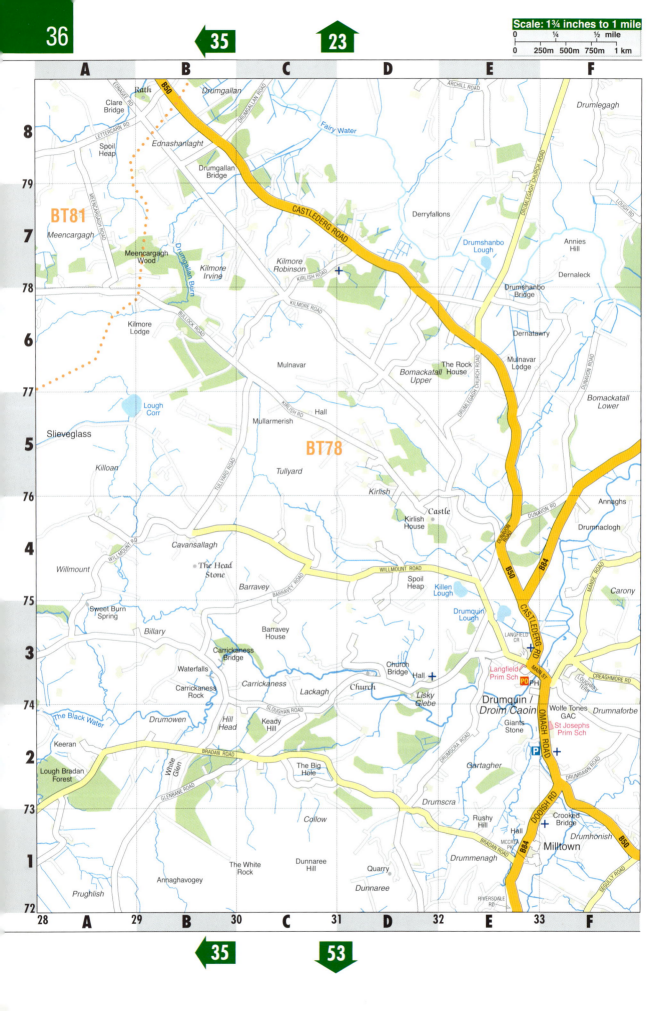

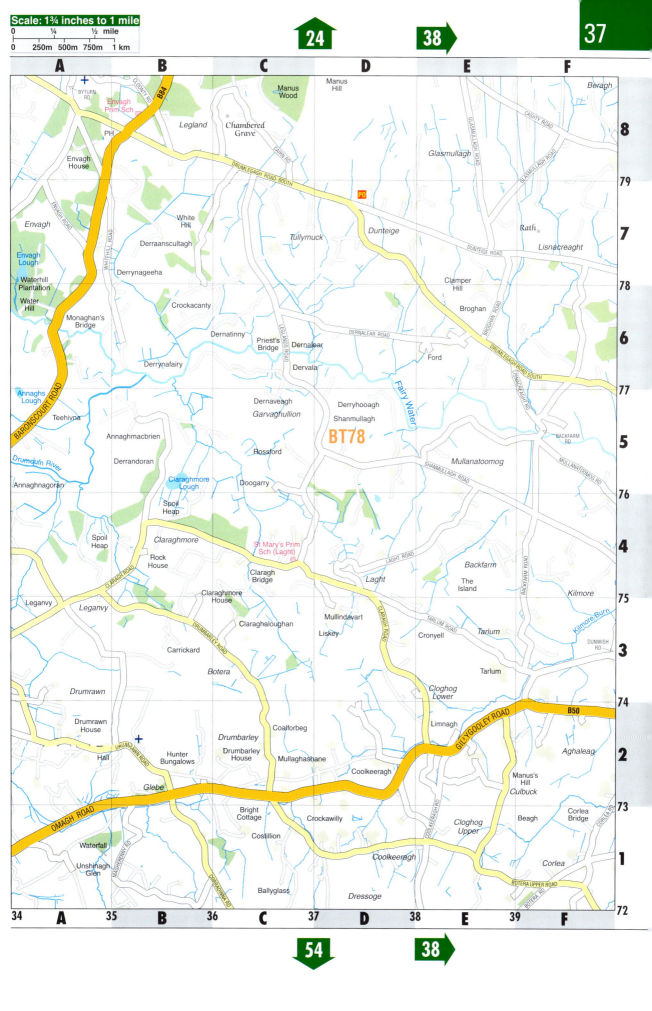

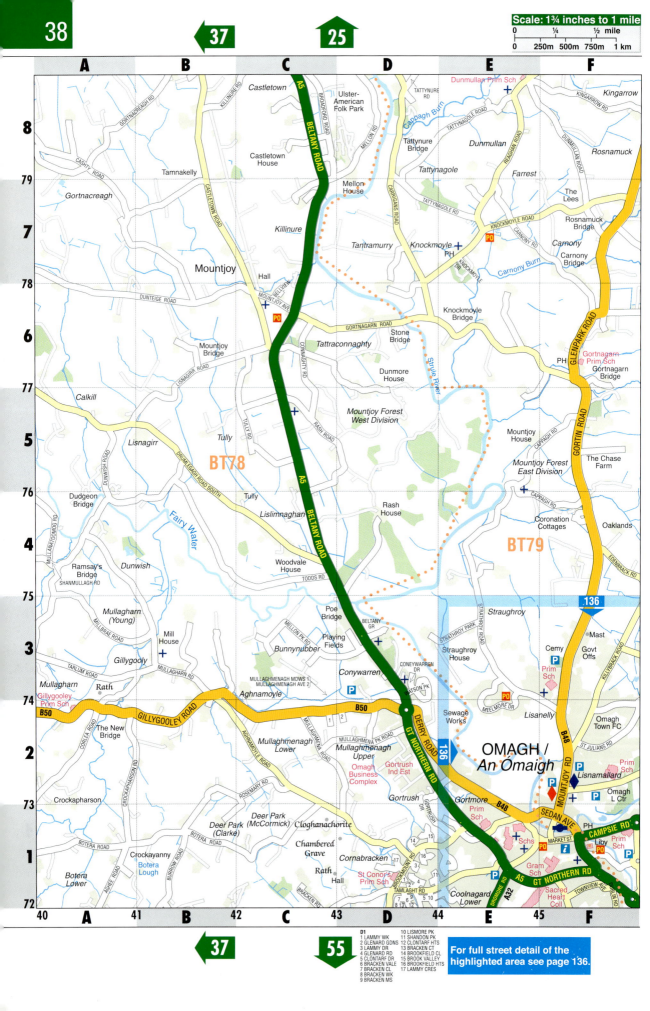

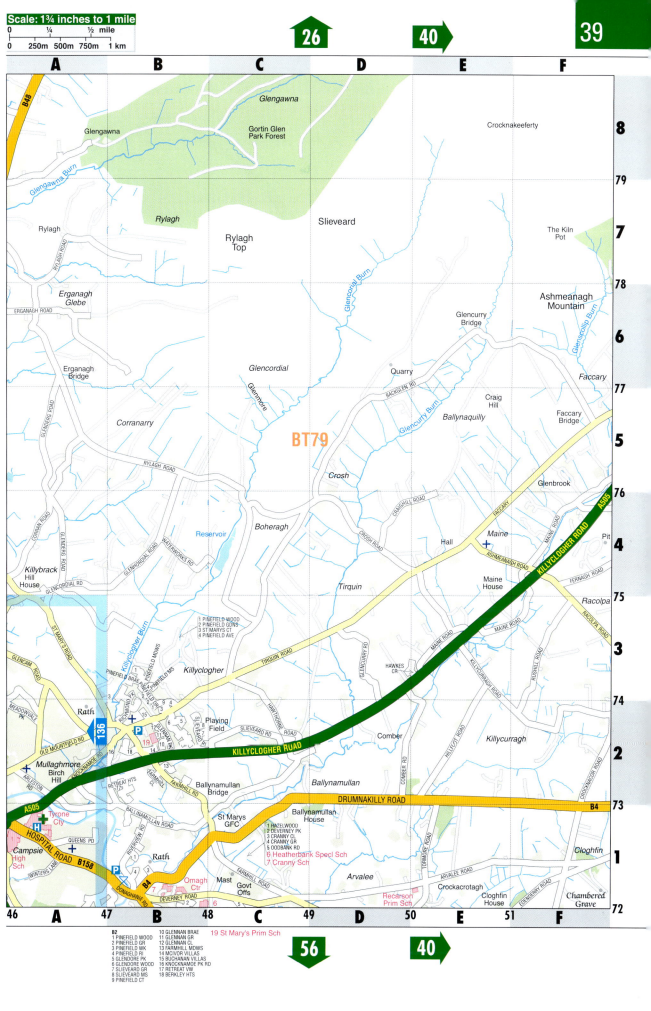

8
79
7
78
6
77
5
76
4
75
3
74
2
73
1
72

Glengawna

Gortin Glen
Park Forest

Crocknakeeferty

Rylagh

Glengawna Burn

Rylagh

Slieveard

The Kiln
Pot

B48

Rylagh

RYLAGH ROAD

Erganagh
Glebe

ERGANAGH ROAD

Erganagh
Bridge

GLENDERG ROAD

Corranarry

Glencordial Burn

Ashmeanagh
Mountain

Glenscollip Burn

Glencurry
Bridge

Quarry

Craig
Hill

Faccary

Faccary
Bridge

BACKGLEN RD

Ballynaquilly

BT79

Glencordial

Glenmore

Glencurry Burn

CORRAN ROAD

GLENDERG ROAD

GLENCORDIAL RD

Killybrack
Hill
House

RYLAGH ROAD

WATERWORKS RD

Reservoir

Boheragh

Crosh

Glenbrook

CRAIGHILL ROAD

Maine

A505

KILLYCLOGHER ROAD

Pit

FACCARY

MAINE ROAD

Hall

ASHMEANAGH ROAD

Maine
House

FERNAGH ROAD

Racolpa

RACOLPA ROAD

Tirquin

CROSH ROAD

MAINE ROAD

GLENCAM ROAD

ST MARYS ROAD

Killyclogher Burn

1 PINEFIELD WOOD
2 PINEFIELD GDNS
3 ST MARYS CT
4 PINEFIELD AVE

TIRQUIN ROAD

GLENCURRY RD

HAWKES
CR

MAINE ROAD

KILLYCURRAGH ROAD

Killycurragh

RUSHILL ROAD

CROCKNACOR ROAD

MEADOWVALE
PK

Rath

136

PINEFIELD BRAE

PINEFIELD MS

Killyclogher

RICHMOND PK

GREENVALE

SLIEVEARD

Playing
Field

SLIEVEARD RD

HAWTHORNE ROAD

Comber

COMBER RD

HILLCOT ROAD

GLENCAM ROAD

P

19

KNOCKNAMOE

KILLYCLOGHER ROAD

Mullaghmore
Birch Hill

RETREAT HTS

FARMHILL CL

FARMHILL RD

Ballynamullan
Bridge

Ballynamullan

Ballynamullan
House

DRUMNAKILLY ROAD

B4

A505

ARLESTON RD

Tyrone
Cty

H

QUEENS PD

BALLINAMULLAN ROAD

St Marys
GFC

1 HAZELWOOD
2 DEVERNEY PK
3 CRANNY CL
4 CRANNY GR
5 OODBANK RD
6 Heatherbank Specl Sch
7 Cranny Sch

TORMORE ROAD

ARVALEE ROAD

Cloghfin

HOSPITAL ROAD

Campsie
High Sch

WINTERS LANE

B158

RIVERVIEW RD

Rath

FARMHILL RD

P

B4

DONAGHANIE RD

Omagh
Ctr

DEVERNEY RD

Mast

Govt
Offs

Arvalee

Recarson
Prim Sch

Crockacrotagh

Cloghfin
House

Cloghfin

EDENDERRY ROAD

Chambered
Grave

B2
1 PINEFIELD WOOD
2 PINEFIELD GR
3 PINEFIELD WK
4 PINEFIELD RI
5 GLENDORE PK
6 GLENDORE WOOD
7 SLIEVEARD GR
8 SLIEVEARD MS
9 PINEFIELD CT
10 GLENNAN BRAE
11 GLENNAN GR
12 GLENNAN CL
13 FARMHILL MDWS
14 MCIVOR VILLAS
15 BUCHANAN VILLAS
16 KNOCKNAMOE PK RD
17 RETREAT VW
18 BERKLEY HTS

19 St Mary's Prim Sch

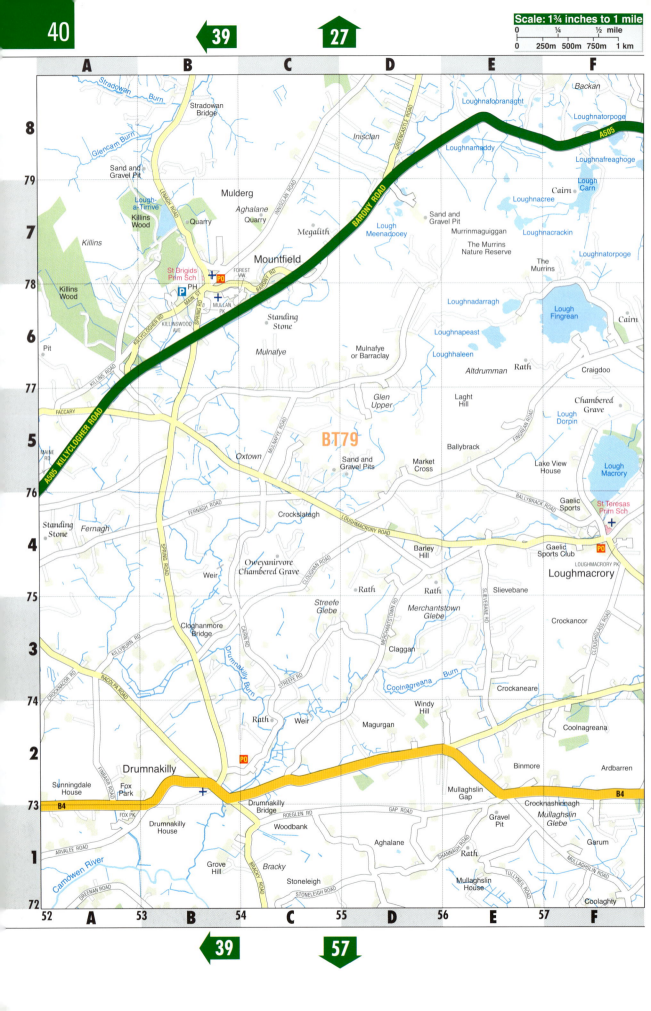

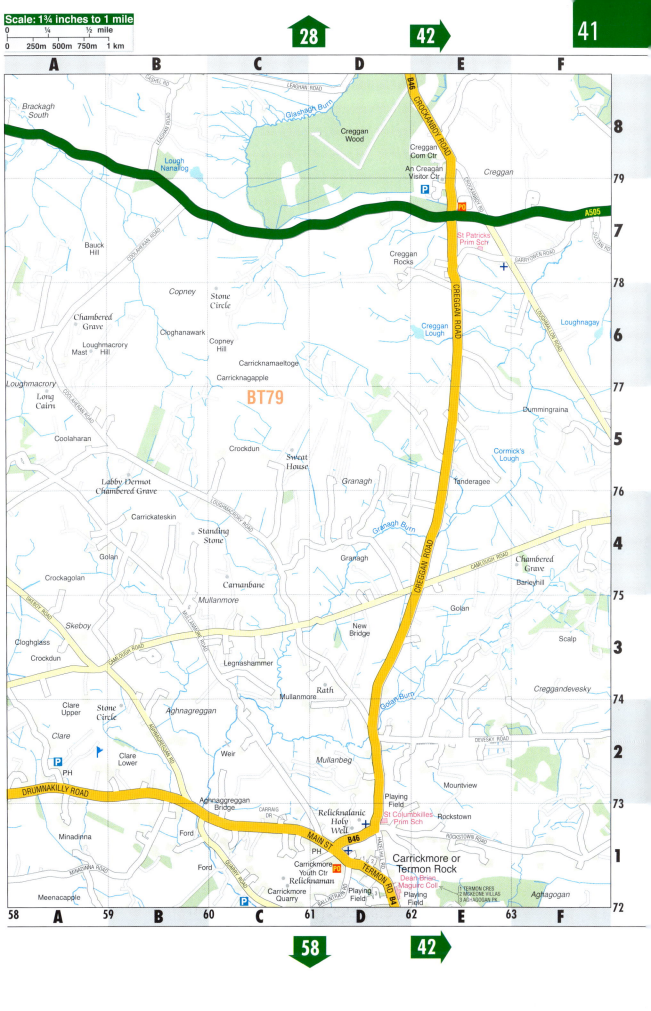

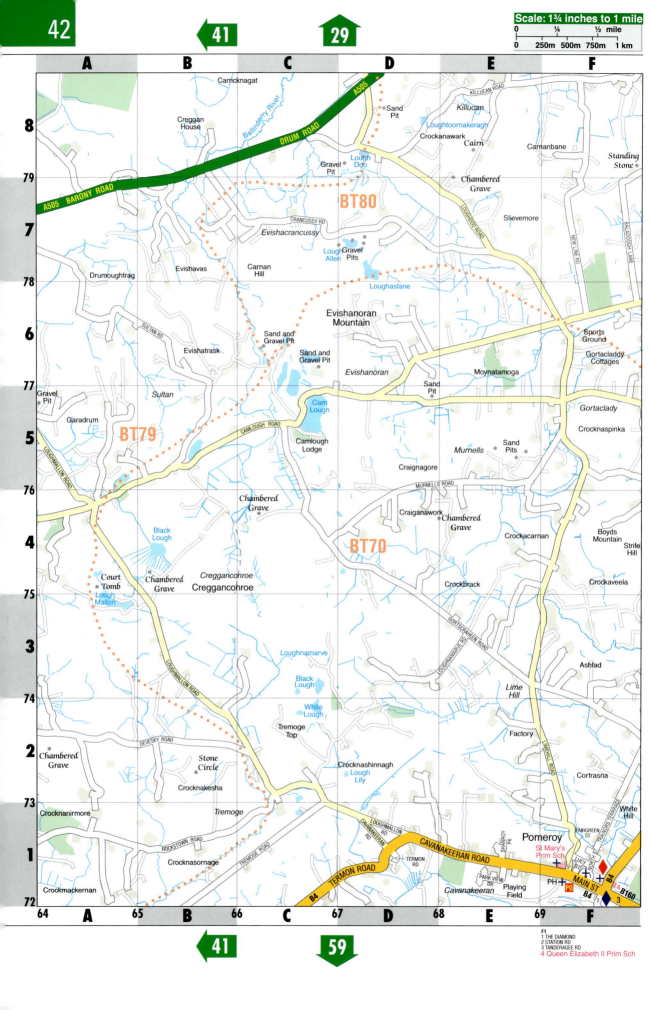

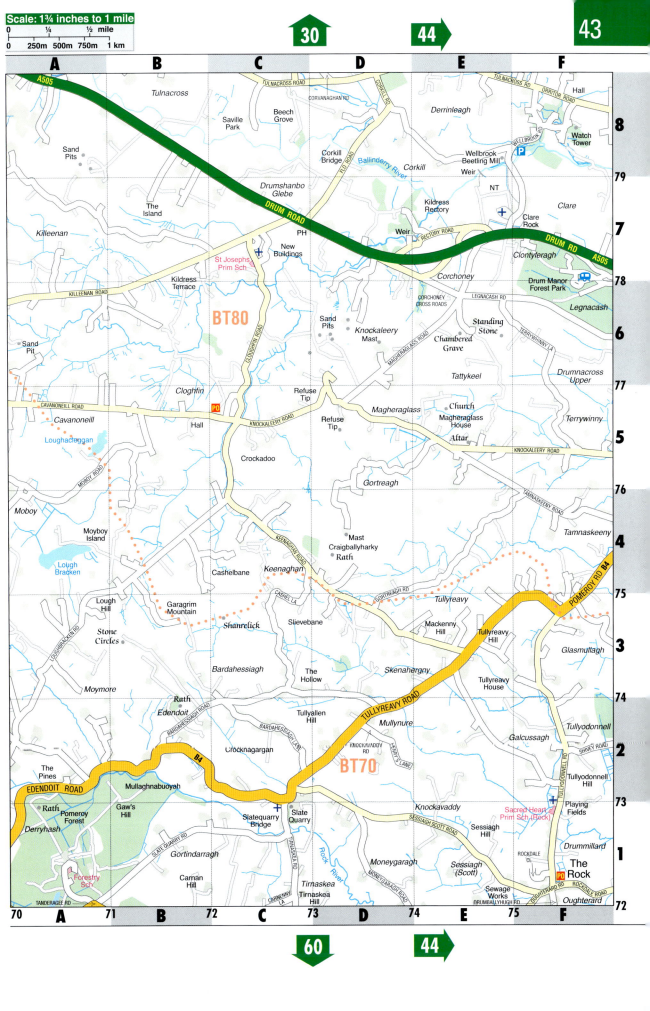

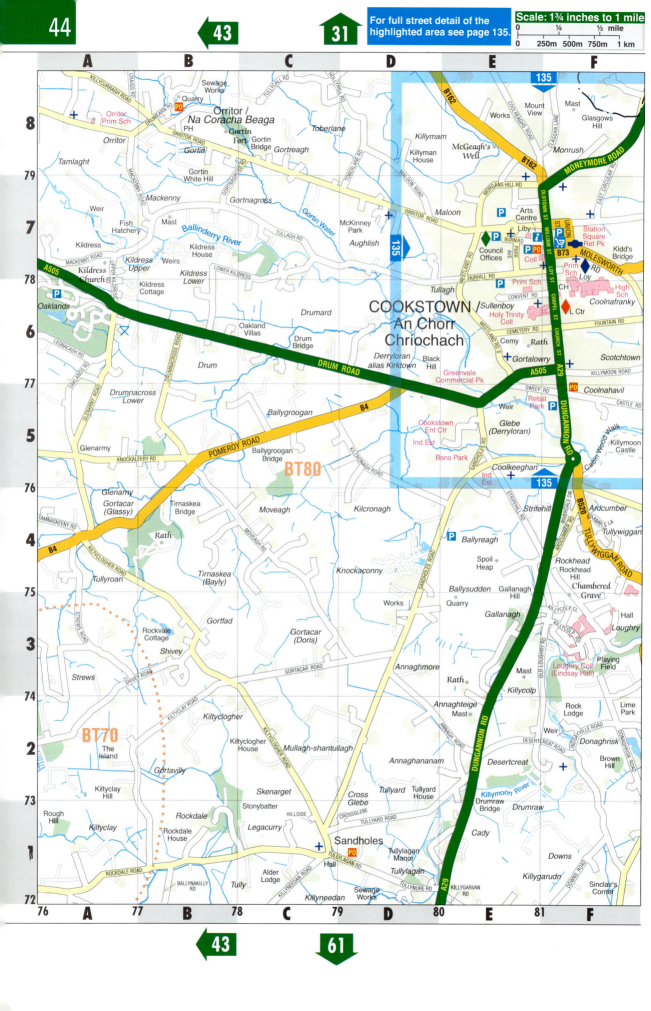

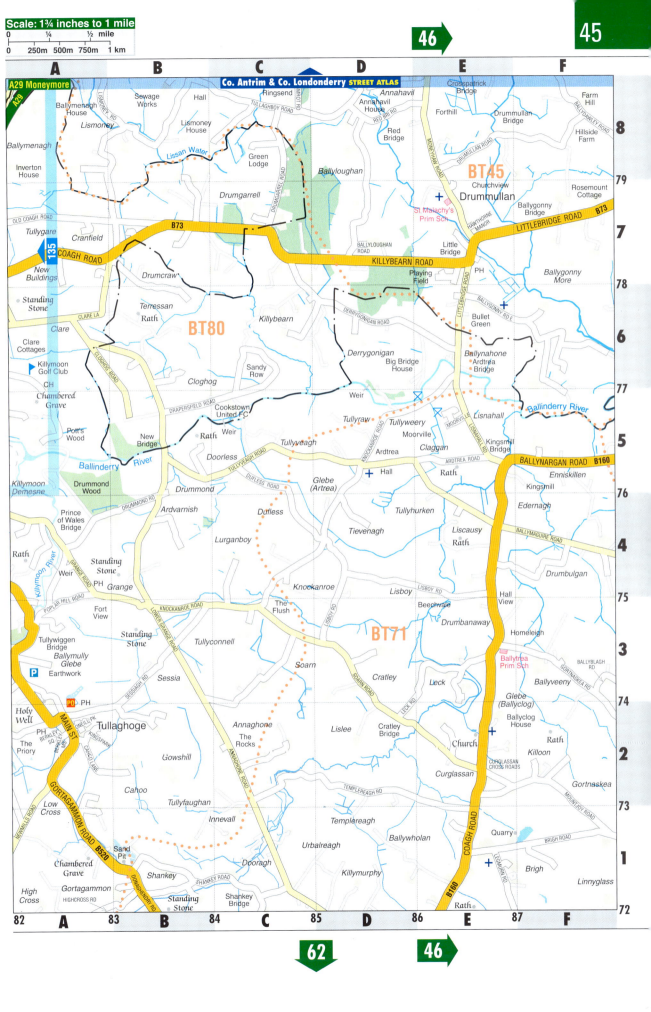

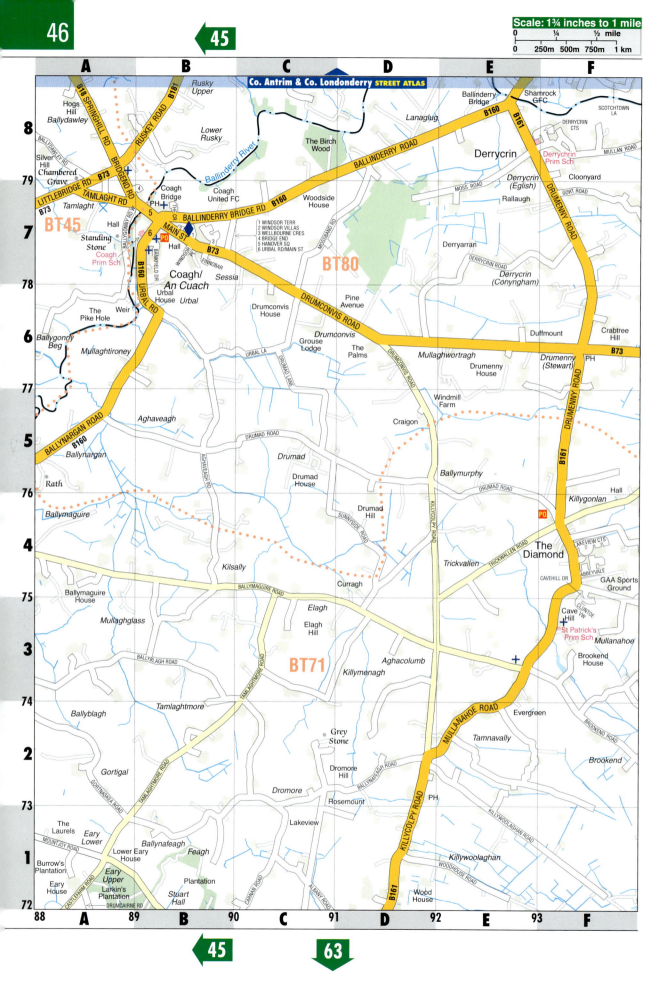

Co. Antrim & Co. Londonderry STREET ATLAS

A   **B**   **C**   **D**   **E**   **F**

Rusky
Upper

Hogs
Hill
Ballydawley

Lower
Rusky

Lanaglug

Ballinderry
Bridge

Shamrock
GFC

SCOTCHTOWN
LA

DERRYCRIN
CTS

MULLAN ROAD

8

SPRINGHILL RD

B73

RUSKEY ROAD

B181

The Birch
Wood

BALLINDERRY ROAD

B160

B161

Derrycrin

Derrychrin
Prim Sch

BALLYDAWLEY RD

Silver
Hill
Chambered
Grave

B73

BRIDGEND RD

LITTLEBRIDGE RD

Coagh
Bridge

Coagh United FC

Woodside
House

MOSS ROAD

Derrycrin
(Eglish)

Rallaugh

Cloonyard

GORT ROAD

79

TAMLAGHT RD

PH

B160

Derryarran

Derrycrin
Road

Duffmount

DRUMENNY ROAD

B73

7

BT45

Tamlaght

Hall

Standing
Stone

Coagh Prim Sch

5

Hall

BALLINDERRY BRIDGE RD

MAIN ST

B73

1 Windsor Terr
2 Windsor Villas
3 Wellbourne Cres
4 Bridge End
5 Hanover Sq
6 Urbal Rd/Main St

MOSSBAND RD

Derrycrin
(Conyngham)

BT80

PO

6

WINDSOR PL

FINNOBAR

Coagh/
An Cuach

Sessia

78

B160

URBAL RD

BALLYGONNY RD

BANKFIELD DR

Urbal
House

Urbal

Drumconvis
House

DRUMCONVIS ROAD

Pine
Avenue

6

Ballygonny
Beg

The
Pike Hole

Weir

Mullaghtironey

Drumconvis

URBAL LA

Grouse
Lodge

The
Palms

DRUMAD LANE

Mullaghwortragh

Drumenny
House

Drumenny
(Stewart)

PH

B73

Crabtree
Hill

77

Windmill
Farm

Craigon

DRUMCONVIS ROAD

DRUMENNY ROAD

B161

5

BALLYNARGAN ROAD

B160

Aghaveagh

Ballynargan

AGHAVEAGH RD

DRUMAD ROAD

Drumad

Drumad
House

Ballymurphy

DRUMAD ROAD

Killygonlan

Hall

76

Rath

Ballymaguire

Drumad
Hill

SUNNYSIDE ROAD

KILLYCOLPY ROAD

PO

LAKEVIEW CTS

The Diamond

4

Kilsally

BALLYMAGUIRE ROAD

Curragh

Trickvallen

TRICKWALLEN ROAD

CAVEHILL DR

ABBEYVALE

GAA Sports
Ground

CLUNTOE

CW

75

Ballymaguire
House

Mullaghglass

Elagh

Elagh
Hill

Cave
Hill

St Patrick's
Prim Sch

Mullanahoe

Brookend
House

3

BALLYBLAGH ROAD

BT71

Killymenagh

Aghacolumb

TAMLAGHTMORE ROAD

74

Ballyblagh

Tamlaghtmore

MULLANAHOE ROAD

Evergreen

Tamnavally

BROOKEND ROAD

2

Gortigal

GORTNASKEA ROAD

Grey
Stone

Dromore
Hill

BALLYNAFEIGH ROAD

Brookend

KILLYCOLPY ROAD

PH

KILLYWOOLAGHAN ROAD

73

The
Laurels

Eary
Lower

Dromore

Rosemount

Lakeview

Killywoolaghan

WOODHOUSE ROAD

1

MOUNTJOY RD

Burrow's
Plantation

Lower Eary
House

Ballynafeagh

Feagh

CARNAN ROAD

ALBANY ROAD

Eary
House

CASTLEFARM RD

Eary
Upper

Larkin's
Plantation

Plantation

Stuart
Hall

B161

Wood
House

72

DRUMCAIRNE RD

Scale: 1¾ inches to 1 mile

0   ¼   ½   mile
0   250m 500m 750m 1 km

A   B   C   D   E   F

Riverside Cottage

KINTURK RD

Kinturk
Factory

Mullan Upper

Kinturk Flat

ANNETER LANE

Kinturk Cultural Centre

The Gort alias Eglish

Anneeter Beg

ANNETER ROAD

Anneeter Point

The Gort Moss Walk

Annaghmore

ANNAGHMORE RD

Works

BT80

Anneeter More

Staniers Point

ANNAGHMORE LA

Derrycarbane

Coyles Cottage

Annaghmore Hill

Blockfield House

TIRNANOG

ANNETER ROAD

Lough Neagh

BATTERY ROAD

Cluntoe (Quin)

TOBIN PK

Moortown

Ardean

The Battery

Drumenny (Conyngham)

PO

B73

St MALACHY'S PK

Clinbo

Tobin Meml Park (GFG)

St Peter's Prim Sch

ARDBOE RD

Moortown GFC

Lifeboat Sta

Kinrush

KINRUSH ROAD

Oughtragh

Claggan

Cluntoe (Richardson)

Sessia

Kinrush

ARDBOE ROAD

Ardboe Abbey Church

Airfield (disused)

Ardboe

Ardboe Cross Point

PH

Works

Ardboe Bsns Pk

Works

Farsnagh

KILMASCALLY ROAD

Resource Ctr

Farsnagh Point

Cave Lodge

Kilmascally

Kilmascally House

BT71

KILLYCANAVAN ROAD

Lurgyroe

Killycanavan Upper

Kiltagh Point

Killycanavan Lower

8 79 7 78 6 77 5 76 4 75 3

94 A 95 B 96 C 97 D 98 E 99 F

94 G H I 97

82

Co. Antrim & Co. Londonderry STREET ATLAS

Killymuck

Lakeside

KILLYMUCK ROAD

Ballinderry River

Taylor's Rock

81

MULLAN ROAD

Mullan Point

SCOTCHTOWN LA

BT80

Lower Mullan

Fish Farm

KINTURK RD

80

94 G 95 H 96 I 97

72

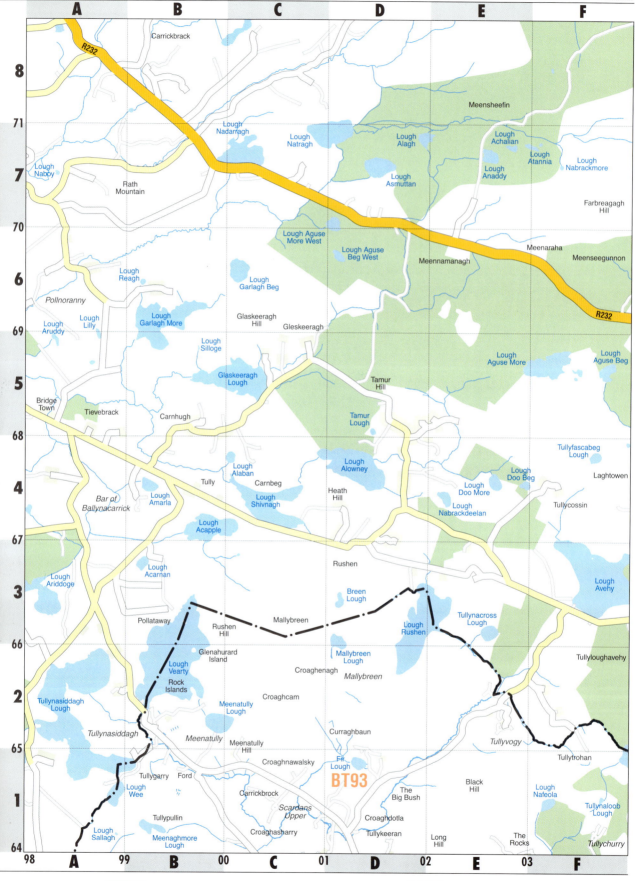

Scale: 1¾ inches to 1 mile

0   ¼   ½   mile
0   250m 500m 750m 1 km

8
71
7
70
6
69
5
68
4
67
3
2
65
1
64

98   A   99   B   00   C   01   D   02   E   03   F

65   66

R232

Carrickbrack

Lough Nadarragh

Lough Natragh

Lough Alagh

Meensheefin

Lough Achalian

Lough Atannia

Lough Nabrackmore

Lough Naboy

Rath Mountain

Lough Asmuttan

Lough Anaddy

Meenaraha

Farbreagagh Hill

Meenseegunnon

Meennamanagh

Lough Reagh

Lough Aguse More West

Lough Aguse Beg West

R232

Pollnoranny

Lough Garlagh Beg

Lough Aruddy

Lough Lilly

Lough Garlagh More

Glaskeeragh Hill

Gleskeeragh

Lough Aguse More

Lough Aguse Beg

Lough Silloge

Glaskeeragh Lough

Tamur Hill

Bridge Town

Tievebrack

Carnhugh

Tamur Lough

Tullyfascabeg Lough

Lough Doo Beg

Laghtowen

Lough Alaban

Carnbeg

Lough Alowney

Lough Doo More

Tullycossin

Bar of Ballynacarrick

Tully

Lough Amarla

Lough Shivnagh

Heath Hill

Lough Nabrackdeelan

Lough Acapple

Rushen

Lough Ariddoge

Lough Acarnan

Lough Avehy

Breen Lough

Tullynacross Lough

Pollataway

Rushen Hill

Mallybreen

Lough Rushen

Glenahurard Island

Mallybreen Lough

Tullyloughavehy

Lough Vearty

Croaghenagh

Mallybreen

Rock Islands

Tullynasiddagh Lough

Meenatully Lough

Croaghcam

Tullyvogy

Tullynasiddagh

Meenatully

Meenatully Hill

Curraghbaun

Tullytrohan

Tullygarry

Ford

Croaghnawalsky

Fir Lough

BT93

Black Hill

Lough Nafeola

Lough Wee

Tullypullin

Carrickbrock

The Big Bush

Tullynaloob Lough

Lough Sallagh

Meenaghmore Lough

Scardans Upper

Croaghasharry

Croaghdotla

Tullykeeran

Long Hill

The Rocks

Tullychurry

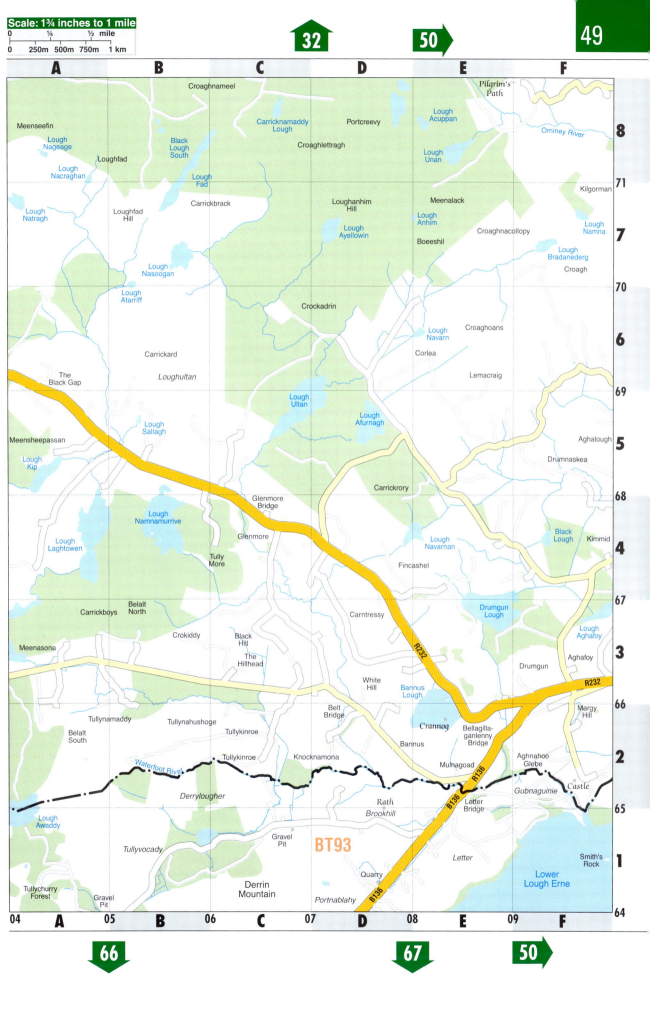

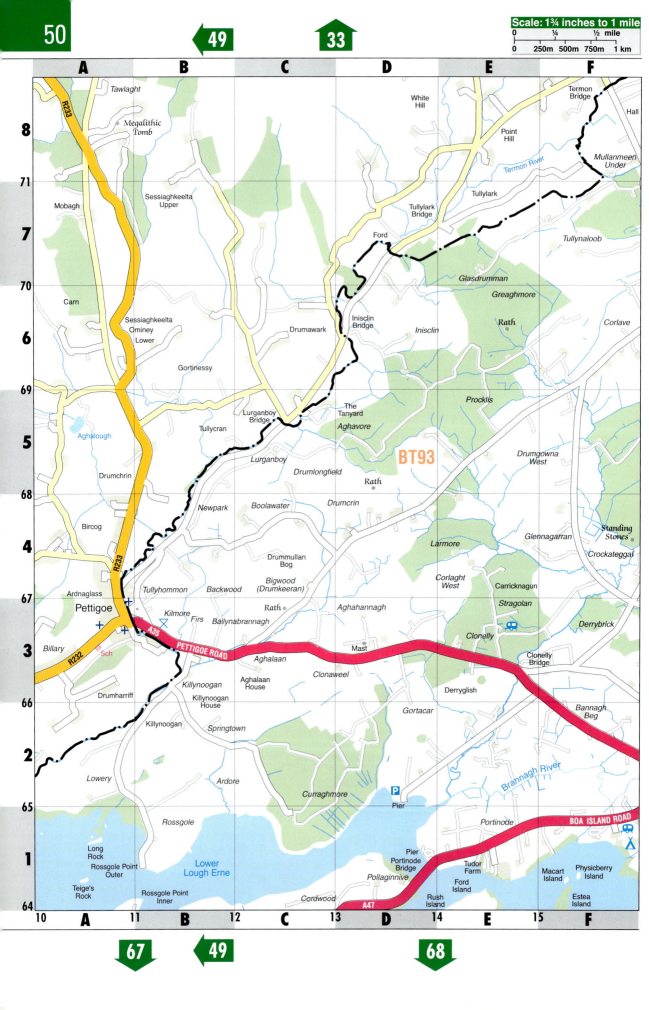

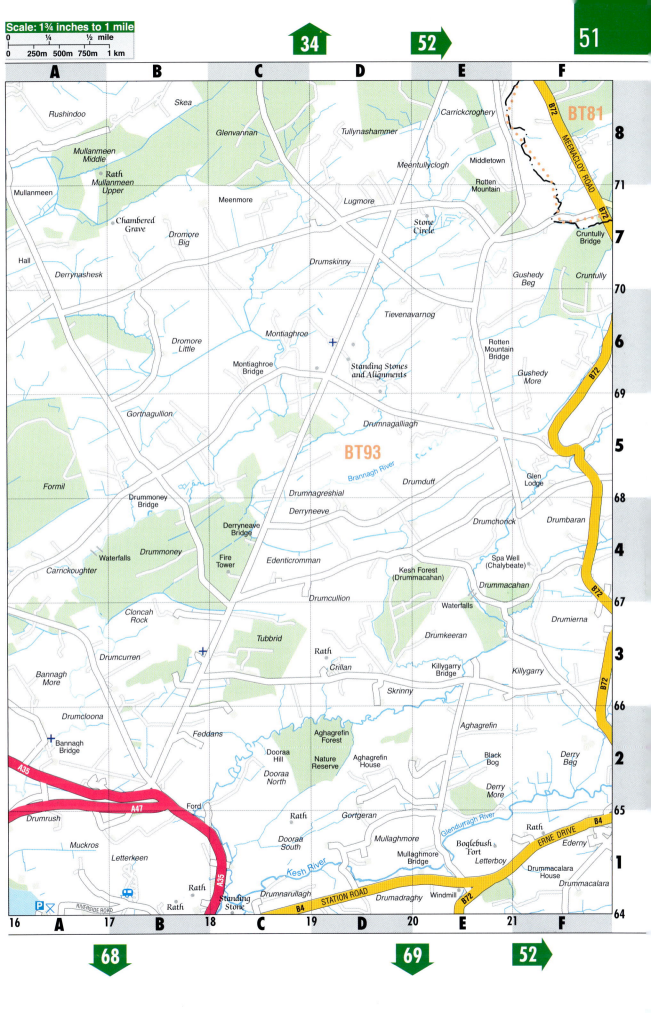

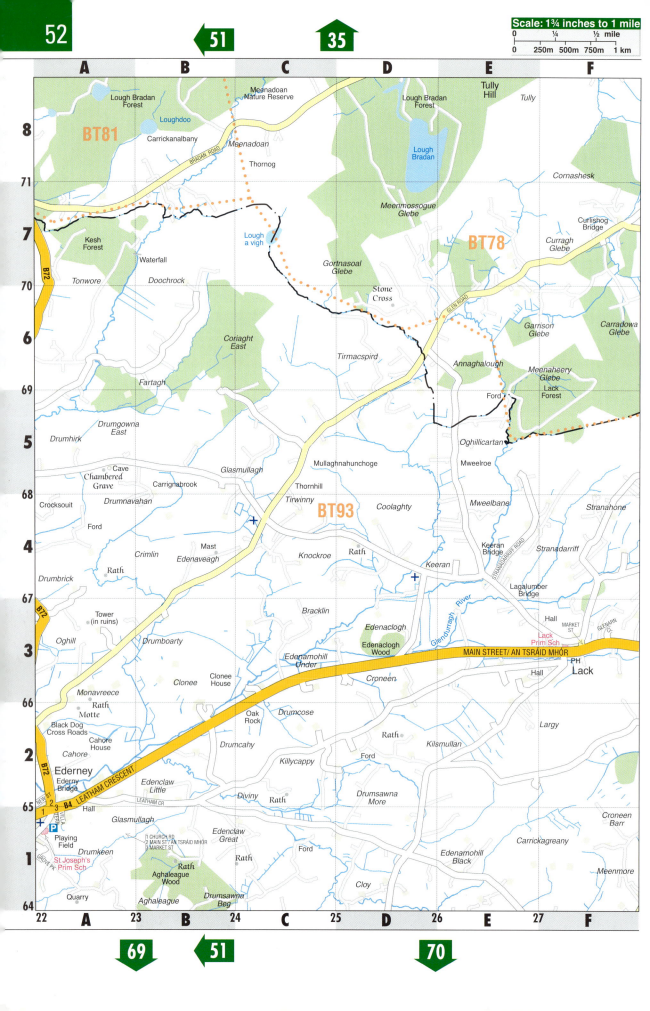

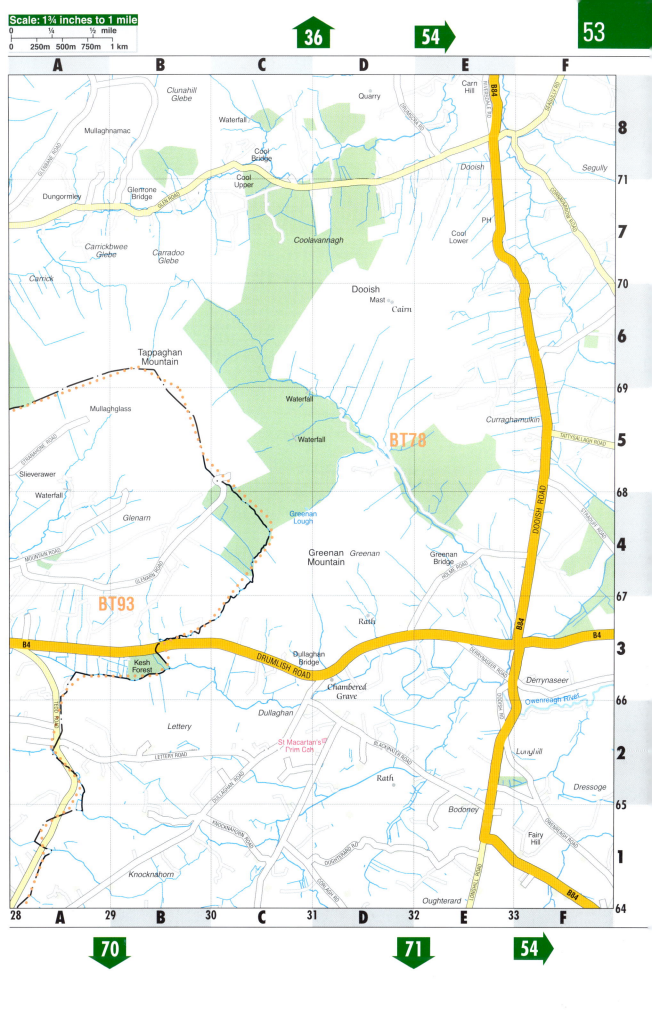

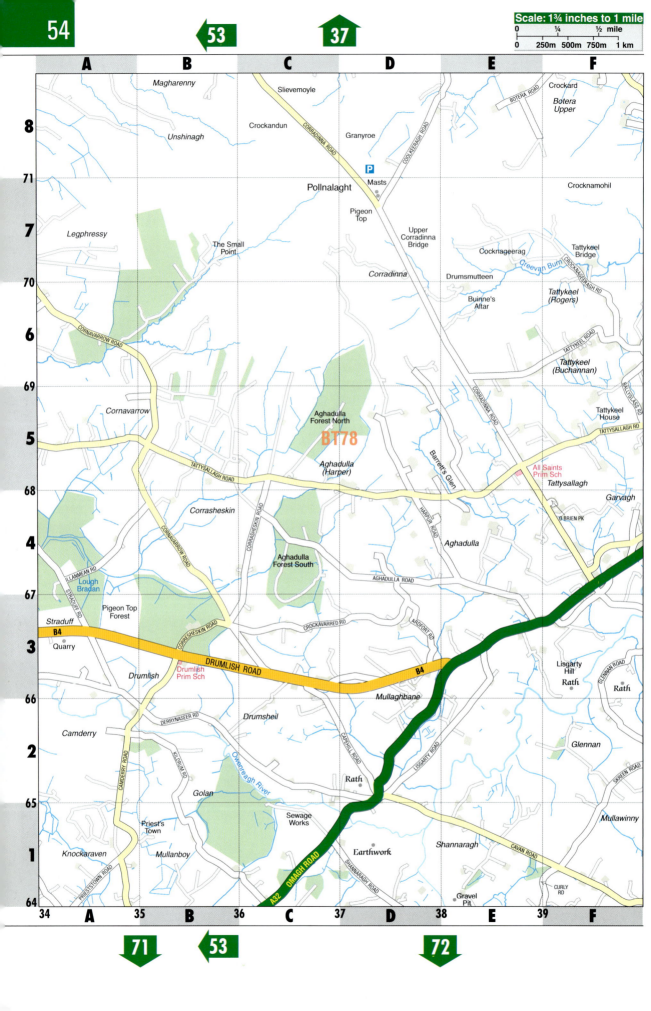

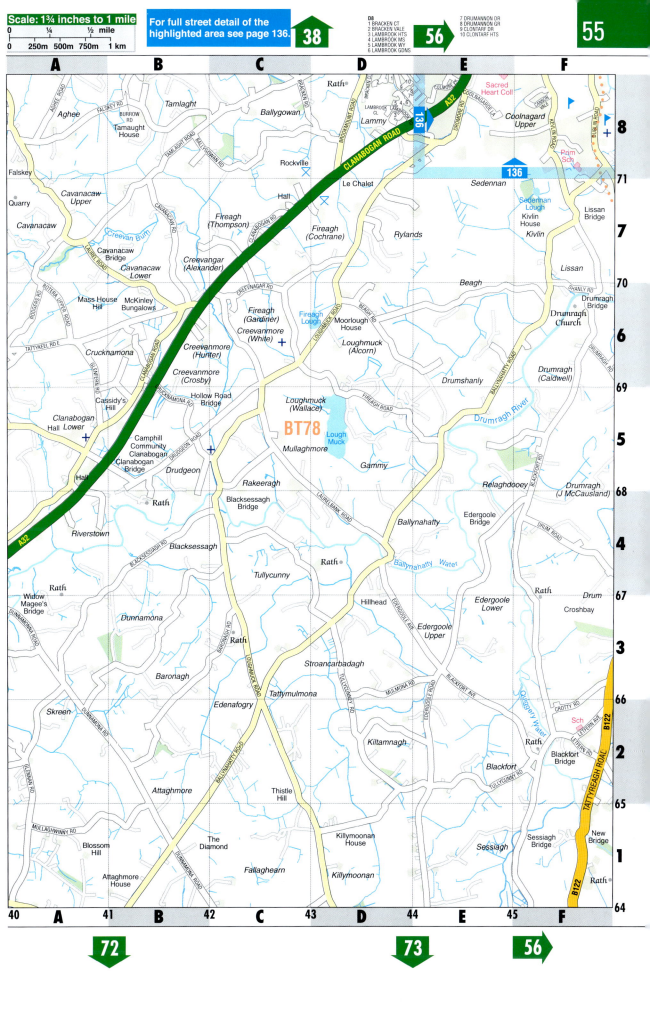

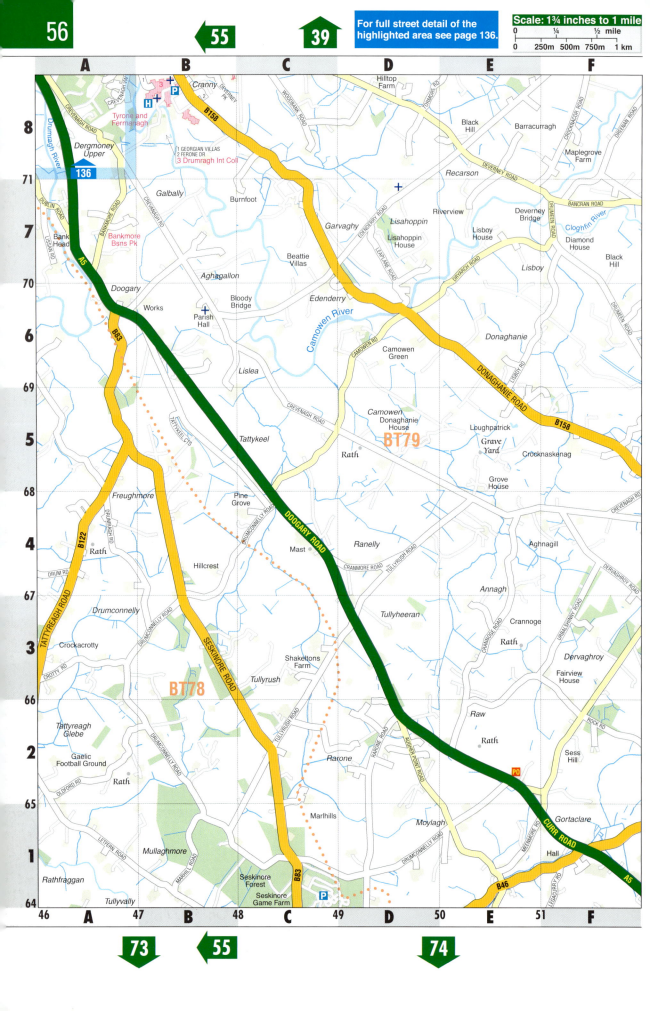

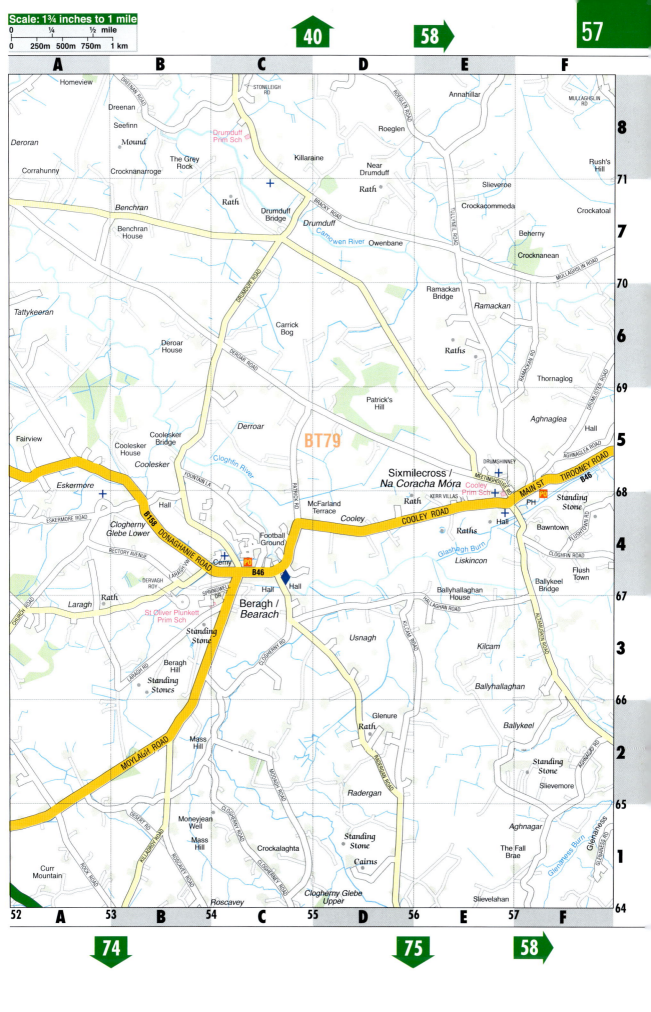

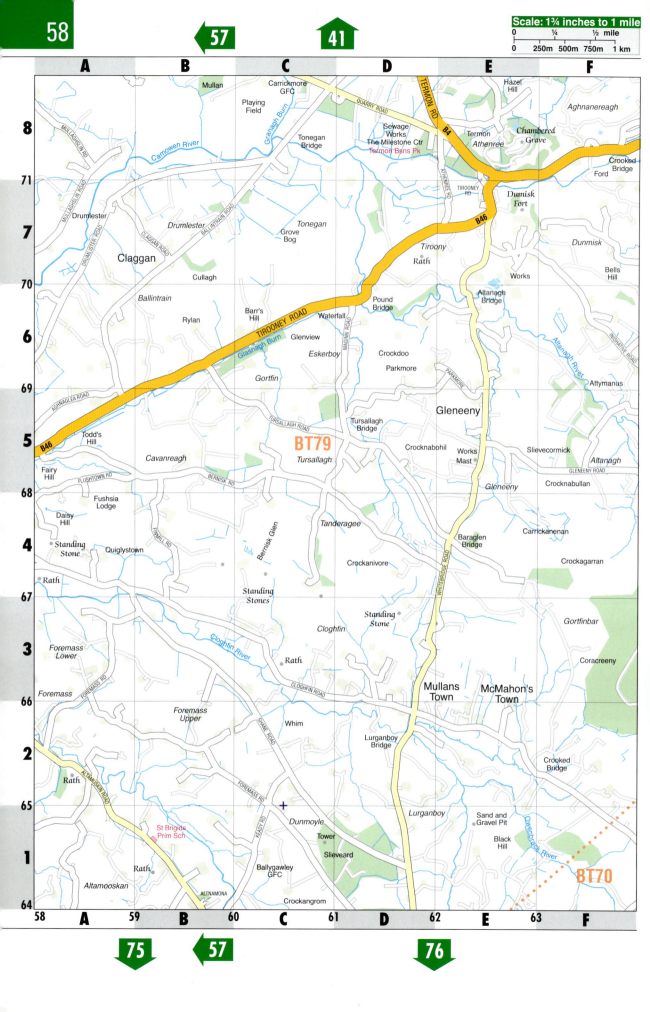

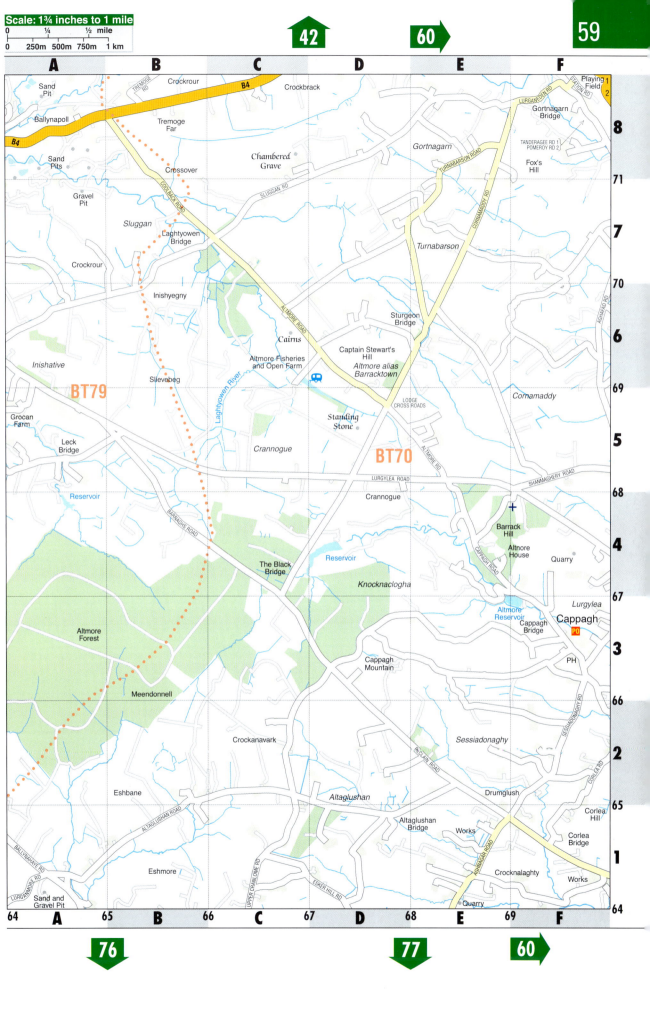

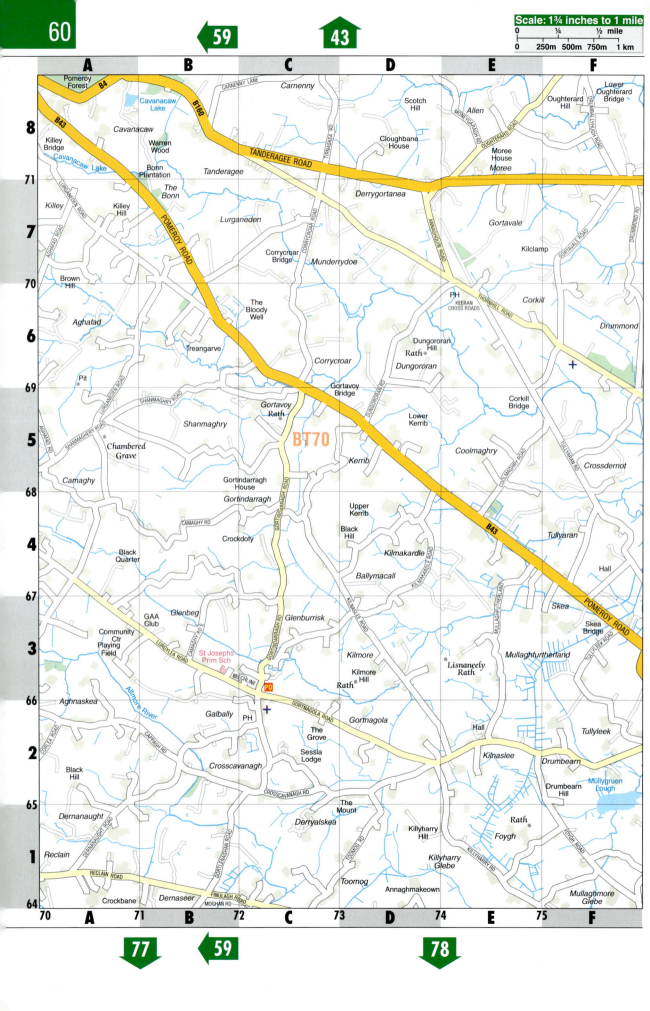

A   B   C   D   E   F

8
71
7
70
6
69
5
68
4
67
3
66
2
65
1
64

A   B   C   D   E   F
70   71   72   73   74   75

Pomeroy Forest
B4
Cavanacaw Lake
Carnenny Lane
Carnenny
Scotch Hill
Allen
Oughterard Hill
Lower Oughterard Bridge
B160
B43
Killey Bridge
Cavanacaw
Warren Wood
Cloughbane House
MONEYGARAGH RD
OUGHTERARD ROAD
DRUMBALLYHUGH ROAD
Moree House
Moree
Cavanacaw Lake
Killey
The Bonn
Bonn Plantation
Tanderagee
TANDERAGEE ROAD
Derrygortanea
TIRNASKEA RD
ANNAGHLUN ROAD
Gortavale
DRUMMOND RD
Killey Hill
Lurganeden
CORRYCROAR ROAD
Kilclamp
GORTAVALE ROAD
AGHAFAD ROAD
LURGANEDEN ROAD
POMEROY ROAD
Corrycroar Bridge
Munderrydoe
PH
KEERAN CROSS ROADS
THORNHILL ROAD
Corkill
Brown Hill
Aghafad
The Bloody Well
Treangarve
Corrycroar
Dungororan Hill
Rath
Dungororan
Drummond
Pit
SHANMAGHRY ROAD
LURGANEDEN ROAD
AGHAFAD RD
Gortavoy Bridge
DUNGORORAN RD
Corkill Bridge
Gortavoy Rath
Lower Kerrib
Corkill Bridge
BT70
Shanmaghry
Chambered Grave
Kerrib
Coolmaghry
Crossdernot
Camaghy
Gortindarragh House
GORTINDARRAGH ROAD
Upper Kerrib
COOLMAGHRY ROAD
TULLYARAN RD
Gortindarragh
CAMAGHY RD
Crockdoty
Black Hill
Kilmakardle
B43
Tullyaran
Black Quarter
KILMAKARDLE ROAD
Ballymacall
Hall
Glenbeg
Glenburrisk
KILNASLEE ROAD
Skea
POMEROY ROAD
GAA Club
LURGYLEA ROAD
CAMAGHY RD
GORTINDARRAGH RD
Kilmore
MULLAGHFURTHERLAND
Skea Bridge
Community Ctr Playing Field
St Josephs Prim Sch
BEECHLINE
Kilmore Hill
Rath
Lisnaneely Rath
Mullaghfurtherland
TULLYLEEK ROAD
Aghnaskea
PO
Galbally
Allmore River
PH
GORTNAGOLA ROAD
Gortnagola
Hall
Tullyleek
CORLEA ROAD
The Grove
Kilnaslee
Drumbearn
CAPPAGH RD
Crosscavanagh
Sessia Lodge
Drumbearn Hill
Mullygruen Lough
Black Hill
CROSSCAVANAGH RD
Derryalskea
Killyharry Hill
Rath
Foygh
Dernanaught
DERNANAUGHT ROAD
The Mount
TOOMOG RD
KILLYHARRY RD
FOYGH ROAD
Reclain
RECLAIN ROAD
GORTLENAGHAN ROAD
FINULAGH ROAD
Killyharry Glebe
Crockbane
Dernaseer
MOGHAN RD
Toomog
Annaghmakeown
Mullaghmore Glebe

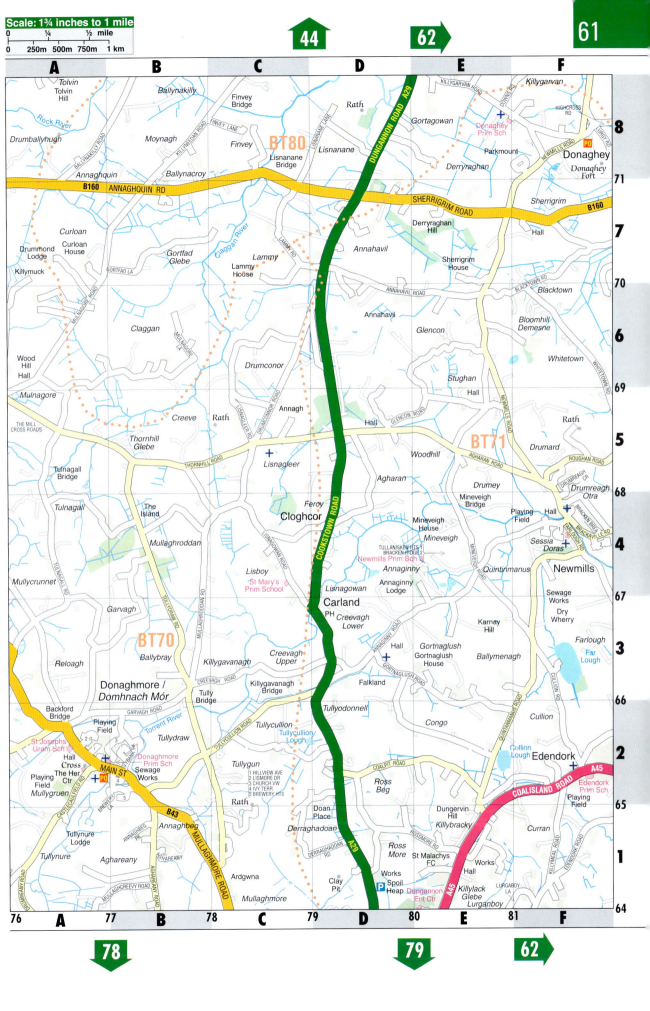

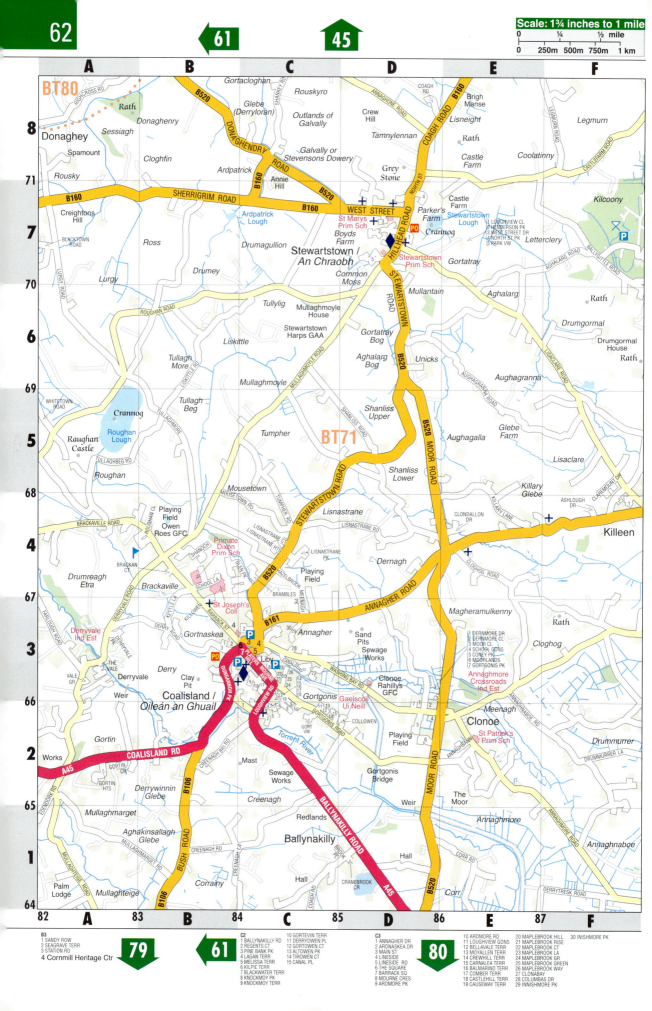

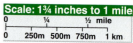

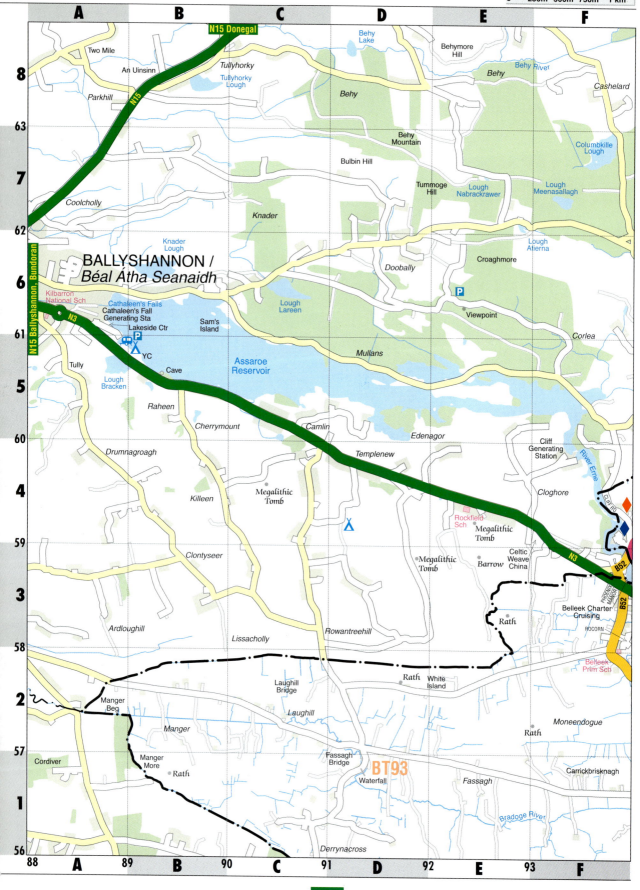

N15 Donegal

Two Mile

An Uinsinn

Tullyhorky

Tullyhorky Lough

Behy Lake

Behymore Hill

Behy

Behy River

Cashelard

Parkhill

N15

Behy

Coolcholly

Behy Mountain

Columbkille Lough

Bulbin Hill

Tummoge Hill

Lough Nabrackrawer

Lough Meenasallagh

Knader

Knader Lough

Knader

Lough Atierna

BALLYSHANNON /
Béal Átha Seanaidh

Doobally

Croaghmore

N15 Ballyshannon, Bundoran

Kilbarron National Sch

Cathaleen's Falls

Cathaleen's Fall Generating Sta

Lakeside Ctr

N3

Sam's Island

Lough Lareen

P

Viewpoint

Corlea

YC

Cave

Assaroe Reservoir

Mullans

Tully

Lough Bracken

Raheen

Cherrymount

Camlin

Edenagor

Templenew

Cliff Generating Station

River Erne

Drumnagroagh

Killeen

Megalithic Tomb

Cloghore

Clontyseer

Megalithic Tomb

Rockfield Sch

Megalithic Tomb

Celtic Weave China

N3

CLIFF RD

B52

B52

Ardloughill

Lissacholly

Rowantreehill

Megalithic Tomb

Barrow

Rath

Belleek Charter Cruising

PHOENIX MANOR

ROCORN

Manger Beg

Laughill Bridge

Rath

White Island

Rath

Moneendogue

Belleek Prim Sch

Manger

Laughill

Rath

Cordiver

Manger More

Rath

Fassagh Bridge

Waterfall

BT93

Fassagh

Carrickbrisknagh

Bradoge River

Derrynacross

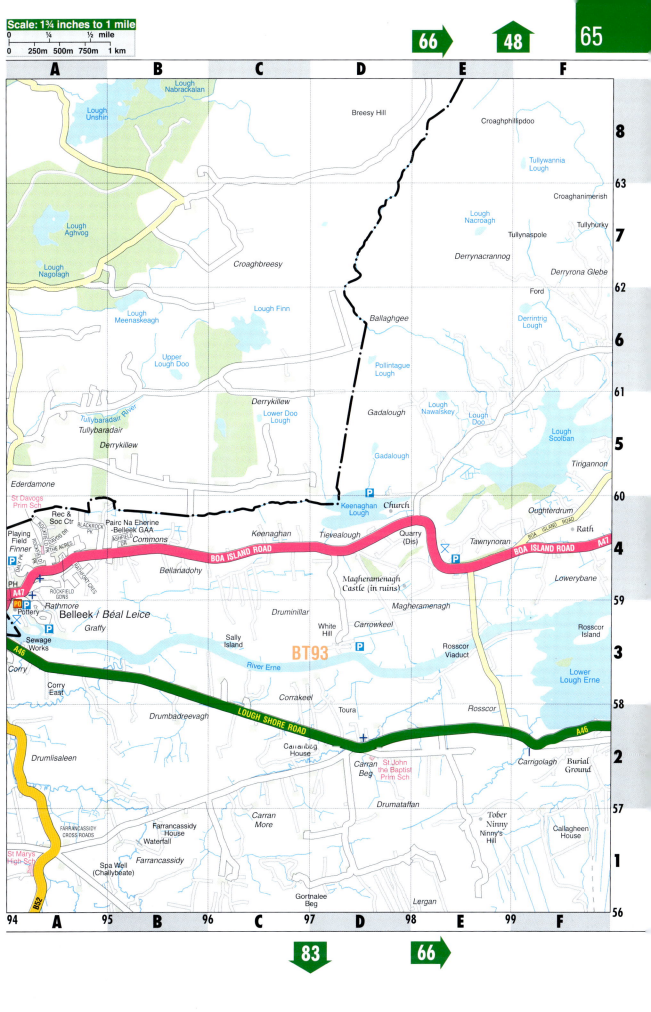

A   B   C   D   E   F

8

Lough Nabrackalan

Breesy Hill

Croaghphillipdoo

Lough Unshin

63

Tullywannia Lough

Croaghanimerish

7

Lough Aghvog

Lough Nacroagh

Tullyhurky

Croaghbreesy

Tullynaspole

Lough Nagolagh

Derrynacrannog

62

Derryrona Glebe

Lough Meenaskeagh

Lough Finn

Ballaghgee

Ford

6

Derrintrig Lough

Upper Lough Doo

Pollintague Lough

61

Derrykillew

Gadalough

Lough Nawalskey

Lough Doo

Tullybaradair River

Lower Doo Lough

Tullybaradair

Lough Scolban

Derrykillew

5

Gadalough

Tirigannon

Ederdamone

60

Keenaghan Lough

Church

Oughterdrum

St Davogs Prim Sch

Rec & Soc Ctr

P

BOA ISLAND ROAD

Rath

Playing Field

Pairc Na Eherine -Belleek GAA

Keenaghan

Tievealough

Quarry (Dis)

Tawnynoran

BOA ISLAND ROAD

A47

Finner

Commons

BOA ISLAND ROAD

4

Blackrock Pk

Bellanadohy

Magheramenagh Castle (in ruins)

P

Lowerybane

A47

Rockfield Gdns

Magheramenagh

59

PH

Druminillar

White Hill

Carrowkeel

Rosscor Island

Rathmore

Belleek / Béal Leice

Graffy

Sally Island

P

BT93

Rosscor Viaduct

3

Sewage Works

River Erne

Corrakeel

A46

Corry

Toura

Rosscor

Lower Lough Erne

Corry East

Drumbadreevagh

LOUGH SHORE ROAD

58

A46

Carrigolagh

Drumlisaleen

Carranbeg House

Carran Beg

St John the Baptist Prim Sch

Burial Ground

2

Drumataffan

57

Farrancassidy Cross Roads

Farrancassidy House Waterfall

Carran More

Tober Ninny

Callagheen House

B52

Ninny's Hill

St Marys High Sch

Farrancassidy

1

Spa Well (Challybeate)

Gortnalee Beg

Lergan

56

94   A   95   B   96   C   97   D   98   E   99   F

A B C D E F

8

Cordwood
Drumgrenaghan   Middletown
A47 BOA ISLAND ROAD A47

Hare
Island

Muckros
Point

Kesh
Water Foot

Kesh River
Kesh /
An Cheis
Rosscah   ERNE PK
Rosscolban

FORTVIEW PK

CREVENISH PK 1
PETTIGOE RD 2
RIVERSIDE RD 3

Kesh
Prim Sch
Playing
Field

63

Gubbakip

Scallan's
Rock

7

Rath
Cruninish
Island

Water
Horse

Black
Rock

Horse
Island

Duck
Island

Rabbit
Island

Crevinish Castle
(in ruins)

Curley's
Rock

Grave
Yard

Crevinish

Lisingle

Rath

Cornacrea

62

Scattered
Rocks

Kinnausy
Island

Camplany

Mullaghfad

BT93

Cady

Rath

6

Gravel
Ridge

Gravel Ridge
Island

Gubbaroe
Point

Grubbaroe

Gorteen

Rath
Standing
Stones

Stallion
Cowes

61

Cleenishmeen
Island

Deerahan
Island

Castle Archdale
Islands Nature
Reserve

Strongbow
Island

Clareview

Ardatrave

Rath

Rath

Drumbarna

5

Creefin
Island

Crevinishaugh
Island

White
Island

Church
(in ruins)

60

Lower
Lough Erne

Cleenishgarve
Island

White
Hill

Inish More or
Davy's Island

Inish Beg or
Tom's Island

Abbey
(remains of)

4

Gay
Island

Castle Archdale
Islands Nature
Reserve

Slevindoo
Point

59

Rossmore

Rossbeg
Point

YH

Wildlife
Area

3

Castle Archdale
Islands Nature
Reserve

Rossmore
Point

Duross
Point

Castle Archdale
Country Park
Duross
Bay

Rossachrin
Rath

58

BT94

Mullies

2

Heron
Island

Gull
Rock

Duross

Tislevin
House

57

Home
Bay

Lignameeltoge
Point

Glenross
Bay

1

Tully

Sand
Bay

Bess
Island

Kerney
Island

Gaffer
Island

Glenross

Lignameeltoge

56

Tully
Point

12 A 13 B 14 C 15 D 16 E 17 F

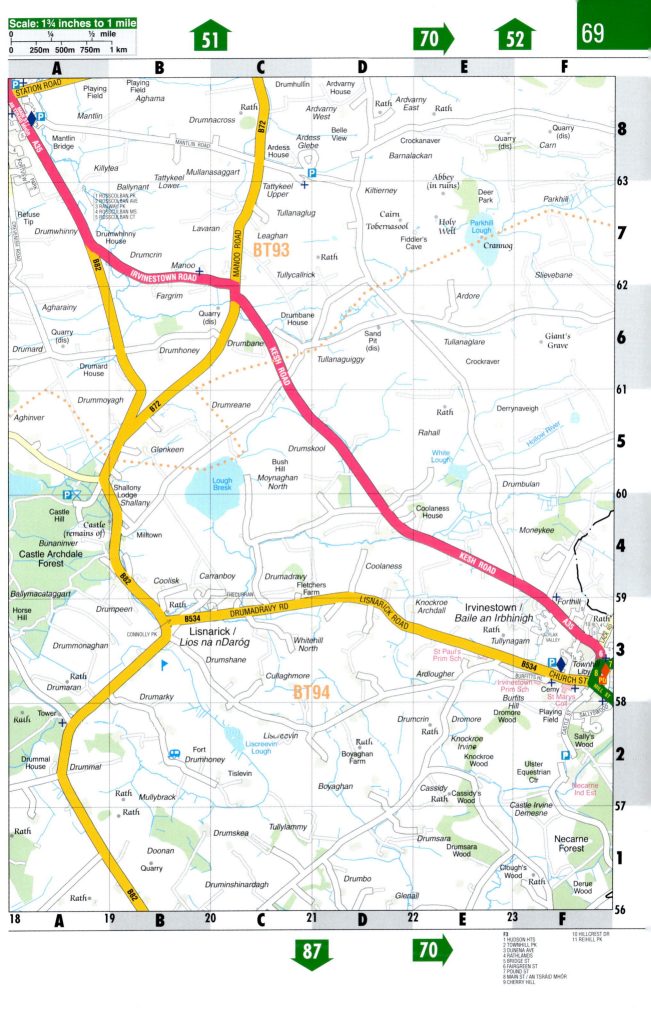

Scale: 1¾ inches to 1 mile

0   ¼   ½ mile
0   250m 500m 750m 1 km

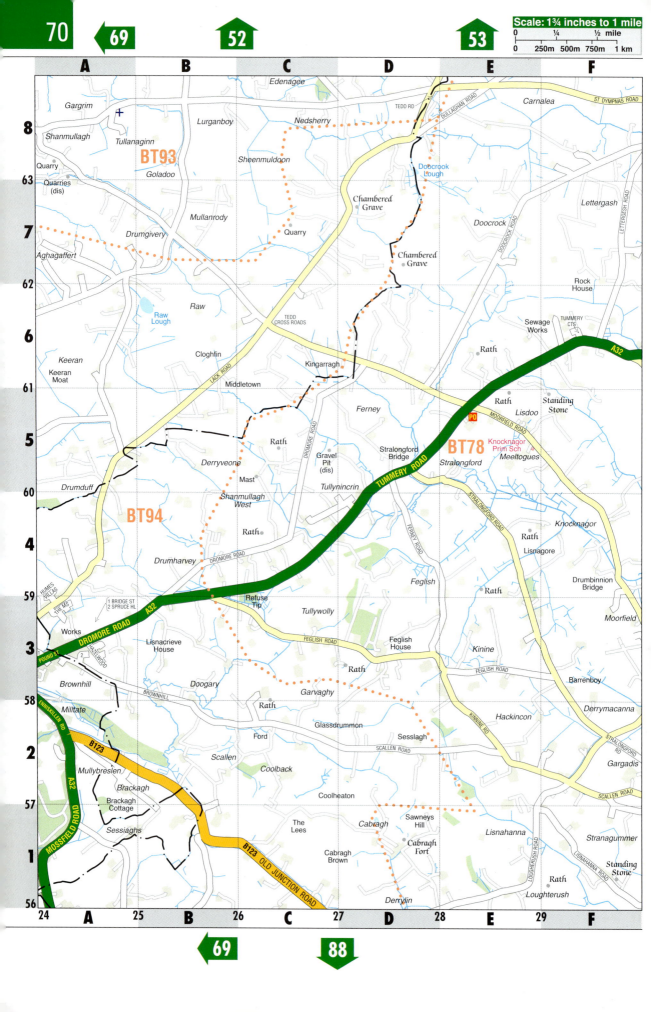

A B C D E F

8

Gargrim

+

Shanmullagh

Tullanaginn

BT93

Lurganboy

Edenagee

Nedsherry

TEDD RD

DULLAGHAN ROAD

Carnalea

ST DYMPNAS ROAD

63

Quarry

Quarries (dis)

Goladoo

Sheenmuldoon

Doocrook Lough

Chambered Grave

Doocrock

Lettergash

DOOCROCK ROAD

LETTERGESH ROAD

7

Aghagaffert

Drumgivery

Mullanrody

Quarry

Chambered Grave

Rock House

62

Raw

Raw Lough

TEDD CROSS ROADS

Sewage Works

TUMMERY CTS

6

Keeran

Keeran Moat

Cloghfin

LACK ROAD

Kingarragh

Rath

A32

61

Middletown

DROMORE ROAD

Ferney

Rath

Lisdoo

Standing Stone

5

Derryveone

Rath

Gravel Pit (dis)

Stralongford Bridge

TUMMERY ROAD

PO

MOORFIELD ROAD

BT78

Knocknagor Prim Sch

Meeltogues

Mast

Stralongford

STRALONGFORD ROAD

60

Shanmullagh West

Tullynincrin

FERNEY ROAD

Knocknagor

Drumduff

Rath

Lisnagore

4

BT94

Drumharvey

DROMORE ROAD

Feglish

Rath

Drumbinnion Bridge

Moorfield

59

HUMES VILLAS

THE MS

Refuse Tip

Tullywolly

Feglish House

Rath

A32

DROMORE ROAD

1 BRIDGE ST
2 SPRUCE HL

HAZELWOOD

FEGLISH ROAD

Kinine

KINNINE RD

3

POUND ST

Works

2

Lisnacrieve House

FEGLISH ROAD

Rath

Barrenboy

STRALONGFORD RD

Derrymacanna

Brownhill

Doogary

BROWNHILL

Garvaghy

Hackincon

58

ENNISKILLEN RD

Milltate

Rath

Glassdrummon

Sesslagh

B123

Ford

SCALLEN ROAD

Lisnahanna

SCALLEN ROAD

Gargadis

2

Mullybreslen

Scallen

Coolback

Coolheaton

Sawneys Hill

Stranagummer

A32

Brackagh

Brackagh Cottage

The Lees

Cabragh

Cabragh Fort

LOUGHERUSH ROAD

LISNAHANNA ROAD

Standing Stone

57

MOSSFIELD ROAD

Sessiaghs

Cabragh Brown

Rath

1

B123 OLD JUNCTION ROAD

Derrylin

Loughterush

56

24 A 25 B 26 C 27 D 28 E 29 F

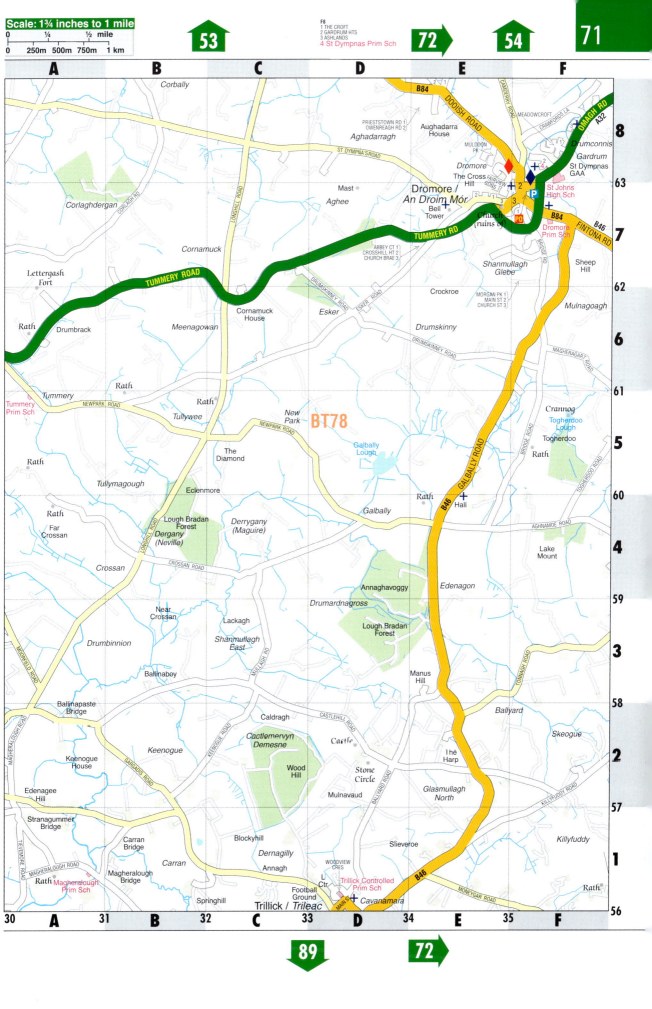

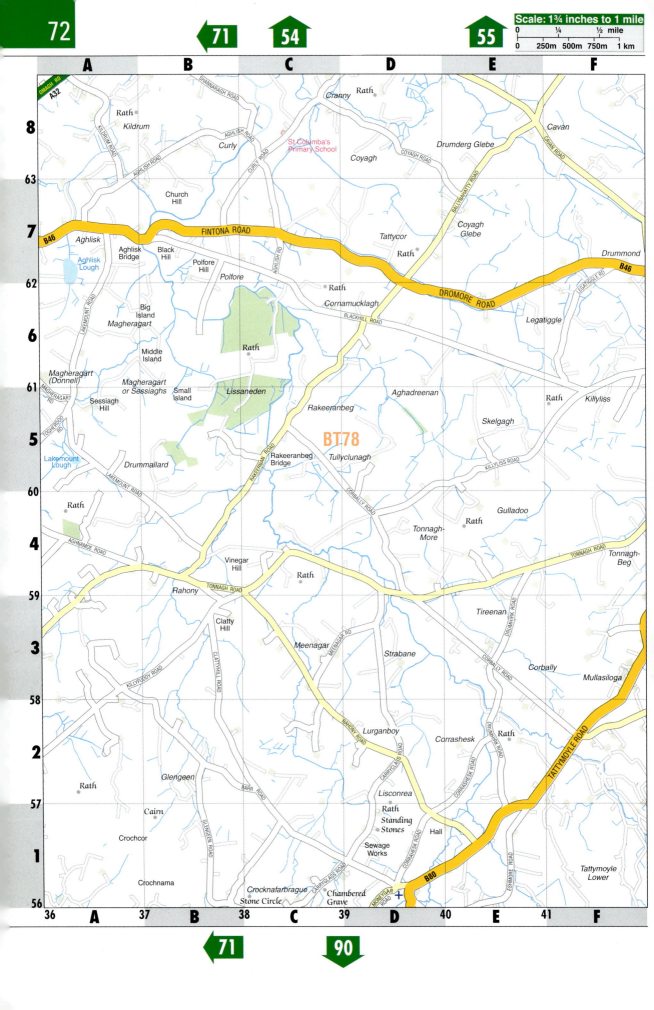

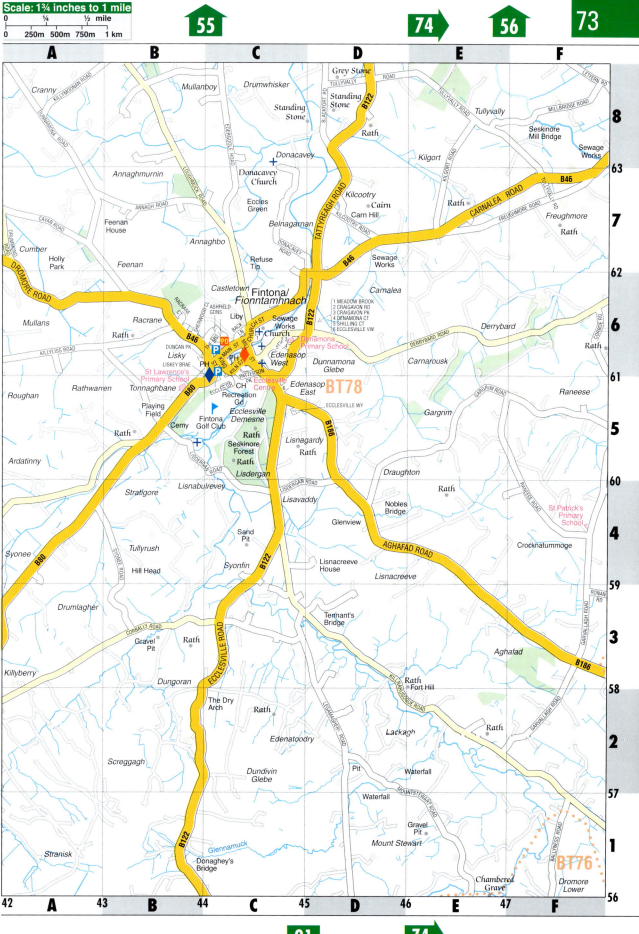

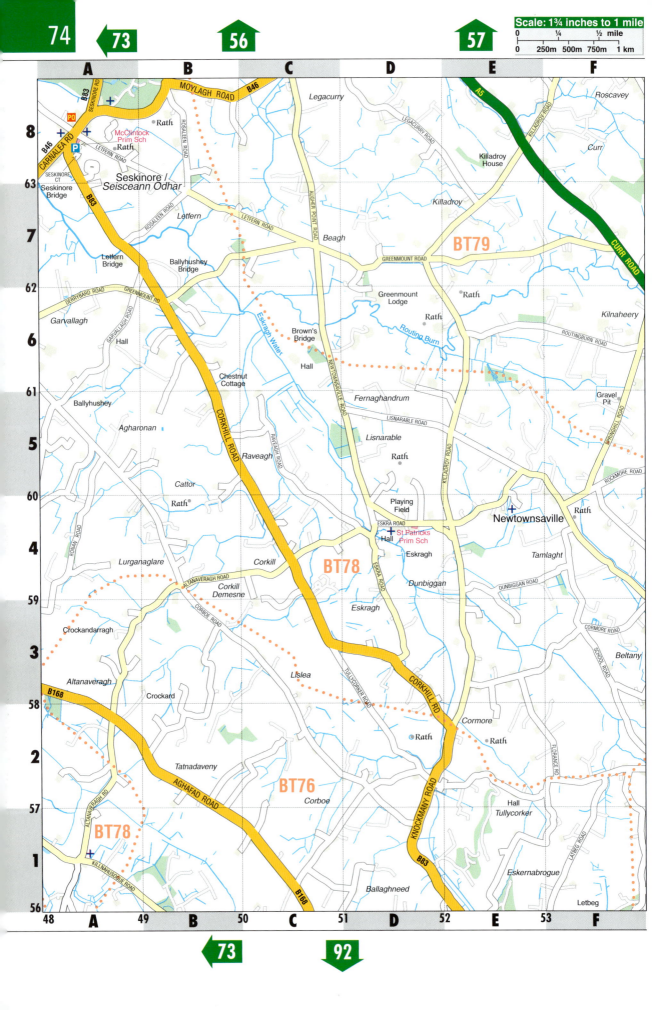

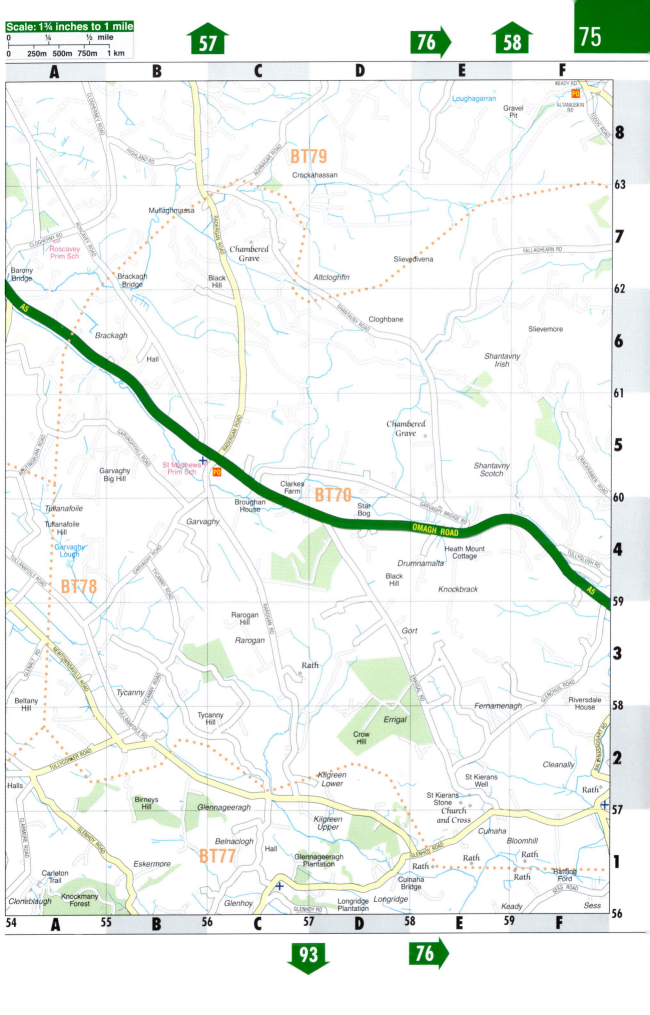

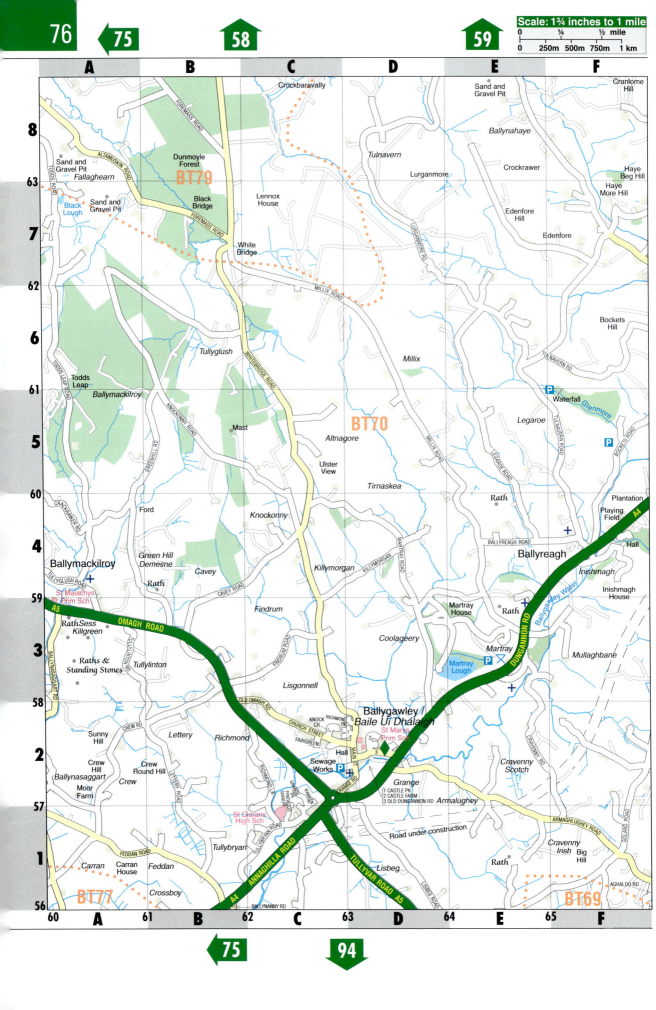

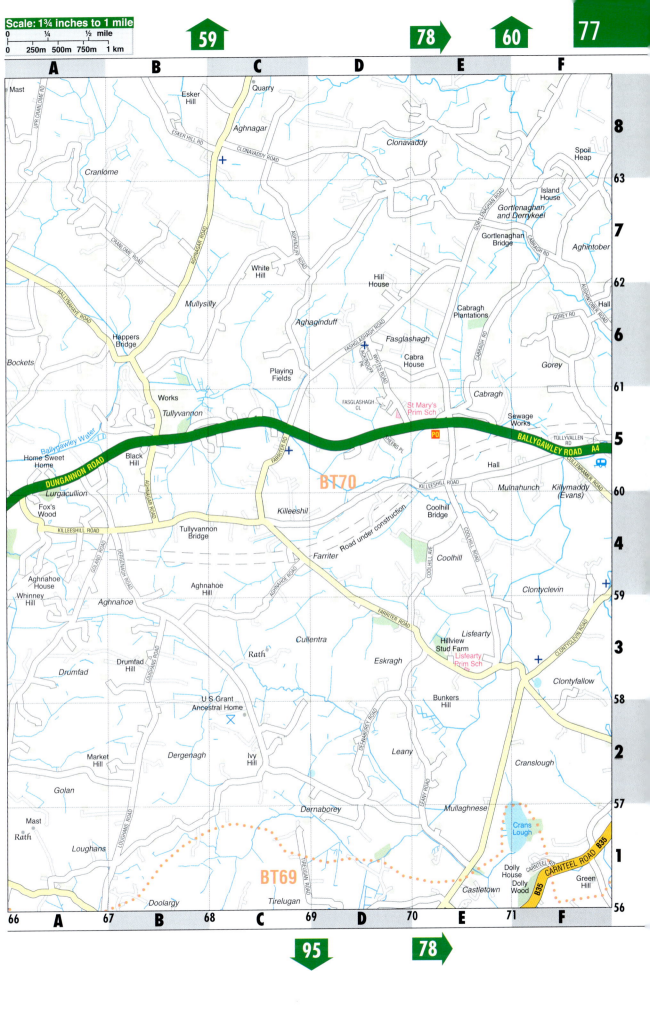

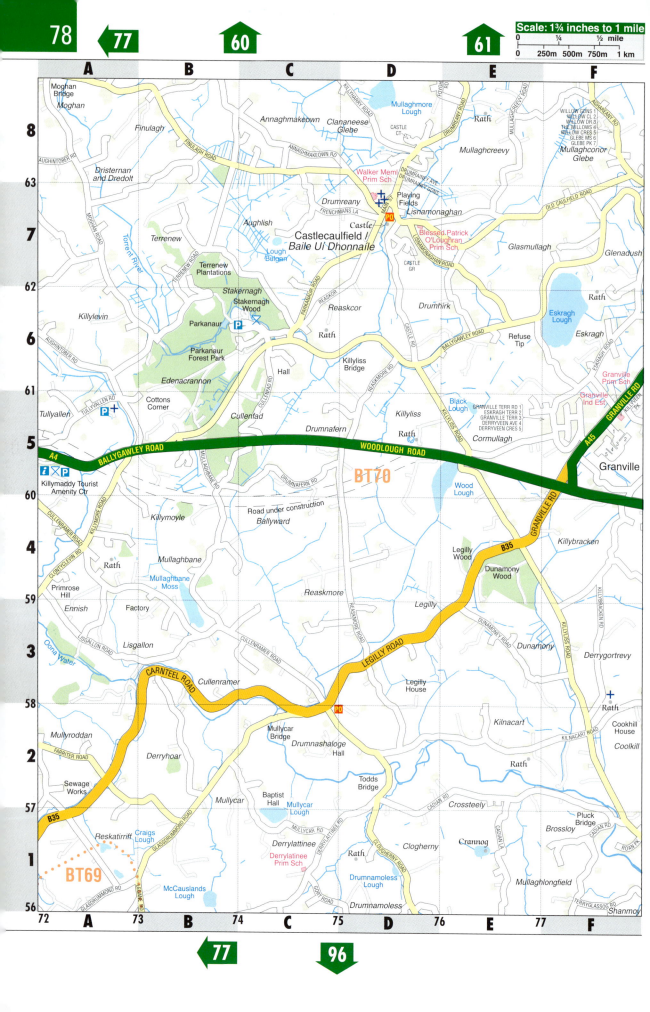

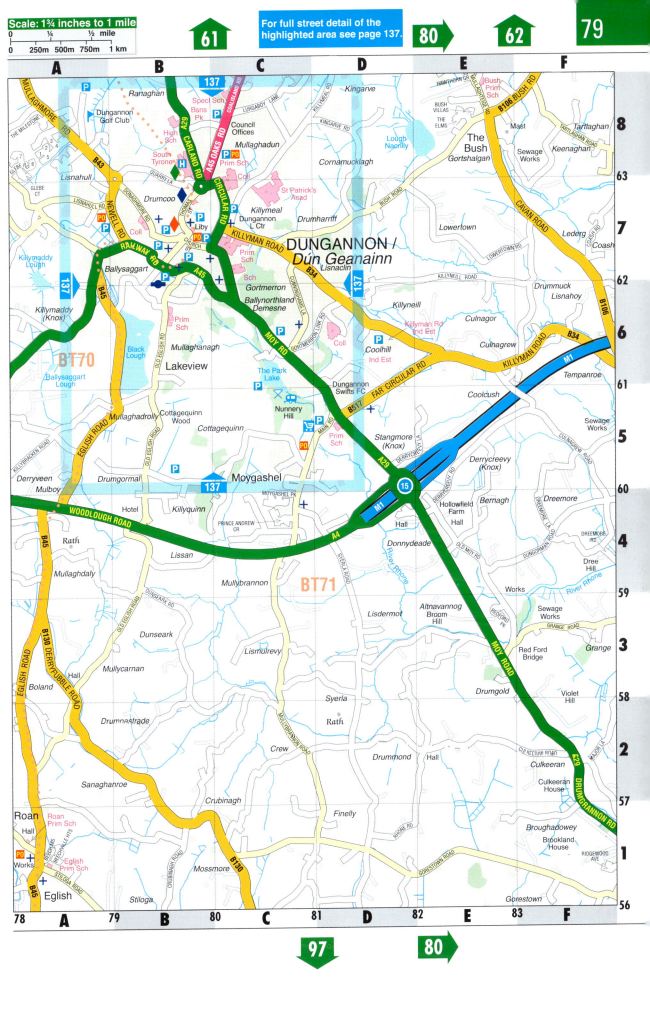

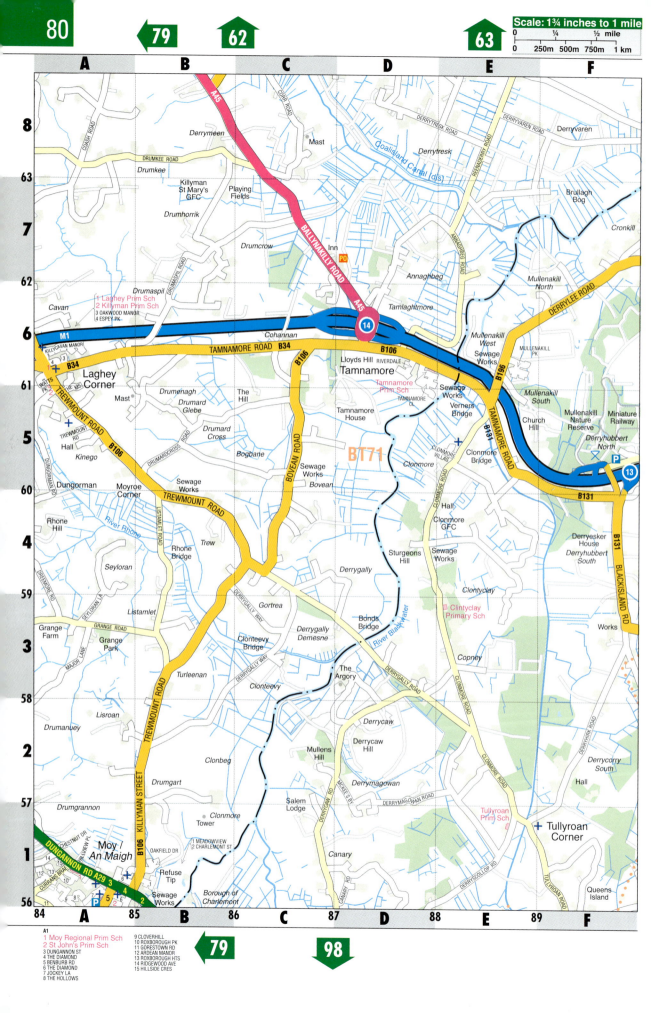

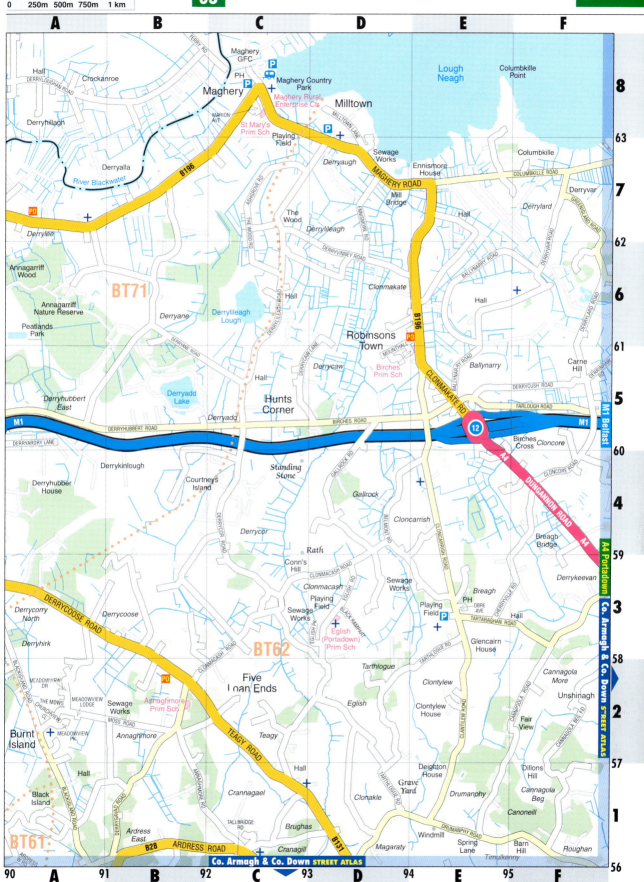

A   B   C   D   E   F

8
63
7
62
6
61
5
60
4
59
3
58
2
57
1
56

Hall
Crockanroe
DERRYLOUGHAN ROAD
Maghery GFC
PH
Maghery
Maghery Country Park
Maghery Rural Enterprise Ctr
Milltown
Lough Neagh
Columbkille Point

Derryhillagh
MARION AVE
St Mary's Prim Sch
Playing Field
Milltown Lane
Sewage Works
Columbkille
Columbkille Road

Derryalla
B196
River Blackwater
Derryaugh
MAGHERY ROAD
Ennismore House
Derryvar
GREENSLAND ROAD

ASHGROVE RD
The Wood
Mill Bridge
Hall
Derrylard
DERRYVAR ROAD

PO
Derrylee
THE WOOD RD
ENNISMORE RD
Derrylileagh
DERRYVINNEY ROAD
Ballynarry Road

Annagarriff Wood
BT71
DERRYLILEAGH ROAD
Hall
Clonmakate
Hall
DERRINREW RD

Annagarriff Nature Reserve
Derryane
Derrylileagh Lough
DERRYCAW LANE
Robinsons Town
B196
Ballynarry
Carne Hill

Peatlands Park
DERRYANE ROAD
Hall
Derrycaw
PO
Mounthall
Birches Prim Sch
DERRYCUSH ROAD
FARLOUGH ROAD

Derryhubbert East
Derryadd Lake
Hunts Corner
DERRYADD
Birches Road
CLONMAKATE RD
BALLYNARRY ROAD
M1 Belfast

M1
DERRYHUBBERT ROAD
12
Birches Cross
Cloncore
M1

DERRYARDRY LANE
Derrykinlough
Standing Stone
GALLROCK RD
A4
DUNGANNON ROAD
Cloncore Road

Derryhubber House
Courtneys Island
DERRYCOR ROAD
Gallrock
A4 Portadown
A4

Derrycor
Cloncarrish
BELMONT RD
CLONCARRISH ROAD
Breagh Bridge
Derrykeevan

Rath
Conn's Hill
CLONMACASH ROAD
EGLISH RD
Sewage Works
Breagh
A4 Portadown | Co. Armagh & Co. Down STREET ATLAS

Derrycorry North
DERRYCOOSE ROAD
Derrycoose
Clonmacash
Playing Field
BLACK RAMPART
PH
OBRE AVE
TARTARAGHAN ROAD

Derryhirk
EGLISH PK
Eglish (Portadown) Prim Sch
Playing Field
CHERRYVILLE RD
Hall

BT62
CLONMACASH ROAD
Sewage Works
Glencairn House

Five Loan Ends
PO
Tarthlogue
Clontylew
TARTHLOGUE RD
Cannagola More
Unshinagh

MEADOWVIEW DR
THE MDWS
MEADOWVIEW LODGE
Sewage Works
Annaghmore Prim Sch
Eglish
Clontylew House
CLANTILEW ROAD
Fair View
CANNAGOLA BEG RD
CANNAGOLA RD

CHURCHVIEW CL
MEADOWVIEW PK
MOSS ROAD
Annaghmore
Teagy
Deighton House

Burnt Island
BLACKISLAND ROAD
Hall
ANNAGHMORE RD
TEAGY ROAD
Hall
Grave Yard
Drumanphy
Dillons Hill
Cannagola Beg

DERRYGAVAD ROAD
Crannagael
Clonakle
TARTHLOGUE RD
Canoneill

Black Island
TALLBRIDGE RD
Brughas
Magaraty
Windmill
DRUMANPHY ROAD
Spring Lane
Barn Hill
Roughan

BT61
ARDRESS RD
B28
ARDRESS ROAD
Cranagill
B131
Timulkenny

Co. Armagh & Co. Down STREET ATLAS

90   A   91   B   92   C   93   D   94   E   95   F   56

64

A   B   C   D   E   F

8

Derrynaseer

Derrynameeo

Ford

55

Abhornaleha Bridge

Viewpoint

Drumnasreane

7

Rusheen Point

Derrynaseer Amenity Area

Friar's Garden

Rosskit Island

Friar's Gap

Muckenagh

Tullymore Upper

Spa Well (Chalybeate)

Waterfall

Tullymore

Lakeview

Inishkeen

Muckenagh Bridge

BT93

54

Inishtemple

Rossmore Point

Melvin Cottage

6

Gubanummera Point

Lough Melvin

Gorminish

Garvros

53

YC

R281

Bilberry Island

Sally Island

Lakeshore Plantation

5

Ballindrehid

Roosky Point

Cloghan

Roosky

52

Glack

4

B53

Shasgar

Viewpoint

County Bridge

51

R282

Standing Stone

Megalithic Tomb

Mollynadinta

Ardagh

Ross Point

3

Megalithic Tomb

Sheenun

Drungan

Mogue Bridge

Dooard

50

Mautiagh

Church

R281

Eden

Lissiniska

Tawnaleck

2

Carrowkeel

Sraud

Ballagh River

Drumanure

Glenaniff River

49

Larganhugh

Rossinver

1

Glenaniff

R282

R281

Sch

48

Aghnahoo

A   B   C   D   E   F

88   89   90   91   92   93

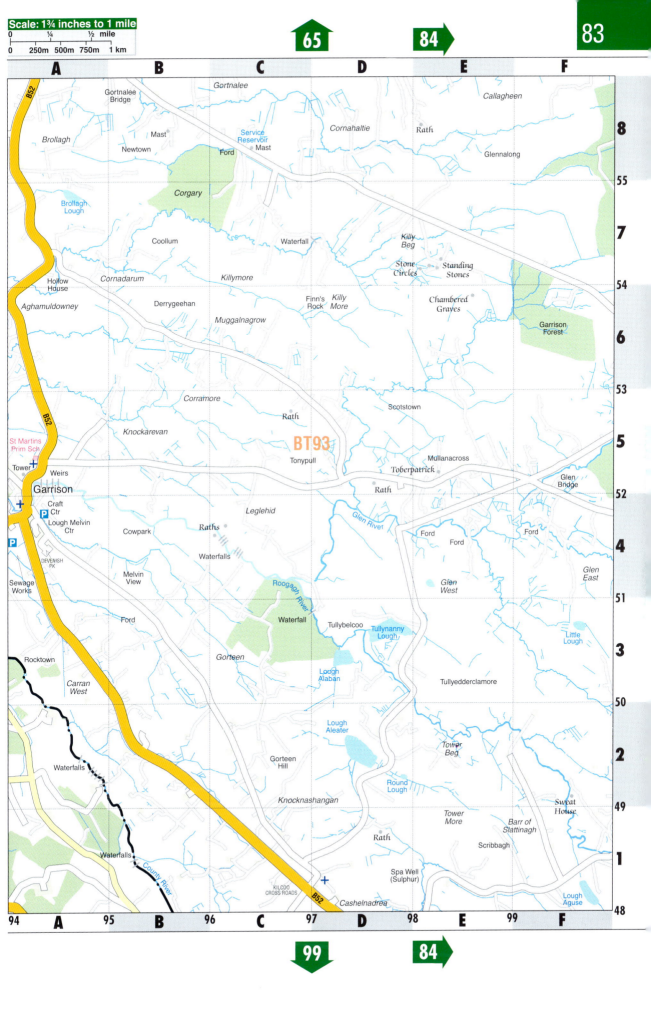

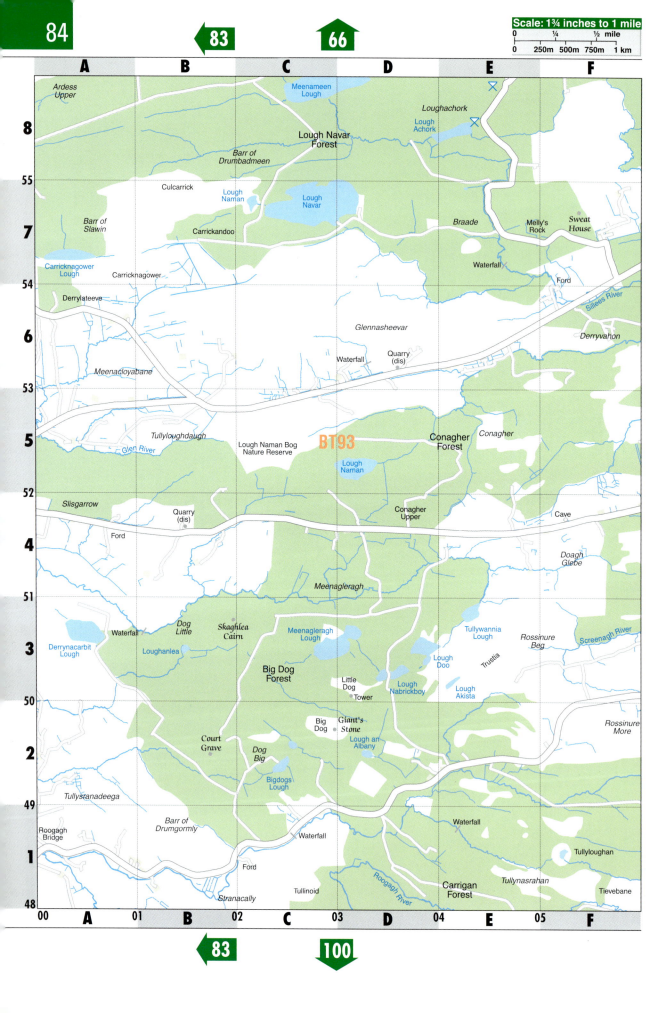

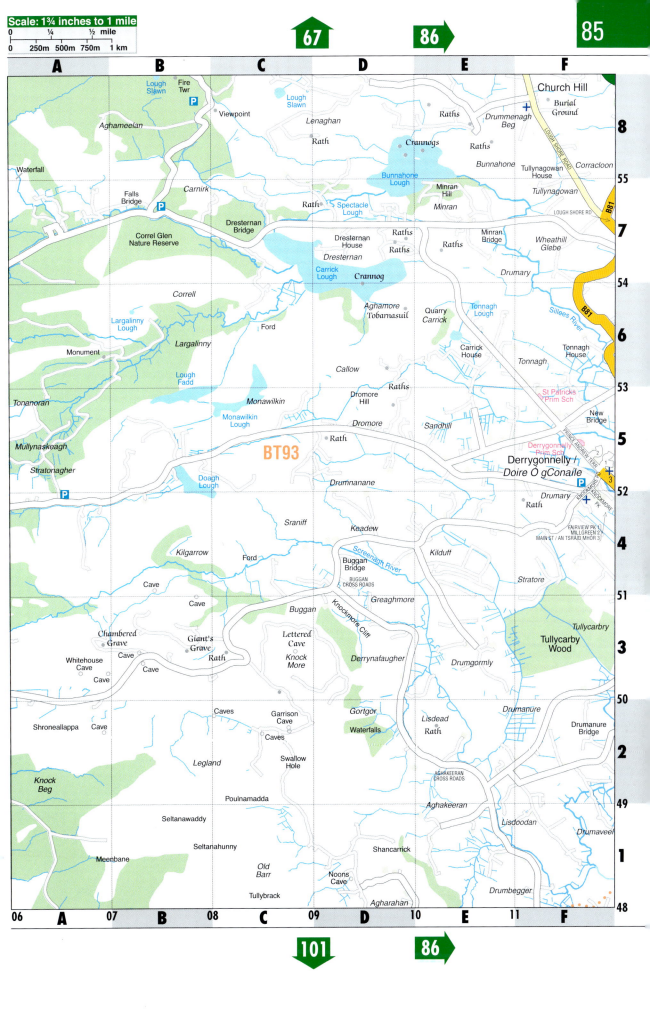

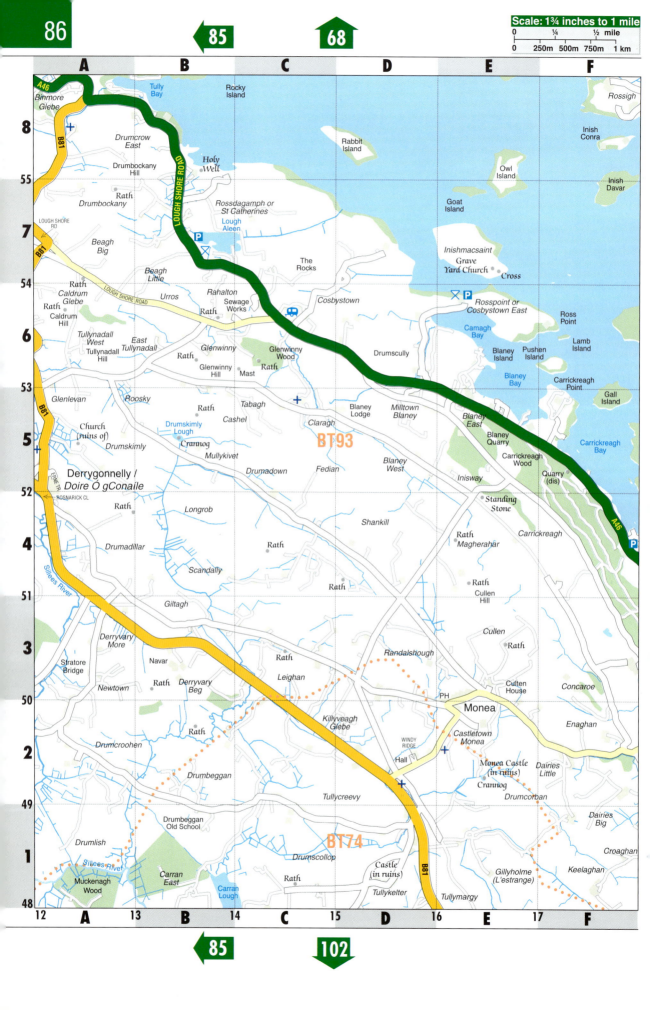

85
68

Scale: 1¾ inches to 1 mile

0   ¼   ½   mile
0   250m 500m 750m 1 km

A   B   C   D   E   F

8

55

A46
Binmore
Glebe
B81

Tully
Bay
Rocky
Island

Rabbit Island

Rossigh

Inish
Conra

Drumcrow
East

Drumbockany
Hill

Holy
Well

Owl
Island

Inish
Davar

7

54

LOUGH SHORE
RD
B81

Rath
Drumbockany

Beagh
Big

Rossdagamph or
St Catherines
Lough
Aleen

Goat
Island

Grave
Yard Church
Cross

LOUGH SHORE ROAD

P

Beagh
Little

Urros

Rath

The
Rocks

Rosspoint or
Cosbystown East

Ross
Point

6

53

Rath Caldrum
Glebe

Rath
Caldrum
Hill

Tullynadall
West
Tullynadall
Hill

East
Tullynadall

Rath

LOUGH SHORE ROAD

Sewage
Works

Rahalton

Rath

Cosbystown

Camagh
Bay

Lamb
Island

Glenwinny

Glenwinny
Wood

Drumscully

Blaney
Island

Pushen
Island

Carrickreagh
Point

Glenlevan

Roosky

Rath

Glenwinny
Hill

Mast

Rath

Blaney
Bay

Gall
Island

5

52

B81

Church
(ruins of)

Drumskimly
Lough

Rath

Cashel

Tabagh

Claragh

BT93

Blaney
Lodge

Milltown
Blaney

Blaney
East

Blaney
Quarry

Carrickreagh
Wood

Carrickreagh
Bay

Drumskimly

Crannog

Mullykivet

Drumadown

Fedian

Blaney
West

Inisway

Quarry
(dis)

Derrygonnelly /
Doire Ó gConaíle
ERNE TR
ROSNARICK CL

4

51

Rath

Longrob

Shankill

Standing
Stone

Rath
Magherahar

Carrickreagh

Drumadillar

Scandally

Rath

Rath

Rath
Cullen
Hill

3

50

Giltagh

Derryvary
More

Navar

Rath
Derryvary
Beg

Rath

Leighan

Randalshough

PH

Cullen

Cullen
House

Rath

Monea

Concaroe

Enaghan

Stratore
Bridge

Newtown

Rath

Killyveagh
Glebe

WINDY
RIDGE
Hall

Castletown
Monea

Monea Castle
(in ruins)
Crannog

Dairies
Little

2

49

Drumcroohen

Rath

Drumbeggan

Tullycreevy

Drumcorban

Dairies
Big

1

48

Silees River

Drumlish

Silees River

Drumbeggan
Old School

Carran
East

Carran
Lough

Rath

Drumscollop

BT74

Castle
(in ruins)

Tullykelter

B81

Tullymargy

Gillyholme
(L'estrange)

Keelaghan

Croaghan

Muckenagh
Wood

A46
P

12   A   13   B   14   C   15   D   16   E   17   F

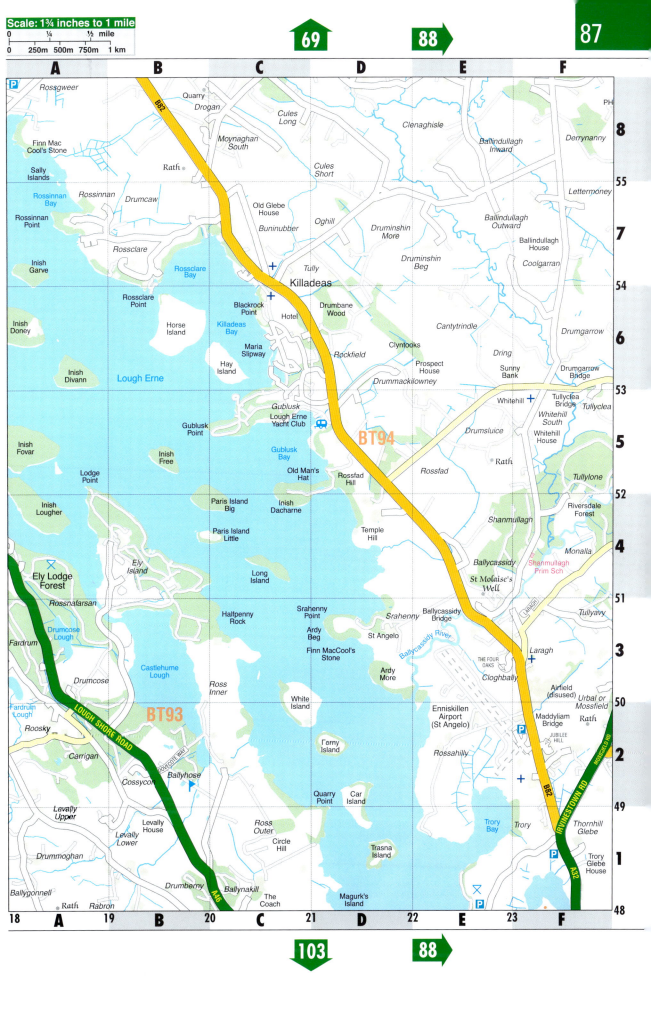

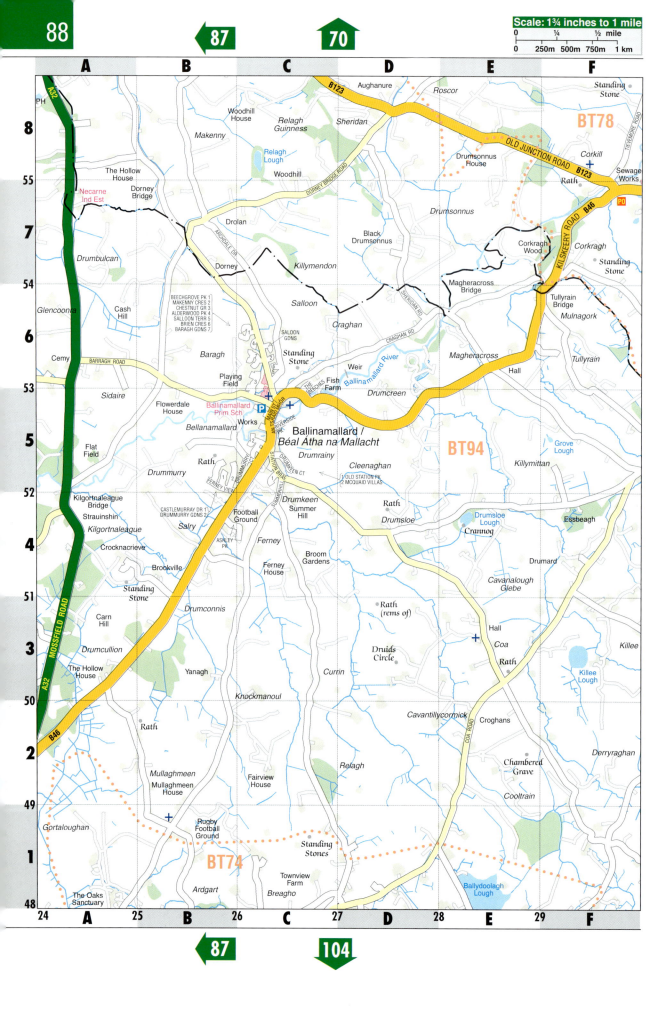

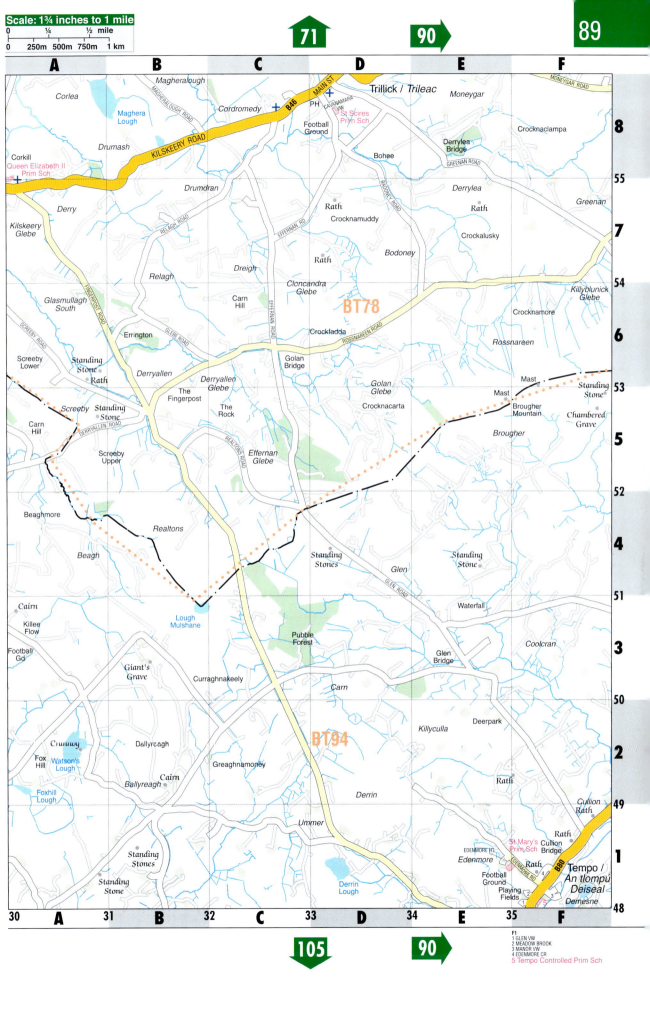

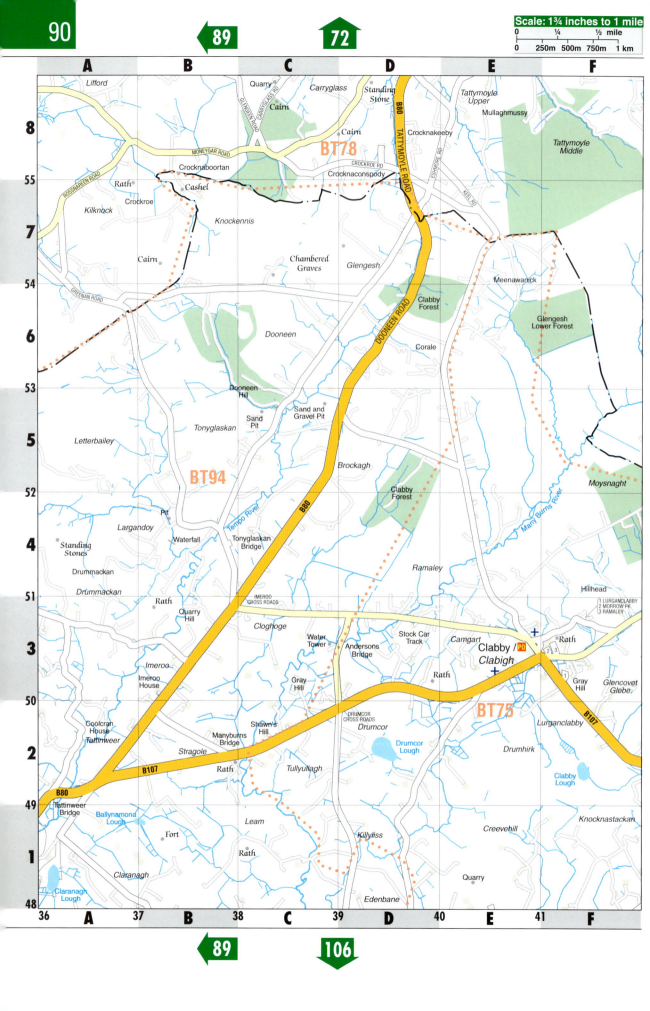

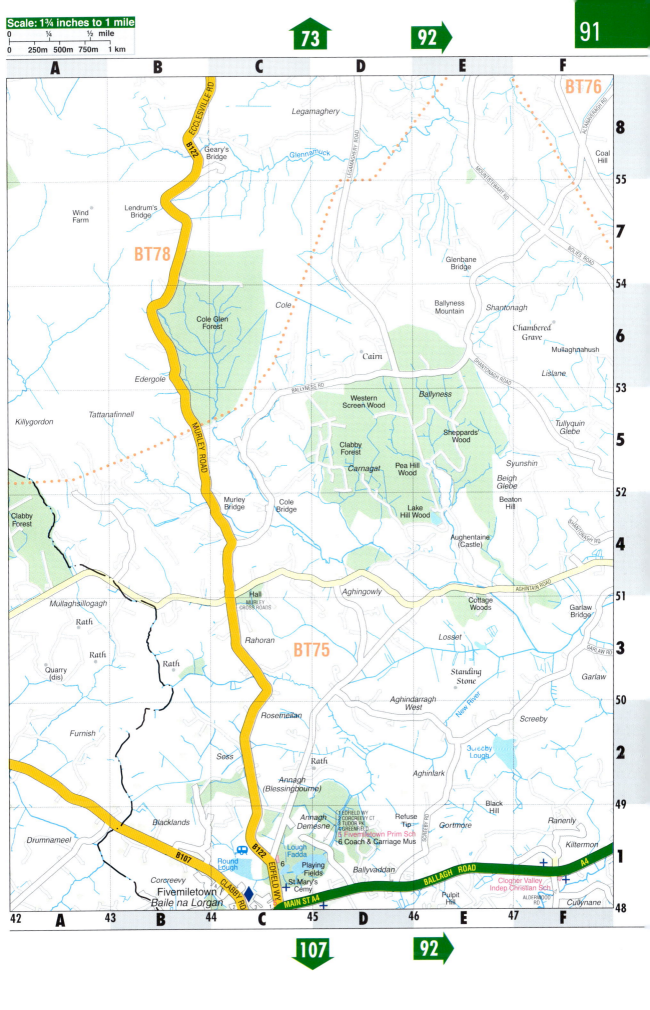

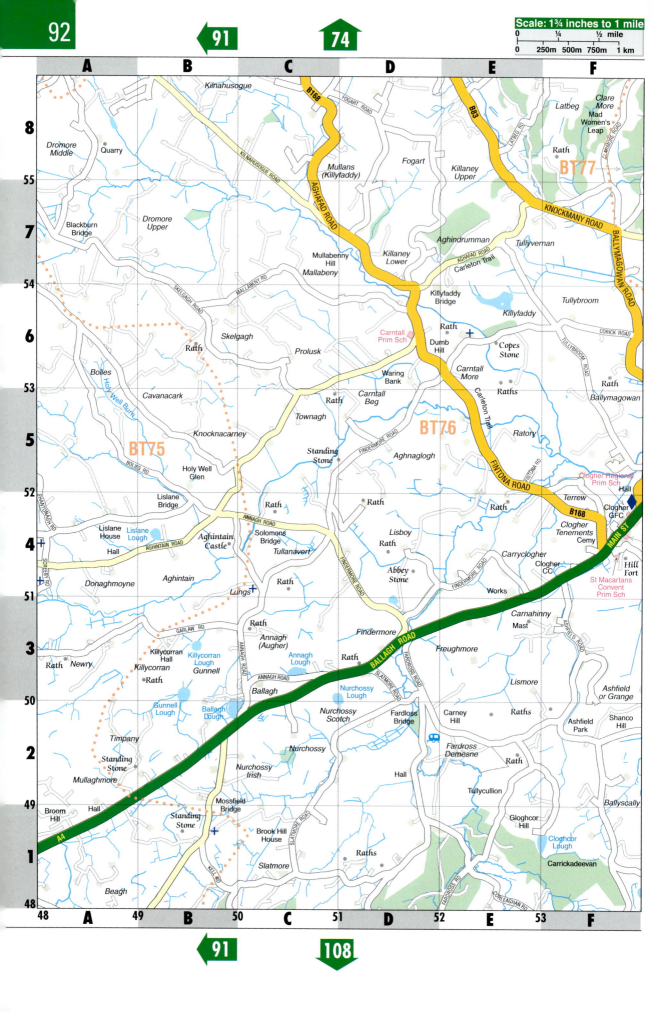

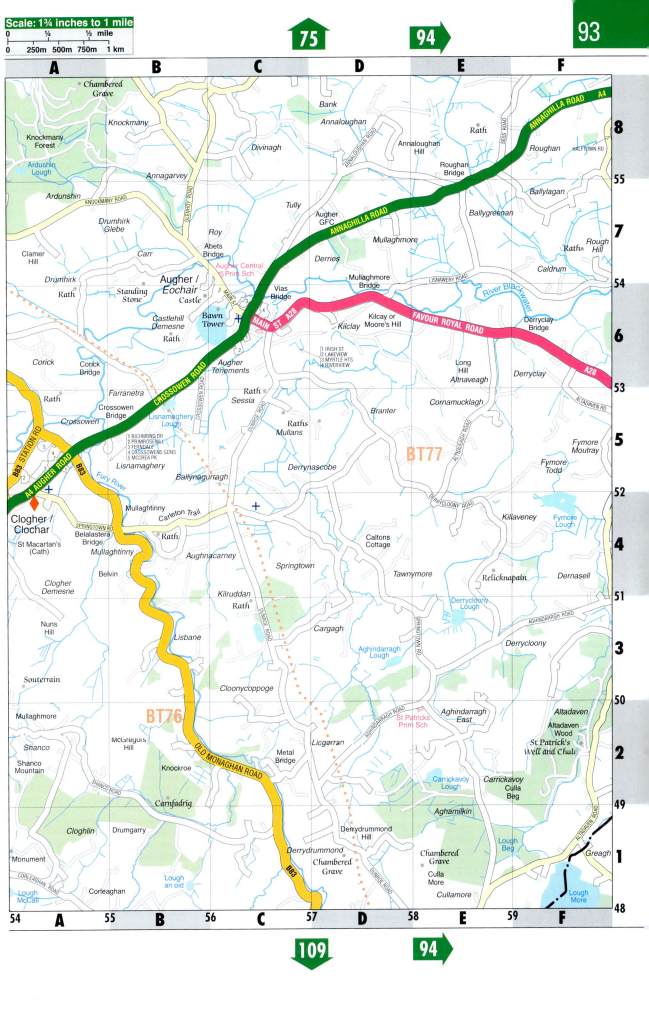

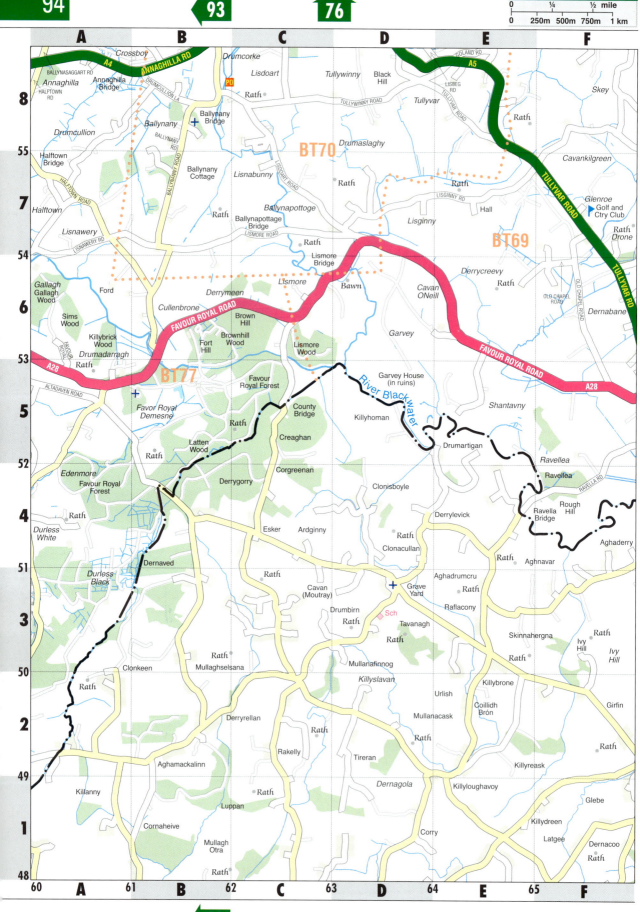

93 76

Scale: 1¾ inches to 1 mile

0   ¼   ½   mile
0   250m 500m 750m 1 km

A B C D E F

Ballynasaggart Rd
Crossboy
Annaghilla
ANNAGHILLA RD
A4
Drumcorke
Lisdoart
Tullywinny
Black Hill
SOLAND RD
A5
Skey

Annaghilla
HALFTOWN RD
Annaghilla Bridge
DRUMCULLION LA
PO
Rath
Lisbeg RD
TULLYVAR ROAD
Rath

Drumcullion
Ballynany
Ballynany Bridge
BT70
Drumaslaghy
Tullyvar
Rath
Cavankilgreen

Halftown Bridge
BALLYNANY RD
Ballynany Cottage
Lisnabunny
LISDOART ROAD
Rath
Lisginny RD
Rath
TULLYVAR ROAD

Halftown
HALFTOWN ROAD
Ballynapottoge
LISMORE ROAD
Rath
Lisginny RD
Hall
Glenroe Golf and Ctry Club

Lisnawery
LISNAWERY RD
Ballynapottage Bridge
Rath
Lisginny
BT69
Rath Drone

Gallagh
Gallagh Wood
Ford
Derrymeen
Lismore Bridge
Lismore
Bawn
Derrycreevy
Rath
Old-Chapel Road
Dernabane

Cullenbrone
FAVOUR ROYAL ROAD
Brown Hill
Cavan O'Neill
FAVOUR ROYAL ROAD
A28
OLD CHAPEL ROAD
TULLYVAR RD

Sims Wood
FAVOUR ROYAL
Brownhill Wood
Garvey

Killybrick Wood
Fort Hill
Lismore Wood
FAVOUR ROYAL ROAD

Drumadarragh
Rath
BT77
Favour Royal Forest
Garvey House (in ruins)
River Blackwater
Shantavny
A28

A28
ALTADAVEN ROAD
Favor Royal Demesne
Rath
County Bridge
Killyhoman
Drumartigan
Ravellea

Latten Wood
Creaghan
Ravellea
RAVELLA RD

Edenmore
Favour Royal Forest
Rath
Corgreenan
Clonisboyle
Ravella Bridge
Rough Hill

Durless White
Derrygorry
Esker
Ardginny
Derrylevick
Rath
Aghaderry

Rath
Dernaved
Rath
Clonacullan
Aghadrumcru
Rath
Aghnavar

Durless Black
Cavan (Moutray)
Grave Yard
Raflacony
Skinnahergna
Rath
Ivy Hill
Ivy Hill

Drumbirn
Sch
Tavanagh
Rath

Clonkeen
Rath
Mullaghselsana
Rath
Mullanafinnog
Killyslavan
Urlish
Mullanacask
Coillidh Brón
Killybrone
Killyreask
Girfin

Rath
Derryrellan
Rath
Rakelly
Tireran
Dernagola
Killyloughavoy
Rath

Killanny
Aghamackalinn
Luppan
Rath
Corry
Killydreen
Latgee
Glebe

Cornaheive
Mullagh Otra
Rath
Dernacoo
Rath

A B C D E F
60 61 62 63 64 65
48 49 50 51 52 53 54 55

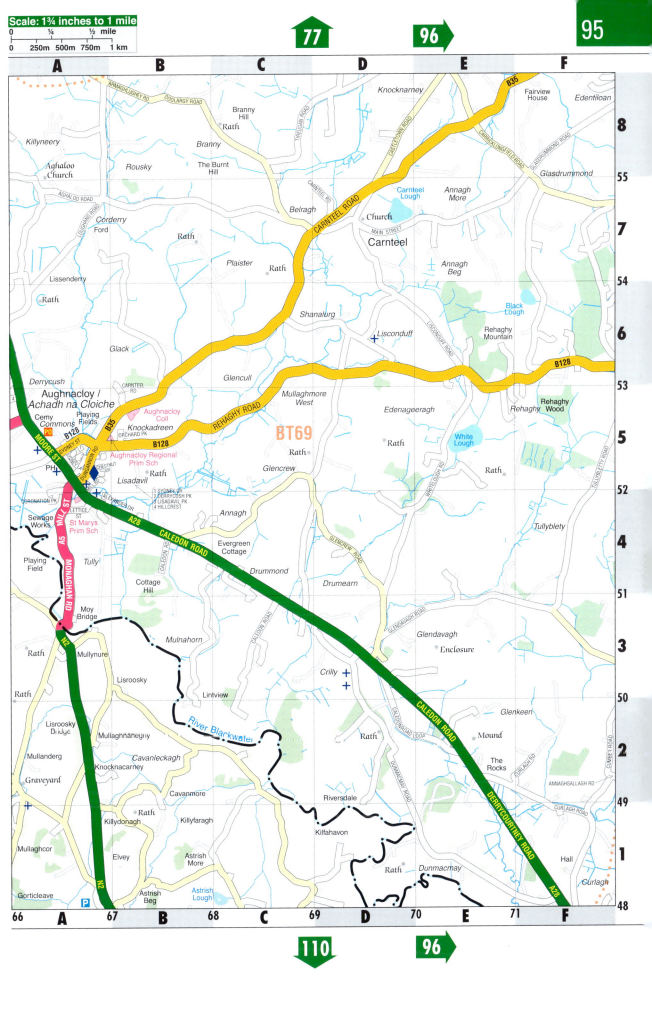

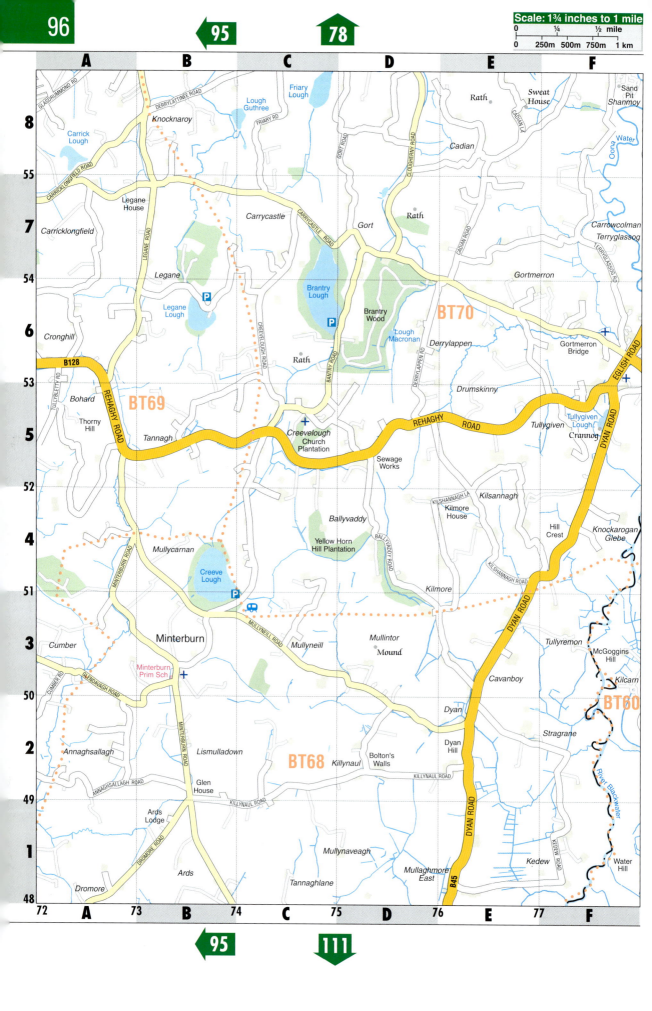

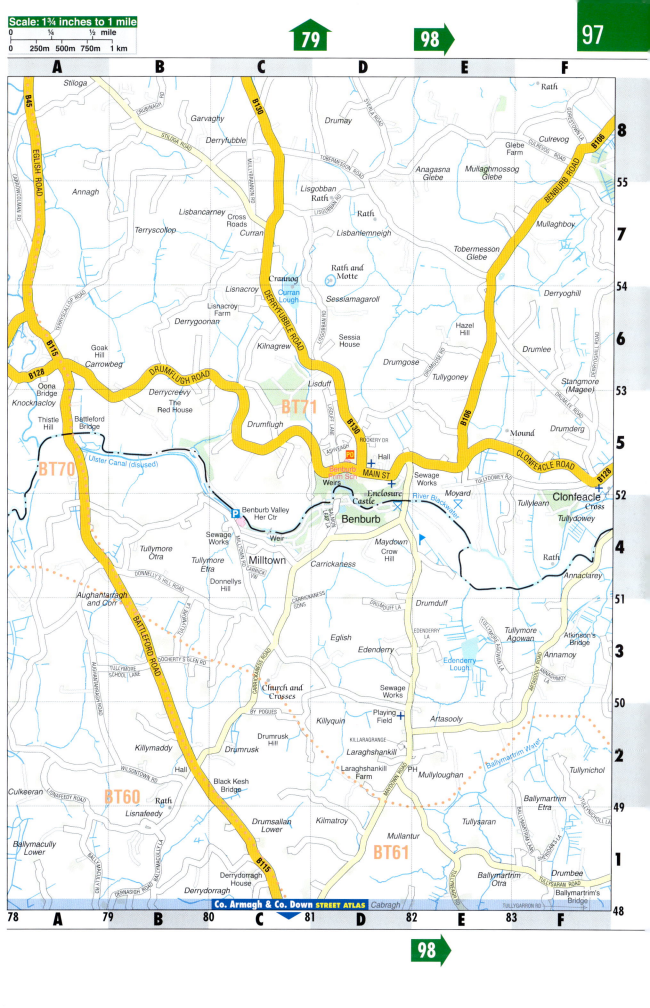

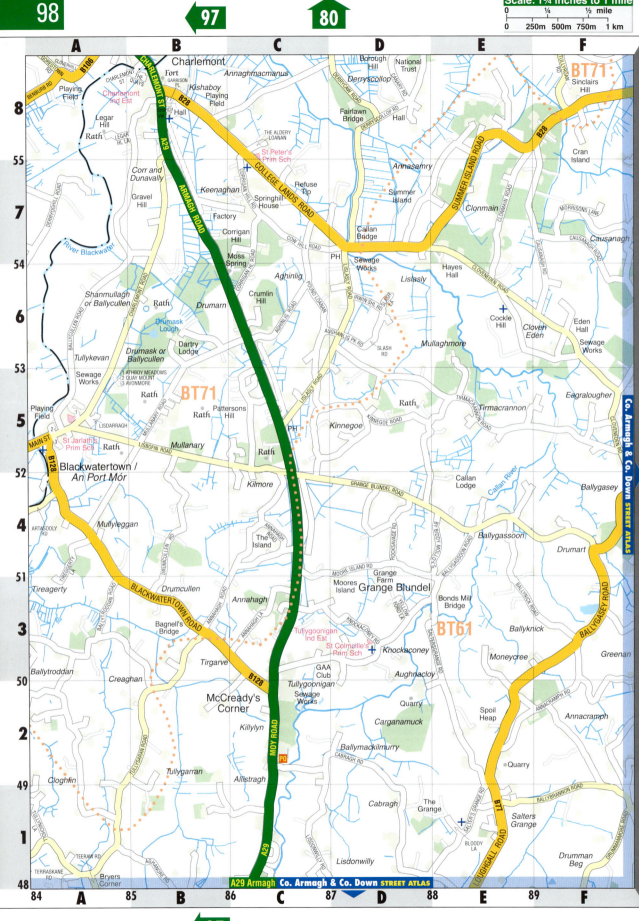

Scale: 1¾ inches to 1 mile

0   ¼   ½   mile
0   250m 500m 750m 1 km

BT71:

Sinclairs Hill

Charlemont

Fort
Charlemont
Ind Est
The Quays
Benburb Rd
Gorestown
Cloverhill Rd

Playing Field

Legar Hill

Rath

Annaghmacmanus

Kishaboy Playing Field

Hall

COLLEGE LANDS ROAD

St Peter's Prim Sch

THE ALDERY LOANAN

Refuse Tip

Springhill House

Factory

Moss Spring

Aghinlig

Corr and Dunavally

Gravel Hill

Keenaghan

Corrigan Hill

CORRIGAN HILL RD

COW HILL ROAD

PH

Sewage Works

Crumlin Hill

AGHINLIG ROAD

POUND LOANAN

IRWIN SHL RD

Drumarn

Lislasly

Aghinlig

Mullaghmore

Borough Hill

National Trust

DERRYCAW ROAD

CANARY RD

Derryscollop

Fairlawn Bridge

Hall

DERRYSCOLLOP ROAD

Annasamry

Summer Island

Callan Bridge

SUMMER ISLAND ROAD

Clonmain

CLONMAIN ROAD

CAUSANAGH RD

MORRISONS LANE

Causanagh

Hayes Hall

CLOVENEDEN ROAD

Cockle Hill

Cloven Eden

Eden Hall

Sewage Works

Eagralougher

Cran Island

River Blackwater

Shanmullagh or Ballycullen

BALLYCULLEN ROAD

DERRYOGHILL ROAD

Tullykevan

Sewage Works

Playing Field

MAIN ST

B128

St Jarlath's Prim Sch

Rath

Blackwatertown / An Port Mór

Rath

Drumask Lough

Drumask or Ballycullen

Dartry Lodge

1 ATHBOY MEADOWS
2 QUAY MOUNT
3 AVONMORE

LISDARRAGH

MULLANARY ROAD

Rath

Mullanary

LISBOFIN ROAD

Pattersons Hill

Rath

PH

Rath

Kinnegoe

KINNEGOE ROAD

LISLASLY ROAD

SLASH RD

Rath

Tirmacrannon

TIRMACRANNON ROAD

Callan River

Ballygasey

Ballygassoon

Drumart

ARTASOOLY RD

Mullyleggan

DRUMCULLEN ROAD

BLACKWATERTOWN ROAD

BALLYTRODDAN ROAD

TIREAGERTY

Tireagerty

Drumcullen

Annahagh

ANNAHAGH ROAD

ANNAHAGH LA

Kilmore

GRANGE BLUNDEL ROAD

Callan Lodge

ROCKSAVAGE RD

MOORE ISLAND RD

Moores Island

Grange Farm

Grange Blundel

BY BIDDY MOLLYS

BALLYGASSON ROAD

Bonds Mil Bridge

PETTERSGRANGE RD

YELLOW FORD LA

Ballygasson

BALLYGASEY ROAD

BALLYKNICK ROAD

Ballyknick

Greenan

Ballytroddan

Creaghan

Bagnell's Bridge

Tirgarve

B128

The Island

ANNAHAGH ROAD

The Island

Tullygoonigan Ind Est

St Colmcille's Prim Sch

GAA Club

Tullygoonigan

Sewage Works

KNOCKACONEY RD

Knockaconey

Aughnacloy

BT61

Moneycree

Spoil Heap

ANNACRAMPH RD

Annacramph

McCready's Corner

Killyln

MOY ROAD

PO

Carganamuck

Quarry

Cloghfin

Tullygarran

Allistragh

LISDONWILLY RD

Ballymackilmurry

CABRAGH RD

Cabragh

The Grange

Quarry

SALTERS GRANGE RD

BLOODY LA

LOUGHGALL ROAD

BT1

Salters Grange

Drumman Beg

TULLYNICHOL RD

TEERAW RD

TERRASKANE RD

Bryers Corner

AGHADOE RD

TULLYGARRAN ROAD

Lisdonwilly

BALLYBRANNON ROAD

Ballybrannon Road

DRUMMANMORE RD

A29

A29 Armagh   Co. Armagh & Co. Down   STREET ATLAS

Co. Armagh & Co. Down   STREET ATLAS

BT71

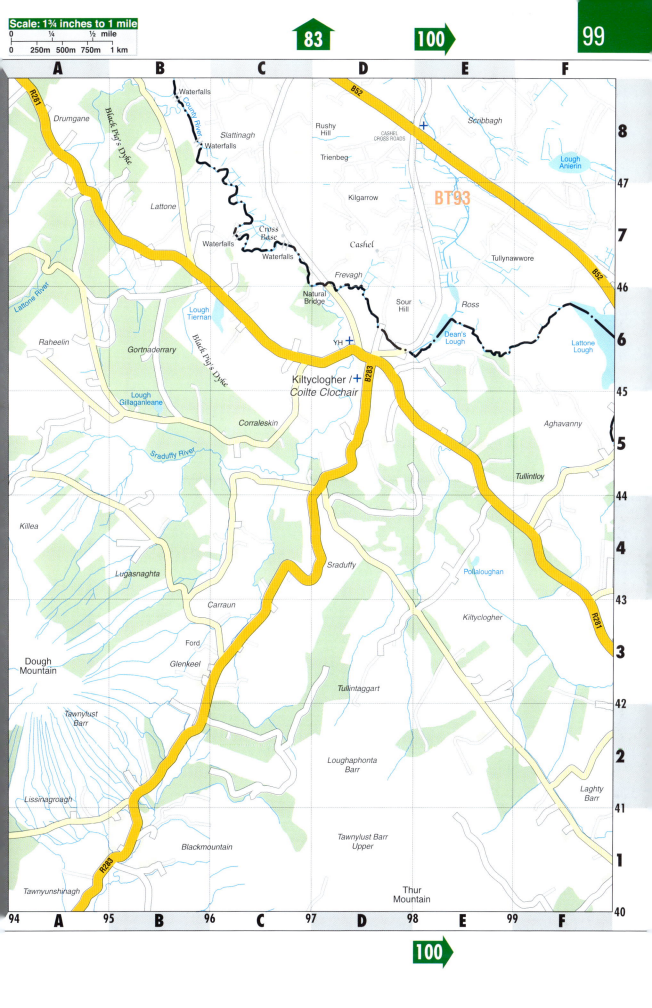

A   B   C   D   E   F

8

Tullygerravra

Clogherycurneen

Carrigan

Crockroe

Carrigan
Forest

Tullinwonny

Lough
Formal

Tullyeenta

47

Tullinteskin

Lough
Avrilleen

Black
Rocks

Carrigan

Carrickwaddyroe

7

Agho

Lattone
Hill

Teebane

Tullyraver

Tievebunnan

Glenmore

Loughanquin

Shaking
Stone

Clogherbog

46

B52

Lattone
Bridge

Lattone

Meennaskeagh

Meenanarvore

Spa Well
(Chalybeate)

Spa Well
(Chalybeate)

Slieveglass

Lough
Namanfin

Carrickory

6

Lattone
Lough

Chambered Grave
Giants Grave

Meenarainy

Pound
Hill

Tieveglass

45

Drumcully

Cornacully

Tullyrossmearan
Forest

Carricknagat

BT93

Slapragh

Waterfall

Tullybrack

Black River

Tullinacambel

Waterfall

Ballintempo

5

Black River

Tullyrossmearan

Waterfall

Stone
Circle

Mullaghmore

44

Lough
Arudda

Tullybellina

Mullynavarnoge

Waterfalls

Corraderrybrock

Lough
Aleagan

Tullylgarran

Tullintuckry

4

Black
Pig's

Drumkeenagh

Dyke

Mullanshellistragh

Black
Bridge

Mullanawinna

Greaghnagleragh

Tullyveeny

Lough
Martincrossagh

Carricknabrock

43

Corracloona

Inishteise

Stable
Park

Greaghaphort

Ford

Tullylanagan

Toppan

3

R281

Meenagh

P

Trawnish
Island

Upper
Macnean
Lough

Killyphort

Coasan

Masanaghran

Carricknamaddaroe

Standing
Stone

2

Meenawargy

Tullynacor

Cashelbane

Corraglass
West
Pollagaddy

41

Carrickduff

P

Mullan

Mullan
Rocks

Waterfalls

1

Glenfarne
Wood

Inishkeen

Corralea
Activity
Ctr

Corralea

Drumelly
Rocks

Drumelly

40

Carrickrevagh

Garrow or
Buck Islands

B52

00   A   01   B   02   C   03   D   04   E   05   F

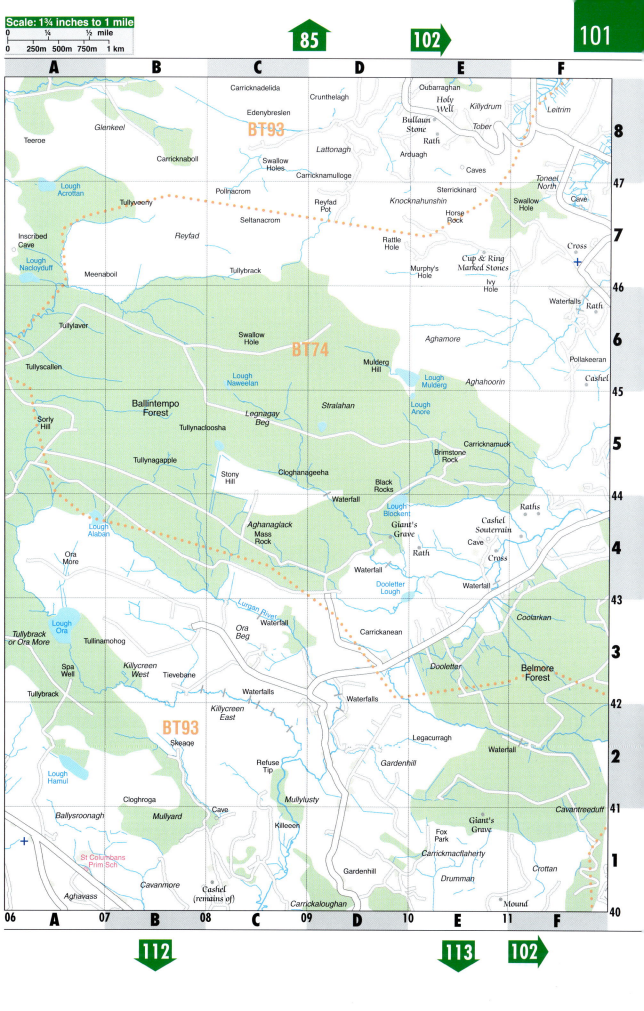

Carricknadelida
Crunthelagh
Oubarraghan
Holy Well
Killydrum
Leitrim

8

Teeroe
Glenkeel
Edenybreslen
BT93
Bullaun Stone
Tober
Rath
Carricknaboll
Lattonagh
Arduagh
Caves

47

Swallow Holes
Carricknamulloge
Sterrickinard
Toneel North

Lough Acrottan
Pollnacrom
Reyfad Pot
Knocknahunshin
Horse Rock
Swallow Hole
Cave

Tullyveeny
Seltanacrom
Rattle Hole

7

Inscribed Cave
Reyfad
Murphy's Hole
Cup & Ring Marked Stones
Cross

Lough Nacloyduff
Tullybrack
Ivy Hole

46

Meenaboil

Tullylaver
Swallow Hole
BT74
Aghamore
Waterfalls
Rath

6

Tullyscallen
Mulderg Hill
Lough Mulderg
Pollakeeran

Lough Naweelan
Aghahoorin
Cashel

45

Ballintempo Forest
Legnagay Beg
Stralahan
Lough Anore

Tullynacloosha

Tullynagapple
Cloghanageeha
Carricknamuck
Brimstone Rock

5

Sorly Hill
Stony Hill
Black Rocks
Waterfall

Aghanaglack Mass Rock
Lough Blockent
Cashel Souterrain
Raths

44

Lough Alaban
Giant's Grave
Cave
Cross

4

Ora More
Rath
Waterfall
Waterfall

Dooletter Lough

43

Lurgan River
Waterfall
Carrickanean
Coolarkan

Tullybrack or Ora More
Lough Ora
Ora Beg
Tullinamohog
Dooletter
Belmore Forest

3

Spa Well
Killycreen West
Tievebane
Waterfalls
Waterfalls
Legacurragh
Waterfall

Tullybrack

42

BT93
Killycreen East
Gardenhill
Waterfall

2

Skeage
Refuse Tip

Lough Hamul
Cloghroga
Legacurragh

Cavantreeduff

41

Ballysroonagh
Mullyard
Cave
Mullylusty
Fox Park
Giant's Grave

Cavanmore
Killeeen
Carrickmacflaherty
Crottan

1

St Columbans Prim Sch
Gardenhill
Drumman

Aghavass
Cashel (remains of)
Carrickaloughan
Mound

40

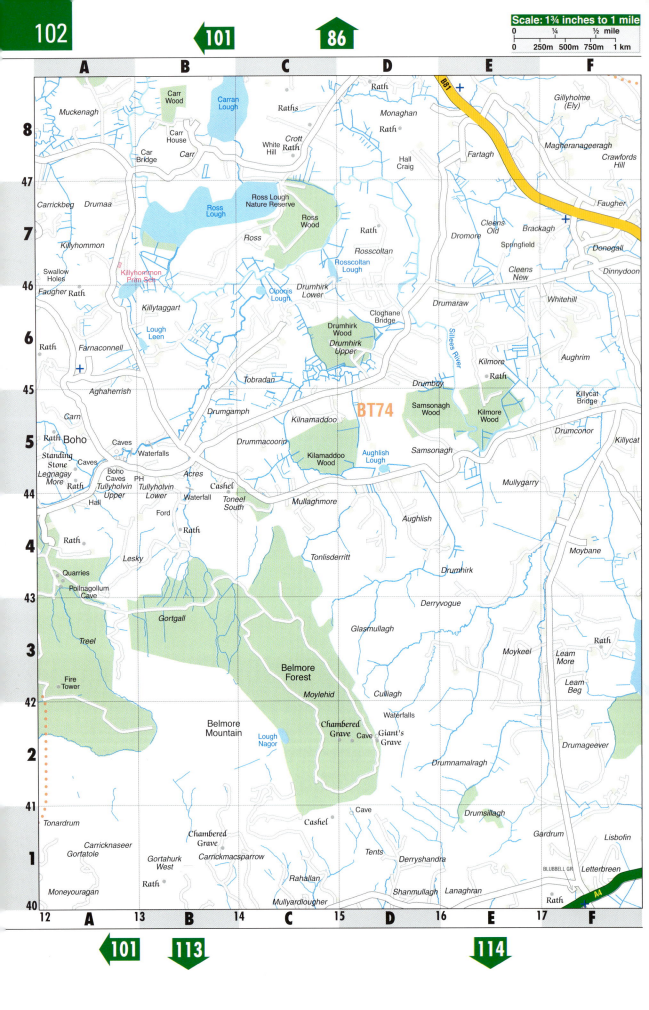

A   B   C   D   E   F

8

47

7

46

6

45

5

44

4

43

3

42

2

41

1

40

Muckenagh

Carr Wood

Carran Lough

Raths

Rath

Monaghan

Rath

Gillyholme (Ely)

Magheranageeragh

Crawfords Hill

Carr House

White Hill

Crott Rath

Hall Craig

Fartagh

B81

Faugher

Carrickbeg

Drumaa

Carr

Car Bridge

Ross Lough

Ross Lough Nature Reserve

Ross Wood

Rath

Cleens Old

Dromore

Springfield

Brackagh

Donegall

Killyhommon

Ross

Rosscoltan

Rosscoltan Lough

Cleens New

Dinnydoon

Swallow Holes

Killyhommon Prim Sch

Cloonis Lough

Drumhirk Lower

Cloghane Bridge

Drumaraw

Whitehill

Faugher   Rath

Killytaggart

Drumhirk Wood

Drumhirk Upper

Silees River

Kilmore

Aughrim

Rath

Farnaconnell

Lough Leen

Rath

Tobradan

Drumboy

Rath

Killycat Bridge

Aghaherrish

Drumgamph

Kilnamaddoo

BT74

Samsonagh Wood

Kilmore Wood

Drumconor

Killycat

Carn

Drummacoorin

Kilamaddoo Wood

Aughlish Lough

Samsonagh

Rath Boho

Caves

Waterfalls

Standing Stone

Caves

Acres

Cashel

Mullygarry

Legnagay More

Boho Caves

PH

Tullyholvin Lower

Tullyholvin Upper

Waterfall

Toneel South

Mullaghmore

Aughlish

Moybane

Hall

Ford

Rath

Rath

Lesky

Tonlisderritt

Drumhirk

Derryvogue

Rath

Quarries

Leam More

Pollnagollum Cave

Gortgall

Glasmullagh

Moykeel

Leam Beg

Treel

Belmore Forest

Moylehid

Culliagh

Drumageever

Fire Tower

Belmore Mountain

Lough Nagor

Chambered Grave

Cave

Giant's Grave

Waterfalls

Drumnamalragh

Tonardrum

Cave

Drumsillagh

Cashel

Gardrum

Lisbofin

Carricknaseer

Gortatole

Chambered Grave

Carrickmacsparrow

Tents

Derryshandra

Blubbell Gr

Letterbreen

Gortahurk West

Rahallan

Shanmullagh

Lanaghran

Rath

A4

Moneyouragan

Rath

Mullyardlougher

12   A   13   B   14   C   15   D   16   E   17   F

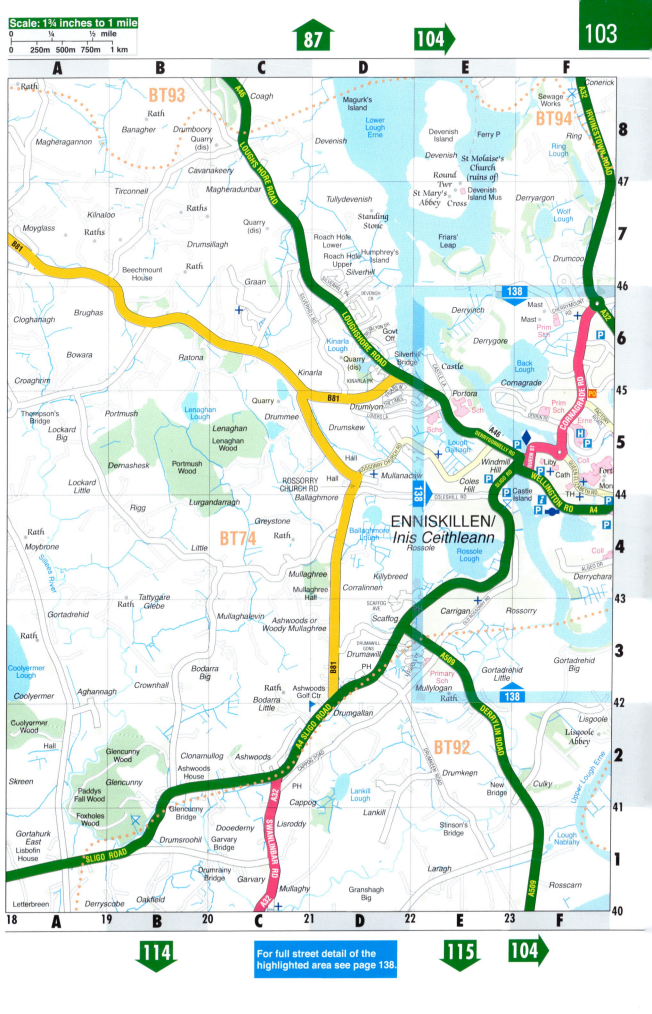

A   B   C   D   E   F

BT93

Rath
Magheragannon
Banagher
Drumboory
Quarry (dis)
Coagh
Magurk's Island
Devenish
Lower Lough Erne
Devenish Island
Ferry P
Ring
Sewage Works
Ring Lough
Conerick

BT94

8

Rath
Cavanakeery
St Molaise's Church (ruins of)
Devenish Island Mus
47

Tirconnell
Magheradunbar
Raths
Round Twr
St Mary's Abbey
Cross
Derryargon
Wolf Lough

Kilnaloo
Raths
Tullydevenish
Standing Stone
Friars' Leap
Drumcoo
7

Moyglass
Drumsillagh
Roach Hole Lower
46

Beechmount House
Rath
Graan
Roach Hole Upper
Silverhill
Humphrey's Island
138

Cloghanagh
Brughas
Silverhill PK
DEVENISH CR
Derryinch
Mast
Mast
CHERRYMOUNT RD
Prim Sch
6

Bowara
Ratona
SILVERHILL RD
LOUGHSHORE ROAD
Kinarla Lough
Quarry (dis)
HOLLYLON DR
Govt Off
Derrygore
Back Lough
Cornagrade
P
PO

Croaghrim
Kinarla
Quarry (dis)
Silverhill Bridge
CASTLE LA
Castle
Portora Sch
Prim Sch
DERRIN RD
FACTORY ROAD
45

Thompson's Bridge
B81
KINARLA PK
FRIARS W
THE LIMES
Schs
Erne
H
Coll
Cath
Fort
Mon

Lockard Big
Portmush
Lenaghan Lough
Drummee
Drumlyon
LOVERS LA
DERRYGONNELLY RD
A46
Schs
QUEEN ST
Lough Galliagh
Liby
QUEEN ELIZABETH RD
5

Lockard Little
Dernashesk
Lenaghan
Lenaghan Wood
Drumskew
Hall
ROSSORRY CHURCH RD
Windmill Hill
WELLINGTON RD
P
TH
P
44

Rigg
Portmush Wood
Lurgandarragh
Hall
Mullanacaw
138
SLIGO RD
Coles Hill
Castle Island
i
P
P

Rath
Moybrone
Greystone
Rath
ROSSORRY CHURCH RD
Ballaghmore
Ballaghmore Lough
COLESHILL RD
ENNISKILLEN/
Inis Ceithleann
A4
4

BT74
Little
Rossole
Rossole Lough
Coll

Rath
Mullaghree
Killybreed
Algeo DR
Derrychara
43

Gortadrehid
Tattygare Glebe
Rath
Mullaghalevin
Mullaghree Hall
Corralinnen
Scaffog AVE
Carrigan
OLD ROSSORRY RD
Rossorry

Coolyermer Lough
Ashwoods or Woody Mullaghree
Scaffog
DRUMAWILL GDNS
Drumawill
PH
A509
Primary Sch
Mullylogan
Gortadrehid Big
3

Coolyermer
Aghannagh
Crownhall
Bodarra Big
PH
CAPPOG RD
Rath
Gortadrehid Little
138

Coolyermer Wood
Clonamullog
Ashwoods
Bodarra Little
Ashwoods Golf Ctr
Drumgallan
DRUMKEEN ROAD
42

Hall
Glencunny Wood
Ashwoods House
B81
Rath
Drumkeen
Lisgoole
Lisgoole Abbey
2

Skreen
Glencunny
Paddys Fall Wood
Foxholes Wood
A32
PH
Cappog
Lankill Lough
Lankill
DERRYLIN ROAD
New Bridge
Culky

Gortahurk East
Lisbofin House
Glencunny Bridge
Drumsroohil
Dooederny
Garvary Bridge
SWANLINBAR RD
Lisroddy
Stinson's Bridge
Lough Nablahy
41

SLIGO ROAD
Drumrainy Bridge
Garvary
Mullaghy
A32
Granshagh Big
Laragh
A509
Rosscarn
1

Letterbreen
Derryscobe
Oakfield
Drumrainy Bridge
BT92
40

18   A   19   B   20   C   21   D   22   E   23   F

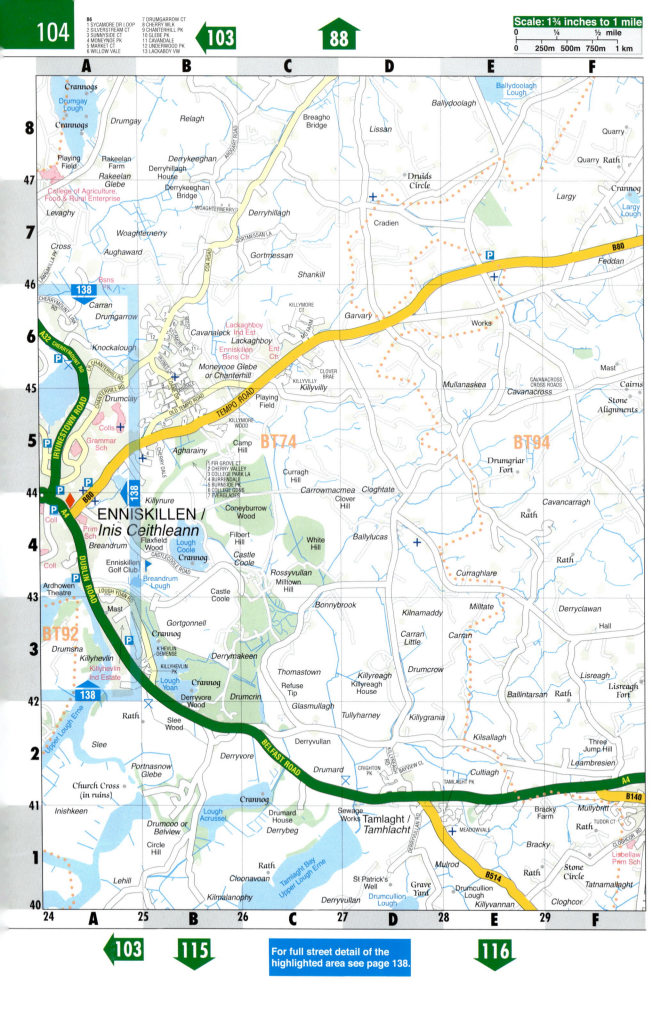

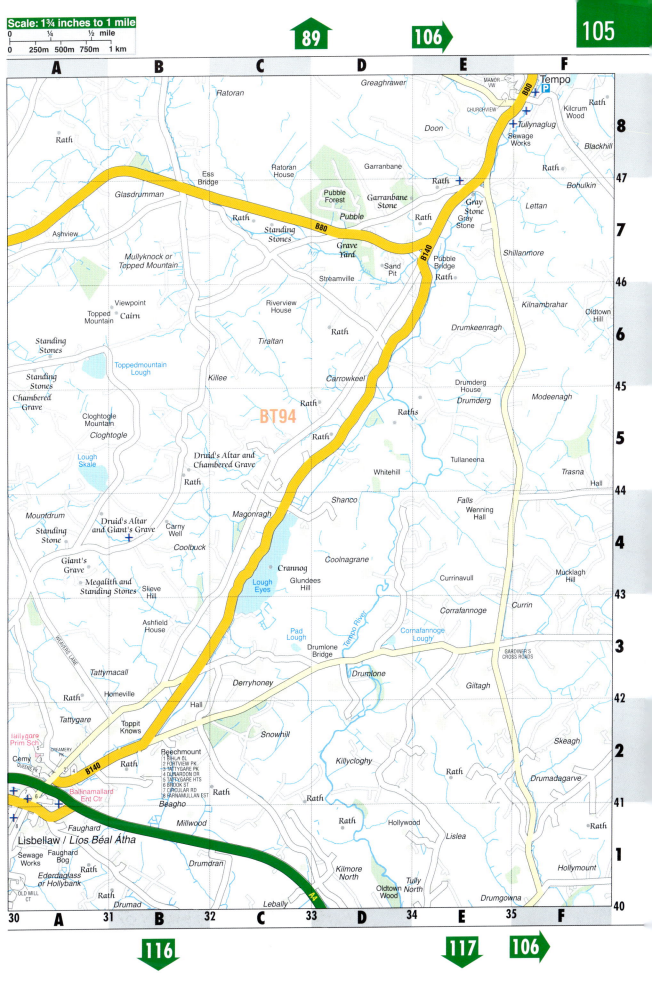

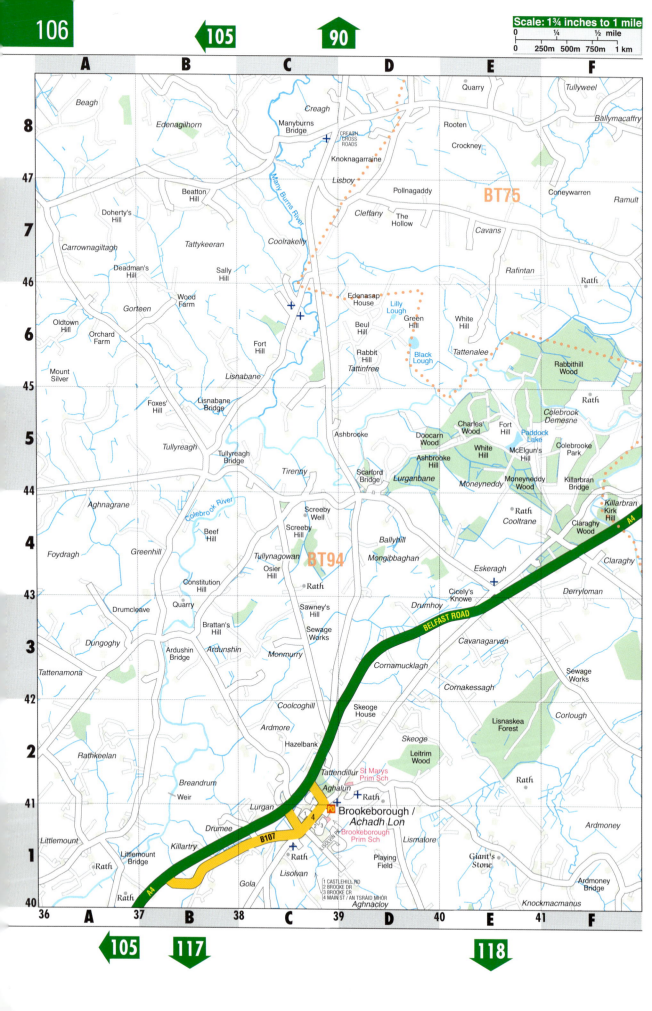

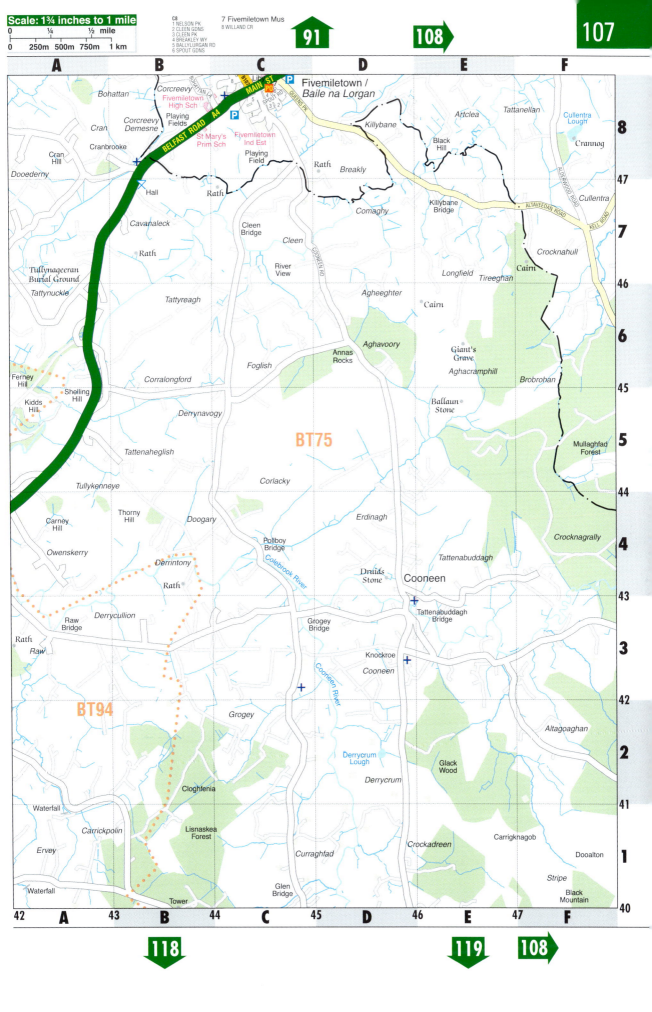

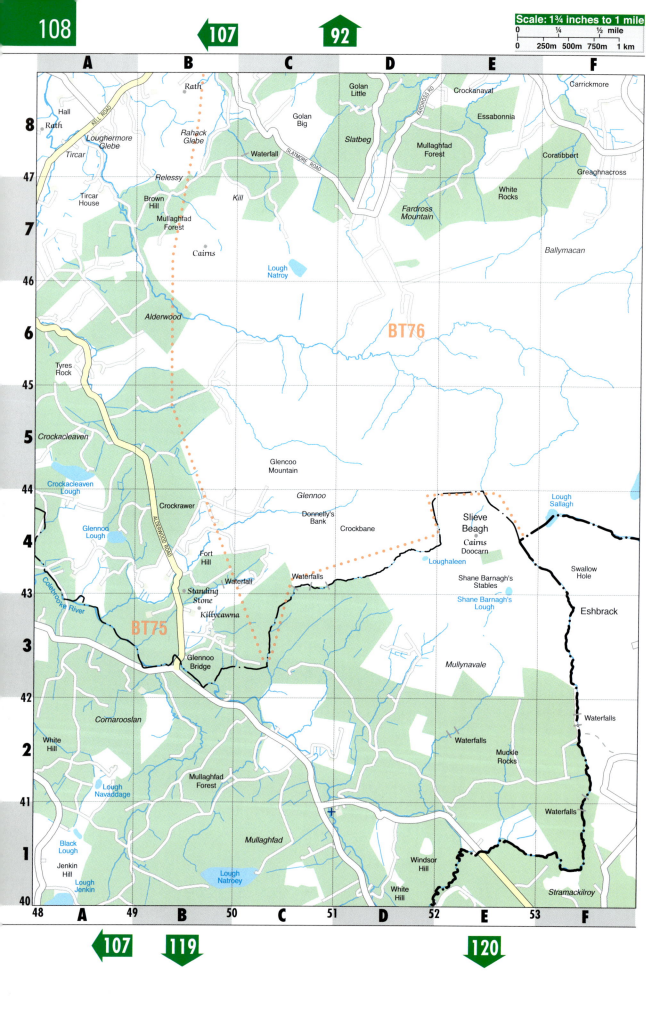

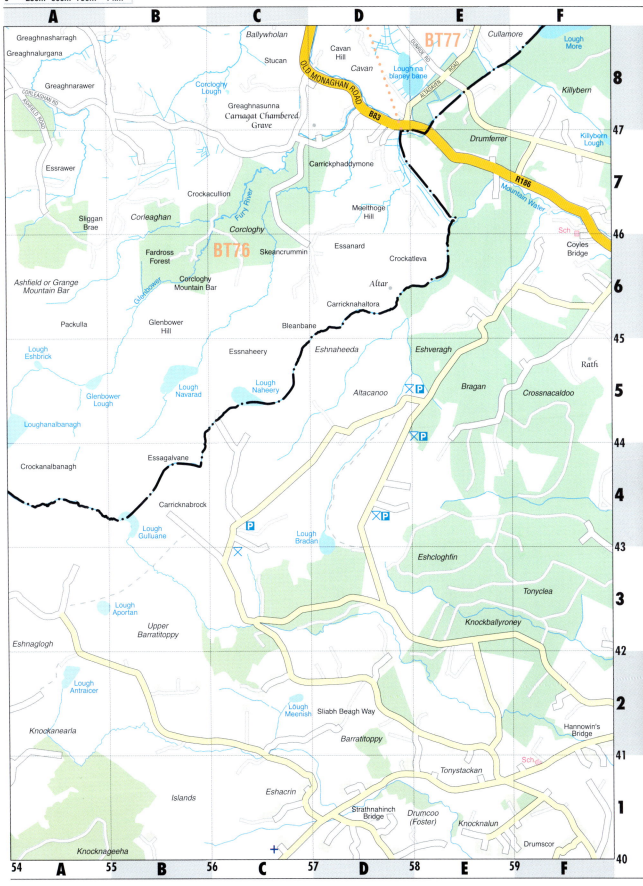

A   B   C   D   E   F

BT77

Cullamore

Lough More

Ballywholan

Stucan

Cavan Hill

Cavan

Lough na blaney bane

Killybern

OLD MONAGHAN ROAD

Corcloghy Lough

Greaghnasharragh

Greaghnalurgana

Greaghnarawer

Greaghnasunna

Carnagat Chambered Grave

B83

DUNROE RD

ALTADAVEN ROAD

Drumferrer

Killybern Lough

8

Corleaghan Ro

Ashfield Road

Essrawer

Carrickphaddymone

R186

Mountain Water

47

7

Crockacullion

Fury River

Meelthoge Hill

Coyles Bridge

Sch

46

Sliggan Brae

Corleaghan

Corcloghy

Skeancrummin

Essanard

Crockatleva

6

Fardross Forest

BT76

Altar

Ashfield or Grange Mountain Bar

Glenbower

Corcloghy Mountain Bar

Carricknahaltora

Rath

45

Packulla

Glenbower Hill

Bleanbane

Eshnaheeda

Eshveragh

Crossnacaldoo

Lough Eshbrick

Essnaheery

Altacanoo

Bragan

5

Glenbower Lough

Lough Navarad

Lough Naheery

44

Loughanalbanagh

Essagalvane

4

Crockanalbanagh

Carricknabrock

Lough Bradan

Eshcloghfin

Tonyclea

43

Lough Gulluane

P

P

3

Lough Aportan

Upper Barratitoppy

Knockballyroney

Eshnaglogh

42

Lough Antraicer

2

Lough Meenish

Sliabh Beagh Way

Hannowin's Bridge

Knockanearla

Barratitoppy

Tonystackan

41

Sch

Islands

Eshacrin

Strathnahinch Bridge

Drumcoo (Foster)

Knocknalun

Drumscor

1

Knocknageeha

40

54   A   55   B   56   C   57   D   58   E   59   F

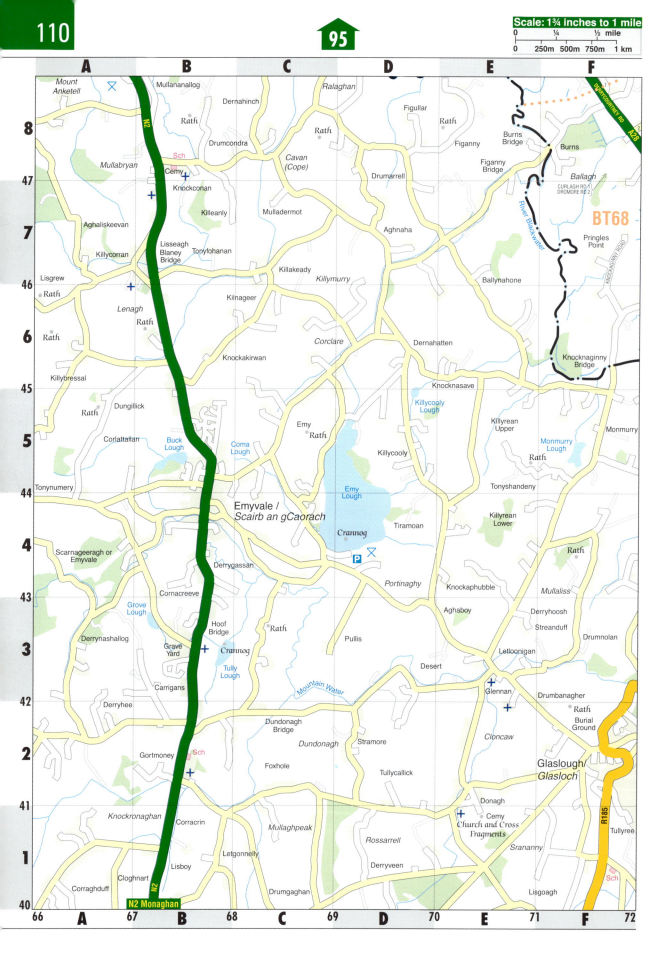

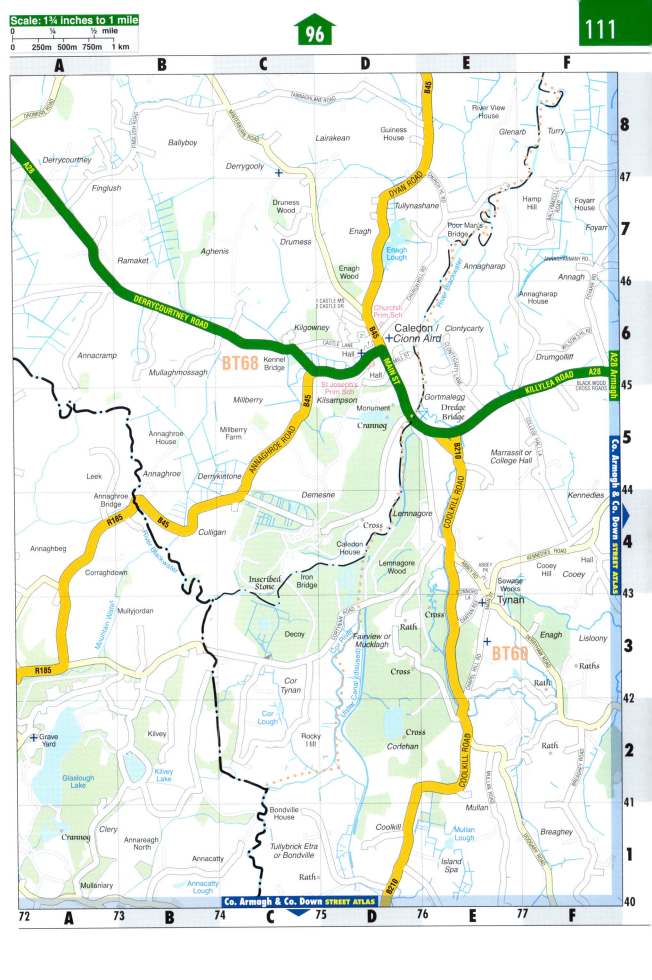

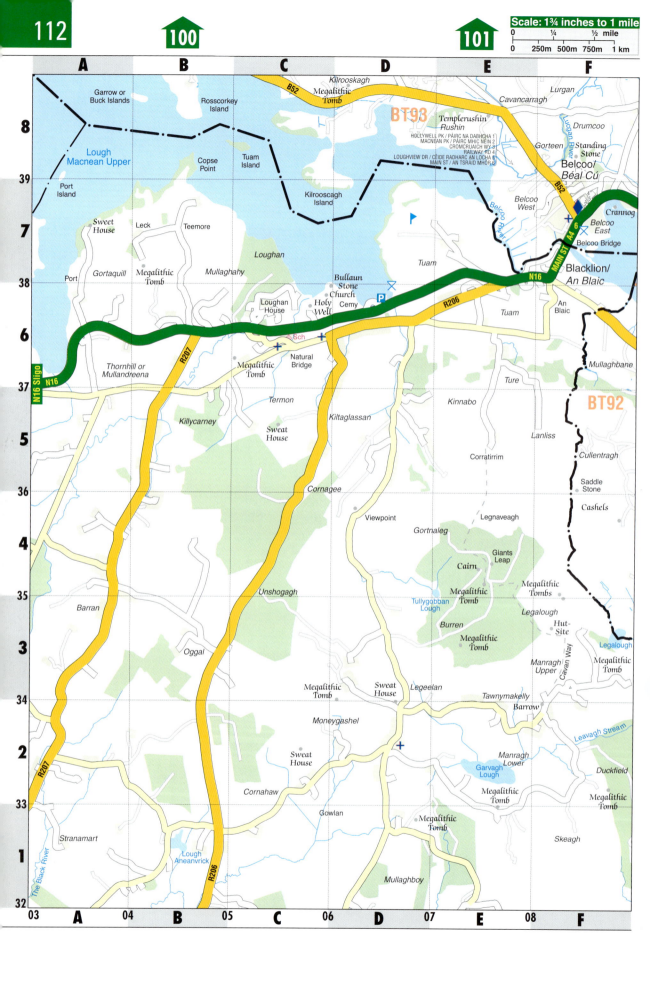

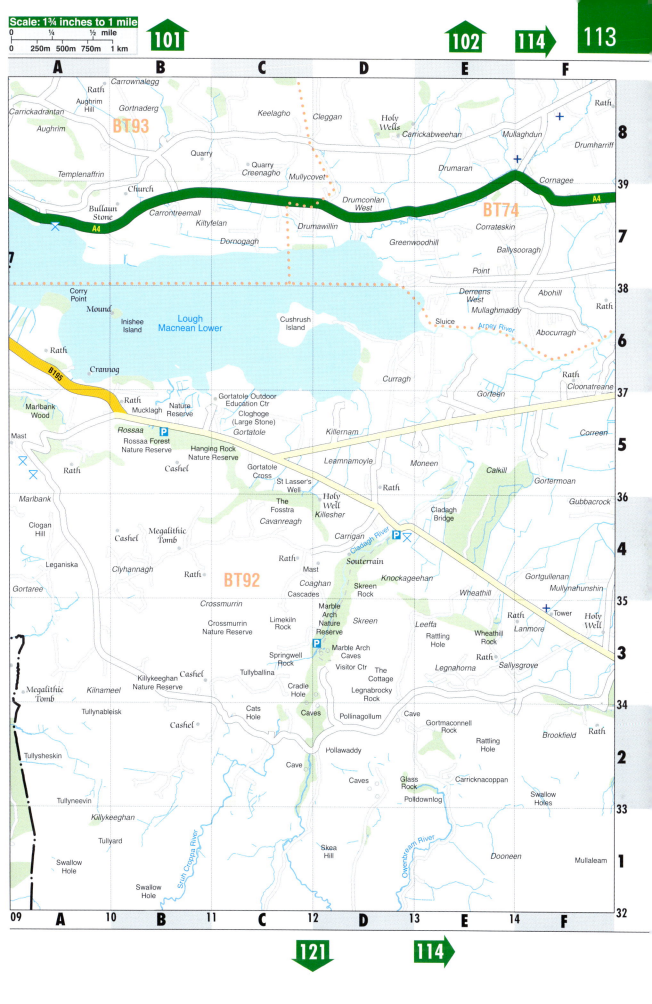

A   B   C   D   E   F

Carrownalegg
Rath
Aughrim Hill
Gortnaderg
BT93   8
Carrickadrantan
Aughrim
Keelagho   Cleggan   Holy Wells   Carrickabweehan   Mullaghdun   Rath
Drumharriff
Quarry
Templenaffrin   Quarry Creenagho   Mullycovet   Drumaran   Cornagee
Church   39   A4
Bullaun Stone   A4   Drumconlan West   BT74
Carrontreemall   Kiltyfelan   Drumawillin   Corrateskin   7
Dornogagh   Greenwoodhill   Ballysooragh
Point   38
Corry Point   Derreens West   Abohill   Rath
Mound   Inishee Island   Lough Macnean Lower   Cushrush Island   Mullaghmaddy   Abocurragh   6
Sluice   Arney River
Rath   Curragh   Gorteen   Rath   Cloonatreane   37
Marlbank Wood   B195   Rath   Mucklagh   Nature Reserve   Gortatole Outdoor Education Ctr   Cloghoge (Large Stone)   Gortatole   Killernam   Correen
Mast   Rossaa   P   Leamnamoyle   Moneen   Calkill   Gortermoan   5
Rath   Rossaa Forest Nature Reserve   Hanging Rock Nature Reserve   Gortatole Cross   St Lasser's Well   Rath   36
Marlbank   Cashel   The Fosstra   Holy Well Killesher   Cladagh Bridge   Gubbacrock
Clogan Hill   Cashel   Megalithic Tomb   Cavanreagh   Carrigan   Cladagh River   P   4
Leganiska   Clyhannagh   Rath   BT92   Rath   Souterrain   Knockageehan   Gortgullenan   Mullynahunshin
Gortaree   Mast   Coaghan Cascades   Skreen Rock   Wheathill   35
Crossmurrin   Marble Arch Nature Reserve   Skreen   Leeffa   Rath   Lanmore   Tower   Holy Well
Megalithic Tomb   Crossmurrin Nature Reserve   Limekiln Rock   Rattling Hole   Wheathill Rock
Kilnameel   Kilmameel   Springwell Rock   P   Marble Arch Caves Visitor Ctr   The Cottage   Legnahorna   Rath   Sallysgrove   3
Cashel   Tullyballina   Cradle Hole   Legnabrocky Rock
Tullysheskin   Tullynableisk   Cashel   Cats Hole   Caves   Pollinagollum   Cave   Gortmaconnell Rock   Rattling Hole   Brookfield   Rath   34
Pollawaddy   Cave   2
Cave   Caves   Glass Rock   Carricknacoppan   Swallow Holes
Killykeeghan   Polldownlog   33
Tullyneevin   Sruh Croppa River   Owenbream River
Tullyard   Skea Hill   Dooneen   Mullaleam   1
Swallow Hole   Swallow Hole   32

09   A   10   B   11   C   12   D   13   E   14   F   32

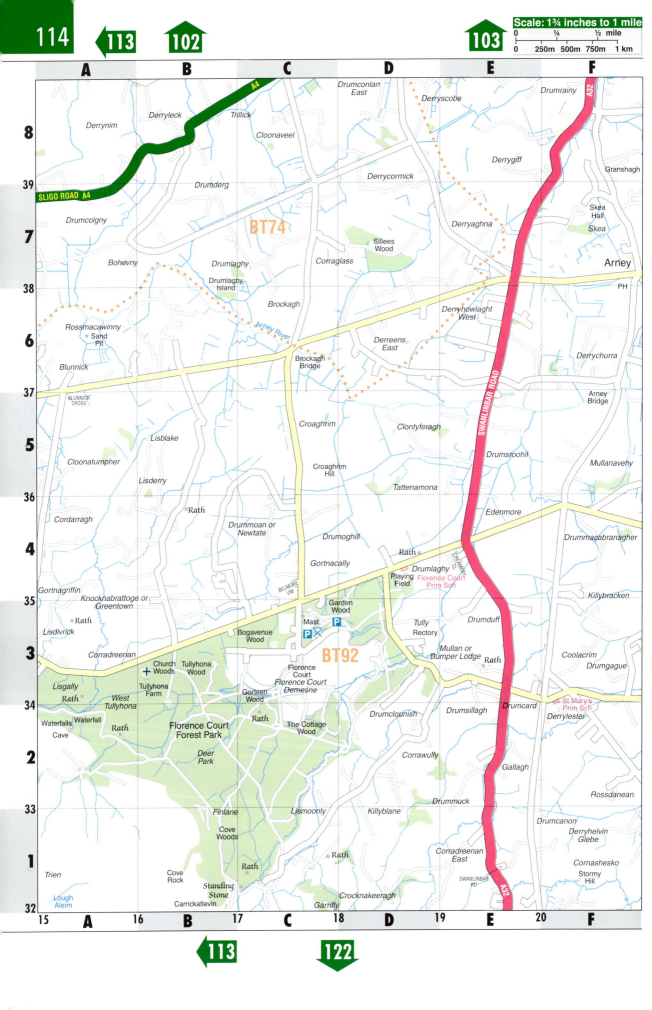

114

113

102

103

Scale: 1¾ inches to 1 mile

0   ¼   ½   mile
0 250m 500m 750m 1 km

A   B   C   D   E   F

8

Drumconlan
East

Derryscobe

Drumrainy

Derrynim

Derryleck

Trillick

A4

Cloonaveel

Derrygiff

Granshagh

39

SLIGO ROAD A4

Drumderg

Derrycormick

Derryaghna

Skea
Hall

Skea

Drumcolgny

BT74

7

Bohevny

Drumlaghy

Sillees
Wood

Arney

PH

38

Drumlaghy
Island

Corraglass

Derryhowlaght
West

6

Rossmacawinny

Sand
Pit

Arney River

Brockagh

Derreens
East

Derrychurra

Blunnick

Brockagh
Bridge

Arney
Bridge

37

BLUNNICK
CROSS

Croaghrim

Clontyferagh

Drumsroohil

5

Lisblake

Mullanavehy

Cloonatumpher

Croaghrim
Hill

Tattenamona

36

Lisderry

Edenmore

Cordarragh

Rath

Drummoan or
Newtate

Rath

Drummacabranagher

Killybracken

4

Gortnagriffin

Gortnacally

Drumlaghy

Drumduff

Coolacrim

Knocknabrattoge or
Greentown

Rath

Playing
Field

Florence Court
Prim Sch

Drumgague

35

Lisdivrick

Rath

BELMORE
VW

Garden
Wood

Tully
Rectory

Drumclounish

St Mary's
Prim Sch

3

Corradreenan

Church
Woods

Tullyhona
Wood

Mast

P

P

BT92

Mullan or
Bumper Lodge

Rath

Drumsillagh

Drumcard

Derrylester

Lisgally
Rath

West
Tullyhona

Tullyhona
Farm

Gorteen
Wood

Florence
Court

Florence Court
Demesne

34

Waterfalls
Cave

Waterfall

Rath

Florence Court
Forest Park

Rath

The Cottage
Wood

Corrawully

Drumcanon

Derryhelvin
Glebe

2

Deer
Park

Drummuck

Gallagh

Rossdanean

33

Finlane

Lismoonly

Killyblane

Cove
Woods

Cornashesko
Stormy
Hill

1

Trien

Cove
Rock

Rath

Corradreenan
East

Lough
Aleim

Standing
Stone

SWANLINBAR
RD

A32

Crocknakeeragh

32

Carrickatlevin

Garrifly

15   A   16   B   17   C   18   D   19   E   20   F

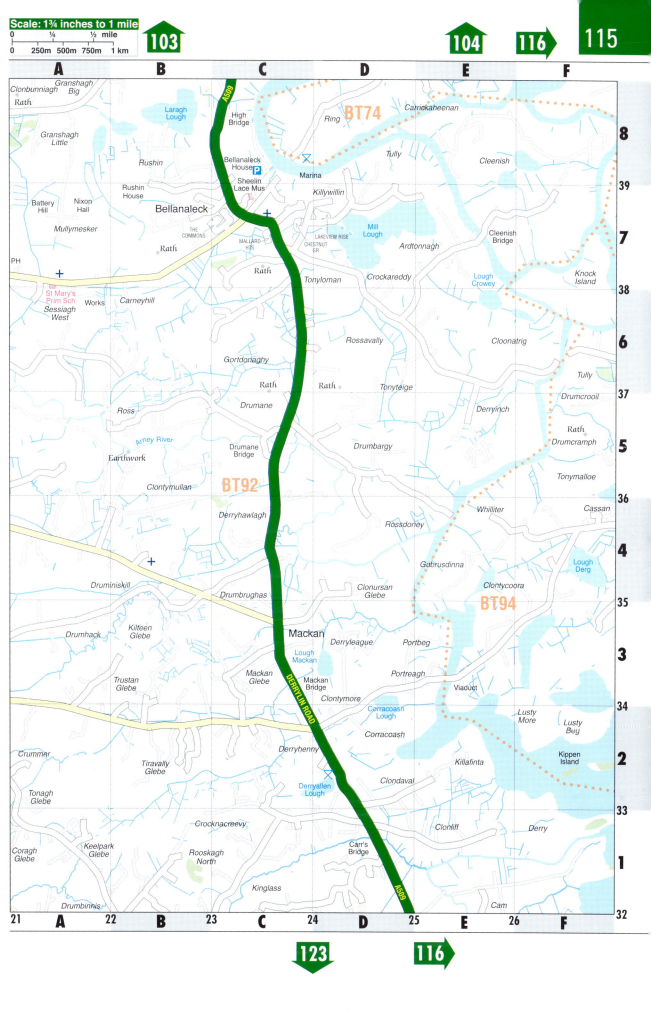

A   B   C   D   E   F

8
39
7
38
6
37
5
36
4
35
3
34
2
33
1
32

Clonbunniagh
Granshagh Big
Rath
Laragh Lough
High Bridge
BT74
Ring
Carrickaheenan
Granshagh Little
Rushin
Bellanaleck House
Sheelin Lace Mus
P
Marina
Tully
Cleenish
Rushin House
Killywillin
Bellanaleck
Cleenish Bridge
THE COMMONS
LAKEVIEW RISE
Mill Lough
Ardtonnagh
Rath
MALLARD HTS
CHESTNUT GR
Mullymesker
Rath
Tonyloman
Crockareddy
Lough Crowey
Knock Island
PH
St Mary's Prim Sch
Works
Carneyhill
Rath
Rossavally
Cloonatrig
Sessiagh West
Gortdonaghy
Tully
Drumcrooil
Ross
Rath
Rath
Tonyteige
Derryinch
Rath
Drumcramph
Arney River
Drumane
Drumbargy
Earthwork
Drumane Bridge
BT92
Cloonatrig
Tonymalloe
Clontymullan
Whilliter
Cassan
Derryhawlagh
Rossdoney
Lough Derg
Druminiskill
Gubrusdinna
Clontycoora
Drumbrughas
Clonursan Glebe
BT94
Drumhack
Kilteen Glebe
Mackan
Derryleague
Portbeg
Lusty More
Lusty Bay
Trustan Glebe
Lough Mackan
Mackan Bridge
Portreagh
Viaduct
Mackan Glebe
Clontymore
Kippen Island
Crummer
DERRYLIN ROAD
Clontymore
Corracoash Lough
Killafinta
Tiravally Glebe
Derryhenny
Corracoash
Clondaval
Tonagh Glebe
Derryallen Lough
Coragh Glebe
Keelpark Glebe
Crocknacreevy
Clonliff
Derry
Rooskagh North
Carr's Bridge
Kinglass
Drumbinnis
A509
Cam

116

115

104

105

Scale: 1¾ inches to 1 mile

0   ¼   ½ mile

0   250m 500m 750m 1 km

A   B   C   D   E   F

8

Drumcullion Lough

Drumcullion

Fyagh

Derrybrusk Church

B514

Drumrainy

Whinnigan Glebe

Farnacht

Cloghcor

Elm Cottage

Rath

Cloon

Cornashannel

39

Coolnashanton

Hall

Hall

Hall

Fort Hill

BT74

Lough Neely

Cappy

Cappy House

Farnamullan

Kiltenamullagh

Drumroo

Drummeer

7

Black Lough

Ring

Derrybrusk

Lough Raymond

Tawnyreagh

Tawnyreagh House

Gola Lough

Gola

Corraclare

Drumleagues Little

Ballina New Bridge

Drumbaghlin

Curryann

38

Arda

Crockaleen

Arda Lough

Drumhirk Lough

Lismoyle

Slipway

Mullaghmakervy

Lough Corban

Clay

Corranewy

6

Drumhirk

Rath

Carry

Fort Hill

Hotel

P

Carry Bridge

Aghnacarra

Aghnaloo

Ederdacurragh

Wood Hill

Rath

Cuil Hill *Littlehill*

37

Aughey

Inishmore

Rath

Lough Nabodeen

Rosse Wood

✚

Derryharney

Mullaghkippin

Acres

Droles

Killyrover

B514

5

Crannog

Lough Barry

✚

Slee

Drummee

Racecourse Hill

Blackbog Wood

Derryharney Wood

Glen Bridge *Glen Bridge Wood* *Wood*

Derryhowlaght Lough

BT94

Derryhowlaght East

Rath

Droles Bridge

Drumcramph

Rath

Ballindarragh

Drummack

36

Belle Isle

Slatequay Bay

Slatequay Wood

Fort Hill

Templehill Wood

Derrycallaghan

Drumharriff

Drumleagues Big

4

Decoy Lough

Cloonacarn

Bunnahesco

Drumhack

35

Sessiagh East

West Island

Inishbeg Hill

Corrard

Drumcoo

Drumcon

3

Killygowan Island

Carrickmacrourk Island

Inishbeg Point

Corrard Bay

Coolbeg

Aghamore North

Drumbad More

Currogs

34

Creaghmacwallen Island

Finnis Island

Inishcreenry

Bunnahola Island

Corrachrow House

Corrachrow

2

Shave Island

Inishcreagh

Castle Hill

Lough Digh

Derryasna

33

Staff Island

Tonregee Island

Bilberry Island

Deal Island

Inishleague

Grey Stone

Kinmore

BT92

1

Corraslough Point

Creaghnarourk Island

Doocharn Island

Inishfausy

Inishroosk

Rossmacole

32

27   A   28   B   29   C   30   D   31   E   32   F

A   B   C   D   E   F

8
39
7
38
6
37
5
36
4
35
3
34
2
33
1
32

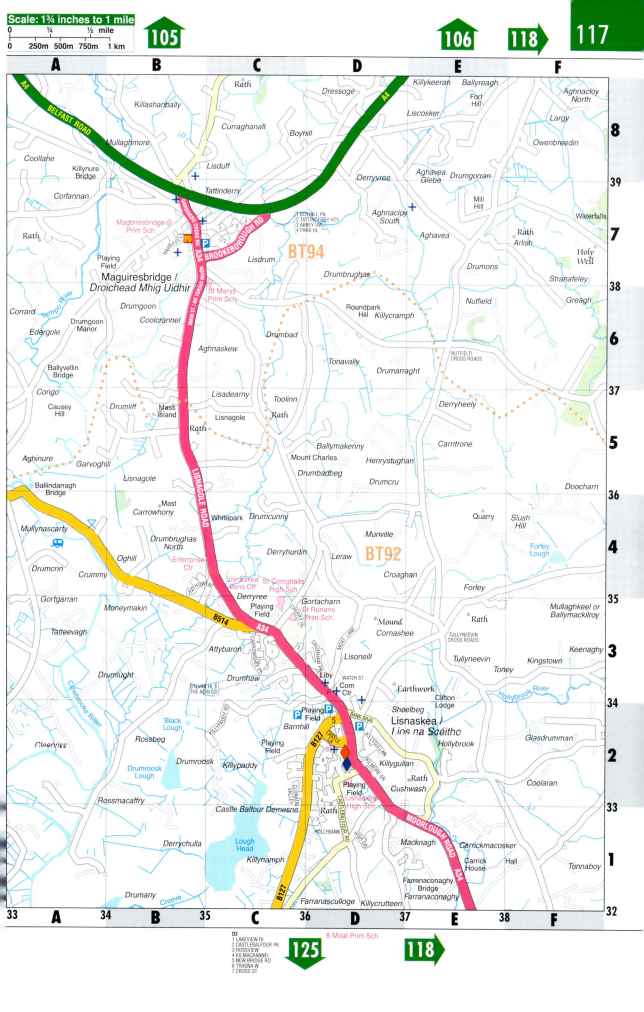

A4
BELFAST ROAD

Rath
Killashanbally
Dressoge
Liscosker
Killykeeran
Ballyreagh
Fort Hill
Aghnacloy North
Largy

Mullaghmore
Curraghanall
Boyhill
A4
Owenbreedin

Coollane
Lisduff
Derryvree
Aghavea Glebe
Drumgorran
Mill Hill

Killynure Bridge
Tattinderry
Aghnacloy South
Aghavea
Waterfalls

Corfannan
1 BOYHILL PK
2 TATTINDERRY HTS
3 ABBEY VW
4 PARK HL
Rath Arlish

Maguiresbridge Prim Sch
BT94
Drumoris
Holy Well

Rath
Lisdrum
Drumbrughas
Roundpark Hill
Killycramph
Nutfield
Stranafeley
Greagh

Maguiresbridge / Droichead Mhig Uidhir
St Marys Prim Sch

Corrard
Drumgoon
Coolcrannel
Aghnaskew
Drumbad
Tonavally
Drumarraght
Nutfield Cross Roads

Edergole
Drumgoon Manor

Ballyvellin Bridge
Lisadearny
Toolinn
Rath
Ballymakenny
Mount Charles
Drumbadbeg
Henrystughan
Drumcru
Derryheely
Carntrone

Congo
Causey Hill
Drumliff
Mass Island
Lisnagole
Rath

Aghinure
Garvoghill
Lisnagole
LISNAGOLE ROAD
Doocharn

Ballindarragh Bridge
Mast Carrowhony
Whitepark
Drumcunny
Quarry
Slush Hill

Mullynascarty
Drumbrughas North
Derryhurdin
BT92
Munville
Forfey Lough

Oghill
Enterprise Ctr
Leraw
Croaghan
Forfey

Drumcrin
Crummy
Lisnaskea Bsns Ctr
St Comghalls High Sch

Gortgarran
Moneymakin
RATHOWEN
Derryree
Playing Field
Gortacharn St Ronans Prim Sch
Mound Cornashee
Rath
Tullyneevin Cross Roads
Mullaghkeel or Ballymackilroy

Tatteevagh
B514
A34
CHERRYHL
Moat Lane
Lisoneill
Tullyneevin
Toney
Kingstown
Keenaghy

Drumlught
Attybaron
DRUMHAW PK
Liby
Water St
Com Ctr
Earthwork
Clifton Lodge
Hollybrook River

SYLVAN HL
THE ACRES
Drumhaw
Black Lough
Sheelbeg
Glasdrumman

Gleenriss
KILLYPADDY RD
Playing Field
Barnhill
BANK BRAE
Lisnaskea / Lios na Scéithe
Hollybrook

Rossbeg
Drumroosk
Killypaddy
Playing Field
B127
CASTLE
5
7
KILLYGULLAN
KILMORE GN
Killygullan

Drumroosk Lough
6
Playing Field
Lisnaskea High Sch
Rath
Cushwash
Coolaran

Rossmacaffry
CLONOGG VALLEY
Rath
MOORLOUGH ROAD

Castle Balfour Demesne
Lough Head
HOLLYBANK
CASTLEBALFOUR RD
HIGH GR
Macnagh
Carrickmacosker
Carrick House
Hall
Tonnaboy

Derrychulla
Killynamph
B127
Farranaconaghy Bridge
Farranaconaghy

Drumany
Creeve
Farranasculloge
Killycrutteen
A34

33   34   35   36   37   38
A   B   C   D   E   F
32

D2
1 LAKEVIEW RI
2 CASTLEBALFOUR PK
3 ROSSVIEW
4 KILMACRANNEL
5 NEW BRIDGE RD
6 TRASNA W
7 CROSS ST

8 Moat Prim Sch

125   118

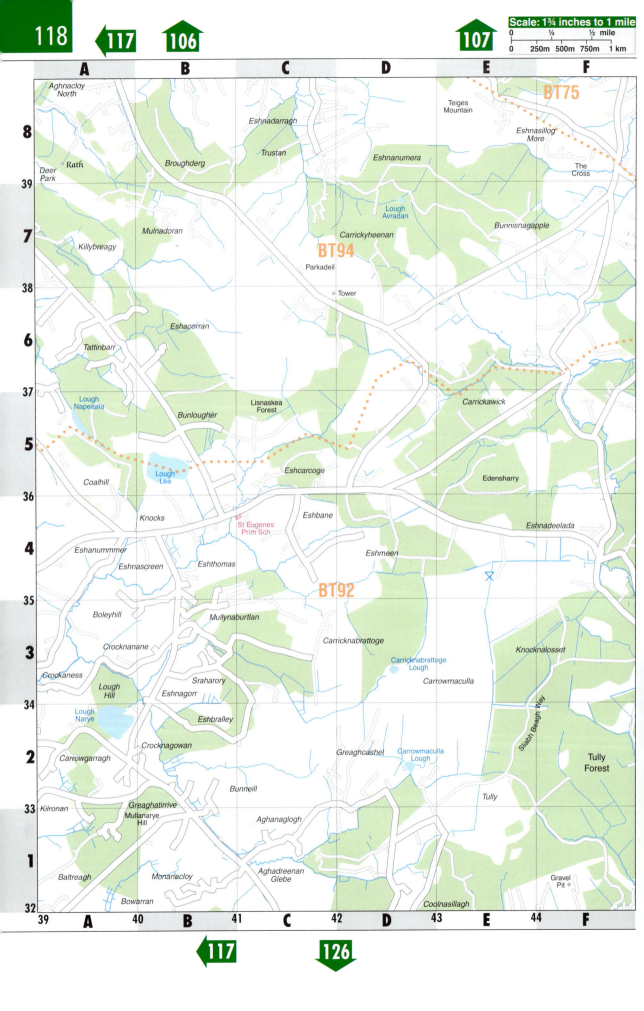

118
117
106
107

Scale: 1¾ inches to 1 mile
0   ¼   ½   mile
0   250m 500m 750m 1 km

A   B   C   D   E   F

Aghnacloy
North

BT75

Teiges
Mountain

Eshnasillog
More

8

Deer
Park
Rath

Broughderg

Eshnadarragh

Trustan

Eshnanumera

The
Cross

39

7

Killybreagy

Mulnadoran

Lough
Avradan

Carrickyheenan

BT94

Bunnisnagapple

38

Parkadeil

Tower

6

Tattinbarr

Eshacorran

37

Lough
Napeasta

Bunlougher

Lisnaskea
Forest

Carrickawick

5

Coalhill

Lough
Lea

Eshcarcoge

Edensharry

36

Knocks

Eshbane

Eshnadeelada

St Eugenes
Prim Sch

4

Eshanummmer

Eshthomas

Eshmeen

Eshnascreen

35

BT92

3

Boleyhill

Mullynaburtlan

Carricknabrattoge

Knocknalosset

Crocknanane

Carricknabrattoge
Lough

Carrowmaculla

Crockaness

Sraharory

34

Lough
Hill

Eshnagorr

Lough
Narye

Eshbralley

Sliabh Beagh Way

2

Carrowgarragh

Crocknagowan

Greaghcashel

Carrowmaculla
Lough

Tully
Forest

Bunneill

Tully

33

Kilronan

Greaghatirrive

Aghanaglogh

Mullanarye
Hill

1

Baltreagh

Monanacloy

Aghadreenan
Glebe

Gravel
Pit

Coolnasillagh

32

39   A   40   B   41   C   42   D   43   E   44   F

A   B   C   D   E   F

Altmartin
Legatillida
Stripe
Lough Jenkin
Lough Cushkeery
Lough Nabraddagh
Sliabh Beagh Way

8

Eshnasillog Beg
Atnamollyboy
BT75
Lough Nadarra
Altawark

39

Coonen Water
Attyclannabryan
Lough Asladee
Lough Tawy
Garrane

7

BT94
Knockanorane

38

Altnaponer
Eshywulligan
The Lodge
Eshnadarragh
Knockannagapple

6

Lough Nabull
Bunlougher

Mullanvaum
Eshekerin
Knockanduff

37

Crocknakelly Glebe
Lough Corry
Knoppane
Bunmichael
Greaghaverrin

5

Doon and Eshcleagh
Lisnaskea Forest
Sliabh Beagh Way
Doocarn
Lisnakea Forest

Mast
BT92

36

Kimran Lough
Carnmore Lough
Ervey
Greaghnagore

4

Eshcleagh Lough
Kimran
Carnmore
Cornamramurry
Bruscarnagh

Errasallagh
Bunnablaneybane
Corrinshigo

35

Mast
Errasallagh Cross Roads
Greaghacholea
Cornacreeve
Corbane

3

Gorteen
Follum Big
Greaghacapple
Crocknagross
Tibberedoge Glebe

34

Corraghy
Corranny
Crockawaddy Glebe
Cortaher
Tonydrummallard

2

Chy
Corlaghaloon
Corranny Lough
Follum Little
Drumerwinter
Feagh

33

Clahernagh
Knockmacaroony Glebe
Derrynacloy

1

Strananerriagh
Cross
Drumbrughas
Cortrasna
Dresternan Lough

Dernabacky
Annaghilly North
Mullavea Glebe
Playing Field

Derrynawilt West
Derrynawilt Cross Roads
B36

Crocknaboghill

45   A   46   B   47   C   48   D   49   E   50   F   32

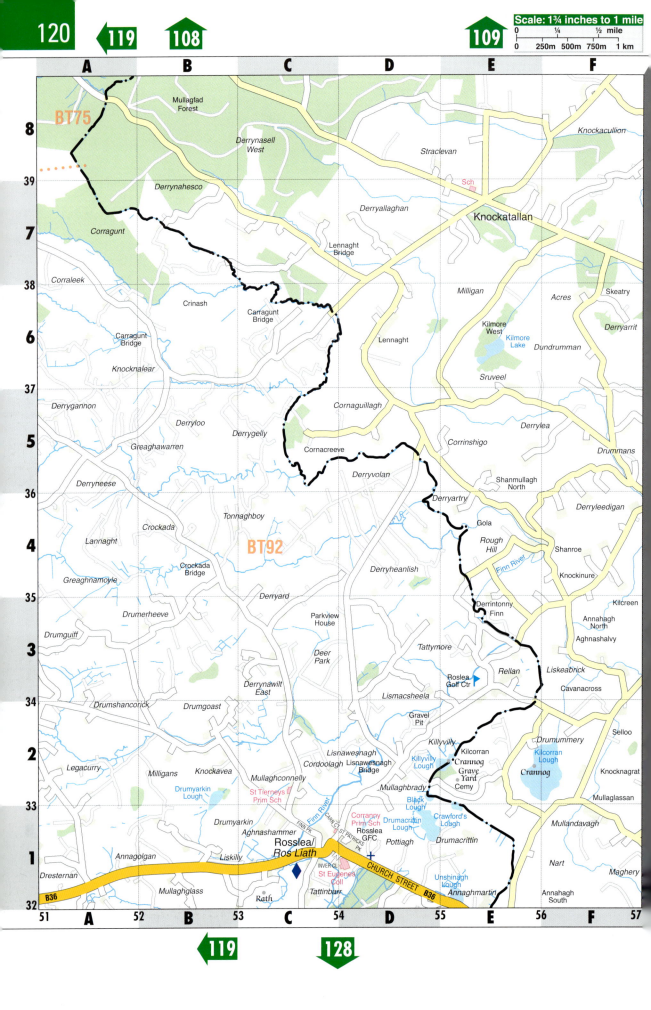

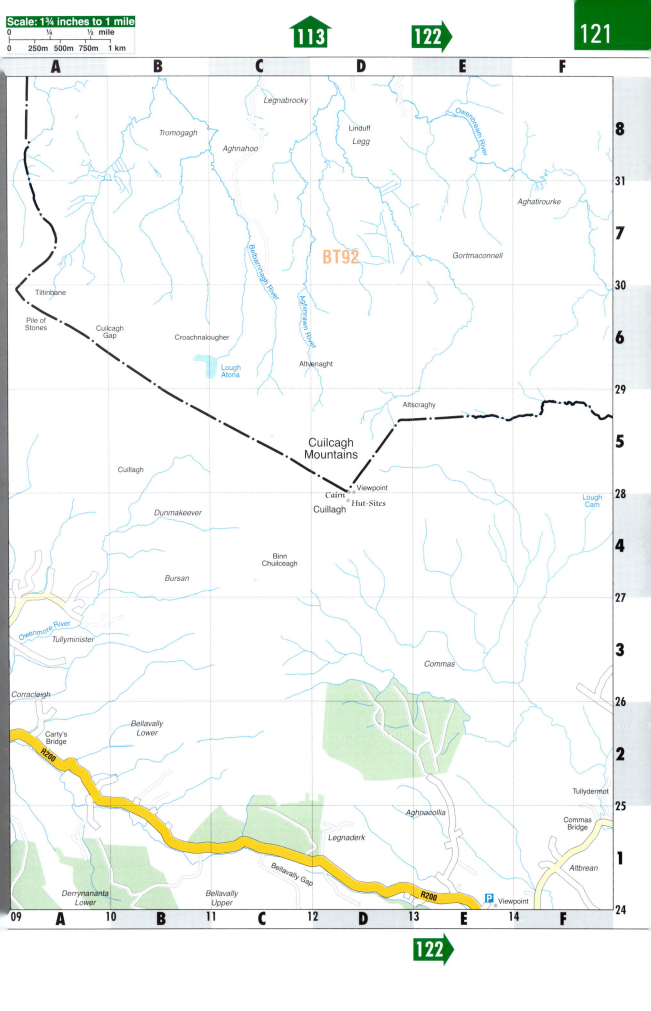

Scale: 1¾ inches to 1 mile
0   ¼   ½   mile
0   250m 500m 750m 1 km

A   B   C   D   E   F

Legnabrocky

Tromogagh

Aghnahoo

Linduff

Legg

Owenbream River

Aghatirourke

BT92

Belbarrinagh River

Gortmaconnell

Tiltinbane

Pile of Stones

Cuilcagh Gap

Aghinrawn River

Croachnalougher

Lough Atona

Altvenaght

Altscraghy

Cuilcagh Mountains

Cuillagh

Viewpoint
Cairn
Cuillagh
Hut-Sites

Lough Cam

Dunmakeever

Binn Chuilceagh

Bursan

Owenmore River

Tullyminister

Commas

Corracleigh

Carty's Bridge

Bellavally Lower

R200

Aghnacollia

Tullydermot

Legnaderk

Commas Bridge

Bellavally Gap

R200

P Viewpoint

Altbrean

Derrynananta Lower

Bellavally Upper

8
31
7
30
6
29
5
28
4
27
3
26
2
25
1
24

09   A   10   B   11   C   12   D   13   E   14   F

Scale: 1¾ inches to 1 mile

0   ¼   ½   mile

0   250m   500m   750m   1 km

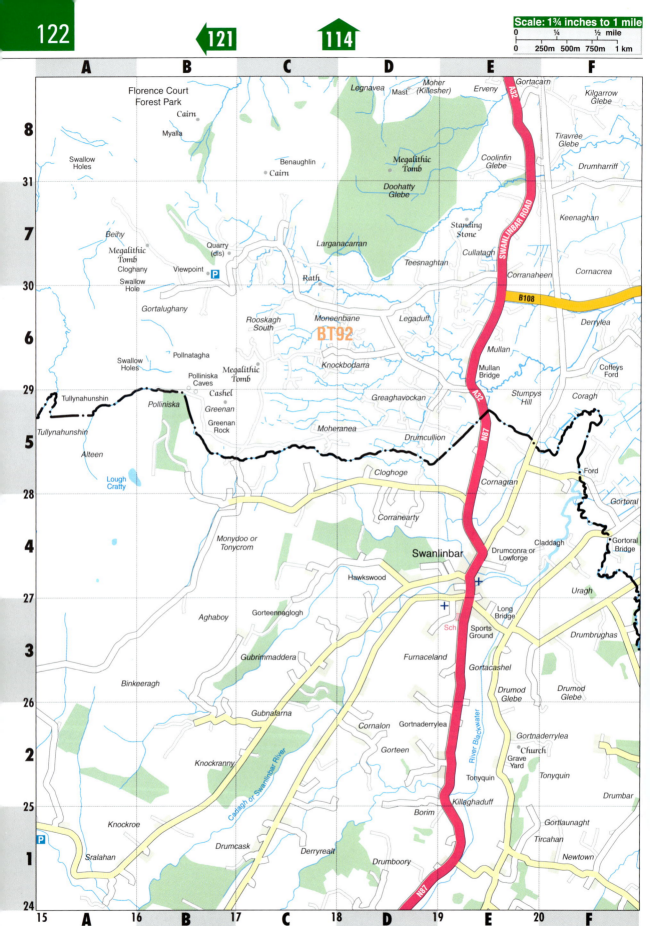

Florence Court
Forest Park

Legnavea   Moher
                  Mast (Killesher)   Erveny   Gortacarn

Cairn   Kilgarrow
                                                                   Glebe
Myalla
                                   Megalithic   Coolinfin   Tiravree
                                   Tomb   Glebe   Glebe
Swallow   Benaughlin   Drumharriff
Holes   Cairn   Doohatty   Keenaghan
                                         Glebe
                                                          Standing
Beihy   Stone   Cullatagh
                                        Larganacarran   Cornacrea
Megalithic   Quarry
Tomb   (dis)   Teesnaghtan   Corranaheen
Cloghany   B108
         Viewpoint   Derrylea
Swallow   Rath   Legaduff
Hole   Moneenbane   Mullan
Gortalughany   Rooskagh   Coffeys
                                  South   BT92   Mullan   Ford
Swallow   Bridge   Stumpys
Holes   Pollnatagha   Megalithic   Knockbodarra   Hill   Coragh
              Polliniska   Tomb
              Caves   Cashel   A32
Polliniska   Greenan   Greaghavockan   Ford
                        Greenan
                        Rock   Moheranea
Tullynahunshin   Drumcullion
                                                                         N87
Tullynahunshin   Alteen   Gortoral
                                      Cloghoge   Cornagran
                                                                              Gortoral
Lough   Corranearty   Bridge
Cratty
                       Monydoo or   Drumconra or   Claddagh
                       Tonycrom   Swanlinbar Lowforge
                                                                              Uragh
                                     Hawkswood
Aghaboy   Gorteennaglogh   Long   Drumbrughas
                                                          Bridge
Gubrimmaddera   Sch   Sports
                                              Ground
Binkeeragh   Furnaceland Gortacashel   Drumod   Drumod
                                                                      Glebe   Glebe
Gubnafarna   Cornalon   Gortnaderrylea
                                                            Gortnaderrylea
              Knockranny   Gorteen   Church
                                                                 Grave
Knockroe   Yard
                                                   Tonyquin   Tonyquin
                                                                                   Drumbar
         Sralahan   Drumcask   River Blackwater Killaghaduff   Gortlaunaght
                               Derryrealt   Tircahan   Newtown
                         Drumboory
                                                                N87

Cadagh or Swanlinbar River

Swanlinbar

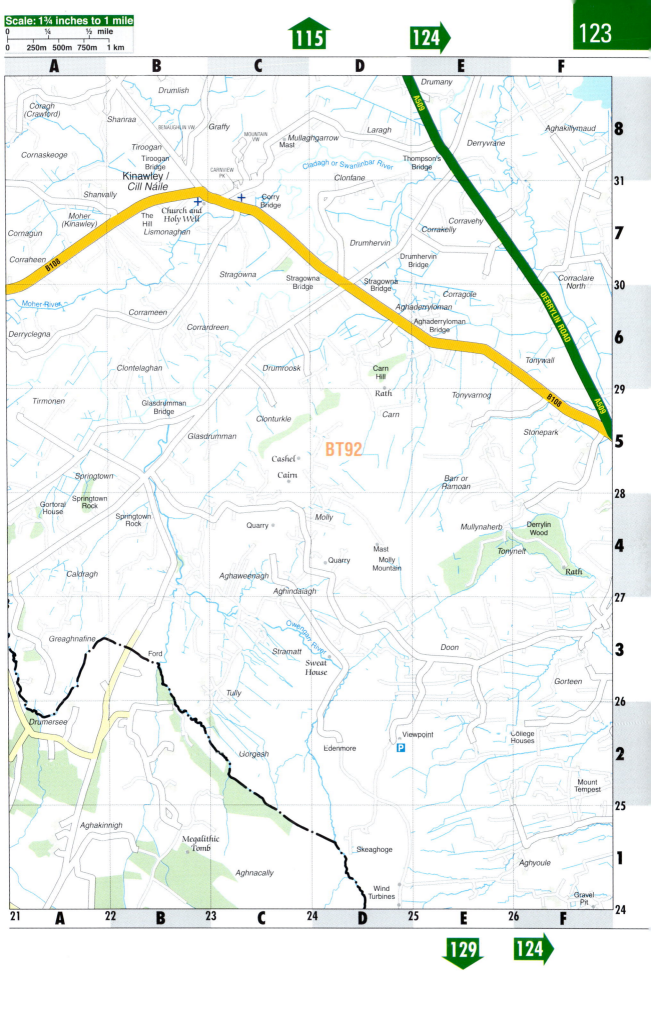

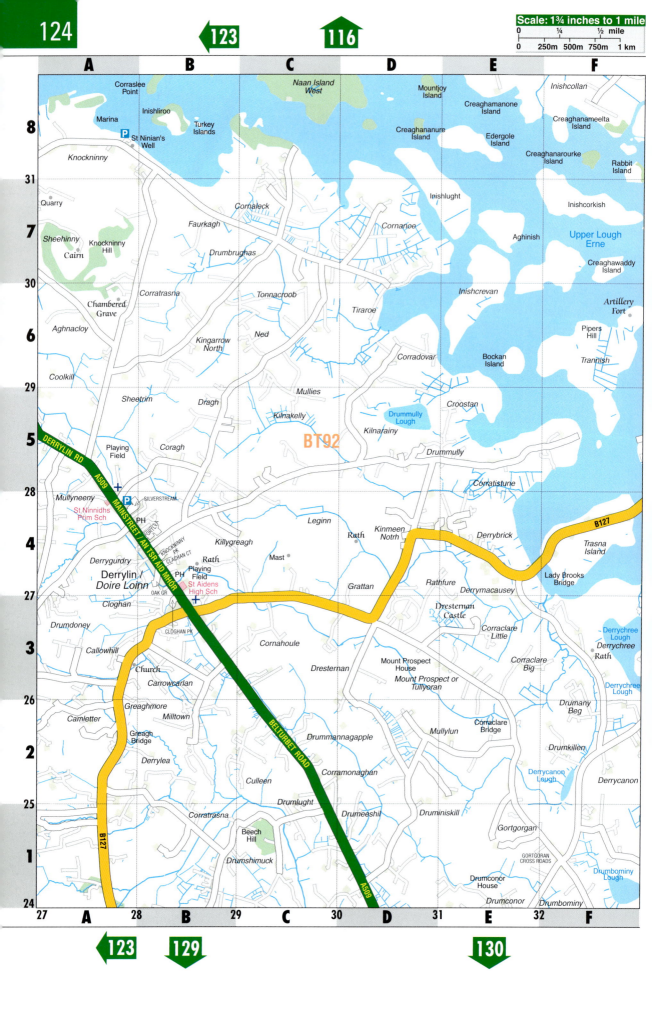

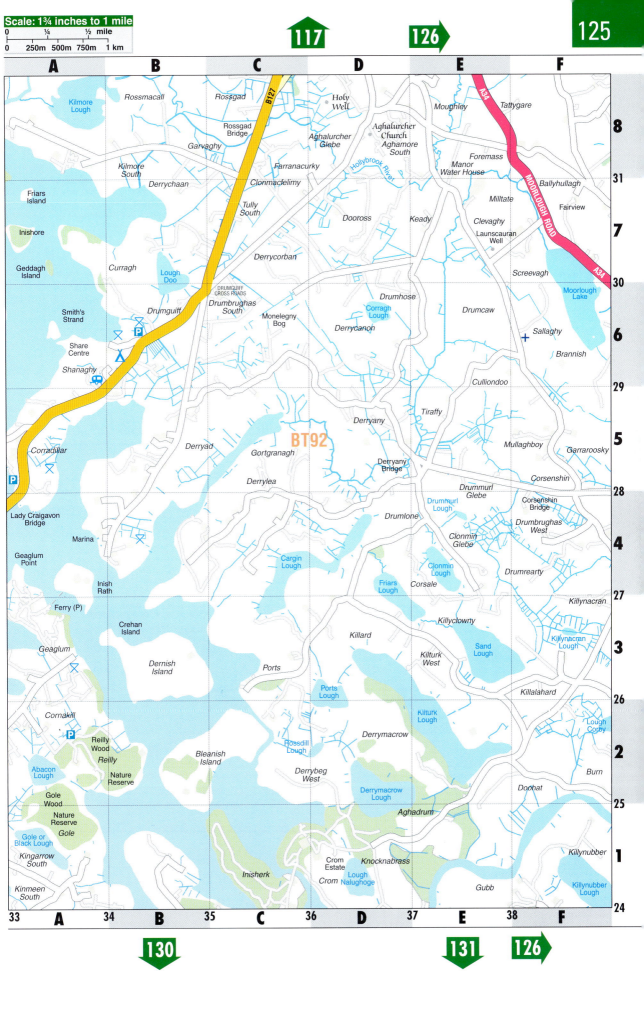

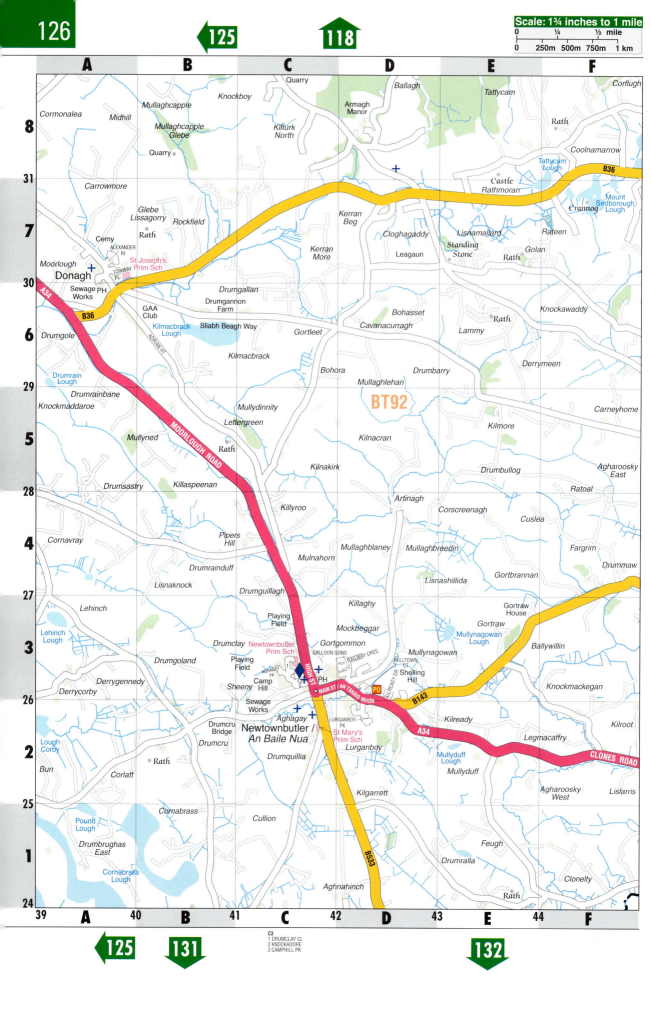

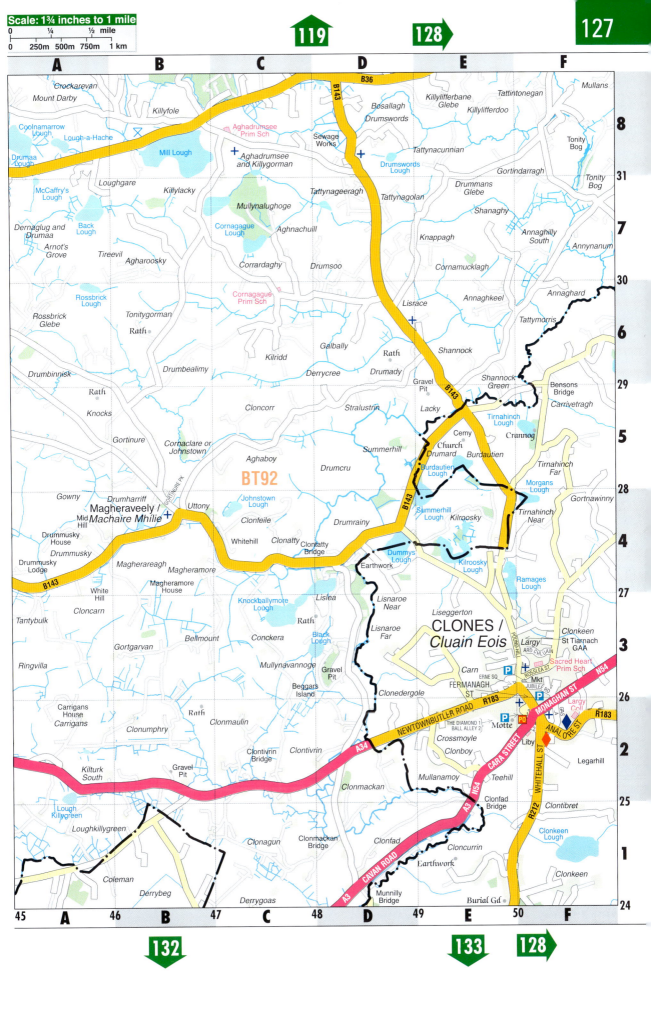

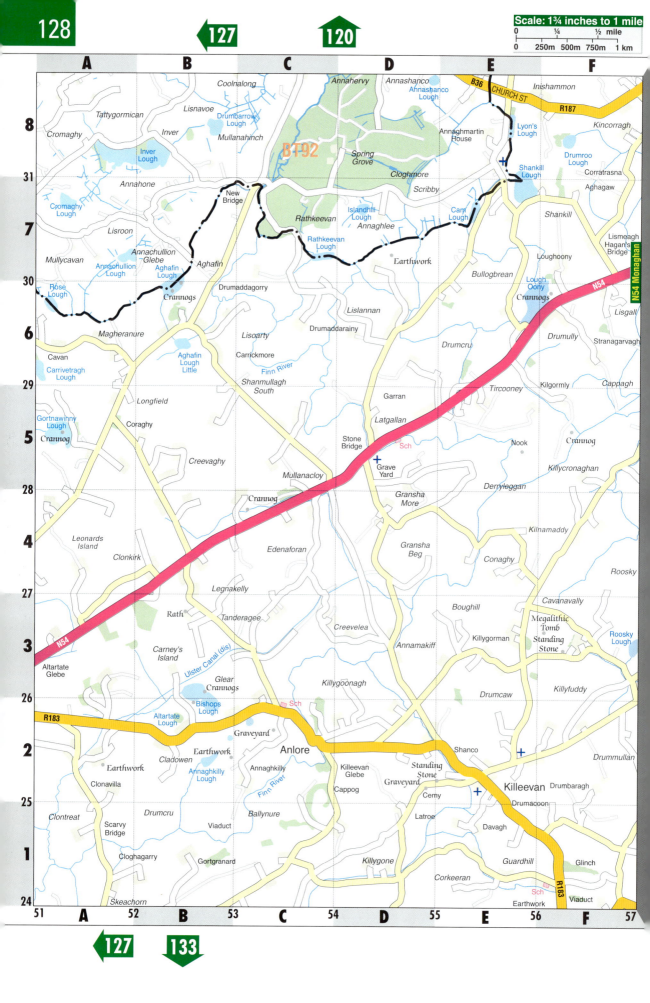

Scale: 1¾ inches to 1 mile

0 ¼ ½ mile
0 250m 500m 750m 1 km

A   B   C   D   E   F

Coolnalong
Annahervy   Annashanco
Annashanco Lough
Inishammon

B36   CHURCH ST
R187

Tattygormican
Lisnavoe
Drumbarrow Lough
Mullanahinch
Spring Grove
Annaghmartin House
Lyon's Lough
Kincorragh

8

Cromaghy
Inver

BT92

Cloghmore
Shankill Lough
Drumroo Lough
Corratrasna

31

Annahone
New Bridge
Rathkeevan
Scribby
Aghagaw

Cromaghy Lough
Islandhill Lough
Annaghlee
Cam Lough
Shankill
Lismeagh
Hagan's Bridge

7

Lisroon
Rathkeevan Lough
Loughoony

Mullycavan
Annachullion Glebe
Aghafin
Earthwork
Lough Oony
Crannogs

N54

Annachullion Lough
Aghafin Lough
Drumaddagorry
Bullogbrean
Lisgall

30

Rose Lough
Crannogs
Drumcru
Drumully
Stranagarvagh

6

Magheranure
Lisoarty
Drumaddarainy
Lislannan
Tircooney
Kilgormly
Cappagh

Cavan
Carrickmore
Aghafin Lough Little
Finn River
Garran
N54

Carrivetragh Lough
Shanmullagh South
Latgallan
Nook
Crannog
Killycronaghan

29

Gortnawinny Lough
Longfield
Coraghy
Stone Bridge
Sch
Derryleggan

5

Crannog
Creevaghy
Mullanacloy
Grave Yard
Gransha More

Crannog
Kilnamaddy

28

Leonards Island
Clonkirk
Edenaforan
Gransha Beg
Conaghy
Roosky

4

Legnakelly
Boughill
Cavanavally
Roosky Lough

27

Rath
Tanderagee
Creevelea
Annamakiff
Killygorman
Megalithic Tomb
Standing Stone

3

N54
Carney's Island
Ulster Canal (dis)
Killygoonagh
Drumcaw
Killyfuddy

Altartate Glebe
Glear Crannogs
Bishops Lough
Sch

26

R183
Altartate Lough
Graveyard
Anlore
Shanco
Drumbaragh
Drummullan

2

Cladowen
Earthwork
Annaghkilly
Annaghkilly Lough
Standing Stone
Killeevan Glebe
Graveyard
Killeevan
Cemy

Clonavilla
Annaghkilly Lough
Finn River
Cappog
Latroe
Drumacoon
Davagh

25

Clontreat
Drumcru
Ballynure
Killygone
Guardhill
Glinch

1

Scarvy Bridge
Viaduct
Gortgranard
Corkeeran
R183

Cloghagarry
Killygone
Earthwork
Viaduct

24

Skeachorn
A   B   C   D   E   F

51   52   53   54   55   56   57

N54 Monaghan

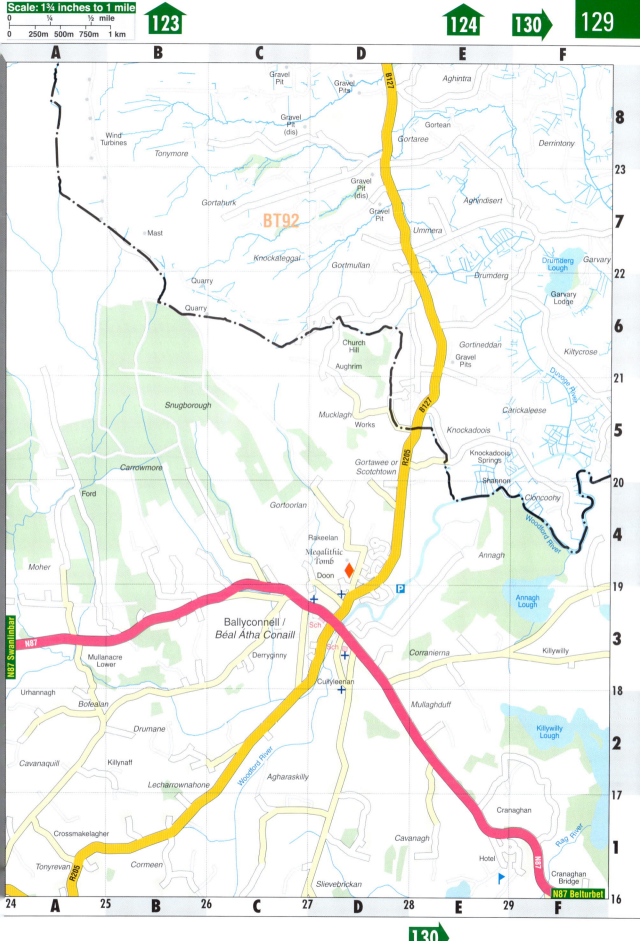

A   B   C   D   E   F

8
23
7
22
6
21
5
20
4
19
3
18
2
17
1
16

Wind Turbines
Tonymore
Gortahurk
BT92
Knockateggal
Gortmullan
Gravel Pit
Gravel Pits
Gravel Pit (dis)
Gravel Pit (dis)
Gravel Pit
Aghintra
Gortean
Gortaree
Ummera
Aghindisert
Derrintony
Drumderg
Drumderg Lough
Garvary
Garvary Lodge
Kiltycrose
Mast
Quarry
Quarry
Snugborough
Carrowmore
Ford
Moher
Church Hill
Aughrim
Mucklagh
Works
Gortawee or Scotchtown
Gortoorlan
B127
R205
Gortineddan
Gravel Pits
Knockadoois
Knockadoois Springs
Shannon
Cloncoohy
Woodford River
Duvoge River
Carickaleese
Annagh
Annagh Lough
Killywilly
Killywilly Lough
Rakeelan
Megalithic Tomb
Doon
Ballyconnell / Béal Átha Conaill
Derryginny
Cullyleenan
Corranierna
Mullaghduff
Sch
Sch
N87 Swanlinbar
N87
Mullanacre Lower
Urhannagh
Bofealan
Drumane
Cavanaquill
Killynaff
Lecharrownahone
Woodford River
Agharaskilly
Slievebrickan
Cavanagh
Cranaghan
Rag River
Hotel
Cranaghan Bridge
N87
N87 Belturbet
Crossmakelagher
Cormeen
Tonyrevan
R205

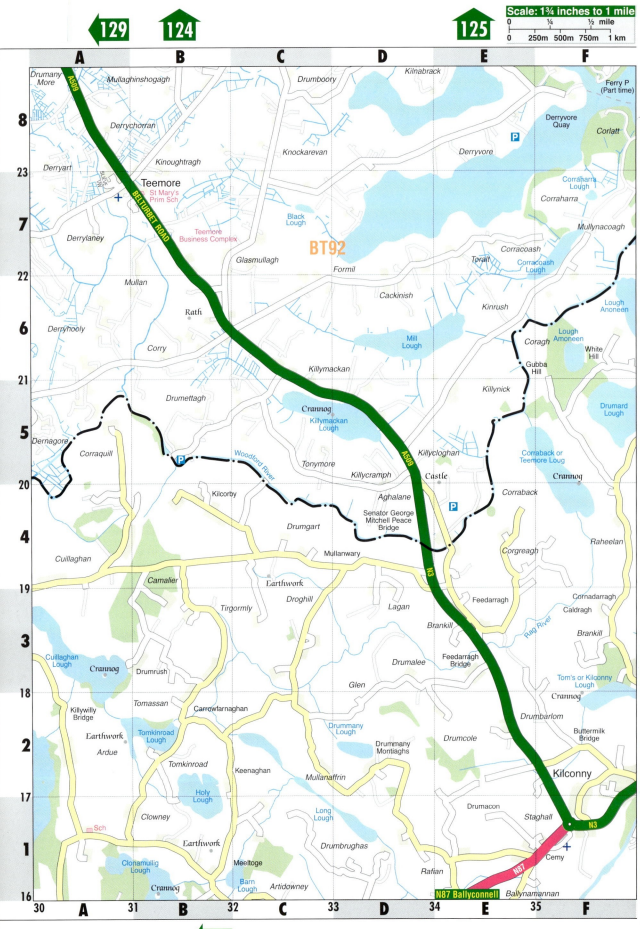

Drumany More
Mullaghinshogagh
Derrychorran
Kinoughtragh
Teemore
St Mary's Prim Sch
BELTURBET ROAD
A509
SLIEVE
Derryart
Derrylaney
Teemore Business Complex
Glasmullagh
Mullan
Rath
Derryhooly
Corry
Drumettagh
Dernagore
Corraquill
Woodford River
Kilcorby
Killymackan
Crannog
Killymackan Lough
Tonymore
Killycramph
Drumgart
Cuillaghan
Camalier
Mullanwary
Earthwork
Droghill
Tirgormly
Lagan
Cuillaghan Lough
Crannog
Drumrush
Killywilly Bridge
Tomassan
Carrowfarnaghan
Earthwork
Ardue
Tomkinroad Lough
Tomkinroad
Keenaghan
Mullanaffrin
Holy Lough
Clowney
Sch
Earthwork
Clonamullig Lough
Crannog
Meeltoge
Barn Lough
Artidowney
Drumbughas
Long Lough
Drummany Lough
Drummany Montiaghs
Glen
Drumalee
Brankill
Kilnabrack
Drumboory
Knockarevan
Black Lough
BT92
Formil
Cackinish
Mill Lough
Killymackan
Senator George Mitchell Peace Bridge
Aghalane
Castle
P
N3
Feedarragh
Brankill
Feedarragh Bridge
Drumcole
Drumacon
Rafian
Derryvore Quay
Corlatt
Corraharra Lough
Corraharra
Mullynacoagh
Corracoash
Toralt
Corracoash Lough
Kinrush
Lough Anoneen
Coragh
Lough Amoneen
White Hill
Gubba Hill
Killynick
Drumard Lough
Killycloghan
Killyclick
Corraback or Teemore Loug
Crannog
Corraback
Corgreagh
Raheelan
Cornadarragh
Caldragh
Brankill
Rag River
Tom's or Kilconny Lough
Crannog
Drumbarlom
Buttermilk Bridge
Kilconny
Staghall
Cemy
N3
N87
N87 Ballyconnell
Ballynamannan
Ferry P (Part time)
Derryvore
P

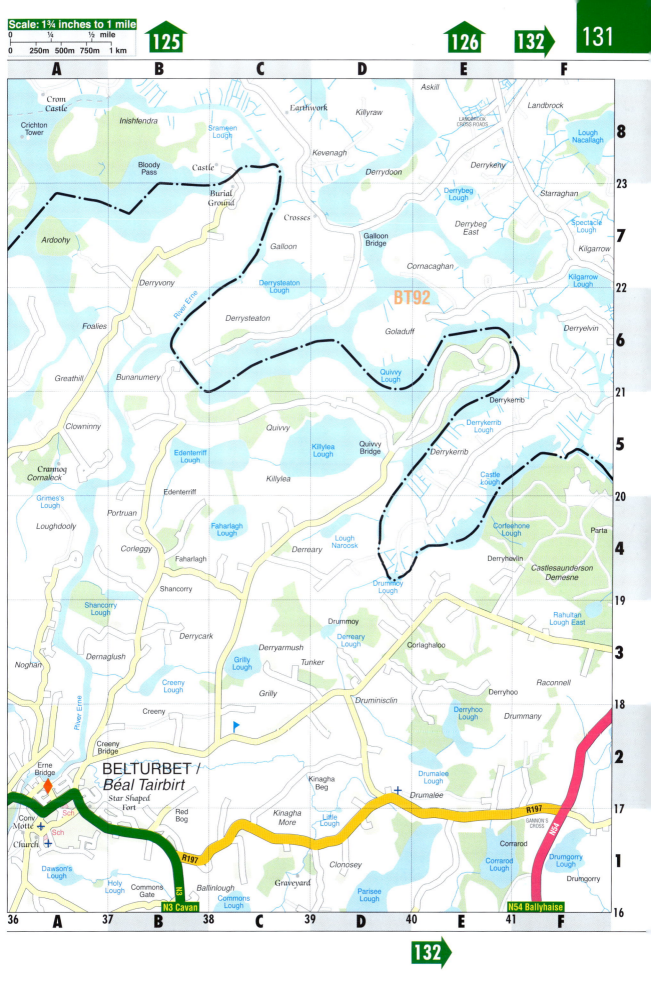

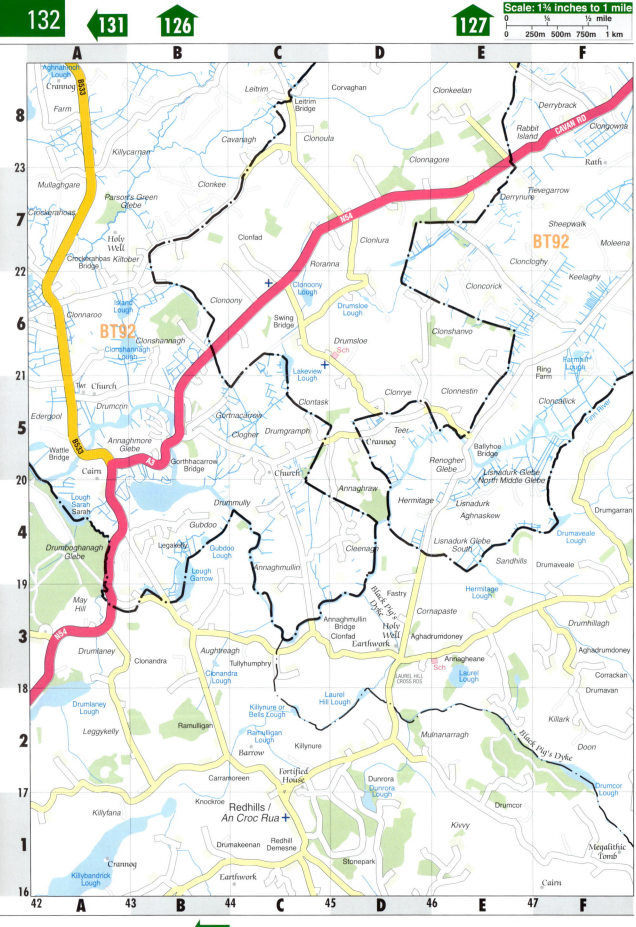

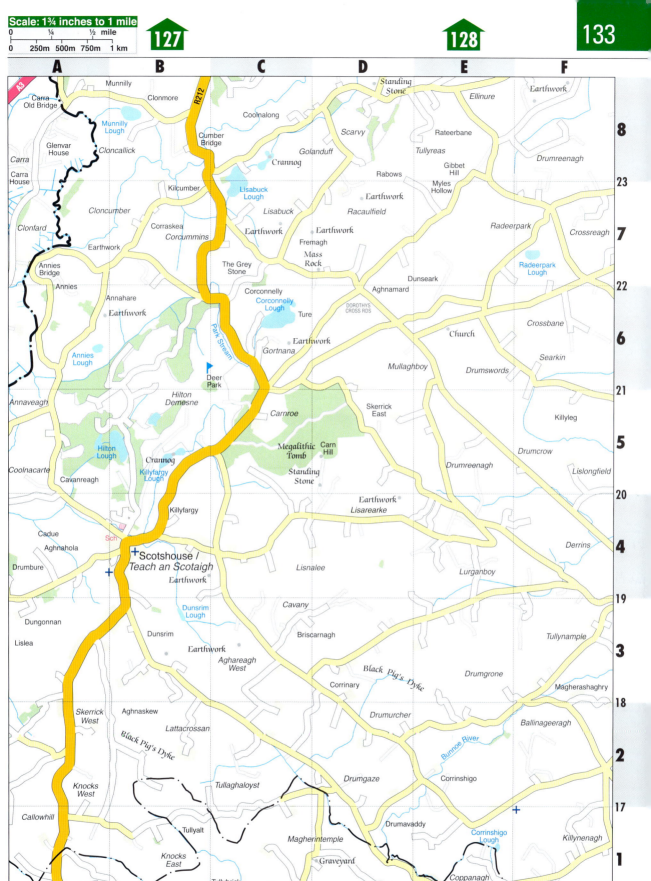

A3

Munnilly

Clonmore

Carra
Old Bridge

Glenvar House

Munnilly Lough

Cloncallick

Carra

Carra House

Cloncumber

Kilcumber

Corraskea
Corcummins

R212

Cumber Bridge

Coolnalong

Crannog

Golanduff

Lisabuck Lough

Lisabuck

Earthwork

Fremagh

Mass Rock

Standing Stone

Scarvy

Rabows

Earthwork

Racaulfield

Ellinure

Rateerbane

Tullyreas

Gibbet Hill

Myles Hollow

Earthwork

Drumreenagh

Radeerpark

Crossreagh

Radeerpark Lough

8
23
7

Clonfard

Earthwork

Annies Bridge

Annies

Annaveagh

Annahare

Earthwork

The Grey Stone

Corconnelly

Corconnelly Lough

Ture

Earthwork

Gortnana

Dunseark

Aghnamard

DOROTHYS CROSS RDS

Church

Mullaghboy

Drumswords

Crossbane

Searkin

22
6

Annies Lough

Park Stream

Deer Park

Hilton Demesne

Carnroe

Skerrick East

Drumreenagh

Killyleg

Drumcrow

Lislongfield

21
5

Coolnacarte

Hilton Lough

Crannog

Killyfargy Lough

Cavanreagh

Killyfargy

Megalithic Tomb

Carn Hill

Standing Stone

Earthwork

Lisarearke

Earthwork

Lurganboy

Derrins

20
4

Cadue

Aghnahola

Drumbure

Sch

Scotshouse / Teach an Scotaigh

Earthwork

Lisnalee

19
3

Dungonnan

Lislea

Dunsrim Lough

Dunsrim

Earthwork

Aghareagh West

Cavany

Briscarnagh

Black Pig's Dyke

Corrinary

Drumgrone

Tullynample

Magherashaghry

18
2

Skerrick West

Aghnaskew

Lattacrossan

Black Pig's Dyke

Drumurcher

Ballinageeragh

Bunnoe River

Knocks West

Callowhill

Tullaghaloyst

Tullyalt

Knocks East

Tullybrick

Drumgaze

Magherintemple

Graveyard

Lattacapple

Drumavaddy

Corrinshigo

Corrinshigo Lough

Coppanagh

Killynenagh

Killynenagh Lough

17
1
16

R212

Drumacleeskin

Killyrue

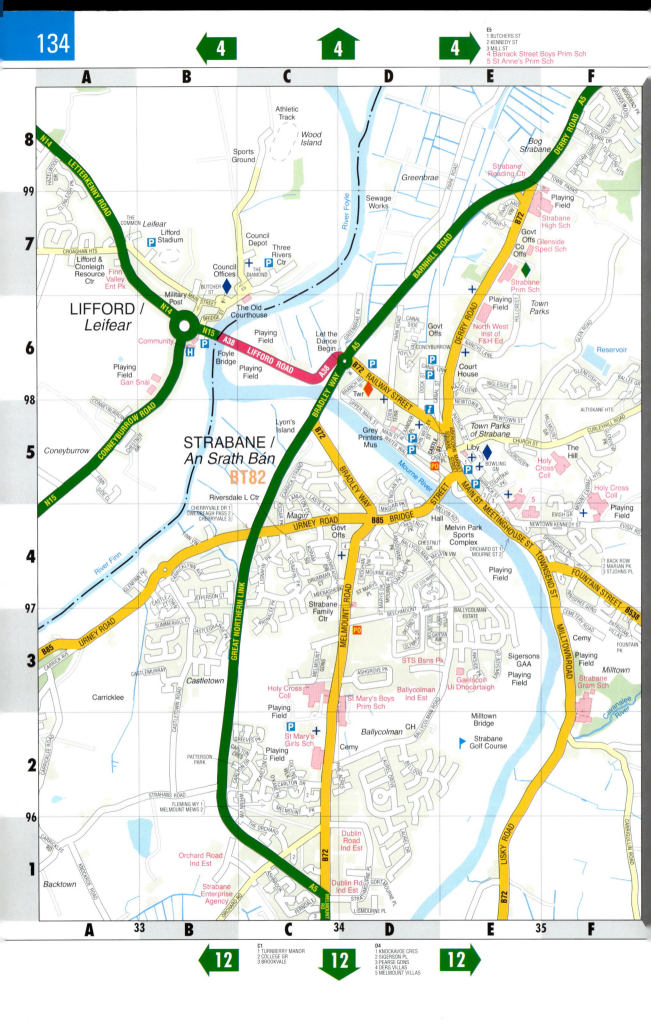

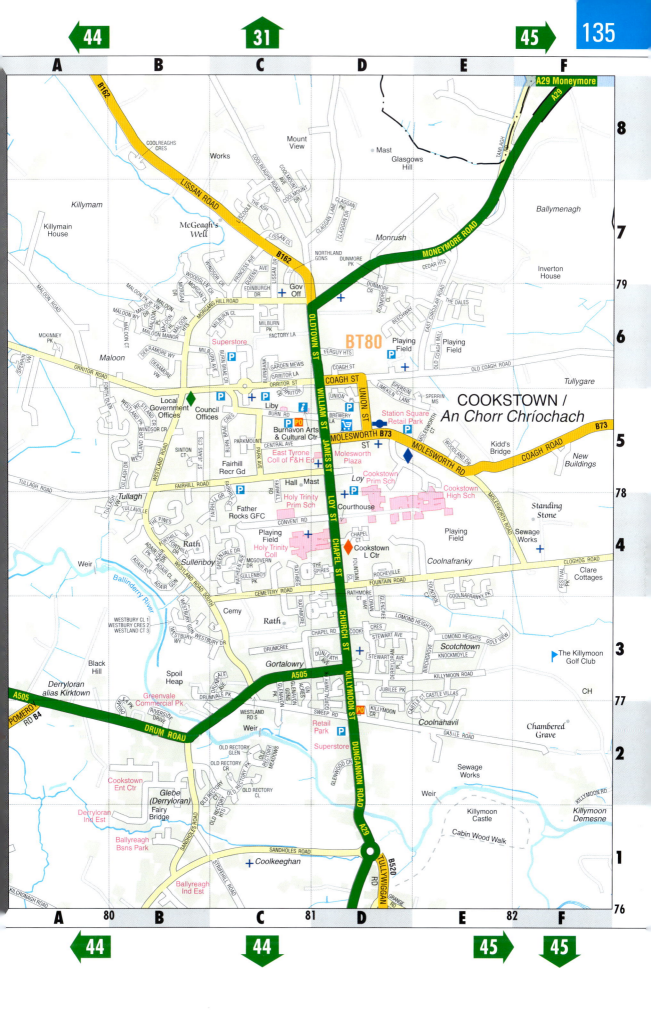

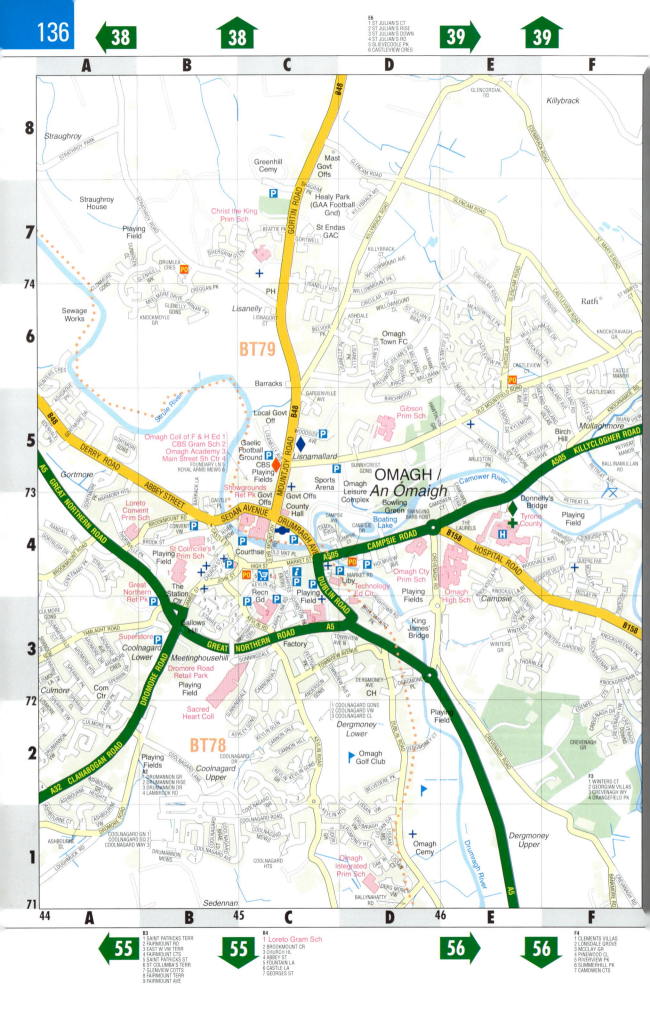

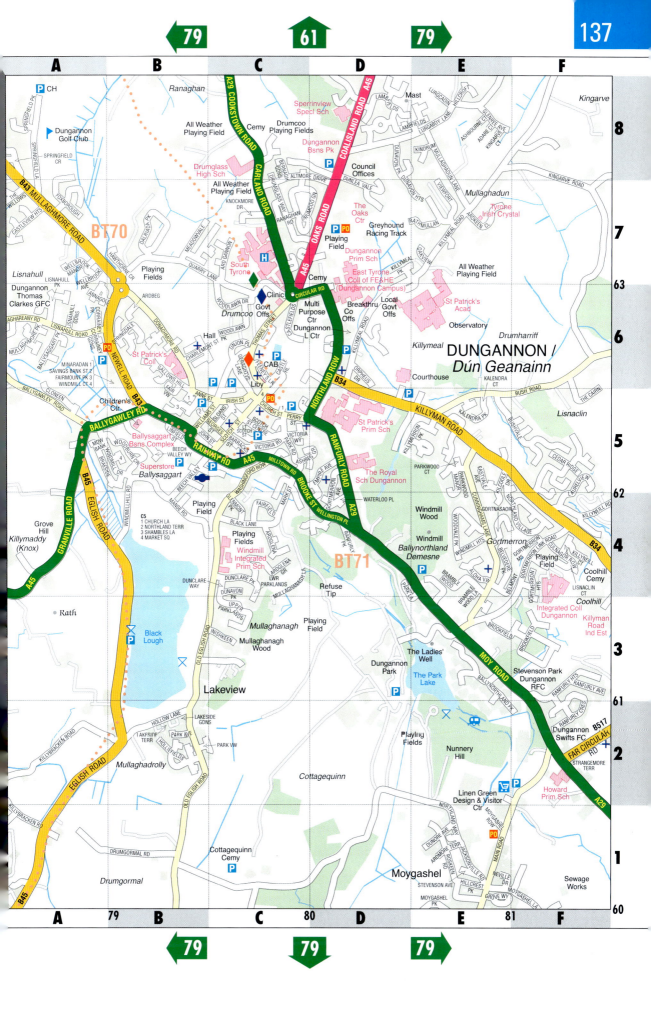

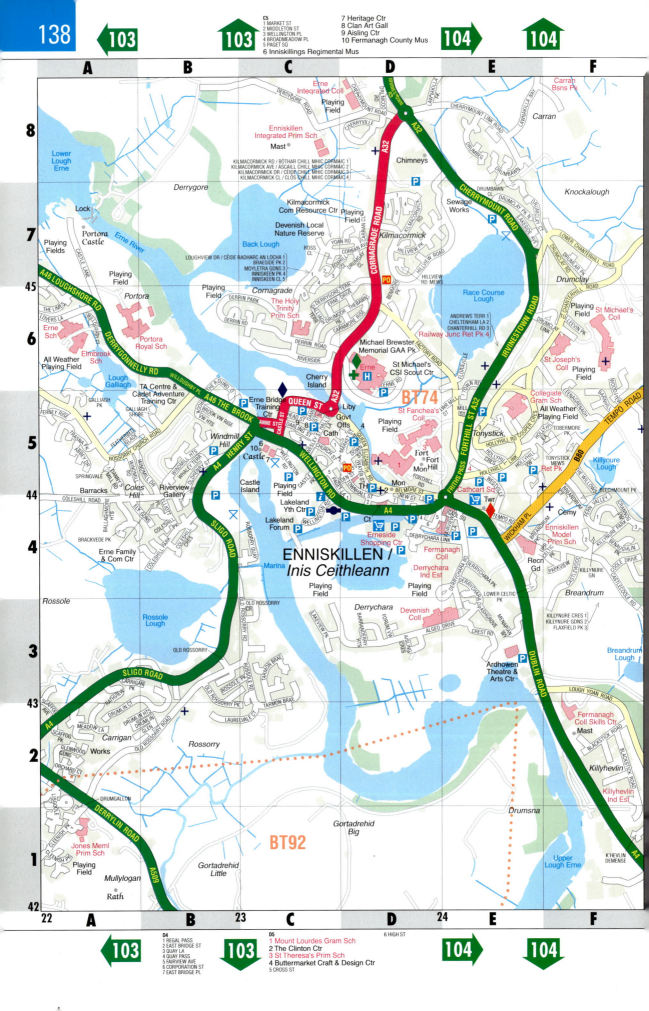

Index

Place name May be abbreviated on the map → Church La **2** Lisburn BT28.........**26 B1**

Location number Present when a number indicates the place's position in a crowded area of mapping

Locality, town or village Shown when more than one place has the same name

Postcode district District for the indexed place

Page and grid square Page number and grid reference for the standard mapping

Cities, towns and villages are listed in CAPITAL LETTERS   **Public and commercial buildings** are highlighted in magenta
Places of interest are highlighted in blue with a star★   **Townlands** are indicated by ❶ in the index and *italic* type on the maps

Abbreviations used in the index

Acad	**Academy**	Comm	**Common**	Gd	**Ground**	L	**Leisure**	Prom	**Promenade**
App	**Approach**	Cott	**Cottage**	Gdn	**Garden**	La	**Lane**	Rd	**Road**
Arc	**Arcade**	Cres	**Crescent**	Gn	**Green**	Liby	**Library**	Recn	**Recreation**
Ave	**Avenue**	Cswy	**Causeway**	Gr	**Grove**	Mdw	**Meadow**	Ret	**Retail**
Bglw	**Bungalow**	Ct	**Court**	H	**Hall**	Meml	**Memorial**	Sh	**Shopping**
Bldg	**Building**	Ctr	**Centre**	Ho	**House**	Mkt	**Market**	Sq	**Square**
Bsns, Bus	**Business**	Ctry	**Country**	Hospl	**Hospital**	Mus	**Museum**	St	**Street**
Bvd	**Boulevard**	Cty	**County**	HQ	**Headquarters**	Orch	**Orchard**	Sta	**Station**
Cath	**Cathedral**	Dr	**Drive**	Hts	**Heights**	Pal	**Palace**	Terr	**Terrace**
Cir	**Circus**	Dro	**Drove**	Ind	**Industrial**	Par	**Parade**	TH	**Town Hall**
Cl	**Close**	Ed	**Education**	Inst	**Institute**	Pas	**Passage**	Univ	**University**
Cnr	**Corner**	Emb	**Embankment**	Int	**International**	Pk	**Park**	Wk, Wlk	**Walk**
Coll	**College**	Est	**Estate**	Intc	**Interchange**	Pl	**Place**	Wr	**Water**
Com	**Community**	Ex	**Exhibition**	Junc	**Junction**	Prec	**Precinct**	Yd	**Yard**

Index of towns, villages, townlands, streets, hospitals, industrial estates, railway stations, schools, shopping centres, universities and places of interest

A

Abbey Ct BT78 . . . . 71 E7
Abbey Dr BT74 . . . . 138 A5
Abbey Pk BT60 . . . . 111 E4
Abbey Rd BT60 . . . . 111 E4
Abbey St **4** BT78 . . . . . . 136 B4
Abbeyvale BT71 . . . . 46 F4
Abbey View BT94 . . . . 117 C7
Abercorn Sq BT82 . . . . 134 E5
Abocurragh❶ BT74 . . . . 113 F6
Abohill❶ BT74 . . . . 113 F6
ACHADH LON
  (BROOKEBOROUGH)
  BT94 . . . . 106 D1
ACHADH NA CLOICHE
  (AUGHNACLOY) BT69 . . . 95 A5
Ackinduff Pk BT70 . . . . 77 D6
Acres❶
  Enniskillen BT74 . . . . . . 102 B5
  Enniskillen BT94 . . . . . . 116 E6
  Knockatallan 120 F6
Acres The
  Belleek BT93 . . . . 65 A4
  Lisnaskea BT92 . . . . 117 C3
Adair Ave BT80 . . . . 135 B4
Adair Cl BT80 . . . . 135 B4
Adair Dr BT80 . . . . 135 B4
Adair Gdns BT80 . . . . 135 B4
Adair Pk BT80 . . . . 135 B4
Adare Ct BT71 . . . . 137 E8
Adrian Hts BT92 . . . . 126 B6
Aghaboy❶
  Enniskillen BT92 . . . . . . 127 C5
  Swanlinbar 122 B3
Aghaboy Lower❶ BT79 . . 27 D2
Aghaboy Rd BT79 . . . . 27 E3
Aghaboy Upper❶ BT79 . . 27 C2
Aghabrack❶ BT82 . . . . 7 B3
Aghabrack Rd
  Omagh BT79 . . . . 15 A8
  Strabane BT82 . . . . 7 A2
Aghacolumb❶ BT71 . . . . 46 D3
Aghacramphill❶ BT75 . . 107 E6
Aghadarragh❶ BT78 . . . 71 D8
Aghaderryloman❶ BT92 123 E6
Aghadreenan❶ BT78 . . . 72 D5
Aghadreenan Glebe❶
  BT92 . . . . 118 C1
Aghadrum❶ BT92 . . . . . 125 E1
Aghadrumsee and
  Killygorman❶ BT92 . . . 127 C8

Aghadrumsee Prim Sch
  BT92 . . . . 127 C8
Aghadulla❶ BT78 . . . . 54 E4
Aghadulla (Harper)❶
  BT78 . . . . 54 C5
Aghadulla Rd BT78 . . . . 54 D4
Aghaessy Rd BT78 . . . . 23 F1
Aghafad❶
  Dungannon BT70 . . . . 60 A6
  Omagh BT78 . . . . 24 D2
  Omagh BT78 . . . . 73 E3
  Strabane BT82 . . . . 7 A4
Aghafad Rd
  Clogher BT76 . . . . 74 B2
  Dungannon BT70 . . . . 60 A7
  Omagh BT78 . . . . 24 D2
  Strabane BT82 . . . . 7 B4
Aghafin❶ 128 B7
Aghagaffert❶ BT94 . . . . . . 70 A7
Aghagallon❶ BT79 . . . . 56 B7
Aghagay❶ BT92 . . . . 126 C2
Aghagay Pk BT92 . . . . 126 C3
Aghaginduff❶ BT70 . . . . . . 77 D6
Aghagogan❶ BT79 . . . . 41 F1
Aghagogan Pk BT79 . . . . . . 41 D1
Aghagrefin❶ BT93 . . . . 51 E2
Aghahannagh❶ BT93 . . . . . 50 D3
Aghaherrish❶ BT74 . . . . . . 102 A5
Aghahoorin❶ BT74 . . . . . . 101 E6
Aghakeeran❶ BT93 . . . . 85 E1
Aghakeeran Cross Roads
  BT93 . . . . 85 E2
Aghakillymaud❶ BT92 . . 123 F8
Aghakinmart❶ BT81 . . . . . 35 F7
Aghakinnigh❶ 123 A1
Aghakinsallagh Glebe❶
  BT71 . . . . 62 B1
Aghalaan❶ BT93 . . . . 50 C3
Aghalane❶
  Enniskillen BT92 . . . . . . 130 D4
  Omagh BT79 . . . . 15 B5
  Omagh BT79 . . . . 40 C7
Aghalarg❶ BT71 . . . . 62 E6
Aghalarg Bog❶ BT71 . . . . . 62 D6
Aghalarg Rd BT71 . . . . 62 F7
Aghaleag❶ BT78 . . . . 37 F2
Aghaleague❶ BT93 . . . . 52 B1
Aghaloo Rd BT70 . . . . 76 F1
Aghalougher❶ BT81 . . . . . 34 C8
Aghalougher Rd BT81 . . . . . 34 D8
Aghalun❶ BT94 . . . . 106 C2
Aghalunny❶ BT81 . . . . 21 B1

Aghalunny Rd BT81 . . . . . . 21 C1
Aghalurcher Church★
  BT92 . . . . 125 D8
Aghalurcher Glebe❶
  BT92 . . . . 125 D8
Aghama❶ BT93 . . . . 69 B8
Aghameelan❶ BT93 . . . . . . 85 B8
Aghamilkin❶ BT77 . . . . . . 93 E1
Aghamore❶
  Castlederg BT81 . . . . 34 E6
  Enniskillen BT74 . . . . . . 101 E6
  Enniskillen BT93 . . . . 85 D6
Aghamore North❶ BT94 116 E3
Aghamore Rd BT81 . . . . 34 E7
Aghamore Rd T BT81 . . . . 35 A6
Aghamore South❶
  BT92 . . . . 125 D8
Aghamuldowney❶ BT93 . . 83 A6
Aghanaglack❶ BT74 . . . . . 101 C4
Aghanaglogh❶ BT92 . . . . 118 C1
Aghannagh❶ BT74 . . . . . . 103 A3
Aghanore Rd BT61 . . . . 98 B1
Agharahan❶ BT93 . . . . 85 D1
Agharainy❶
  Enniskillen BT74 . . . . . . 104 B5
  Enniskillen BT93 . . . . 69 A6
Agharan❶ BT71 . . . . 61 D5
Agharan Rd BT71 . . . . 61 E5
Agharaskilly❶ 129 C2
Aghareagh West❶ 133 C3
Aghareany❶ 61 B1
Aghareany❶ BT70 . . . . 61 B1
Aghareany Rd BT70 . . . . . 137 A6
Agharonan❶ BT78 . . . . 74 A5
Agharoosky❶ BT92 . . . . . 127 B7
Agharoosky East❶ BT92. 126 F5
Agharoosky West❶
  BT92 . . . . 126 F2
Aghascrebagh❶
  Castlederg BT81 . . . . 35 A7
  Omagh BT79 . . . . 28 D4
Aghascrebagh Rd
  Castlederg BT81 . . . . 34 F7
  Omagh BT79 . . . . 28 E4
Aghasessy❶ BT78 . . . . 23 F2
Aghatirourke❶ BT92 . . . . 121 F7
Aghavanny❶ 99 F5
Aghavass❶ BT93 . . . . 101 A1
Aghaveagh❶ BT94 . . . . . . 117 E7
Aghaveagh❶ BT80 . . . . 46 B5
Aghaveagh Rd BT80 . . . . . . 46 B5
Aghavea Glebe❶ BT94 . . 117 E8
Aghavoory❶ BT75 . . . . . . 107 D6

Aghavore❶ BT93 . . . . 50 D5
Aghaweenagh❶ BT92 . . . 123 C4
Aghee❶
  Omagh BT78 . . . . 55 A8
  Omagh BT78 . . . . 71 D7
Agheeghter❶ BT75 . . . . . . 107 D6
Aghee Rd BT78 . . . . 55 A8
Aghenis❶ BT68 . . . . 111 B7
Aghindaiagh❶ BT92 . . . . 123 C4
Aghindarragh East❶
  BT77 . . . . 93 E2
Aghindarragh Rd BT77 . . . 93 D2
Aghindarragh West❶
  BT75 . . . . 91 D2
Aghindarrgh Rd BT77 . . . . . 93 F3
Aghindisert❶ BT92 . . . . . . 129 E2
Aghindrumman❶ BT76 . . . 92 E7
Aghinduff Rd BT70 . . . . 77 C7
Aghingowly❶ BT75 . . . . . . 91 D4
Aghinlark❶ BT75 . . . . 91 E2
Aghinlig❶ BT71 . . . . 98 C6
Aghinlig Rd BT71 . . . . 98 C6
Aghintain❶ BT75 . . . . 92 B4
Aghintain Castle★ BT75 . . 92 B4
Aghintain Rd BT75 . . . . 91 F4
Aghintober❶ BT70 . . . . 77 F7
Aghintra❶ BT92 . . . . 129 E8
Aghinure❶ BT94 . . . . 117 A5
Aghinver❶ BT94 . . . . 69 A5
Aghlish Rd BT78 . . . . 72 B8
Aghlisk❶ BT78 . . . . 72 A7
Aghnablaney❶ BT93 . . . . . 67 A8
Aghnacally❶ 123 C1
Aghnacarra❶ BT94 . . . . . 116 D6
Aghnachuill❶ BT92 . . . . . 127 C7
Aghnacloy❶
  Enniskillen BT92 . . . . . . 124 A6
  Enniskillen BT94 . . . . . . 106 D1
Aghnacloy North❶
  Enniskillen BT94 . . . . . . 117 F8
  Enniskillen BT94 . . . . . . 118 A8
Aghnacloy South❶
  BT94 . . . . 117 D7
Aghnacollia❶ 121 E1
Aghnagar❶
  Dungannon BT70 . . . . 77 C8
  Omagh BT79 . . . . 57 F1
Aghnagar Rd
  Dungannon BT70 . . . . 77 B7
  Omagh BT79 . . . . 75 C8
Aghnaglea❶ BT79 . . . . 57 F5
Aghnaglea Rd BT79 . . . . . . 57 F5
Aghnaglogh❶ BT76 . . . . . . 92 D5

Abb–Alt

Aghnagrane❶ BT94 . . . . 106 A4
Aghnagreggan❶ BT79 . . . 41 B2
Aghnagreggan Rd BT79 . . 41 B2
Aghnahinch❶ BT92 . . . . . 126 D1
Aghnahoe❶ BT70 . . . . 77 B3
Aghnahoe Rd BT70 . . . . 77 C4
Aghnahoo❶
  Castlederg BT81 . . . . 22 A1
  Enniskillen BT92 . . . . . . 121 C8
  Rossinver 82 A1
Aghnaloo❶ BT94 . . . . 116 D6
Aghnaloo Rd BT81 . . . . 22 A1
Aghnamirigan❶ BT79 . . . 27 E3
Aghnamirigan Rd BT79 . . 27 E2
Aghnamoe Rd BT78 . . . . . . 71 F4
Aghnamoyle❶ BT78 . . . . . 38 C3
Aghnamoyle Rd BT78 . . . . 38 C2
Aghnanereagh❶ BT79 . . . 58 F8
Aghnashammer❶ BT92 . 120 C1
Aghnaskea❶ BT70 . . . . 60 A2
Aghnaskew❶
  Enniskillen BT92 . . . . . . 132 E4
  Enniskillen BT94 . . . . . . 117 C6
Agho❶ BT93 . . . . 100 A7
Aghyaran❶ BT81 . . . . 21 C2
Aghyaran Rd BT81 . . . . 21 C1
Aghyaran Rd Upper BT81 . 21 C2
Aghyoule❶ BT92 . . . . 123 F1
Aisling Cres BT74 . . . . 138 D3
Albany Rd BT71 . . . . 46 C1
Albert Pl BT82 . . . . 12 D5
Alder Rd BT82 . . . . 1 E2
Alderwood❶ BT75 . . . . . . 108 B6
Alderwood Pk BT94 . . . . . . 88 C6
Alderwood Rd BT75 . . . . . 107 F8
Aldery Loanan The BT71 . . 98 C8
Alexander Dr BT69 . . . . 95 A4
Alexander Pk BT81 . . . . 22 D5
Alexander Pl BT82 . . . . . . 134 D5
Alexander Rise BT92 . . . . 126 A7
Algeo Dr BT74 . . . . 138 D3
Allan Pk BT82 . . . . 6 C8
Allen❶ BT70 . . . . 60 E8
Allistragh❶ BT61 . . . . 98 C2
All Saints Prim Sch BT78 . 54 F5
Ally❶ BT78 . . . . 35 D2
Aloha View BT71 . . . . 137 E4
Altacamcosy❶ BT79 . . . . . 28 A7
Altacanoo❶ 109 D5
Altadaven❶ BT77 . . . . 93 F2

Altadaven Rd BT77.... 93 F1
Altaghoney BT47......7 F6
Altaghoney Rd BT47.....7 E6
Altaglushan BT70..... 59 D2
Altaglushan Rd BT70.. 59 B1
Altagoaghan BT75 ... 107 F2
Altamooskan BT79.... 58 A1
Altamullan BT81.... 20 F2
Altamullan Rd BT81.... 21 A3
Altamuskin Rd BT79.... 58 A2
Altanagh BT79....... 58 F5
Altanaveragh BT76.... 74 A3
Altanaveragh Rd
  Clogher BT76........ 91 F8
  Omagh BT78 .... 74 B4
Altaveedan Rd BT75... 107 F7
Altawark BT75 ...... 119 D8
Altbrean 121 F1
Altcloghfin BT79.... 75 D7
Altdoghal BT78 .... 25 C5
Altdoghal Rd BT78.... 25 D5
Altdrumman BT79.... 40 E6
Alteen 122 A5
Altgolan BT81....... 34 F5
Altinaghree Castle★ BT82 .. 6 F8
Altinure Lower BT47 ....8 F7
Altinure Pk BT47.......8 F7
Altinure Rd BT47.......9 B7
Altinure Upper BT47 ....8 F8
Altishahane BT82.......6 E3
ALTISHANE BT82.........6 E4
Altishane Prim Sch BT82 ...6 E3
Altiskane Hts BT82..... 134 F5
Altmartin BT75 ...... 119 A8
Altmore alias Barracktown
  BT70 .... 59 D6
Altmore Dr BT71....... 137 C8
Altmore Rd BT70....... 59 C6
Altnageerog BT82........6 B4
Altnamona BT79 .... 58 B1
Altnaponer BT94...... 119 A6
Altnavannog BT71 .... 79 E3
Altnaveagh BT77..... 93 E6
Altnaveagh Rd BT77.... 93 E5
Altowen Pk 13 BT71.... 62 C2
Altrest BT82.............1 F2
Altrest Rd
  Londonderry BT47........ 2 A3
  Strabane BT82...........1 F2
Alwories BT79 ...... 28 B6
Anagasna Glebe BT71 .. 97 E8
Analore St 127 F2
AN BAILE NUA
  (NEWTOWNBUTLER)
  Newtownbutler BT92....126 C2
  Newtownstewart BT78 .. 25 A6
AN BLAIC (BLACKLION)
  BT93 .... 112 F7
AN CHEIS (KESH) BT93 ... 68 F8
AN CHORR CHRÍOCHACH
  (COOKSTOWN) BT80....135 E5
AN CHRAOBH
  (STEWARTSTOWN)
  BT71 .... 62 C7
An Creagán Visitor Ctr★
  BT79 .... 41 E8
AN CROC RUA
  (REDHILLS)
  BT93 .... 132 C1
AN CUACH (COAGH) BT80 .. 46 B7
Anderson Gdns BT74.... 136 C3
Andrews Terr BT74 .... 138 E5
AN DROIM MÓR (DROMORE)
  BT78 .... 71 E7
ANLORE................ 128 C2
AN MAIGH (MOY) BT71 ... 80 A1
Annachullion Glebe
  BT92 .... 128 B7
Annaclarey BT71..... 97 F4
Annacramp BT68 .... 111 A6
Annacramph BT61 .... 98 F2
Annacramph Rd BT61.... 98 F2
Annagarvey BT77 .... 93 B8
Annagh
  Armagh BT60......... 111 F7
  Aughnacloy BT69...... 95 C4
  Ballyconnell........ 129 E4
  Dungannon BT71....... 97 A7
  Omagh BT79 .... 56 E4
Annaghalough BT93.... 52 E6
Annaghananam BT80.... 44 D2
Annaghannany Rd BT60 . 111 F7
Annagharap BT60..... 111 F7
Annaghard BT92 .... 127 F6
Annagh (Augher) BT76. 92 C3
Annaghbann BT71..... 62 E2
Annaghbeg
  Dungannon BT70....... 61 B1
  Dungannon BT71....... 80 D7
Annagh Beg BT69.... 95 E2
Annaghbeg Pk BT70..... 61 B1
Annaghbeg Rd BT71 .... 80 E7
Annagh (Blessingbourne)
  BT75 .... 91 C2
Annaghbo BT78..... 73 B7
Annagh Demesne BT75. 91 D1
Annagher BT71....... 62 C3
Annagher Dr 1 BT71.... 62 C3
Annagher Rd BT71..... 62 D3
Annaghilla BT77..... 94 A3
Annaghilla Rd BT77.... 93 F8
Annaghilly North
  BT92 .... 119 D1
Annaghilly South
  BT92 .... 127 F7

Annaghkeel BT92 ..... 127 E6
Annaghlee BT92 ..... 128 D7
Annaghmacmanus
  BT71 .... 98 C8
Annaghmakeown BT70. 78 C8
Annaghmakeown Rd
  BT70 .... 78 C8
Annaghmartin BT92... 120 E1
Annaghmore
  Cookstown BT80....... 44 D3
  Cookstown BT80....... 47 A7
  Craigavon BT62....... 81 B2
  Dungannon BT71....... 62 E1
Annagh More BT69.... 95 E2
Annaghmore Crossroads Ind
  Est BT71 .... 62 E3
Annaghmore Glebe
  BT92 .... 132 A5
Annaghmore La BT80 ... 47 A7
Annaghmore Prim Sch
  BT62 .... 81 B2
Annaghmore Rd
  Cookstown BT80....... 47 B7
  Craigavon BT62....... 81 B1
  Dungannon BT71....... 62 F1
Annaghmoy La BT71..... 97 F3
Annaghmullin BT92... 132 C4
Annaghmurnin BT78 .. 73 B7
Annaghnaboe BT71.... 62 F1
Annaghnaboe Rd BT71 .. 62 E3
Annaghone BT80...... 45 C2
Annaghone Rd
  Cookstown BT80....... 45 C2
  Dungannon BT71....... 62 D8
Annaghquin BT80..... 61 A8
Annaghquin Rd
  Cookstown BT80....... 61 B7
  Dungannon BT70....... 60 D7
Annaghraw 132 D4
Annagh Rd
  Clogher BT76........ 92 C3
  Cookstown BT80....... 44 E2
  Fivemiletown BT75.... 92 C4
  Omagh BT78 .... 73 B7
Annaghroe BT68..... 111 B5
Annaghroe Rd BT68..... 111 C5
Annaghsallagh BT68 .. 96 A2
Annaghsallagh Rd
  Aughnacloy BT69...... 95 F2
  Caledon BT68........ 96 A2
Annaghteige BT80 ... 44 E2
Annaginny BT71...... 61 D4
Annaginny Rd BT71 .... 61 D3
Annagole BT70 .... 137 A6
Annagolgan BT92.... 120 A1
Annahagh BT71....... 98 C3
Annahagh La BT71..... 98 C3
Annahagh Rd BT71 .... 98 B3
Annahavil
  Dungannon BT71....... 61 D7
  Magherafelt BT45..... 45 D8
Annahavil Rd BT71..... 61 D6
Annahervy BT92 .... 128 C8
Annahone BT92...... 128 B7
Annaloughan BT77.... 93 D8
Annaloughan Rd BT77.. 93 D8
Annamakiff 128 D3
Annamoy BT71....... 97 F3
Annasamry BT61..... 98 D7
Annashanco BT92.... 128 D8
Annaveagh 133 A5
Anneeter Beg BT80 ... 47 C7
Anneeter More BT80.. 47 C7
Anne St
  Dungannon BT70....... 137 B5
  Enniskillen BT74..... 138 C5
Anneter La BT80 ..... 47 B7
Anneter Rd BT80...... 47 C6
Annynanum BT92 .... 127 F7
AN OMAIGH (OMAGH)
  BT79 .... 136 D5
AN PORT MÓR
  (BLACKWATERTOWN)
  BT71 .... 98 A5
AN SRATH BÁN (STRABANE)
  BT82 .... 134 B5
AN TLOMPÚ DEISEAL
  (TEMPO) BT94 .... 89 F1
An Tsráid Mhór (Main St)
  Ballinamallard BT94 .. 88 C5
  Brookeborough BT94...106 C1
  Enniskillen BT92..... 124 A4
  Enniskillen BT93..... 52 E3
  Enniskillen BT93..... 85 F5
  Enniskillen BT94..... 117 B6
  8 Irvinestown BT94... 69 C3
  Kesh BT93 .... 69 A8
  Newtownbutler BT92...126 D3
Archdale Dr BT94...... 88 B7
Archill BT78....... 23 E1
Archill Rd BT78....... 23 E1
Arda BT94......... 116 A6
Ardagh 82 D3
Ardarver BT81...... 21 B3
Ardarver Rd BT81..... 21 B3
Ardatinny BT78..... 73 A5
Ardatrave BT93 .... 68 E5
Ardbarren Lower BT81. 35 D8
Ardbarren Rd BT81..... 35 C7
Ardbarren Upper BT81. 35 D8
Ardbeg BT70....... 137 B6
ARDBOE BT80......... 47 C4
Ardboe Abbey★ BT71 ... 47 C4
Ardboe Bsns Pk BT71 ... 47 A4
Ardboe Rd BT71...... 47 C4
Ardcame BT82.........2 E1
Ardcame Rd BT82.........2 E1
Ard Chluain 127 F3

Ardcumber BT80 ..... 44 F4
Ardcumber Rd BT80.... 44 F4
Ardean BT80........ 47 C6
Ardean Manor 12 BT71 .. 80 A1
Ardees Lower BT93 .. 66 B2
Ardess Glebe BT93... 69 C8
Ardess Upper BT93... 84 A8
Ardfort Rd BT78 ...... 54 D3
Ard Gannon BT70 ..... 137 C7
Ardgart
  Enniskillen BT74..... 88 B1
  Enniskillen BT93..... 66 A1
Ardgart Rd BT74...... 104 B8
Ardglena BT71........ 137 C4
Ardglena Gr BT71..... 137 C4
Ardground BT47..........3 E4
Ardground Rd BT47......3 F5
Ardhowen Theatre & Arts
  Ctr★ BT74........... 138 E3
Ardkeen Cl BT71...... 137 E7
Ardkill BT47.........3 B7
Ardkill Rd BT47..........3 B7
Ardlougher BT94..... 69 E3
Ardloughill 64 A3
Ardmoney BT94...... 106 F1
Ardmore
  Enniskillen BT94..... 106 C2
  Londonderry BT47........ 2 A3
Ardmore Ave BT78 .... 136 A3
Ardmore Cres BT78 ... 136 A3
Ardmore Dr BT78 ..... 136 A3
Ardmore Hts BT78 .... 136 A3
Ardmore Pk 9 BT71 ... 62 C3
Ardmore Rd
  10 Coalisland BT71 ... 62 C3
  Londonderry BT47........ 3 D7
Ardmore Terr BT71 .... 137 C1
Ardnalee Pk BT82..... 134 C3
Ardnaskea Dr 2 BT71... 62 C3
Ardoohy 131 A7
Ardore
  Enniskillen BT93..... 50 B2
  Enniskillen BT94..... 69 E6
Ardpatrick BT71..... 62 B8
Ardrdmoney Rd
  Enniskillen BT94..... 69 C5
Ardress East BT62... 81 B1
Ardress Rd BT62...... 81 B1
Ardress W Rd BT61.... 81 A1
Ards BT68 .... 96 B1
Ardshankill BT93.... 67 F8
ARD STRATHA (ARDSTRAW)
  BT78 .... 24 B7
ARDSTRAW (ARD STRATHA)
  BT78 .... 24 B8
Ardstraw Prim Sch BT78. 24 B8
Ardtonnagh BT92.... 115 C7
Ardtrea Rd BT71...... 45 E5
Ardue 130 A2
Ardunshin
  Augher BT77......... 93 A7
  Enniskillen BT94..... 106 B3
Ardvarnish BT80..... 45 B4
Ardvarny East BT93.. 69 D8
Ardvarny West BT93 . 69 D8
Arleston Dr BT79 .... 136 E5
Arleston Pk BT79 .... 136 E5
Arleston Rd BT79 .... 136 E5
Arlish BT94........ 117 F7
Armaghlughey Rd
  Aughnacloy BT69...... 95 A8
  Dungannon BT79...... 76 F1
Armagh Rd BT71....... 98 B7
Armalughey BT70 ... 76 E2
ARNEY BT92.......... 114 F7
Arnot's Grove BT92 . 127 A4
Artasooly BT71..... 97 E2
Artasooly Rd BT71.... 97 F3
Artclea BT75....... 107 E8
Artidowney 130 C1
Artigarvan BT82......5 B5
ARTIGARVAN BT82.......5 B5
Artigarvan Prim Sch BT82 .5 B5
Artinagh BT92 ..... 126 D4
Art Rd BT82 ....5 C5
Arvalee BT79 ...... 39 D1
Arvalee Rd BT79 ..... 39 E1
Ascaill Chill Mhic Cormaic
  (Kilmacormick Ave)
  BT74................ 138 D7
Ash Ave BT78 ....1 C2
Ashbeg Gr BT71...... 137 C5
Ashbourne Cl BT78.... 136 A1
Ashbourne Ct
  Dungannon BT71...... 137 E8
  Omagh BT78 .... 136 A1
Ashbourne Gr BT78 ... 136 A1
Ashbourne Hts BT78 .. 136 A2
Ashbourne View BT78.. 136 A1
Ashbrook BT82........ 134 C1
Ashburn Pk BT81 ..... 22 D5
Ashdale BT74......... 104 B5
Ashdale Ct BT79...... 136 D6
Ashfield Dr BT93..... 65 B4
Ashfield Gds BT78 ... 73 B6
Ashfield or Grange
  BT76................ 92 F3
Ashfield or Grange Mountain
  Bar BT76.......... 109 A6
Ashfield Rd BT76..... 92 F3
Ashgrove BT74........ 138 E3
Ashgrove Pk
  Omagh BT78 .... 136 A5
  Strabane BT82....... 134 D3
Ashgrove Rd BT71..... 81 C7
Ashlands 3 BT78 ..... 71 F8
Ashley Gdns BT78 ... 136 B2
Ashley Pk BT94...... 88 B4
Ashlough Dr BT71..... 62 F4

Ashmeanagh Rd BT79 ... 39 E4
Ash The BT80......... 135 C7
Ashveagh BT71........ 97 D5
Ashwoods BT74..... 103 C2
Ashwoods Golf Ctr BT74 103 C3
Ashwoods or Woody
  Mullaghree BT74 ... 103 C3
Askill BT92........ 131 E8
Athabryanmore BT81... 33 A6
Athboy Mdws BT71..... 98 A5
Athenree BT79...... 58 E8
Athenree Rd BT79..... 58 E8
Atnamollyboy BT75 .. 119 B8
Attagh BT79 .... 27 E2
Attaghmore BT78 ... 55 B2
Attybaron BT92 .... 117 C4
Attyclannabryan BT75. 119 A7
Aughagalla BT71..... 62 E5
Aughagranna BT71.... 62 E6
Aughagranna Rd BT71.. 62 E6
Aughamullan BT71.... 63 A3
Aughamullan Prim Sch
  BT71................ 63 B3
Aughanlig Pk Rd BT71.. 98 C6
Aughantarragh and Corr
  BT60................ 97 A3
Aughantarragh Rd BT60. 97 A3
Aughaward BT74..... 104 A7
Augher Central Prim Sch
  BT77................ 93 C2
AUGHER (EOCHAIR) BT77.. 93 B7
Augher Point Rd BT79 . 56 D2
Augher Rd BT76....... 93 A5
Augher Tenements
  BT77................ 93 C6
Aughey BT94....... 116 A5
Aughintober Rd BT70 .. 78 A8
Aughlish
  Cookstown BT80....... 44 D7
  Dungannon BT70...... 78 C7
  Enniskillen BT74..... 102 D4
  Londonderry BT47.......9 F6
Aughnacarney BT76... 93 B4
Aughnacloy Rd BT61... 98 D3
AUGHNACLOY (ACHADH NA
  CLOICHE) BT69 ...... 95 A5
Aughnacloy Coll BT69.. 95 B5
Aughnacloy Regional Prim
  Sch BT69........... 95 A5
Aughrim
  Enniskillen BT74..... 102 F6
  Enniskillen BT93..... 113 A8
Aughrimderg BT71.... 63 A5
Aughtermoy BT82......6 D7
Aughtreagh 132 B3
Avery Pk 1 BT78 ..... 25 A6
Avonmore BT71........ 98 A5
Backan BT79 .... 40 F8
Backfarm BT78 ..... 37 E4

B

Backfarm Rd BT78 ..... 37 F4
Backfence BT82.........4 E5
Backglen Rd BT79..... 39 D5
Backhill BT71...... 22 F1
Backhill Rd BT81..... 22 F1
Back Lower BT71.... 63 D7
Backlower Rd BT71.... 63 D7
Back Row BT82........ 134 F4
Backtown BT82..... 134 A1
Back Upper BT71.... 63 C6
Backwood BT93..... 59 D4
Badoney Rd BT78 ..... 89 D7
BAILE AN IRBHINIGH
  (IRVINESTOWN) BT94 .. 69 E3
BAILE NA LORGAN
  (FIVEMILETOWN) BT75 . 107 C8
BAILE UÍ DHÁLAIGH
  (BALLYGAWLEY) BT70 .. 76 D2
BAILE UÍ DHONNAÍLE
  (CASTLECAULFIELD)
  BT70................ 78 D7
Baladoogh La BT80 ... 42 F7
Balbane Rd BT82........ 6 D1
Balix Lower BT82 .....7 A2
Balix Upper BT79 ... 14 F7
Ballagh
  Caledon BT68........ 110 F8
  Clogher BT76........ 92 C3
  Enniskillen BT92..... 126 D8
Ballaghalare BT82 .....5 F7
Ballaghgee BT93..... 65 D6
Ballaghmore Hts BT74. 138 A4
Ballaghneed BT76 ... 74 D1
Ballagh Rd
  Clogher BT76........ 92 D3
  Fivemiletown BT75.... 91 E1
Ball Alley 127 F2
Ballaun Stone★ BT75 .. 107 E5
Ballbeg BT71....... 63 C4
BALLEE BT82...........5 B4
Ballee Gr BT82....... 134 F6
Ballee Rd BT82....... 5 A4
Ballinageeragh 133 F2
BALLINAMALLARD (BÉAL
  ÁTHA NA MALLACHT)
  BT94................ 88 C5
Ballinamallard Ent Ctr
  BT94................ 105 A2
Ballinamallard Prim Sch
  BT94................ 88 B5
Ballinamullan Rd BT79. 136 F5
Ballindarragh BT74 .. 116 F5
Ballinderry Bridge Rd
  BT80................ 46 B7

Ballinderry Rd BT80... 46 D8
BALLINDRAIT 4 A4
Ballindrehid 82 B5
Ballindullagh Inward
  BT94................ 87 E8
Ballindullagh Outward
  BT94................ 87 E7
Ballinlough 131 C1
Ballintarsan BT94... 104 E3
Ballintempo BT93... 100 F4
Ballintrain BT79 ... 58 B6
Ballintrain Rd
  Carrickmore BT79.... 41 D1
  Omagh BT79 .... 58 B7
Ballought BT82..... 12 D3
Balloughry Rd BT48......1 E8
Ballyard BT78...... 71 E2
Ballyard Rd BT78 .... 71 D2
Ballyarton BT47..... 3 F3
Ballyarton Rd
  Londonderry BT47.......3 F2
  Strabane BT82........ 7 C8
Ballybeeny BT82 .....1 E4
Ballybeeny Rd BT82.....1 E4
Ballybeg Rd BT71..... 63 B4
Ballyblagh BT71.... 46 A2
Ballyblagh Rd BT71.... 46 B3
Ballybogie Rd BT47 .....2 F8
Ballyboy BT68...... 111 B8
Ballybrack Rd BT79 ... 40 E4
Ballybrannon Rd BT61... 98 F1
Ballybray BT70..... 61 B3
Ballybriest BT80 ... 31 A8
Ballybriest Rd BT80 .. 31 A8
Ballycallaghan BT47 ....3 C2
Ballycassidy BT94... 87 E4
Ballycolman BT82... 134 D2
Ballycolman Ave BT82. 134 D4
Ballycolman Est BT82. 134 E3
Ballycolman Ind Est
  BT82................ 134 D3
Ballycolman Rd BT82.. 134 D2
BALLYCONNELL 129 C3
Ballycullen Rd BT71... 98 A6
Ballydawley BT45 ... 46 A8
Ballydawley Rd BT45... 45 F8
Ballydonaghy BT79 ...5 A8
Ballydonegan BT47 ... 9 D6
Ballydoolagh BT74.. 104 E8
Ballyfatten BT82 ... 12 D7
Ballyfatten Pk 1 BT82. 12 D6
Ballyfolliard BT82... 23 B8
Ballygasey BT61.... 98 F4
Ballygasey Rd BT61.... 98 E4
Ballygassoon BT61... 98 E4
Ballygassoon Rd BT61. 98 E3
Ballygawley BT70 ... 76 D2
BALLYGAWLEY (BAILE UÍ
  DHÁLAIGH) BT70..... 76 D2
Ballygawley Rd BT70 .. 77 F5
Ballygittle BT71.... 63 A6
Ballygittle Rd BT71... 62 F7
Ballyglass Rd BT78.... 54 F6
Ballygonnell BT93... 87 A1
Ballygonny Beg BT45. 46 A6
Ballygonny More BT45. 45 F7
Ballygonny Rd E BT45 . 45 E6
Ballygonny Rd W BT45. 46 A7
Ballygowan BT78 ... 55 C8
Ballygowan Rd BT78 .. 55 B8
Ballygreenan BT77... 93 E7
Ballygroogan BT80... 44 C5
Ballyhallaghan BT79. 57 E3
Ballyheather BT82 ....5 C8
Ballyheather Rd BT82....5 B7
Ballyhill BT94...... 106 D4
Ballyhose BT93 .... 87 B2
Ballyhullagh BT92... 125 F7
Ballykeel
  Omagh BT78 .... 25 C4
  Omagh BT79 .... 57 F2
Ballykeery BT82.......6 C1
Ballykeery Rd BT82.... 13 F6
Ballyknick BT61.... 98 E3
Ballylagan BT77 .... 93 F7
Ballylaw BT82........ 5 D7
Ballylaw Rd BT82..... 5 D7
Ballylennan Mercer
  BT81................ 22 F4
Ballylennan Rd BT81... 22 E3
Ballylennan Scott BT81. 22 E3
Ballyloughan BT45... 45 D8
Ballyloughan Rd BT45.. 45 D7
Ballylucas BT74..... 104 D4
Ballylurgan Rd 5 BT75. 107 C8
Ballymacaffry BT75 . 106 F8
Ballymacall BT76.... 60 D4
Ballymacan BT76.... 108 F7
Ballymacataggart BT94. 69 A4
Ballymacavany 32 F1
Ballymackilmurry BT61. 98 D2
BALLYMACKILROY BT70 .. 76 A4
Ballymackilroy BT70.. 76 A5
Ballymacully La BT60 .. 97 B1
Ballymacully Lower
  BT60................ 97 A1
Ballymacully Rd BT60 . 111 F7
Ballymaghran BT93... 66 B5
Ballymagorry BT82.....5 A6
BALLYMAGORRY BT82......5 B6
Ballymagowan BT76 .. 92 F5
Ballymagowan Rd BT76. 92 F7
Ballymagrane BT71... 46 A4
Ballymaguire Rd BT71.. 46 C4
Ballymakenny BT92 .. 117 D5
Ballymartrim Etra BT61 97 F2
Ballymartrim La BT61.. 97 F1

Ballymartrim Otra❶ BT61 . 97 E1
Ballymenagh❶
 Cookstown BT80 . . . . 135 F7
 Dungannon BT71. . . . . 61 E3
Ballymongan❶ BT81 . . . . 33 F5
Ballymongan Rd BT81 . . . 33 D6
Ballymullarty❶ BT82 . . . . 13 C2
Ballymullarty Rd
 Omagh BT78 . . . . 25 A8
 Strabane BT82 . . . . 13 D2
Ballymully Glebe❶ BT80 . 45 A3
Ballymurphy❶ BT71 . . . . . 46 E5
Ballynabrannagh❶ BT93 . 50 C3
Ballynabwee❶ BT47 . . . . . . 2 A2
Ballynacross❶ BT82 . . . . . 7 C7
Ballynacross Rd BT82 . . . . 7 C8
Ballynacroy❶ BT80 . . . . . . 61 B8
Ballynafeagh❶ BT71 . . . . . 46 B1
Ballynafeagh Rd BT71 . . . . 46 D2
Ballynagilly❶ BT80 . . . . . 30 E5
Ballynagilly La BT80 . . . . . 31 B4
Ballynagilly Rd BT80 . . . . 30 E5
Ballynagowan Rd BT71 . . . 63 C7
BALLYNAGRAN BT82 . . . . . . 5 F4
Ballynagurragh❶ BT76 . . . 93 B5
Ballynahatty❶ BT78 . . . . . 55 E4
Ballynahatty Rd BT78 . . . . 55 E5
Ballynahaye❶ BT70 . . . . . . 76 E8
Ballynahaye Rd BT70 . . . . 77 A6
Ballynahone❶ BT45 . . . . . 45 E6
Ballynakill❶ BT93 . . . . 87 C1
Ballynakilly❶ BT80 . . . . . 61 B8
BALLYNAKILLY BT71 . . . . . 62 C1
Ballynakilly Rd
 ❶ Coalisland BT71 . . . . . . 62 C2
 Cookstown BT80 . . . . 61 A8
 Dungannon BT71. . . . . 80 C7
Ballynaloan❶ BT81 . . . . . 23 C5
Ballynaloan Rd BT81 . . . . 23 C4
BALLYNAMALLAGHT BT82 . . 7 B4
Ballynamannan❶ 130 E1
Ballynamullan❶ BT79 . . . 39 D2
Ballynant❶ BT93 . . . . 69 B7
Ballynany❶ BT70 . . . . 94 B8
Ballynany Rd BT70 . . . . . . 94 B8
Ballynapottoge❶ BT70 . . . 94 C7
Ballynaquilly❶ BT79 . . . . 39 E5
Ballynargan❶ BT80 . . . . . 46 A5
Ballynargan Rd
 Cookstown BT80 . . . . 46 A5
 Dungannon BT71. . . . . 45 F5
Ballynarry❶ BT62 . . . . . . 81 E5
Ballynarry Rd BT62 . . . . . 81 E5
Ballynasaggart❶ BT70 . . 76 A2
Ballynasaggart Rd
 Augher BT77 . . . . 94 A8
 Dungannon BT70 . . . . 76 A3
Ballynasollus❶ . . . .
 Cookstown BT80 . . . . 30 C4
 Omagh BT79 . . . . 14 B5
Ballynasollus Rd
 Cookstown BT80 . . . . 30 C3
 Omagh BT79 . . . . 14 C4
Ballynatubbrit❶ BT79 . . . 25 E4
Ballyneaner❶ BT82 . . . . . . 7 C8
Ballyness❶ BT75 . . . . 91 E5
Ballyness Rd
 Clogher BT76 . . . . 73 F1
 Fivemiletown BT75 . . . . . . 91 C5
Ballynick Rd BT61 . . . . . . 98 E3
Ballynorthland Demesne❶
 BT71 . . . . 137 E4
Ballynorthland Pk BT71 . 137 E3
Ballynure❶ 128 C1
Ballyreagh❶ BT80 . . . . . . 44 E4
BALLYREAGH BT70 . . . . 76 E4
Ballyreagh❶
 Enniskillen BT94 . . . . 89 B2
 Enniskillen BT94 . . . . . . 117 E8
Ballyreagh Bsns Pk
 BT80 . . . . 135 B1
Ballyreagh Ind Est BT80 . 135 B1
Ballyreagh Rd BT70 . . . . . 76 E4
Ballyreenan Rd BT78 . . . . 24 D4
Ballyrenan❶ BT78 . . . . . . 24 D3
Ballyrory❶ BT47 . . . . 8 C8
Ballyrory Rd BT47 . . . . 8 C8
Ballysaggart❶ BT71 . . . . 137 B5
Ballysaggart Bsns Complex
 BT71 . . . . 137 B5
Ballysaggart Pk BT70 . . . 137 A6
Ballyscally❶ BT76 . . . . . . 92 F2
BALLYSHANNON (BÉAL ÁTHA
 SEANAIDH) B6
Ballyskeagh❶ BT82 . . . . . . 5 D5
Ballyskeagh Rd BT82 . . . . . 5 D5
Ballysooragh❶ BT74 . . . . 113 F7
Ballysroonagh❶ BT93 . . . 101 A1
Ballysudden❶ BT80 . . . . . 44 E4
Ballytrea Prim Sch BT71 . 45 E3
Ballytroddan❶ BT71 . . . . 98 A3
Ballytroddan Rd BT71 . . . 98 A3
Ballyure Rd BT71 . . . . 21 D4
Ballyvaddan❶ BT75 . . . . . 91 D1
Ballyvaddy❶ BT70 . . . . . . 96 D4
Ballyvaddy Rd BT70 . . . . . 96 D4
Ballyveeny❶ BT71 . . . . . . 45 F3
Ballyward❶ BT70 . . . . 78 C4
Ballywholan❶
 Clogher BT76 . . . . 109 C8
 Dungannon BT71. . . . . 45 D1
Balmarino Terr ❶❻ BT71 . 62 C3
Baltreagh❶ BT92 . . . . . . 118 A1
Banagher❶ BT93 . . . . . . 103 B8
Banagher Rd BT47 . . . . . . 10 A8

Bancran Rd BT79 . . . . 56 F7
Bank❶ BT77 . . . . 93 D8
Bank Brae BT92 . . . . 117 D2
Bankfield Dr BT80 . . . . . . 46 B7
Bankmore Bsns Pk BT79 . 56 A7
Bankmore Rd BT79 . . . . . . 56 A7
Bannagh Beg❶ BT93 . . . . 50 F2
Bannagh More❶ BT93 . . . 51 A3
Bantry Rd BT70 . . . . 96 C6
Baragh❶ BT94 . . . . 88 B6
Baragh Gdns BT94 . . . . . . 88 C6
Bardahessiagh❶ BT70 . . . 43 C3
Bardahessiagh La BT70 . . 43 C2
Bardahessiagh Rd BT70 . . 43 B2
Barley Hill❶ BT82 . . . . 1 D1
Barleyhill Rd BT81 . . . . . . 22 C8
Barnaghs Rd BT79 . . . . . . 59 B4
Barnalackan❶ BT93 . . . . . 69 D8
Barnes Rd BT47 . . . . 9 A6
Barnhill BT74 . . . . 138 F5
Barnhill❶ BT82 . . . . 117 C2
Barnhill Ct BT82 . . . . 134 E7
Barnhill Rd BT82 . . . . . . 134 D7
Bar of Ballynacarrick❶ . . 48 A4
Baronagh❶ BT78 . . . . 55 B3
Baronagh Rd BT78 . . . . . . 55 C3
Barons Court❶ BT78 . . . . 24 C3
Baronscourt Rd BT78 . . . . 24 D4
Barony Rd BT79 . . . . 40 D7
Barrack La BT79 . . . . 136 B4
Barrack St Boys Prim Sch ❹
 BT82 . . . . 134 E5
Barrack Sq ❼ BT71 . . . . . 62 C3
Barracks St BT70 . . . . . . 137 C5
Barrack St
 Coalisland BT71 . . . . 62 B3
 Strabane BT82 . . . . 134 E5
Barragh Rd BT94 . . . . 88 A6
Barran❶
 Gubaveeny 112 A3
 Strabane BT82 . . . . 6 A5
Barranderry Hts BT74 . . . 138 D3
Barratitoppy❶ 109 D2
Barravey❶ BT78 . . . . 36 C4
Barravey Rd BT78 . . . . 36 C4
Barr of Bolusty More❶
 BT93 . . . . 66 D1
Barr of Drumbadmeen❶
 BT93 . . . . 84 C8
Barr of Drumgormly❶
 BT93 . . . . 84 B1
Barr of Slattinagh❶ BT93 . 83 F1
Barr of Slawin❶ BT93 . . . . 84 A7
Barron Rd BT82 . . . . 6 A6
Barrontop Fun Farm★
 BT82 . . . . 6 A6
Barr or Ramoan❶ BT92 . . 123 E5
Barr Rd BT78 . . . . 72 B2
Battery Rd BT80 . . . . 47 A6
Battleford Rd BT60 . . . . . . 97 B3
Bawn The BT74 . . . . 138 D6
Bawn Twr★ BT77 . . . . 93 B6
Bayview Cl BT74 . . . . 104 D2
Beagh❶
 Enniskillen BT94 . . . . 89 A4
 Enniskillen BT94 . . . . . . 106 A8
 Fivemiletown BT75 . . . . . . 92 A1
 Omagh BT78 . . . . 55 E6
 Omagh BT79 . . . . 74 C7
 Strabane BT82 . . . . 13 D4
Beaghbeg❶ BT80 . . . . 29 D2
Beaghbeg Rd BT80 . . . . . . 29 C2
Beagh Big❶ BT93 . . . . 86 A7
Beagh Little❶ BT93 . . . . . 86 B7
Beagh More❶ BT80 . . . . . . 29 D4
Beaghmore Rd BT80 . . . . . 29 D3
Beaghmore Stone Circles;
 Alignments & Cairns★
 BT80 . . . . 29 F5
Beagho❶ BT94 . . . . 105 B1
Beagh Rd
 Omagh BT78 . . . . 55 D6
 Strabane BT82 . . . . 13 D3
BÉAL ÁTHA NA MALLACHT
 (BALLINAMALLARD)
 BT94 . . . . 88 C3
BÉAL ÁTHA SEANAIDH
 (BALLYSHANNON) B6
BÉAL CÚ (BELCOO) BT93 . . 112 F8
BÉAL LEICE (BELLEEK)
 BT93 . . . . 65 A3
BÉAL TAIRBIRT
 (BELTURBET) 131 A2
BEARACH (BERAGH)
 BT79 . . . . 57 C3
Bearney Glebe❶ BT82 . . . 13 A5
Bearney Rd BT82 . . . . 12 F6
Beattie Pk BT79 . . . . 136 C7
Beeches The BT94 . . . . . . 88 C5
Beech Gr BT79 . . . . 136 E6
Beechgrove Pk BT94 . . . . . 88 C6
Beech Hill BT74 . . . . 104 B6
Beechlawn Dr BT81 . . . . . 22 F5
Beechline BT70 . . . . 60 B3
Beech Mews BT71 . . . . 79 A1
Beechmount Ave BT82 . . 134 D3
Beechmount Pk BT74 . . . 138 F5
Beech Pk BT82 . . . . 12 D6
Beech Valley BT71 . . . . . . 137 B5
Beech Valley Way BT71 . . 137 B5
Beechville Hts BT71 . . . . . 79 A1
Beechway BT80 . . . . 135 D6
Behy❶ 64 D8
Beigh Glebe❶ BT75 . . . . . 91 E5
Beihy❶ BT92 . . . . 122 A7
BELCOO (BÉAL CÚ) BT93 . . 112 F8
Belcoo East❶ BT93 . . . . . 112 F7
Belcoo West❶ BT93 . . . . 112 E7

Beleevna-Beg❶ BT80 . . . . 29 F4
Beleevna-More❶ BT79 . . . 30 B5
Belfast Rd
 Enniskillen BT74 . . . . . . 104 C2
 Fivemiletown BT75 . . . . . 107 B8
Bellanadohy❶ BT93 . . . . . 65 B4
BELLANALECK❶ BT92 . . . 115 B7
Bellanaleck❶ BT92 . . . . . 115 C8
Bellanamallard❶ BT94 . . . 88 B5
Bellavale Terr ❶❷ BT71 . . 62 C3
Bellavally Lower❶ 121 B2
Bellavally Upper❶ 121 C1
Belldoo BT82 . . . . 134 D2
BELLEEK (BÉAL LEICE)
 BT93 . . . . 65 A3
Belleek Charter Cruising
 (Boat Hire)★ BT93 . . . . . 64 F3
Belleek Prim Sch BT93 . . . 64 F2
Belle Isle❶ BT94 . . . . . . 116 B4
Bellmount❶ BT92 . . . . . . 127 B3
Bellmount alias
 Ballynagowan Upper❶
  BT71 . . . . 63 B7
Bell Rd BT82 . . . . 12 A7
Bells Ct 11 F7
Bellsgrove alias
 Ballynagowan Lower❶
  BT71 . . . . 63 D7
Bellspark❶ BT82 . . . . 12 A6
Bellspark Rd
 Sion Mills BT82 . . . . 12 C5
 Strabane BT82 . . . . 11 F7
Bellview BT78 . . . . 38 C6
Bellview Ct BT79 . . . . 26 D6
Belmont BT71 . . . . 137 F4
Belmont Rd BT62 . . . . 81 D4
Belmore St BT71 . . . . 138 D5
Belmore View BT92 . . . . . 114 C4
Belnaclogh❶ BT77 . . . . . . 75 C1
Belnagarnan❶ BT78 . . . . . 73 C7
Belragh❶ BT69 . . . . 95 C7
Beltany❶
 Omagh BT78 . . . . 25 A2
 Omagh BT78 . . . . 74 F3
Beltany Gr BT78 . . . . 38 D3
Beltany Rd
 ❶❶ Omagh BT78 . . . . . . 25 A6
 Omagh BT78 . . . . 25 B3
Beltonanean❶ BT80 . . . . . 30 B3
Beltonanean La BT80 . . . . 30 C3
Beltonanean Rd BT80 . . . . 30 B3
Beltrim❶ BT79 . . . . 26 C5
Beltrim Cres BT79 . . . . . . 26 D7
BELTURBET (BÉAL
 TAIRBIRT) 131 A2
Belturbet BT92 . . . . 124 C2
Belvedere Pk
 Dungannon BT71 . . . . . . 137 E4
 Omagh BT78 . . . . 136 D2
Belvoir Pk BT71 . . . . 136 C6
Benaughlin Pk BT74 . . . . 138 F4
Benaughlin View BT92 . . 123 B8
BENBURB❶ BT71 . . . . 97 D4
Benburb❶ BT71 . . . . 97 D5
Benburb Prim Sch BT71 . 97 D5
Benburb Rd BT71 . . . . 97 F7
Benburb Valley Heritage
 Ctr★ BT71 . . . . 97 C4
Benchran❶ BT79 . . . . 57 B7
Benmore Pk BT74 . . . . . . 138 D6
Beragh❶
 Omagh BT78 . . . . 37 F8
 Omagh BT79 . . . . 57 C3
BERAGH (BEARACH)
 BT79 . . . . 57 C3
Berkley Hts ❶❽ BT79 . . . 39 B2
Berkley Mews BT80 . . . . . 45 A2
Berkley Sq BT80 . . . . 45 A2
Bernagh❶ BT71 . . . . 79 E4
Bernagh Gdns BT71 . . . . 137 C8
Bernisk Rd BT79 . . . . 58 B5
Berryhill Rd BT82 . . . . 5 F1
Berrysfort❶ BT81 . . . . . . 22 F4
Bessybell Ct BT78 . . . . . . 24 F6
Bigwood (Drumkeeran)❶
 BT93 . . . . 50 C4
Bigwood Rd
 Londonderry BT47 . . . . . . 3 A7
 Strabane BT82 . . . . 2 E4
Bigwood (Templecarn)❶
 BT93 . . . . 66 F7
Billary❶
 Omagh BT78 . . . . 36 B3
 Pettigoe 50 A3
Binbunnifh❶ BT82 . . . . . . 7 A3
Binkeeragh❶ 122 B3
Binmore Glebe❶ BT93 . . . 86 A8
Binnafreaghan❶ BT79 . . . 27 E1
Binnawooda❶ BT81 . . . . . 35 C6
Binnelly❶ BT82 . . . . 6 B8
Binnelly Rd BT82 . . . . 6 B7
Birch Cl BT94 . . . . 105 A2
Birches Prim Sch BT62 . . 81 D5
Birches Rd BT62 . . . . 81 D5
Birchgrove BT80 . . . . 135 E3
Birch Rd
 Londonderry BT47 . . . . . . 3 E8
 Strabane BT82 . . . . 5 A6
Birchwood BT79 . . . . 136 D5
Birchwood Dr BT79 . . . . . 136 D6
Birnaghs❶ BT78 . . . . 24 D7
Blabreenagh❶ 32 B7
Blackbog Rd BT79 . . . . . . 28 F2
Blackburn Rd BT82 . . . . . 13 F5
Blackfort❶ BT78 . . . . 55 E2
Blackfort Ave BT78 . . . . . 55 E3
Blackfort Rd BT78 . . . . . . 55 F5
Blackhill BT94 . . . . 105 F4

Blackhill Rd BT78 . . . . . . 72 C6
Blackisland Rd BT71 . . . . 80 F4
Black La BT71 . . . . 137 C4
Blacklands❶ BT75 . . . . . 91 B1
BLACKLION (AN BLAIC) . . 112 F7
Blackmountain❶. 99 B1
Black Rampart BT62 . . . . 81 D3
Blackrock Pk BT93 . . . . . . 65 A4
Blackrock Rd BT78 . . . . . . 29 E6
Blacksessiagh❶ BT78 . . . . 55 B4
Blacksessiagh Rd BT78 . . . 55 B4
Blackslee❶ BT93 . . . . 67 C1
Blackstick Rd BT74 . . . . . 138 F2
Blackstone Pk BT47 . . . . . . 1 F7
Blacktown❶ BT71 . . . . 61 F6
Blacktown Rd BT71 . . . . . . 61 F6
Blackwater Rd BT78 . . . . . 53 D2
Blackwater Terr ❼ BT71 . . 62 C2
BLACKWATERTOWN (AN
 PORT MÓR) BT71 . . . . . . 98 A5
Blackwatertown Rd BT71 . 98 B3
Black Wood Cross Roads
 BT60 . . . . 111 F6
Blane Rd BT81 . . . . 21 D5
Blaney East❶ BT93 . . . . . 86 D5
Blaney West❶ BT93 . . . . . 86 D5
Bleanish Island❶ BT92 . . 125 C2
Blessed Patrick O'loughran
 Prim Sch BT70 . . . . 78 E7
Bloody La BT61 . . . . 98 E1
Bloomhill❶ BT70 . . . . 75 F1
Bloomhill Demesne❶
 BT71 . . . . 61 F6
Bloomry❶ BT78 . . . . 25 B5
Blubbell Gr BT74 . . . . 102 F1
Bluebell Ave BT47 . . . . 2 A4
Blunnick❶ BT92 . . . . 114 A6
Blunnick Cross BT92 . . . . 114 A5
Boa Island Rd BT93 . . . . . 65 F4
Bockets❶ BT70 . . . . 77 A6
Bockets Rd BT70 . . . . 76 F5
Bodarra Big❶ BT74 . . . . . 103 B3
Bodarra Little❶ BT74 . . . 103 C3
Bodoney❶
 Omagh BT78 . . . . 53 E1
 Omagh BT78 . . . . 89 D7
Bofealan❶ 129 A2
Bogagh❶ BT47 . . . . 2 B7
Bogbane❶ BT71 . . . . 80 C5
Bohard❶ BT69. . . . . 96 A5
Bohasset❶ BT92 . . . . 126 D6
Bohattan❶ BT75 . . . . 107 B8
Bohattan La BT75 . . . . . . 107 B8
Boheragh❶ BT79 . . . . 39 C4
Bohevny❶
 Enniskillen BT74 . . . . . . 114 A7
 Enniskillen BT93 . . . . 67 D1
BOHO BT74 . . . . 102 A5
Bohora❶ BT92 . . . . 126 C6
Bohulkno❶ BT94 . . . . . . 105 F7
Bolaght❶ BT81 . . . . 35 E6
Bolaght Rd BT81 . . . . 35 E7
Boland❶ BT71 . . . . 79 A3
Boleyhill❶ BT92 . . . . 118 A3
Bolies❶ BT75 . . . . 92 A6
Bolies Rd BT75 . . . . 92 A5
Bolusty Beg❶ BT93 . . . . . 66 F1
Bolusty More❶ BT93 . . . . 66 D2
Bomackatall Lower❶
 BT78 . . . . 36 F5
Bomackatall Upper❶
 BT78 . . . . 36 F5
Bonds Glen Rd BT47 . . . . . 3 D3
Bonnybrook❶ BT74 . . . . . 104 C3
Boolawater❶ BT93 . . . . . 50 C4
Boorin Nature Reserve★
 BT79 . . . . 26 D5
Borim❶ 122 D1
Borough of Charlemont❶
 BT71 . . . . 80 B1
Bosallagh❶ BT92 . . . . . . 127 D8
Botera❶ BT78 . . . . 37 C3
Botera Lower❶ BT78 . . . . 38 A1
Botera Rd BT78 . . . . 38 A1
Botera Upper❶ BT78 . . . . 54 F8
Botera Upper Rd BT78 . . . 37 E1
Bóthar Chill Mhic Cormaic
 (Kilmacormick Rd)
 BT74 . . . . 138 D7
Boughill❶ 128 E3
Bovean❶ BT71 . . . . 80 C5
Bovean Rd BT71 . . . . 80 C5
Bowara❶ BT74 . . . . 103 A6
Bowarran❶ BT92 . . . . . . 118 A1
Bowling Gn BT82 . . . . . . 134 E5
Boyaghan❶ BT94 . . . . 69 D2
Boyds Farm❶ BT71 . . . . . 62 D7
Boyhill❶ BT94 . . . . 117 C8
Boyhill Pk BT94 . . . . 117 C7
Braade❶ BT93 . . . . 84 E7
Brackagh❶
 Cookstown BT80 . . . . 31 B5
 Dungannon BT70 . . . . 75 B6
 Enniskillen BT74 . . . . . . 102 E7
 Enniskillen BT94 . . . . 70 A2
Brackagh North❶ BT79 . . 18 A3
Brackagh South❶ BT79 . . 41 A8
Brackan Ct BT71 . . . . 62 A4
Brackaville❶ BT71 . . . . . . 62 B4
Brackaville Rd BT71 . . . . . 61 F4
Bracken Brea BT71 . . . . . 61 F4
Bracken Cl
 ❼ Omagh BT78 . . . . 38 D1
 Omagh BT78 . . . . 55 D8
Bracken Ct
 ❶❸ Omagh BT78 . . . . . . 38 D1

Bracken Ct continued
 ❶ Omagh BT78 . . . . 55 D8
Bracken Mews ❾ BT78 . . 38 D1
Bracken Rd BT78 . . . . 55 C8
Bracken Ridge BT71 . . . . . 61 F4
Bracken Vale
 ❻ Omagh BT78 . . . . 38 D1
 ❷ Omagh BT78 . . . . 55 D8
Bracken Wlk ❽ BT78 . . . . 38 D1
Brackfield BT47 . . . . 3 F7
Bracklin❶ BT93 . . . . 52 C3
Brackvede Pk BT74 . . . . . 138 A4
Bracky❶
 Enniskillen BT74 . . . . . . 104 E1
 Omagh BT79 . . . . 40 C1
Bracky Rd BT79 . . . . 40 C1
Bradan Rd
 Castlederg BT81 . . . . 52 B8
 Omagh BT78 . . . . 36 B2
Bradkeel❶ BT79 . . . . 15 D6
Bradkeel Rd BT79 . . . . 15 B7
Bradley Way BT71 . . . . . . 134 C5
Braeside BT71 . . . . 137 A5
Braeside Pk BT74 . . . . . . 138 C7
Bragan❶ 109 E5
Bramble La BT80 . . . . 44 F4
Brambles BT71 . . . . 62 C4
Brambles The BT82 . . . . . . 5 A5
Bramble Wood BT71 . . . . 137 E4
Bramble Wood La BT71 . . 137 E4
Branch Rd BT82 . . . . 134 D6
Brankill❶
 Belturbet 130 E3
 Belturbet 130 F3
Brannish❶ BT92 . . . . 125 F6
Branny❶ BT69 . . . . 95 B8
Branter❶ BT77 . . . . 93 D5
BREADY BT82 . . . . 1 D4
Bready Jubilee Prim Sch
 BT82 . . . . 1 C5
Breagh❶ BT62 . . . . 81 E3
Breaghey❶ BT60 . . . . 111 F1
Breaghey Rd BT60 . . . . . . 111 F2
Breagho❶ BT74 . . . . 88 C1
Breakley Way ❹ BT75 . . 107 C8
Breakly❶ BT75 . . . . 107 D8
Breandrum❶
 Enniskillen BT74 . . . . . . 138 F4
 Enniskillen BT94 . . . . . . 106 B2
Breandrum Ct BT74 . . . . 138 F5
Breandrum Pk BT74. . . . . 138 E4
Breen❶ BT82 . . . . 12 E3
Breen Pk BT82 . . . . 12 E3
Breenvale BT82 . . . . 12 E3
Breezemount Pk
 ❶❶ Castlederg BT81 . . . . 22 E5
 Omagh BT78 . . . . 136 D3
Brewery Hts BT70 . . . . . . 61 B2
Brewery La
 Cookstown BT80 . . . . . . 135 D5
 Dungannon BT70 . . . . 61 A2
Bridge End BT45 . . . . 46 B7
Bridgehill Prim Sch BT81 . 23 A1
Bridgend Rd BT45 . . . . . . 46 A8
Bridge Rd BT78 . . . . 71 F7
Bridge St
 ❺ Irvinestown BT94 . . . . . 69 F3
 Lifford 134 B6
 Omagh BT78 . . . . 136 C4
 Strabane BT82 . . . . 134 D4
Bridgetown❶ BT81 . . . . . 22 E4
Brien Cres BT94 . . . . 88 C6
Brigh❶ BT71 . . . . 45 F1
Brigh Rd BT71 . . . . 45 F1
Broadford Rd BT78 . . . . . . 25 C1
Broadmeadow Pl ❹
 BT74 . . . . 138 C5
Brobrohan❶ BT75 . . . . . . 107 F6
BROCKAGH BT71 . . . . 63 B5
Brockagh❶
 Enniskillen BT74 . . . . . . 114 C6
 Enniskillen BT94 . . . . 90 D5
Brocklis❶ BT82 . . . . 23 F8
Brocklis Rd BT82 . . . . 12 C1
Broghan Rd BT78 . . . . 37 E6
Brollagh❶ BT93 . . . . 83 A8
BROOKEBOROUGH (ACHADH
 LON) BT94 . . . . 106 D1
Brookeborough Prim Sch
 BT94 . . . . 106 D1
Brookeborough Rd BT94 . 117 B7
Brooke Cres BT94 . . . . . . 106 C1
Brooke Dr BT94 . . . . 106 C1
Brookend❶ BT71 . . . . 46 F2
Brookend Rd BT71 . . . . . . 46 F2
Brooke Pk BT81 . . . . 22 E6
Brooke St BT71 . . . . 137 C5
Brookfield❶ BT71 . . . . . . 137 E4
Brookfield❶ BT92 . . . . . . 113 F2
Brookfield BT47 . . . . 1 F7
Brookfield Cl ❶❹ BT78 . . . 38 D1
Brookfield Hts ❶❻ BT78 . . 38 D1
Brookhill❶ BT93 . . . . 49 D1
Brookmount Cres ❷
 BT78 . . . . 136 B4
Brookmount Rd BT78 . . . . 38 D1
Brook Pl BT71 . . . . 62 D1
Brook Rd BT82 . . . . 6 C6
Brook St
 Enniskillen BT94 . . . . . . 105 A2
 Omagh BT78 . . . . 136 B4
Brook The BT74 . . . . 138 B5
Brookvale BT82 . . . . 12 D7
Brook Valley ❶❺ BT78 . . . 38 D1
Brook View Hts BT74 . . . 138 B5

Brook View Rise BT74 . . . 138 B5
Brossloy🔵 BT70 . . . . 78 F1
Broughadowey🔵 BT71 . . 79 F1
Broughderg🔵
  Enniskillen BT94 . . . . . . 118 B8
  Omagh BT79 . . . . 29 C7
Broughderg Rd BT79 . . . 28 F6
Brougher🔵 BT94 . . . . . . 89 E5
Brownhill BT94 . . . . 70 B3
Brownhill🔵
  Irvinestown BT94 . . . . . . 70 A3
  Strabane BT82 . . . . .5 F5
Brownhill Pk BT82 . . . . . . .5 F4
Brughas🔵
  Craigavon BT62 . . . . 81 C1
  Enniskillen BT74 . . . . . . 103 A6
Bruscarnagh🔵 BT92 . . 119 F4
Buchanan Villas 15 BT79 . 39 B2
Buggan🔵 BT93 . . . . 85 C3
Buggan Cross Roads
  BT93 . . . . 85 D4
Bullock Park🔵 BT81 . . . 35 F7
Bullock Rd BT81 . . . . 35 F6
Bullogbrean🔵 128 E7
Bun🔵 BT92 . . . . 126 A2
Bunaninver🔵 BT94 . . . . 69 A4
Bunanumery🔵 131 B6
Bunderg🔵 BT82 . . . . 13 B1
Bunderg Rd
  Omagh BT78 . . . . 24 E8
  Strabane BT82 . . . . 13 B1
Bungalows Rd 3 BT82 . . 12 D6
Buninubber🔵 BT94 . . . . 87 C7
Buninver Rd BT79 . . . . . . 26 F7
Bunlougher🔵
  Enniskillen BT92 . . . . . . 119 E6
  Enniskillen BT94 . . . . . . 118 B5
Bunmichael🔵 BT92 . . . 119 E5
Bunnablaneybane🔵
  BT92 . . . . 119 D4
Bunnahesco🔵 BT94 . . . 116 E4
Bunnahone🔵 BT93 . . . . 85 E8
Bunneill🔵 BT92 . . . . . . 118 C2
Bunnisnagapple🔵 BT94 118 E7
Bunnynubber🔵 BT78 . . . 38 C3
Bunowen🔵 BT82 . . . . .6 D8
Burdautien🔵 127 E5
Burfits Hill BT94 . . . . 69 E3
Burfitts Hill BT94 . . . . . . 69 F3
Burn🔵 BT92 . . . . 125 F2
Burnavon Arts & Cultural
  Ctr ★ BT80 . . . . 135 C5
Burnbank BT80 . . . . 135 C6
Burn Brae Cres BT80 . . 135 C5
Burnhead Rd BT79 . . . . . 26 B6
Burn Rd BT80 . . . . 135 C5
Burnside Pk BT74 . . . . . 104 B5
Burnside Villas 7 BT81 . 22 E5
BURNT ISLAND BT71 . . . 81 A2
Burn View BT79 . . . . 136 F5
Burren🔵 112 E3
Burrendale BT74 . . . . . . 104 B5
Burrow Rd BT78 . . . . 38 B1
Bursan🔵 121 B4
Bushfield Mill 4 BT47 . . .8 E7
Bush Prim Sch BT71 . . . . 79 E8
Bush Rd BT71 . . . . 62 B1
Bushvale BT71 . . . . 137 E5
Bush Villas BT71 . . . . 79 E8
Butchers St 1 BT82 . . . . 134 E5
Butcher St 134 B7
Butterlope Rd BT79 . . . . 15 B6
Buttermarket Craft & Design
  Ctr ★ 4 BT74 . . . . 138 D5
By Biddy Molloy's BT61 . 98 E4
By Mckee's BT71 . . . . . . 80 D2
By Pogues BT61 . . . . 97 C2
Byturn🔵 BT78 . . . . 24 A1
Byturn Rd BT78 . . . . 24 A1
Cabragh🔵
  Armagh BT61 . . . . 97 D1
  Armagh BT61 . . . . 98 D1
  Dungannon BT70 . . . . . . 77 E5
  Enniskillen BT94 . . . . . . 70 D1

C

Cabragh Rd
  Armagh BT61 . . . . 98 D2
  Dungannon BT70 . . . . . . 77 E6
Cackinish🔵 BT92 . . . . . 130 D6
Cadian🔵 BT70 . . . . 96 E8
Cadian La BT70 . . . . 78 E1
Cadian Rd BT70 . . . . 78 F1
Cady🔵
  Cookstown BT80 . . . . . . 44 E1
  Enniskillen BT93 . . . . . . 68 E7
Cahoo🔵 BT80 . . . . 45 B2
Cahoo La BT80 . . . . 45 A2
Cahore🔵 BT93 . . . . 52 A2
Cairn Pk BT79 . . . . 26 C6
Cairn Rd
  Omagh BT78 . . . . 37 C8
  Omagh BT79 . . . . 40 C3
Cairn The BT71 . . . . 137 F5
CAISLEÁNA DEIRGE
  (CASTLEDERG) BT81 . . . 22 E5
Caldragh🔵 BT92 . . . . . 123 A4
Caldrum🔵 BT77 . . . . 93 F7
Caldrum Glebe🔵 BT77 . . 86 A6
Caledon🔵 BT68 . . . . . . 111 D6
CALEDON (CIONN AIRD)
  BT68 . . . . 111 D6
Caledon Rd BT69 . . . . 95 B4

Caledon Rd Loop BT69 . . . 95 D2
Calherne🔵 BT82 . . . . . . .5 A2
Calkill🔵
  Enniskillen BT92 . . . . . . 113 C6
  Omagh BT78 . . . . 38 A5
Callagheen🔵 BT93 . . . . 83 E8
Callow🔵 BT93 . . . . 85 D6
Callowhill🔵
  Enniskillen BT92 . . . . . . 124 A3
  Scotshouse 133 A1
Cam🔵 BT92 . . . . 115 E1
Camaghy🔵 BT70 . . . . . . 60 A5
Camaghy Rd BT70 . . . . . . 60 B4
Camaghy Rd S BT70 . . . . 60 B3
Camalier🔵 130 B4
Camcosy Rd BT79 . . . . . . 27 D7
Camderry🔵 BT78 . . . . . . 54 A2
Camderry Rd BT78 . . . . . 54 A2
Camgart🔵 BT75 . . . . 90 E3
Camletter🔵 BT92 . . . . . 124 A2
Camlin🔵 64 C5
Camlough Rd
  Dungannon BT70 . . . . . . 42 C5
  Omagh BT79 . . . . 41 B3
Camowen🔵 BT79 . . . . . . 56 D5
Camowen Cotts 7 BT79. 136 F4
Camowen Ct BT79 . . . . . 136 E4
Camowen Rd BT79 . . . . . 56 D6
Camowen Terr BT79 . . . 136 F4
Campbell Terr BT79 . . . . 14 F4
Camphill Pk 3 BT92 . . . 126 C3
Camplagh🔵 BT93 . . . . . 34 E1
Camplany🔵 BT93 . . . . . 68 E7
Campsie🔵 BT79 . . . . . . 136 E3
Campsie Ave BT79 . . . . 136 C4
Campsie Cres BT79 . . . . 136 C4
Campsie Ct BT79 . . . . . 136 D4
Campsie Dr BT79 . . . . . 136 C4
Campsie Rd BT79 . . . . . 136 D4
Camus Park🔵 BT82 . . . . 12 F5
Camus Rd BT82 . . . . 13 A3
Canal Link BT82 . . . . . . 134 D6
Canal Pl 16 BT71 . . . . . . 62 C2
Canalquay BT71 . . . . 62 C3
Canal Side BT82 . . . . . . 134 D6
Canal St BT82 . . . . 134 D5
Canary🔵 BT71 . . . . 80 D1
Canary Rd BT71 . . . . 80 D1
Caneese🔵 BT80 . . . . 31 F4
Cannagola Beg🔵 BT62 . . 81 F1
Cannagola Beg Rd BT62 . 81 F2
Cannagola More🔵 BT62 . 81 F2
Cannagola Rd BT62 . . . . . 81 F2
Cannondale BT78 . . . . . 136 C3
Cannon Hill BT78 . . . . . 136 C2
Cannon Vale BT78 . . . . . 136 C2
Canoneill🔵 BT62 . . . . . . 81 F1
Cantytrindle🔵 BT94 . . . 87 E6
Capehill Rd BT78 . . . . . . 54 D2
Cappagh🔵 BT70 . . . . 59 E3
Cappagh🔵 BT70 . . . . 59 F3
CAPPAGH BT70 . . . . . . 128 F6
Cappagh Rd
  Dungannon BT70 . . . . . . 59 E4
  Omagh BT79 . . . . 38 E4
Cappog🔵 BT92 . . . . 103 C2
Cappog Rd BT92 . . . . . . 103 C2
Cappy🔵 BT74 . . . . 116 C7
Caranbane🔵 BT47 . . . . . .8 B8
Cara St 127 E2
Cargagh🔵 BT77 . . . . 93 D3
Carganamuck🔵 BT61 . . . 98 D2
Carickaleese🔵 BT92 . . 129 F5
CARLAND BT71 . . . . 61 D3
Carland Rd BT71 . . . . . . 137 C8
Carlton Cres BT82 . . . . . 134 C2
Carlton Ct BT82 . . . . 134 C2
Carlton Dr BT82 . . . . 134 B2
Carn🔵
  Clones 127 E3
  Enniskillen BT74 . . . . . . 102 A5
  Enniskillen BT92 . . . . . . 123 D5
  Enniskillen BT93 . . . . . . 69 F8
  Enniskillen BT94 . . . . . . 89 D3
Carnafarn🔵 BT47 . . . . . . 2 D7
Carnagribban🔵 BT82 . . .6 F7
Carnahinny🔵 BT76 . . . . 92 E3
Carnalea🔵
  Omagh BT78 . . . . 70 E8
  Omagh BT78 . . . . 73 D6
Carnalea Rd BT78 . . . . . . 73 E7
Carnalea Terr 15 BT71 . . 62 C3
Carnan🔵 BT71 . . . . 63 C8
Carnanbane🔵 BT47 . . . . 10 B8
Carnan Pk BT79 . . . . 136 B6
Carnanransy🔵 BT79 . . . 28 D6
Carnan Rd BT71 . . . . 46 C1
Carnanreagh Rd BT47 . . . 8 A5
Carnargan🔵 BT78 . . . . . 14 C3
Carnargan Rd BT78 . . . . . 14 A1
Carnarousk🔵 BT78 . . . . 73 E6
Carnaveagh🔵 BT78 . . . . 25 C6
Carncorn Rd BT81 . . . . . . 23 B2
Carncorran Glebe🔵 BT81 . 23 B3
Carn Ct BT92 . . . . 120 C1
Carndreen Rd BT81 . . . . . 22 A6
Carnenny🔵 BT70 . . . . . . 60 C8
Carnenny La BT70 . . . . . . 60 B8
Carneyhill🔵 BT92 . . . . . 115 B6
Carneyhome🔵 BT92 . . . 126 F5
Carney's Island🔵 128 B3
Carnirk🔵 BT93 . . . . 85 B7
Carnkenny🔵 BT78 . . . . . 24 A6
Carnkenny Rd BT78 . . . . 23 F4
Carnmore🔵 BT92 . . . . . 119 C4

Carnmore Rise BT74 . . . 138 C6
Carnony🔵 BT79 . . . . 38 F7
Carnony Rd BT79 . . . . . . 38 E7
Carnoughter🔵 BT81 . . . . 21 F7
Carnoughter Rd BT81 . . . 21 F8
Carn Rd
  Castlederg BT81 . . . . . . 21 E4
  Omagh BT79 . . . . 14 F1
Carnreagh🔵 BT47 . . . . . .8 A5
Carnroe🔵 133 C5
Carntall Beg🔵 BT76 . . . . 92 D5
Carntall More🔵 BT76 . . . 92 E6
Carntall Prim Sch BT76 . . 92 D6
CARNTEEL BT69 . . . . 95 D7
Carnteel Rd
  Aughnacloy BT69 . . . . . . 95 C7
  Dungannon BT70 . . . . . . 78 B3
Carntrone🔵 BT92 . . . . . 117 E5
Carnview Pk BT92 . . . . . 123 C8
Carony🔵 BT78 . . . . 36 F4
Car Pk Link Rd BT78 . . . 136 C3
Carr🔵
  Augher BT77 . . . . 93 B7
  Enniskillen BT74 . . . . . . 102 B8
Carra🔵 BT92 . . . . 133 A8
Carrackadartan Rd BT81 . 23 A3
Carracoghan🔵 BT81 . . . . 21 C3
Carradoo Glebe🔵 BT77 . 53 B7
Carradowa Glebe🔵 BT78 . 52 F6
Carraig Dr BT79 . . . . 41 C1
Carran🔵
  Dungannon BT70 . . . . . . 76 A1
  Enniskillen BT74 . . . . . . 104 E3
  Enniskillen BT74 . . . . . . 138 F8
  Omagh BT78 . . . . 71 B1
Carran Beg🔵 BT93 . . . . . 65 D2
Carranboy🔵 BT94 . . . . . 69 C4
Carran Cl BT74 . . . . 138 D7
Carran East🔵 BT74 . . . . . 86 B1
Carran Little🔵 BT74 . . . 104 D3
Carran More🔵 BT93 . . . . 65 C1
Carran West🔵 BT93 . . . . 83 A3
Carraun🔵 99 C3
Carrick🔵
  Enniskillen BT93 . . . . . . 85 E6
  Omagh BT78 . . . . 53 A7
Carrickabweehan🔵
  BT74 . . . . 113 E8
Carrickadartan🔵 BT81 . . . 23 A3
Carrickadrantan🔵 BT93 . 113 A8
Carrickagreany🔵 BT93 . . 52 F1
Carrickaheenan🔵 BT92 . 115 E8
Carrickaholten🔵 BT81 . . . 34 D5
Carrickaloughan🔵 BT93 101 D1
Carrickaness🔵
  Dungannon BT71 . . . . . . 97 D4
  Omagh BT78 . . . . 36 C3
Carrickaness Gdns BT71 . 97 C3
Carrickaness Rd BT61 . . . 97 C3
Carrickatane🔵 BT82 . . . . 2 D3
Carrickatane Rd BT82 . . . 2 D3
Carrick Ave BT82 . . . . . . .4 C1
Carrickavoy🔵 BT77 . . . . 93 E2
Carrickawick🔵 BT92 . . . 118 E5
Carrickayne🔵 BT47 . . . . .7 E3
Carrickayne Rd BT47 . . . .7 D3
Carrickbeg🔵 BT74 . . . . . 102 A7
Carrickbwee Glebe🔵
  BT78 . . . . 53 A7
Carrickcroghery🔵 BT93 . 51 E8
Carricklee BT82 . . . . 134 A1
Carricklongfield🔵 BT69 . 96 A7
Carricklongfield Rd BT69 . 95 E8
Carricklynn Ave BT82 . . . 134 B4
Carrickmacflaherty🔵
  BT93 . . . . 101 E1
Carrickmacosker🔵
  BT92 . . . . 117 E1
Carrickmacsparrow🔵
  BT74 . . . . 102 B1
Carrickmore🔵
  Omagh BT79 . . . . 41 C1
  St Johnstown 1 A2
CARRICKMORE OR TERMON
  ROCK BT79 . . . . 41 E1
Carricknabrattoge🔵
  BT92 . . . . 118 D3
Carricknaseer🔵 BT74 . . 102 A1
Carrickone🔵 BT82 . . . . . 12 B6
Carrickoughter🔵 BT93 . . 51 A4
Carrickpolin🔵 BT94 . . . 107 A1
Carrickrevagh🔵 BT93 . . . 86 F4
Carrickrevagh🔵 100 B1
Carrick Strand BT82 . . . 134 C5
Carrick View BT71 . . . . . . 97 C4
Carrickyheenan🔵 BT94 . 118 D7
Carrigan🔵
  Enniskillen BT74 . . . . . . 138 A2
  Enniskillen BT92 . . . . . . 113 D4
  Enniskillen BT93 . . . . . . 87 A2
  Enniskillen BT93 . . . . . . 100 E7
Carrigan Pk BT74 . . . . . 138 A3
CARRIGANS 1 C8
Carrigans🔵
  Enniskillen BT92 . . . . . . 127 A2
  Omagh BT78 . . . . 25 C2
Carrigans Pk BT79 . . . . . 25 C1
Carrigans Rd BT79 . . . . . 25 C3
Carrigolagh🔵 BT93 . . . . 65 F2
Carrigullin🔵 BT82 . . . . . 13 A6
Carrigullin Rd BT82 . . . . 134 F1
Carrivetragh🔵 127 F5
Carronreemall🔵 BT93 . . 113 B7
Carrowbeg🔵 BT71 . . . . . 97 A6
Carrowcarlan🔵 BT70 . . . 96 F7
Carrowcolman🔵 BT70 . . 96 F7
Carrowcolman Rd BT70 . . 97 A8

Carrowgarragh🔵 BT92 . 118 A2
Carrowhony🔵 BT92 . . . 117 B4
Carrowkeel🔵
  Belleek 82 C2
  Enniskillen BT93 . . . . . . 65 D3
  Enniskillen BT94 . . . . . . 105 D6
Carrowmacmea🔵 BT74 . 104 C5
Carrowmaculla🔵 BT92 . 118 E3
Carrowmore🔵
  Ballyconnell 129 B5
  Enniskillen BT74 . . . . . . 104 A7
Carrownagiltagh🔵 BT94 106 A7
Carrownalegg🔵 BT93 . . 113 B8
Carrowoaghtragh🔵 BT79. 17 F7
Carrowshee Pk BT92 . . . 117 C3
Carry🔵 BT94 . . . . 116 B6
CARRY BRIDGE BT94 . . 116 C6
Carrycastle🔵 BT70 . . . . . 96 C7
Carrycastle Rd BT70 . . . . 96 C7
Carryclass🔵 BT78 . . . . . 72 D2
Carryclogher🔵 BT76 . . . 92 E4
Carryglass🔵 BT78 . . . . . 90 C8
Carryglass Rd BT78 . . . . . 72 C1
Cashel🔵
  Enniskillen BT93 . . . . . . 86 B5
  Omagh BT78 . . . . 28 A2
Cashelard🔵 64 F8
Cashelbane Cairn ★ BT82 . .7 D6
Cashel Cross Roads BT93. 99 D8
Cashel La BT70 . . . . 43 C4
Cashelnadrea🔵 BT93 . . . 83 D1
Cashel Rd BT79 . . . . 27 F1
Cashty🔵 BT78 . . . . 24 C2
Cashty Rd BT78 . . . . 24 D1
CASLEÁN NA FINNE
  (CASTLEFINN) BT82 . . . 11 B8
Casorna🔵 BT79 . . . . 27 E5
Cassan🔵 BT94 . . . . 115 F4
Cassidy🔵 BT74 . . . . 69 E2
Castle Archdale Country Pk ★
  BT94 . . . . 68 F3
Castle Archdale Islands
  Nature Reserve ★ BT94. 68 D5
Castle Balfour Demesne🔵
  BT92 . . . . 117 C1
Castlebalfour Pk 2
  BT92 . . . . 117 D2
Castlebalfour Rd BT92 . . 117 D2
Castlebane🔵 BT81 . . . . . 23 A4
Castlebane Rd BT81 . . . . 23 A3
Castle Brae 9 BT82 . . . . 25 A6
Castlecaldwell National
  Nature Reserve ★ BT93 . 66 B4
CASTLECAULFIELD (BAILE UÍ
  DHONNAÍLE) BT70 . . . . . 78 D7
Castlecaulfield Rd BT70 . . 61 A1
Castle Coole🔵 BT74 . . . 104 C4
Castlecoole Rd BT74 . . . 104 B4
Castlecraig🔵 BT78 . . . . . 35 E4
Castle Ct
  Cookstown BT80 . . . . . . 135 D2
  Dungannon BT70 . . . . . . 78 D8
  Omagh BT78 . . . . 24 F6
Castledamph🔵 BT79 . . . 15 E5
Castledamph Rd BT79 . . . 15 E5
Castle Dr BT68 . . . . 111 D6
Castle Farm BT70 . . . . . . 76 D2
Castle Farm🔵 BT71 . . . . 62 E8
Castlefarm Rd BT71 . . . . 62 F8
Castlefields BT71 . . . . . 137 C6
Castlefin Pk BT81 . . . . . . 22 E5
Castlefin Rd BT81 . . . . . . 11 B1
Castlefin Rd T 2 BT81 . . 22 E5
Castlegore🔵 BT81 . . . . . 22 D4
Castlegore Rd BT81 . . . . 22 D4
Castle Gr
  Dungannon BT70 . . . . . . 78 D7
  Omagh BT79 . . . . 136 F6
Castlegrange Pk BT82 . . 134 B3
Castle Hill BT71 . . . . 137 C6
Castlehill Demesne🔵
  BT77 . . . . 93 B6
Castlehill Rd
  Brookeborough BT94 . . . 106 C1
  Omagh BT78 . . . . 71 D2
Castlehill Terr 18 BT71 . . 62 C3
Castle Irvine Demesne🔵
  BT94 . . . . 69 F1
Castle La
  Caledon BT68 . . . . 111 D6
  Enniskillen BT74 . . . . . . 138 A7
  Lisnaskea BT92 . . . . . . 117 D2
  6 Omagh BT78 . . . . 136 B4
Castle Manor BT79 . . . . 136 F6
Castlemellan🔵 BT82 . . . . 2 D2
Castlemervyn Demesne🔵
  BT78 . . . . 71 C2
Castle Mews BT68 . . . . . 111 D6
Castlemurray BT82 . . . . 134 A3
Castlemurray Dr BT94 . . . 88 B5
Castleoaks BT79 . . . . . . 136 F5
Castle Pk
  Ballygawley BT70 . . . . . . 76 D2
  Enniskillen BT74 . . . . . . 138 C5
Castle Pl
  Omagh BT78 . . . . 136 B4
  Strabane BT82 . . . . 134 D5

Castle Rd
  Cookstown BT80 . . . . . . 135 E2
  Dungannon BT70 . . . . . . 78 D6
Castleroddy Glebe🔵
  BT79 . . . . 26 A3
Castleroddy Rd BT79 . . . 25 F2
Castlesaunderson
  Demesne🔵 131 F4
Castlesessagh🔵 BT81 . . 22 D6
Castle St
  Enniskillen BT74 . . . . . . 138 C5
  Irvinestown BT94 . . . . . . 69 F2
  Omagh BT78 . . . . 136 B4
  Strabane BT82 . . . . 134 D5
Castletown🔵
  Aughnacloy BT69 . . . . . . 77 E1
  Fintona BT78 . . . . 73 C6
  Omagh BT78 . . . . 38 C8
  Strabane BT82 . . . . .5 A3
  Strabane BT82 . . . . 134 B3
Castletown Ct BT82 . . . . 134 B4
Castletown Monea🔵
  BT93 . . . . 86 E2
Castletown Rd
  Aughnacloy BT69 . . . . . . 95 D8
  Omagh BT78 . . . . 25 A4
  Strabane BT82 . . . . 134 B2
Castleview BT78 . . . . 24 F6
Castleview Cres 6 BT79 . 136 E6
Castleview Ct BT79 . . . . 136 E6
Castleview Hts BT70 . . . 137 A7
Castleview Pk BT79 . . . . 136 E6
Castleview Rd BT79 . . . . 136 F6
Castle Villas BT80 . . . . . 135 E3
Castlewarren🔵 BT82 . . . .3 A3
Castlewarren Rd BT82 . . . .2 F4
Castle Way BT71 . . . . 63 C5
Castlewood BT74 . . . . . . 138 F4
Cathcart Sq BT74 . . . . . 138 C5
Cattor🔵 BT78 . . . . 74 B5
Causanagh🔵 BT61 . . . . . 98 F7
Causanagh Rd BT61 . . . . 98 F7
Causeway Terr 19 BT71 . . 62 C3
Causey Rd BT81 . . . . 11 C1
Cavan🔵
  Castlederg BT81 . . . . . . 22 B6
  Clogher BT76 . . . . 109 D8
  Dungannon BT71 . . . . . . 80 A6
  Omagh BT78 . . . . 72 E8
  Rossgeir 4 B6
Cavanacark🔵 BT75 . . . . 92 B5
Cavanacaw🔵
  Dungannon BT70 . . . . . . 60 A8
  Omagh BT78 . . . . 55 A7
Cavanacaw Lower🔵 BT78 55 B7
Cavanacaw Rd BT78 . . . . 55 B8
Cavanacaw Upper🔵 BT78 55 A7
Cavanacor View BT82 . . . .5 A6
Cavanacross🔵 BT94 . . . 104 E5
Cavanacross Cross Roads
  BT94 . . . . 104 F6
Cavanacurragh🔵 BT92 . 126 D6
Cavanagarvan🔵 BT94 . . 106 E3
Cavanagh🔵
  Ballyconnell 129 C1
  Enniskillen BT92 . . . . . . 132 C8
Cavanakeeran🔵 BT70 . . . 42 E1
Cavanakeeran Rd BT70 . . 42 D1
Cavanakeery🔵 BT74 . . . 103 E3
Cavanaleck🔵
  Enniskillen BT74 . . . . . . 104 B6
  Fivemiletown BT75 . . . . 107 B7
Cavanalee🔵 BT82 . . . . . 13 B8
Cavanalough Glebe🔵
  BT94 . . . . 88 E4
Cavanamara🔵 BT92 . . . . 71 D1
Cavanamara View BT78 . . 89 D8
Cavanaquill🔵 129 A2
Cavanavally🔵 128 F3
Cavanboy🔵 BT68 . . . . . . 96 E3
Cavancarragh🔵
  Enniskillen BT93 . . . . . . 112 E8
  Enniskillen BT94 . . . . . . 104 F4
Cavan (Cope)🔵 110 C8
Cavancreagh🔵 BT82 . . . .2 C2
Cavancreagh Rd BT47 . . . .2 C2
Cavandale 11 BT74 . . . . 104 B6
Cavandarragh🔵 BT81 . . . 23 D3
Cavandarragh Rd BT81 . . 23 E3
Cavankilgreen🔵 BT69 . . 94 F7
Cavanleckagh🔵 95 B2
Cavanlee Rd BT82 . . . . . 13 A8
Cavanmore🔵 BT93 . . . . 101 B1
Cavanoneill🔵 BT80 . . . . 43 A5
Cavan ONeill🔵 BT69 . . . 94 D6
Cavanoneill Rd BT80 . . . . 43 A5
Cavan Rd
  Castlederg BT81 . . . . . . 21 F7
  Dungannon BT71 . . . . . . 79 F7
  Enniskillen BT92 . . . . . . 132 F8
  Omagh BT78 . . . . 54 E1
Cavanreagh🔵
  Enniskillen BT92 . . . . . . 113 C3
  Omagh BT79 . . . . 58 B5
Cavans🔵 BT75 . . . . 106 F2
Cavansallagh🔵 BT78 . . . 36 B4
Cavantillycormick🔵 BT94 88 D2
Cavantreeduff🔵 BT93 . . 101 F1
Cavany🔵 133 C3
Cavehill Dr BT71 . . . . 46 F4
Cavey🔵 BT70 . . . . 76 B4
Cavey Rd BT70 . . . . 76 B4
Cedar Hts BT80 . . . . 135 E7
Cedar Pk BT82 . . . . 134 C4
Cedar Ridge BT71 . . . . . 137 E5
Céide Chill Mhic Cormaic
  (Kilmacormick Dr)
  BT74 . . . . 138 D7

Céide Radharc An Locha
  (Loughview Dr) BT74 . . . . 138 C7
Celtic Weave China★ 64 E3
Cemetery Rd
  Cookstown BT80 . . . . 135 C3
  Strabane BT82 . . . . 134 F3
Centenary Pk BT78 . . . . . . 136 A4
Central Ave BT80 . . . . 135 C5
Chanterhill Pk 9 BT74 . . 104 B6
Chanterhill Rd BT74 . . . . . 138 E5
Chapel Ct BT80 . . . . 135 D4
Chapel Hill Rd BT60 . . . . . 111 E3
Chapel La BT79 . . . . 26 D6
Chapel Rd BT80 . . . . 135 D3
Chapel St BT80 . . . . 135 D4
CHARLEMONT BT71 . . . . . . 98 B8
  Charlemont Ind Est BT71 . 98 A8
Charlemont St
  Dungannon BT70 . . . . 137 B6
  Moy BT71 . . . . 98 A8
Cheltenham La BT74 . . . . . 138 C5
Cherry Dale BT74 . . . . 104 B5
Cherry Hill
  Irvinestown BT94 . . . . 69 F3
  Lisnaskea BT92 . . . . 117 C3
Cherrymount★ 64 B5
Cherrymount Link Rd
  BT74 . . . . 138 E8
Cherrymount Rd BT74 . . 138 D8
Cherryvale BT82 . . . . 134 C4
Cherryvale Dr BT82 . . . . . 134 C4
Cherry Valley BT74 . . . . . 104 B5
Cherryville BT74 . . . . 138 D8
Cherryville Rd BT62 . . . . . . 81 E3
Cherry Wlk 8 BT74 . . . . 104 B6
Chestnut Dr BT71 . . . . 80 A1
Chestnut Gr
  Aughnacloy BT69 . . . . 95 A5
  Ballinamallard BT94 . . . . . 88 C6
  Enniskillen BT92 . . . . 115 D7
  Lifford 134 A5
  Strabane BT82 . . . . 134 D4
Chestnut Pk BT82 . . . . . . 134 D4
Chestnut Rd BT82 . . . . 5 C5
Christian Brothers Gram Sch
  BT78 . . . . 136 C3
Christ the King Prim Sch
  BT79 . . . . 136 B7
Church Brae BT78 . . . . 71 E7
CHURCH HILL BT93 . . . . . . 85 F8
Church Hill 3 BT78 . . . . 136 B4
Church Hill BT68 . . . . 2 F2
Church Hill Rd BT68 . . . . . 111 E7
Churchill Prim Sch BT68 111 D6
Church La 1 BT71 . . . . . 137 C5
Church Rd
  Castlederg BT81 . . . . 21 C2
  Ederney BT93 . . . . 52 A1
  Omagh BT79 . . . . 57 A3
Churchside Ct 2 BT82 . . . 12 C6
Church Sq BT82 . . . . 12 D6
Church St
  Ballygawley BT70 . . . . 76 C2
  Cookstown BT80 . . . . 135 D3
  Dromore BT78 . . . . 71 F7
  Dungannon BT70 . . . . . . 137 C5
  Enniskillen BT74 . . . . 138 C5
  Enniskillen BT92 . . . . 120 D1
  Fintona BT78 . . . . 73 C6
  Irvinestown BT94 . . . . 69 F3
  Omagh BT78 . . . . 136 B4
  Strabane BT82 . . . . 134 E5
Churchtown BT81 . . . . 22 E5
Churchtown Pk BT81 . . . . . 22 E6
Christ Churchtown Prim Sch
  BT80 . . . . 31 E3
Churchtown Rd BT80 . . . . . 31 E3
CHURCHTOWN (TULAIGH AN
  LÚIR) BT80 . . . . 31 E3
Churchview
  Enniskillen BT94 . . . . 105 E8
  Strabane BT82 . . . . 134 E5
Church View
  Dungannon BT70 . . . . 61 B2
  Moy BT71 . . . . 98 B8
  Strabane BT82 . . . . 5 B5
Churchview Cl BT62 . . . . . . 81 A2
CILL NÁILE (KINAWLEY)
  BT92 . . . . 123 B8
CIONN AIRD (CÁLEDON)
  BT68 . . . . 111 D6
Circular Rd
  Dungannon BT71 . . . . 137 C6
  Enniskillen BT94 . . . . 105 A2
  Omagh BT79 . . . . 136 D6
CLABBY (CLABIGH) BT75 . . 90 E3
Clabby Rd BT75 . . . . 91 C1
CLABIGH (CLABBY) BT75 . . 90 E3
Cladowen★ 128 B2
Clady Blair BT82 . . . . 12 F1
CLADY (CLÓIDGH) BT82 . . . 11 F6
Clady Haliday BT82 . . . . . . 12 E1
Clady Hood★ BT82 . . . . . . 12 E2
Clady Johnston★ BT82 . . . 12 E2
Clagan BT80 . . . . 31 C5
Clagernagh★ BT81 . . . . . . 20 F1
Claggan★ BT80 . . . . 31 F1
CLAGGAN BT80 . . . . 47 B5
Claggan★
  Cookstown BT80 . . . . 61 B6
  Dungannon BT71 . . . . 45 C5
CLAGGAN BT79 . . . . 58 A7
Claggan Dr BT80 . . . . 135 D7
Claggan La BT80 . . . . 135 D7
Claggan North★ BT82 . . . . . 7 B6
Claggan Pk BT80 . . . . 135 D7

Claggan Rd
  Cookstown BT80 . . . . 31 C5
  Omagh BT79 . . . . 58 B7
Claggan South★ BT82 . . . . 6 F3
Clahernagh★ BT92 . . . . . 119 C1
Clampernow★ BT47 . . . . . . 1 F7
Clampernow Rd BT47 . . . . . 2 A6
Clanabogan Lower★
  BT78 . . . . 55 A5
Clanabogan Rd BT78 . . . . . 55 D8
Clananeese Glebe★ BT70 78 D8
Clan Art Gall★ 8 BT74 . . 138 C5
Clantilew Rd BT62 . . . . 81 E2
Claragh★ BT93 . . . . 86 C5
Claraghmore★ BT78 . . . . . 37 B4
Claragh Rd BT78 . . . . 37 A4
Claraghy★ BT94 . . . . 106 F4
Claranagh★ BT94 . . . . 90 A1
Clare★
  Cookstown BT80 . . . . 43 F7
  Cookstown BT80 . . . . 45 A6
  Omagh BT79 . . . . 41 A2
Clare La BT80 . . . . 45 A6
Claremore★ BT81 . . . . 35 F8
Clare More★ BT76 . . . . 92 F8
Claremore Rd BT81 . . . . . . 22 F1
Clare Upper★ BT81 . . . . . . 35 E8
Clareview★ BT93 . . . . 68 E6
Clarmore Rd BT77 . . . . 75 A1
Clattyhill Rd BT78 . . . . 72 B3
Clay★ BT94 . . . . 116 F6
Cleanally★ BT70 . . . . 75 F2
Cleenagh★ BT92 . . . . 132 D4
Cleenaghan★ BT94 . . . . . . 88 D5
Cleen Gdns 2 BT75 . . . . 107 C8
Cleenish★ BT92 . . . . 115 E8
Cleenish Pk BT92 . . . . 138 A1
Cleen Pk 3 BT75 . . . . . . 107 C8
Cleenriss★ BT92 . . . . 117 A2
Cleens New★ BT74 . . . . . . 102 E7
Cleens Old★ BT74 . . . . 102 E7
Cleffany★ BT75 . . . . 106 D7
Cleggan★ BT74 . . . . 113 D8
Clements Villas 1 BT79 . 136 F4
Clenaghisle★ 87 E8
Clery★ 111 A1
Clevaghy★ BT92 . . . . 125 E7
Cliff Rd BT93 . . . . 64 F4
Clinton Ctr The★ 2
  . . . . 138 D5
Clintyclay Prim Sch BT71 . 80 E3
Clintycracken★ BT71 . . . . . 63 B5
CLOCHAR (CLOGHER)
  BT76 . . . . 93 A4
Cloghaçarah Standing
  Stone★ BT79 . . . . 27 F2
Cloghagaddy★ BT92 . . . . 126 D7
Cloghan★
  Buckode 82 A5
  Enniskillen BT92 . . . . 124 A3
Cloghanachorite★ BT78 . . 38 C1
Cloghanagh★ BT74 . . . . . 103 A6
Cloghbally★ BT94 . . . . 87 E3
Cloghboy★ BT82 . . . . 1 B5
Cloghboy Rd BT82 . . . . 1 C5
CLOGHCOR★ BT70 . . . . 61 C4
Cloghcor★
  Enniskillen BT74 . . . . 104 F1
  Enniskillen BT94 . . . . 116 C8
CLOGHCOR BT82 . . . . 5 B8
Cloghcor Rd BT74 . . . . . . 104 F1
Clogher★ BT92 . . . . 132 C5
Cloglerbog★ BT93 . . . . . . 100 F6
CLOGHER (CLOCHAR)
  BT76 . . . . 93 A4
Clogher Demesne★ BT76 93 A4
Clogherny Rd BT79 . . . . . . 75 A8
Clogherny★
  Dungannon BT70 . . . . 78 D1
  Strabane BT82 . . . . 15 B8
Clogherny Glebe★ BT79 . 16 D4
Clogherny Glebe Lower★
  BT79 . . . . 57 B4
Clogherny Glebe Upper★
  BT79 . . . . 57 D1
Clogherny Rd BT79 . . . . . . 57 D1
Clogher Regional Prim Sch
  BT76 . . . . 92 F5
Clogher Tenements★
  BT76 . . . . 92 F4
Clogher Valley Indep
  Christian Sch BT75 . . . . 91 F1
Cloghfin★
  Armagh BT61 . . . . 98 A2
  Cookstown BT80 . . . . 43 B5
  Dungannon BT71 . . . . 62 B8
  Omagh BT79 . . . . 39 F1
  Omagh BT79 . . . . 58 C3
Cloghfin Rd BT79 . . . . 57 F4
Cloghlin★ BT76 . . . . 93 A1
Cloghmore★ BT92 . . . . . . 128 D8
Cloghmore Chambered
  Grave★ BT79 . . . . 28 E6
Cloghog★
  Cookstown BT80 . . . . 45 B6
  Dungannon BT71 . . . . 62 F3
Cloghoge★
  Enniskillen BT94 . . . . 90 C3
  Swanlinbar 122 D5
Cloghog★ BT82 . . . . 1 E5
Cloghog Lower★ BT78 . . . . 37 E3
Cloghog Rd
  Cookstown BT80 . . . . 135 F4
  Dungannon BT71 . . . . 62 F4
Cloghog Upper★ BT78 . . . . 37 E1
Cloghore★ 64 F4

Cloghornagh★ BT47 . . . . . . 9 E2
Cloghtate★ BT74 . . . . 104 D5
Cloghtogle★ BT94 . . . . . . 105 A5
CLÓIDIGH (CLADY) BT82 . . 11 F6
Clonabay 27 BT71 . . . . 62 C3
Clonagun★ BT92 . . . . 127 C1
Clonakle★ BT62 . . . . 81 D1
Clonamullog★ BT74 . . . . . 103 B2
Clonaog Valley BT92 . . . . 117 C2
Clonatty★ BT92 . . . . 127 C4
Clonavaddy★ BT70 . . . . . . 77 D8
Clonavaddy Rd BT70 . . . . . 77 C8
Clonaweel★ BT93 . . . . 50 C3
Clonbeg★ BT71 . . . . 80 B2
Clonboy★ 127 E2
Clonbunniagh★ BT92 . . . . 115 A8
Cloncah Rock★ BT93 . . . . . 51 B3
Cloncallick★
  Clones 133 B8
  Enniskillen BT92 . . . . 132 F5
Cloncandra Glebe★ BT78 89 C6
Cloncarn★ BT92 . . . . 127 A3
Cloncarrish★ BT62 . . . . . . 81 E4
Cloncarrish Rd BT62 . . . . . 81 E4
Cloncaw★ 110 E2
Cloncloghy★ BT92 . . . . . . 132 E7
Cloncoohy★ BT92 . . . . 129 F4
Cloncore★ BT62 . . . . 81 F5
Cloncore Rd BT62 . . . . 81 F4
Cloncorick★ BT92 . . . . . . 132 E6
Cloncorr★ BT92 . . . . 127 C5
Cloncumber★ 133 A7
Cloncurrin★ 127 E1
Clondallon Dr BT71 . . . . . . 62 E4
Clondaval★ BT92 . . . . 115 D2
Cloneblaugh★ BT77 . . . . . . 75 A1
Clonedergole★ 127 D3
Clonee★ BT93 . . . . 52 B3
Cloneen BT70 . . . . 137 A5
Clonelly★ BT93 . . . . 50 E3
Clonelty★ BT92 . . . . 126 F1
CLONES (CLUAIN EOIS) . . 127 E3
Clones Rd BT92 . . . . 126 F2
Clonfad★ BT92 . . . . 127 D1
Clonfane★ BT92 . . . . 123 D7
Clonfard★ BT92 . . . . 133 A7
CLONFEACLE BT71 . . . . 97 F4
Clonfeacle Rd BT71 . . . . . . 97 F5
Clonfeile★ BT92 . . . . 127 C4
Clongowna★ BT92 . . . . . . 132 F5
Clonkee★ BT92 . . . . 132 B7
Clonkeelan★ 132 E8
Clonkeen★
  Clones 127 F1
  Clones 127 F3
Clonkirk★ 128 A4
Clonleigh Pk 134 A7
Clonliff★ BT92 . . . . 115 E1
Clonlura★ 132 D7
Clonmacash★ 81 D3
Clonmacash Rd BT62 . . . . . 81 B2
Clonmacfelimy★ BT92 . . . 125 C7
Clonmackan★ BT92 . . . . . 127 D2
Clonmain★ BT61 . . . . 98 E7
Clonmain Rd BT61 . . . . 98 E7
Clonmakate★ BT62 . . . . . . 81 D6
Clonmakate Rd BT62 . . . . . 81 E5
Clonmaulin★ BT92 . . . . . . 127 C2
Clonmeen Cotts BT71 . . . . 62 F4
Clonmin Glebe★ BT92 . . . 125 E4
Clonmore★
  Dungannon BT71 . . . . 80 B1
  Dungannon BT71 . . . . 80 D5
Clonmore Gdns BT79 . . . . 136 A7
Clonmore Rd BT71 . . . . . . 80 D5
Clonmore Villas BT71 . . . . 80 E5
Clonnagore★ 132 D8
Clonnaroo★ BT92 . . . . . . 132 A6
Clonnestin★ 132 E5
CLONOE BT71 . . . . 62 E2
Clonoony★ 132 B6
Clonosey★ 131 D1
Clonoula★ 132 C8
Clonrye★ 132 D5
Clonshannagh★ BT92 . . . 132 B6
Clonshanvo★ 132 E6
Clontarf Dr
  5 Omagh BT78 . . . . 38 D1
  9 Omagh BT78 . . . . 55 D8
Clontarf Hts
  12 Omagh BT78 . . . . 38 D1
  10 Omagh BT78 . . . . 55 D8
Clontask★ 132 C5
Clonteevy★ BT71 . . . . 80 C3
Clontelaghan★ BT92 . . . . 123 B6
Clontibret★ 127 F1
Clontivrin★ BT92 . . . . 127 C2
Clontreat★ 128 A1
Clonturkle★ BT92 . . . . . . 123 C5
Clontycarty★ BT60 . . . . . . 111 E6
Clontycarty La BT60 . . . . . 111 E6
Clontyclay★ BT71 . . . . 80 E4
Clontyclevin★ BT70 . . . . . . 77 F4
Clontyclevin Rd BT70 . . . . 77 F3
Clontycoora★ BT94 . . . . . 115 E4
Clontyfallow★ BT70 . . . . . 77 F3
Clontyferagh★
  Cookstown BT80 . . . . 43 F7
  Enniskillen BT92 . . . . 114 D5
Clontylew★ BT62 . . . . 81 E2
Clontymore★ BT92 . . . . . . 115 D3
Clontymullan★ BT92 . . . . 115 B5
Clontyseer★ 64 B3
Clonumphry★ BT92 . . . . . 115 D4
Clonursan Glebe★ BT92 115 D4
Cloon★ BT94 . . . . 116 D8
Cloonacarn★ BT94 . . . . . . 116 D4
Cloonatreane★ BT92 . . . . 113 F6

Cloonatrig★ BT92 . . . . . . 115 E6
Cloonatumpher★ BT92. . 114 A5
Cloonaveel★ BT74 . . . . . . 114 C8
Cloonavoan★ BT74 . . . . . 104 C1
Cloonty★ BT78 . . . . 24 C1
Cloonty Rd BT78 . . . . 24 B1
Cloonycoppoge★ BT76 . . . 93 C3
Cloony Rd BT81 . . . . 22 C6
Clós Chill Mhic Cormaic
  (Kilmacormick Cl)
  BT74 . . . . 138 D7
Cloughan Rd BT79 . . . . 40 C4
Cloughcor Rd BT82 . . . . 5 B8
Clougherny Rd BT70 . . . . . 78 D1
Cloughfin Rd BT80 . . . . 43 C6
Cloughglass Rd BT79 . . . . 40 F3
Cloven Eden★ BT61 . . . . . 98 F6
Cloveneden Rd BT61 . . . . . 98 E6
Clover Brae BT74 . . . . 104 C6
Cloverhill BT71 . . . . 98 A8
Clowney★ 130 B1
Clowninny★ 131 A5
Cloy★ BT93 . . . . 52 D1
CLUAIN EOIS (CLONES) . . 127 E3
Clunahill Glebe★ BT78 . . . 53 B8
Cluntoe (Quin)★ BT80 . . . 47 B6
Cluntoe (Richardson)★
  BT80 . . . . 47 C5
Cluntoe View BT71 . . . . . . 46 F3
Cluntydoon★ BT80 . . . . . . 31 A2
Cluntyganny★ BT80 . . . . . . 31 B2
Cluny Gdns 11 F7
Clyhannagh★ BT92 . . . . . 113 B4
Coa★ BT94 . . . . 88 E3
Coagh★
  Cookstown BT80 . . . . 46 C7
  Enniskillen BT93 . . . . 103 C8
Coaghan★ BT92 . . . . 113 D4
COAGH (AN CUACH) BT80. . 46 B7
Coagh Prim Sch BT45 . . . . 46 A7
Coagh Rd
  Cookstown BT80 . . . . 135 F5
  Dungannon BT71 . . . . 62 D8
Coagh St BT80 . . . . 135 D6
Coalhill★ BT92 . . . . 118 A5
COALISLAND (OILEÁN AN
  GHUAIL) BT71 . . . . 62 B3
Coalisland Rd BT71 . . . . . 137 D8
Coalpit Rd BT71 . . . . 61 D2
Coa Rd BT74 . . . . 104 B7
Coasan★ BT93 . . . . 100 C2
Coash★ BT71 . . . . 79 F7
Coash Rd BT71 . . . . 79 F7
Cohannan★ BT71 . . . . 80 C6
COILTE CLOCHAIR
  (KILTYCLOGHER) 99 D6
Cole★ BT78 . . . . 91 C6
Colebrook Demesne★
  BT94 . . . . 106 F5
Coleman★ 127 A1
Coles Hill★ BT74 . . . . 138 A5
Coleshill Cres BT74 . . . . . 138 B4
Coleshill Pk BT74 . . . . 138 B4
Coleshill Rd BT74 . . . . 138 A4
College Gdns BT74 . . . . . . 104 B5
College Gr 2 BT82 . . . . . 134 C1
College Hall La BT60 . . . . 111 F5
College Lands Rd BT71 . . . 98 C7
College of Agriculture, Food
  & Rural Enterprise
  BT74 . . . . 104 A7
College Pk La BT74 . . . . . 104 B5
Collegiate Gram Sch
  BT74 . . . . 138 F5
Collins Wlk BT82 . . . . 134 C2
Collow★ BT78 . . . . 36 C1
Collowen★ BT71 . . . . 62 D2
Columbas Dr 28 BT71 . . . 62 C3
Columbkille Rd BT62 . . . . . 81 F7
Comaghy★ BT75 . . . . 107 D7
Comber Rd BT79 . . . . 39 D2
Comber Terr 17 BT71 . . . . 62 C3
Commas★ 121 E3
Common★ BT81 . . . . 21 E4
Common Moss★ BT71 . . . . 62 D7
Commons★
  Aughnacloy BT69 . . . . 95 A5
  Belleek BT92 . . . . 65 B4
Commons The BT92 . . . . . 115 B7
Common The 134 A7
Community Hospl 134 B4
Conagher★ BT93 . . . . 84 E5
Conaghy★ 128 E4
Concaroe★ BT93 . . . . 86 F3
Concess★ BT82 . . . . 12 C3
Concess Rd BT82 . . . . 12 D3
Conckera★ BT92 . . . . 127 C3
Conerick★ BT94 . . . . 103 F8
Coneyburrow★ 134 A5
Coneyburrow BT82 . . . . . . 134 B6
Coney Pk BT71 . . . . 62 D2
Coney Twr★ 63 F1
Coneywarren Dr BT78 . . . . 38 D3
Congo★
  Dungannon BT71 . . . . 61 E2
  Enniskillen BT94 . . . . 117 A5
Connaghty Rd BT78 . . . . . . 38 C6
Conneyburrow 134 A5
Connolly Pk BT94 . . . . 69 B3
Connors La BT60 . . . . 111 E3
Conthem Rd BT81 . . . . 12 F6
Convent Rd BT80 . . . . 135 C4
Convent View BT78 . . . . . 136 B4
Conway Cl BT80 . . . . 29 F1
Conway Pl BT82 . . . . 126 A7
Conywarren★ BT78 . . . . . . 38 D3
Cooey★ BT60 . . . . 111 F4
Cooke Cres BT80 . . . . 135 D3

Cookstown BT80 . . . . 135 D6
COOKSTOWN (AN CHORR
  CHRÍOCHACH) BT80 . . . . 135 E5
Cookstown Ent Ctr BT80 135 B2
Cookstown High Sch
  BT80 . . . . 135 E5
Cookstown Leisure Ctr
  BT80 . . . . 135 D4
Cookstown Prim Sch
  BT80 . . . . 135 D5
Cookstown Rd BT71 . . . . . 137 C8
Coolacrim★ BT92 . . . . 114 F3
Coolageery★ BT70 . . . . . . 76 D3
Coolaghty★ BT93 . . . . 52 F4
Coolaghty Rd BT78 . . . . . . 24 A8
Coolaghy★ BT78 . . . . 24 D5
Coolaheran Rd BT79 . . . . . 41 B7
Coolaness★ BT94 . . . . 69 D4
Coolaran★ BT92 . . . . 117 F2
Coolarkan★ BT74 . . . . 101 F3
Coolatinny★ BT71 . . . . 62 E8
Coolavannagh★ BT78 . . . . 53 D7
Coolback★ BT94. . . . . 70 C2
Coolback Rd BT79 . . . . 59 B7
Coolbeg★ BT94. . . . . 116 D3
Coolbuck★ BT94 . . . . 105 B4
Coolcholly★ 64 A7
Coolcoghill★ BT94 . . . . . . 106 C2
Coolcran★ BT94. . . . . 89 F3
Coolcrannel★ BT94 . . . . . 117 B6
Coolcreaghy★ BT81 . . . . . 35 C7
Coolcreaghy Rd BT81 . . . . 35 C7
Coolcush★ BT71. . . . . 79 E5
Coole★ BT71 . . . . 63 A4
Coole Dr BT74 . . . . 138 C4
Coole Rd BT71 . . . . 63 A4
Coolermoney★ BT82. . . . . . . 5 C7
Coolermoney Rd BT82. . . . . 5 C8
Coolesker★ BT79 . . . . 57 B5
Cooley★ BT79. . . . . 57 D4
Cooley Prim Sch BT79 . . . . 57 E5
Cooley Rd BT79 . . . . 57 D4
Coolgarran★ BT94 . . . . 87 F7
Coolhill★
  Dungannon BT70 . . . . 77 E4
  Dungannon BT71 . . . . 137 F3
Coolhill Ave BT70 . . . . 77 E4
Coolhill Rd BT70 . . . . 77 E4
Coolinfin Glebe★ BT92 . . 122 E8
Coolisk★ BT94 . . . . 69 A4
Coolkeeghan★ BT80 . . . . 135 C1
Coolkeeragh★ BT78 . . . . . 37 D1
Coolkeeragh Rd BT78 . . . . 37 E1
Coolkill★
  Armagh BT60. . . . . 111 D1
  Dungannon BT70 . . . . 78 F2
  Enniskillen BT92 . . . . 124 A6
Coolkill Rd BT60 . . . . 111 E2
Coollane★ BT94 . . . . 117 A8
Coolmaghery★ BT82. . . . . . . 1 F6
Coolmaghry★ BT70. . . . . . 60 E5
Coolmaghry Rd BT70. . . . . 60 E5
Coolmount Ave BT80 . . . . 135 C8
Coolmount Dr BT80 . . . . . 135 C7
Coolnacarte★ 133 A5
Coolnacrunaght★ BT81. . . 23 B1
Coolnafranky★ BT80. . . . . 135 E3
Coolnafranky Pk BT80. . . 135 E3
Coolnagard Ave BT78 . . . 136 B1
Coolnagard Brae BT78 . . . 136 B1
Coolnagard Cl BT78 . . . . . 136 C2
Coolnagard Ct BT78 . . . . . 136 B1
Coolnagard Dr BT78 . . . . . 136 B2
Coolnagard Gdns BT78 . . 136 B1
Coolnagard Gn BT78 . . . . 136 B1
Coolnagard Gr BT78 . . . . . 136 C2
Coolnagard Hts BT78 . . . . 136 C1
Coolnagard La BT78 . . . . . 136 B2
Coolnagard Lower★
  BT78 . . . . 136 B3
Coolnagard Mdws BT78 . 136 C2
Coolnagard Rd BT78 . . . . 136 C1
Coolnagard Sq BT78 . . . . 136 B1
Coolnagard Upper★
  BT78 . . . . 136 B2
Coolnagard View BT78. . . 136 C2
Coolnagard Way BT/8. . . 136 B1
Coolnagrane★ BT94 . . . . . 105 D4
Coolnahavil★ BT80 . . . . . 135 E2
Coolnaherin Park BT81. . 23 A1
Coolnalong★ BT92 . . . . . . 128 B8
Coolnamarrow★ BT92 . . . 126 F8
Coolnamonan★ BT47 . . . . . 9 C8
Coolnashanton★ BT74 . . 116 A7
Coolnasillagh★ BT92 . . . . 118 E1
Coolough Dr BT71 . . . . 63 A5
Coolrakelly★ BT74 . . . . . . 106 C7
Coolreaghs★ BT80 . . . . 31 E1
Coolreaghs Cres BT80. . . 135 B8
Coolreaghs Rd BT80 . . . . 135 C8
Cooltrain★ BT94 . . . . 88 E2
Cooltrane★ BT94 . . . . 106 E4
Coolyermer★ BT74 . . . . . . 103 A3
Cooneen★ BT75 . . . . 107 D3
COONEEN BT75. . . . . 107 E4
Cooneen Rd BT75 . . . . 107 C7
Cooper Cres BT74. . . . . . . 138 C5
Copes Stone★ BT76. . . . . . 92 E6
Copney★
  Dungannon BT71. . . . . 80 E3
  Omagh BT79 . . . . 41 B6
Coppanagh★ 133 E1
Coragh★
  Belturbet 130 F6
  Enniskillen BT92 . . . . 122 F5

Coragh continued
Enniskillen BT92 . . . . 124 B5
Coragh (Crawford) 🔵
BT92 . . . . 123 A8
Coragh Glebe 🔵 BT92 . . . 115 A1
Corbally 🔵
Omagh BT78 . . . . 71 B8
Omagh BT78 . . . . 72 E3
Corbally Rd BT78 . . . . 72 C5
Corban Ave BT74 . . . . 138 D7
Corbane 🔵 BT92 . . . . 119 F3
Corboe 🔵 BT76 . . . . 74 C2
Corboe Rd
Clogher BT76 . . . . 74 B3
Omagh BT78 . . . . 73 F6
Corby Rd BT80 . . . . 30 D4
Corchoney 🔵 BT80 . . . . 43 E7
Corchoney Cross Roads
BT80 . . . . 43 E6
Corclare 🔵 110 C6
Corcloghy 🔵 BT76 . . . . . . 109 C7
Corcreevy 🔵 BT75 . . . . 91 B1
Corcreevy Ct BT75 . . . . 91 C1
Corcreevy Demesne 🔵
BT75 . . . . 107 B8
Corcummins 🔵 133 B7
Cordarragh 🔵 BT92 . . . . . 114 A4
Corderry 🔵 BT69 . . . . 95 B7
Cordoolagh 🔵 BT92 . . . . . 120 C2
Cordromedy 🔵 BT78 . . . . . . 89 C8
Cordwood 🔵 BT93 . . . . 50 C1
Corfannan 🔵 BT94 . . . . . . 117 A7
Corfehan 🔵 BT60 . . . . 111 D2
Corflugh 🔵 BT92 . . . . 126 F8
Corgary 🔵 BT93 . . . . 83 B7
Corgary Rd BT81 . . . . 20 D6
Corgreagh 🔵 130 E4
Coriaght East 🔵 BT93 . . . . . 52 C6
Corick 🔵 BT76 . . . . 93 A6
Corickmore 🔵 BT78 . . . . . . 14 C1
Corick Rd BT76 . . . . 74 D3
Corkan Isle 🔵 4 F7
Corkeeran 🔵 128 E1
Corkhill Rd BT78 . . . . 74 D3
Corkill 🔵
Cookstown BT80 . . . . 43 E8
Dungannon BT70 . . . . 60 E6
Omagh BT78 . . . . 74 C4
Omagh BT78 . . . . 88 F8
Corkill Demesne 🔵 BT78 . . 74 B4
Corkill Rd BT80 . . . . 43 D8
Corkragh 🔵 BT78 . . . . 88 F7
Corlacky 🔵 BT75 . . . . 107 C5
Corlaghaloon 🔵 BT92 . . . 119 B2
Corlaghdergan 🔵 BT78 . . . 71 A7
Corlagh Rd BT78 . . . . 71 B7
Corlaght West 🔵 BT93 . . . . 50 E4
Corlatt 🔵
Enniskillen BT92 . . . . 126 A2
Enniskillen BT92 . . . . 130 F8
Corlave 🔵 BT93 . . . . 50 F6
Corlea 🔵
Ballyshannon 64 F6
Omagh BT78 . . . . 37 F1
Omagh BT78 . . . . 89 A8
Corleaghan 🔵 BT76 . . . . . 109 B7
Corleaghan Rd BT76 . . . . . 92 C1
Corlea Rd
Dungannon BT70 . . . . 59 F2
Omagh BT78 . . . . 37 F1
Corleggy 🔵 131 B4
Corlough 🔵 BT94 . . . . 106 F2
Cormeen 🔵 129 B1
Cormonalea 🔵 BT92 . . . . . 126 A8
Cormore 🔵 BT78 . . . . 74 E2
Cormore Rd BT78 . . . . 74 F3
Cormullagh 🔵 BT70 . . . . . . 78 E5
Cornabracken 🔵 BT78 . . . . 38 D1
Cornabrass 🔵 BT92 . . . . . 126 B1
Cornacaghan 🔵 BT92 . . . . 131 E7
Cornaclare or Johnstown 🔵
BT92 . . . . 127 B5
Cornacrea 🔵
Enniskillen BT92 . . . . 122 F7
Enniskillen BT93 . . . . 68 F7
Cornacreeve 🔵 BT92 . . . . 119 E3
Cornacully 🔵 BT93 . . . . . . 100 C6
Cornadarum 🔵 BT93 . . . . . 83 B7
Cornagague Prim Sch
BT92 . . . . 127 C6
Cornagee 🔵
Blacklion 112 C5
Enniskillen BT74 . . . . 113 F8
Cornagrade 🔵 BT74 . . . . . 138 C6
Cornagrade Rd BT74 . . . . 138 D7
Cornagran 🔵 122 E5
Cornaguillagh 🔵 120 D5
Cornagun 🔵 BT92 . . . . . . 123 A7
Cornahaltie 🔵 BT93 . . . . . . 83 D8
Cornahaw 🔵 112 C2
Cornahawla 🔵 BT94 . . . . . 114 A7
Cornahoule 🔵 BT92 . . . . . 124 C3
Cornakessagh 🔵 BT94 . . . 106 E3
Cornakill 🔵 BT92 . . . . 125 A2
Cornaleck 🔵
Belturbet 131 A5
Enniskillen BT92 . . . . 124 C7
Cornalon 🔵 122 D2
Cornamaddy 🔵 BT70 . . . . . . 59 F5
Cornamaddy Rd BT70 . . . . . 59 E7
Cornamurry 🔵 BT92 . . . . . 119 F1
Cornamuck 🔵 BT78 . . . . . . 71 B7
Cornamucklagh 🔵
Augher BT77 . . . . 93 E5
Enniskillen BT92 . . . . 127 E7

Cornamucklagh continued
Enniskillen BT94 . . . . 106 D3
Omagh BT78 . . . . 72 C6
Cornanoe 🔵 BT92 . . . . 124 D7
Cornapaste 🔵 132 D3
Cornarooslan 🔵 BT75 . . . 108 A2
Cornashannel 🔵 BT94 . . . 116 E8
Cornashee 🔵 BT92 . . . . . . 117 D3
Cornashesko 🔵 BT78 . . . . . 52 F8
Cornashesko 🔵 BT92 . . . . 114 F1
Cornaskeoge 🔵 BT92 . . . . 123 A8
Cornavarrow 🔵 BT78 . . . . . 54 A5
Cornavarrow Rd BT78 . . . . 53 F7
Cornavray 🔵 BT92 . . . . . . 126 A4
Cornmill Her Ctr 4 BT71 . 62 B3
Coronation Pk
Aughnacloy BT69 . . . . 95 A4
5 Sion Mills BT82 . . . . 12 D6
Corporation St 6 BT74 . . 138 D4
Corr 🔵 BT71 . . . . 62 E1
Corraback 🔵 130 E4
Corrachrow 🔵 BT92 . . . . . 116 E2
Corraclare 🔵 BT94 . . . . . . 116 D7
Corraclare Big 🔵 BT92 . . . 124 E3
Corraclare Little 🔵 BT92 . 124 E3
Corraclare North 🔵 BT92 . 123 F7
Corracleigh 🔵 121 A3
Corracloon 🔵 BT93 . . . . . . 85 F8
Corracloona 🔵 100 A3
Corracoash 🔵
Enniskillen BT92 . . . . 115 D2
Enniskillen BT92 . . . . 130 D8
Corraderrybrock 🔵 BT93 . 100 D4
Corradillar 🔵 BT92 . . . . . . 125 A5
Corradinna 🔵 BT78 . . . . 54 D7
Corradinna Rd BT78 . . . . . 37 B1
Corradovar 🔵 BT92 . . . . . 124 D6
Corradreenan 🔵 BT92 . . . 114 A3
Corradreenan East 🔵
BT92 . . . . 114 E1
Corrafannoge 🔵 BT94 . . . 105 E3
Corraghy 🔵 BT92 . . . . 119 B2
Corraglass 🔵 BT74 . . . . . . 114 C7
Corraglass West 🔵 BT93 . 100 F1
Corragole 🔵 BT92 . . . . 123 E6
Corragunt 🔵 BT92 . . . . . . 120 A7
Corraharra 🔵 BT92 . . . . . . 130 F7
Corraheen 🔵 BT92 . . . . . . 123 A7
Corrahesk Rd BT78 . . . . . . 72 D1
Corrainey Gdns BT70 . . . . 137 A6
Corrainey Pk BT70 . . . . . . 137 A6
Corrainy 🔵 BT71 . . . . 62 B1
Corrakeel 🔵 BT93 . . . . 65 C3
Corrakelly 🔵 BT92 . . . . . . 123 E7
Corralea 🔵 BT93 . . . . 100 E1
Corralea Activity Ctr ★
BT93 . . . . 100 E1
Corraleek 🔵 BT92 . . . . 120 A7
Corraleskin 🔵 99 C5
Corralinnen 🔵 BT74 . . . . . 103 D4
Corralongford 🔵 BT75 . . . 107 B6
Corrameen 🔵 BT92 . . . . . . 123 B6
Corramonaghan 🔵 BT92 . 124 D2
Corramore 🔵
Enniskillen BT93 . . . . 83 B5
Omagh BT79 . . . . 16 F4
Corramore Rd BT79 . . . . . 16 C3
Corranaheen 🔵 BT92 . . . . 122 E7
Corranarry 🔵 BT79 . . . . . . 39 B5
Corr and Dunavally 🔵
BT71 . . . . 98 B7
Corranearty 🔵 122 D4
Corranewy 🔵 BT94 . . . . . . 116 F6
Corranierna 🔵 129 E3
Corranny 🔵 BT92 . . . . 119 C2
Corran Rd BT79 . . . . 39 A4
Corraquill 🔵 130 A5
Corrard 🔵
Enniskillen BT94 . . . . 116 C3
Enniskillen BT94 . . . . 117 A6
Corrardaghy 🔵 BT92 . . . . 127 C7
Corrardreen 🔵 BT92 . . . . . 123 B6
Corrashesk 🔵 BT78 . . . . . . 72 D2
Corrasheskin 🔵 BT78 . . . . 54 B4
Corrashesk Rd BT78 . . . . . 72 D2
Corratary 🔵 BT79 . . . . 17 D6
Corrateskin 🔵 BT74 . . . . . 113 E7
Corratistune 🔵 BT92 . . . . 124 E5
Corratrasna 🔵
Enniskillen BT92 . . . . 124 B1
Enniskillen BT92 . . . . 124 B6
Corravehy 🔵 BT92 . . . . . . 123 E7
Corrawully 🔵 BT92 . . . . . . 114 D2
Correen 🔵 BT92 . . . . 113 F5
Corresheskin Rd BT78 . . . . 54 B3
Corrickbeg 🔵 BT78 . . . . . . 14 D1
Corrickmore Ave BT78 . . . . 14 C1
Corrigan Hill Rd BT71 . . . . 98 C6
Corrinshigo 🔵
Enniskillen BT92 . . . . 119 F3
Knockatallan 120 E5
Corr Rd BT71 . . . . 62 E1
Corry 🔵
Belleek BT93 . . . . 65 A3
Enniskillen BT92 . . . . 130 B6
Corrycroar 🔵 BT70 . . . . . . 60 C6
Corrycroar Rd BT70 . . . . . . 60 C7
Corsale 🔵 BT92 . . . . 125 E4
Corscreenagh 🔵 BT92 . . . 126 E4
Corsenshin 🔵 BT92 . . . . . 125 F5
Cortaher 🔵 BT92 . . . . 119 E3
Cortrasna 🔵 BT92 . . . . . . 119 F1
Cor Tynan 🔵 BT68 . . . . . . 111 C3
Cortynan Rd BT68 . . . . . . 111 D3
Corvanaghan 🔵 BT80 . . . . 30 D2
Corvanaghan Rd BT80 . . . . 29 F2

Cosbystown 🔵 BT93 . . . . . . 86 D6
Cossycon 🔵 BT93 . . . . 87 B2
Cottagequinn 🔵 BT71 . . . 137 D2
Court Grave ★ BT93 . . . . . . 84 B2
Courtrai Pk BT82 . . . . 134 E5
Cow Hill Rd BT71 . . . . 98 C7
Coxtown 🔵 1 B8
Coyagh 🔵 BT78 . . . . 72 D8
Coyagh Glebe 🔵 BT78 . . . . 72 E7
Coyagh Rd BT78 . . . . 72 D8
Crackrawer Rd BT70 . . . . . 75 F5
Craghan 🔵 BT94 . . . . 88 B4
Craghan Rd BT94 . . . . 88 B4
CRAIG BT47 . . . . 7 E2
Craigatuke 🔵 BT82 . . . . . . 14 C6
Craigavon Pk BT78 . . . . . . 73 C6
Craigavon Rd BT78 . . . . . . 73 C6
Craighill Rd BT79 . . . . 39 D4
Craigmonaghan (Funston) 🔵
BT81 . . . . 22 F6
Craigmonaghan (Nelson) 🔵
BT81 . . . . 22 F5
Craigmont La BT81 . . . . . . 22 F5
Craignagapple 🔵 BT82 . . . . 6 B1
Craigna Rd BT82 . . . . 5 C2
Craigs 🔵 BT80 . . . . 31 B1
Craigs Rd BT80 . . . . 31 A2
Craigtown 🔵 BT47 . . . . 2 A5
Cran 🔵 BT75 . . . . 107 A8
CRANAGH BT79 . . . . 16 E5
Cranagill 🔵 BT62 . . . . 81 C1
Crancussy Rd BT80 . . . . . . 42 C7
Crandreen 🔵 BT81 . . . . 22 A5
Cranebrook Cres BT71 . . . 62 D1
Cranfield 🔵 BT80 . . . . 45 A7
Cranlome 🔵 BT70 . . . . 77 A8
Cranlome Rd BT70 . . . . 77 B7
Cranmore Rd BT79 . . . . . . 56 D4
Crannagael 🔵 BT62 . . . . . . 81 C1
Crannoge 🔵 BT79 . . . . 56 E3
Crannogue 🔵 BT79 . . . . . . 59 C5
Crannog View BT74 . . . . . 138 F4
Cranny 🔵
Omagh BT78 . . . . 72 C8
Omagh BT78 . . . . 73 A8
Omagh BT78 . . . . 56 B8
Cranny Cl 3 BT79 . . . . 39 B1
Cranny Gr 4 BT79 . . . . 39 B1
Cranny Sch 7 BT79 . . . . . . 39 B1
Cranslough 🔵 BT70 . . . . . . 77 F2
Cratley 🔵 BT71 . . . . 45 D3
Cravenny Irish 🔵 BT70 . . . 76 F1
Cravenny Rd BT70 . . . . 76 E2
Cravenny Scotch 🔵 BT70 . 76 E2
Crawfords Hill 🔵 BT74 . . . 102 F8
Crawfords La BT78 . . . . . . 71 F8
Creagh 🔵 BT94 . . . . 106 C8
Creaghan 🔵 BT71 . . . . 98 A2
Creaghan Glebe 🔵 BT82 . . . 6 D8
Creaghcor 🔵 BT92 . . . . 1 C6
Creagh Cross Roads
BT94 . . . . 106 D8
Creaghmore Rd BT78 . . . . 36 F3
Creamery Cl BT92 . . . . 114 E4
Creamery Pk BT94 . . . . . . 105 A2
Creeduff 🔵 BT81 . . . . 22 A2
Creeduff Rd BT81 . . . . 21 F2
Creenagh 🔵 BT71 . . . . 62 C2
Creenagh Bridge Rd BT71 62 B2
Creenagh La BT71 . . . . 62 B1
Creenagho 🔵 BT93 . . . . . . 113 C8
Creenagh Rd BT71 . . . . 62 B1
Creevagh 🔵 BT80 . . . . 31 B3
Creevagh La BT80 . . . . 31 C3
Creevagh Lower 🔵 BT71 . . 61 D3
Creevagh Rd
Cookstown BT80 . . . . 30 F3
Dungannon BT70 . . . . 61 B3
Creevagh Upper 🔵 BT70 . . 61 C7
Creevaghy 🔵 128 B5
Creevangar (Alexander) 🔵
BT78 . . . . 55 B7
Creevanmore (Crosby) 🔵
BT78 . . . . 55 B6
Creevanmore (Hunter) 🔵
BT78 . . . . 55 B6
Creevanmore (White) 🔵
BT78 . . . . 55 C6
Creeve 🔵
Cookstown BT80 . . . . 31 C4
Dungannon BT70 . . . . 61 B5
Creevedonnell 🔵 BT47 . . . . 2 D6
Creevehill 🔵 BT75 . . . . 90 E1
Creevelea 🔵 128 D3
Creevelough 🔵 BT70 . . . . . 96 C5
Creevelough Rd BT70 . . . . 96 C6
Creevnagar Rd BT78 . . . . . 55 C6
Creevy 🔵 BT81 . . . . 23 C2
Creevy Lower 🔵 BT81 . . . . 22 E7
Creevy Rd BT81 . . . . 23 C2
Creevy Upper 🔵 BT81 . . . . 22 E8
Creggan 🔵 BT79 . . . . 41 E8
Cregganconroe 🔵 BT70 . . . 42 B4
Creggandevesky 🔵 BT79 . . 41 F3
Creggan Pk BT79 . . . . 136 B6
Creggan Rd BT79 . . . . 41 E4
Crescent The BT80 . . . . 46 B7
Crest Rd BT74 . . . . 138 E3
Crevanagh Rd BT79 . . . . . . 56 A8
Crevenagh Downs BT79 . . 136 F2
Crevenagh Dr BT79 . . . . . . 136 F2
Crevenagh Gr BT79 . . . . . . 136 F2
Crevenagh View BT79 . . . . 136 F2
Crevenagh Way 3 BT79 . . . 36 F2
Crevinish Pk BT93 . . . . 68 F8
Crevinish Rd BT93 . . . . 69 A7
Crevinish 🔵 BT93 . . . . 68 E7

Crevinish Castle (in ruins) ★
BT93 . . . . 68 E7
Crew 🔵
Dungannon BT70 . . . . 76 A2
Dungannon BT71 . . . . 79 C7
Crewhill Terr 14 BT71 . . . . 62 C3
Crew Lower 🔵 BT82 . . . . . . 23 D6
Crew Rd
Dungannon BT70 . . . . 76 A2
Strabane BT82 . . . . 23 C7
Crew Upper 🔵 BT82 . . . . . . 23 C6
Crievagh Prim Sch BT80 . . 31 A3
Crighdenis 🔵 BT81 . . . . 33 E6
Crighshane 🔵 BT81 . . . . . . 33 D6
Crighton Pk BT74 . . . . 104 D2
Crillan 🔵 BT93 . . . . 51 D3
Crilly 🔵
Aughnacloy BT69 . . . . 95 D3
Pettigoe 34 C3
Crilly Pk BT81 . . . . 21 E1
Crilly's Hill 🔵 BT81 . . . . . . 34 E8
Crillys Hill Rd BT81 . . . . . . 34 E8
Crimlin 🔵 BT93 . . . . 52 B4
Croaghan 🔵
Enniskillen BT92 . . . . 117 D4
Enniskillen BT93 . . . . 86 F1
Croaghan Hts 134 A7
Croaghbrack 🔵 32 C5
Croaghbreesy 🔵 65 C7
Croaghnakern 🔵 19 B1
Croaghrim 🔵
Enniskillen BT74 . . . . 103 A6
Enniskillen BT92 . . . . 114 C5
Crockacleaven 🔵 BT75 . . . 108 A5
Crockada 🔵 BT92 . . . . 120 B4
Crockadreen 🔵 BT75 . . . . 107 E1
Crockahilly Rd BT47 . . . . 9 A4
Crockaleen 🔵 BT94 . . . . . . 116 A6
Crockanboy Rd BT79 . . . . . 26 F6
Crockaness 🔵 BT92 . . . . . 118 A3
Crockan Rd BT82 . . . . 5 F8
Crockapharson Rd BT78 . . 38 A1
Crockareddy 🔵 BT92 . . . . 115 D7
Crockarevan 🔵 BT92 . . . . 127 A8
Crockatanty 🔵
Omagh BT78 . . . . 17 A1
Omagh BT79 . . . . 28 C8
Crockateggal 🔵 BT78 . . . . . 50 F4
Crockatore Rd BT78 . . . . . . 13 F2
Crockavarred Rd BT78 . . . . 54 C3
Crockawaddy Glebe 🔵
BT92 . . . . 119 D2
Crockbane Rd BT80 . . . . . . 29 C2
Crockerahoas 🔵 BT92 . . . 132 A7
Crockett Pk 9 BT81 . . . . . . 22 E5
Crockmore Rd BT47 . . . . 8 A5
Crocknaboghill 🔵 BT92 . . 119 C1
Crocknacor Rd BT79 . . . . . 56 F8
Crocknacreevy 🔵 BT92 . . 115 C1
Crocknafarbrague 🔵
BT78 . . . . 72 C1
Crocknageeragh Rd BT78 . 54 F7
Crocknagowan 🔵 BT92 . . . 118 B2
Crocknagrally 🔵 BT75 . . . 107 F4
Crocknagross 🔵 BT92 . . . 119 F3
Crocknahull 🔵 BT75 . . . . . 107 F7
Crocknakeeragh 🔵 BT92 . 114 D1
Crocknakelly Glebe 🔵
BT92 . . . . 119 B5
Crocknanane 🔵 BT92 . . . . 118 A3
Crockroe Rd BT78 . . . . 90 D8
Crockrour Rd BT79 . . . . . . 14 F8
Croft The 1 BT78 . . . . 71 F8
Croghan View BT82 . . . . . . 134 D4
Crom 🔵 BT92 . . . . 125 D1
Cromaghy 🔵 BT92 . . . . . . 128 A8
Crom Castle ★ BT92 . . . . . 131 A8
Cromcruaich Way BT93 . . 112 F7
Crom Est & Gdn ★ BT92 . 125 D1
Cronalaghy 🔵 21 C7
Croneen 🔵 BT93 . . . . 52 D3
Croneen Barr 🔵 BT93 . . . . 52 F1
Cronghill 🔵 BT69 . . . . 96 A6
Cronkill 🔵 BT71 . . . . 80 F7
Croostan 🔵 BT92 . . . . 124 E5
Crosh 🔵
Omagh BT78 . . . . 25 B8
Omagh BT79 . . . . 39 D5
Croshballinree 🔵 BT78 . . . 25 A7
Crosh Rd
Omagh BT78 . . . . 25 C8
Omagh BT79 . . . . 39 D4
Cross 🔵 BT74 . . . . 104 A7
Crossan 🔵 BT78 . . . . 71 B4
Crossan Rd BT78 . . . . 71 B4
Crossbane 🔵 133 F6
Crossboy 🔵 BT70 . . . . 76 B7
Crosscavanagh 🔵 BT70 . . . 60 B2
Crosscavanagh Rd BT70 . . 60 C2
Crossdernot 🔵 BT70 . . . . . 60 F5
Crossglebe 🔵 BT80 . . . . . . 44 D1
Cross Glebe 🔵 BT80 . . . . . 44 D2
Crosshill Hts BT78 . . . . 71 E7
Crossmoyle 🔵 127 E2
Crossmurrin 🔵 BT92 . . . . 113 C3
Crossmurrin Nature
Reserve ★ BT92 . . . . 113 C3
Crossnacaldoo 🔵 109 F5
Crossowen 🔵 BT76 . . . . 93 A5
Crossowen Rd BT77 . . . . . . 93 B5
Crossowens Gdns BT76 . . . 93 A5
Crossreagh 🔵 133 F7
Cross St
5 Enniskillen BT74 . . . . . 138 D5
Lisnaskea BT92 . . . . 117 D2
Crossteely 🔵 BT70 . . . . 78 E2
Crott 🔵 BT74 . . . . 102 C8

Crottan 🔵 BT93 . . . . 101 F1
Crotty Rd BT78 . . . . 55 F2
Crouck 🔵 BT79 . . . . 28 E5
Crouck Rd BT79 . . . . 29 A5
Crouk Rd BT79 . . . . 28 E4
Crowhill Rd BT78 . . . . 25 E6
Crownhall 🔵 BT71 . . . . 79 B1
Cruckaclady 🔵 14 E5
Crucknamona 🔵 BT78 . . . . 55 B6
Crucknamona Rd BT78 . . . 55 B6
Crumlin Rd BT82 . . . . 7 A8
Crummer 🔵 BT92 . . . . 115 A2
Crummy 🔵 BT92 . . . . 117 A4
Cruntully 🔵 BT93 . . . . 51 F7
Cuillaghan 🔵 130 A4
Culbuck 🔵 BT78 . . . . 37 C2
Cules Long 🔵 BT94 . . . . . . 87 C8
Cules Short 🔵 BT94 . . . . . . 87 D8
Culkeeran 🔵
Armagh BT60 . . . . 97 A2
Dungannon BT71 . . . . 79 F2
Culkeeran Rd BT71 . . . . . . 79 F2
Culky 🔵 BT92 . . . . 103 F2
Cullaghmore 🔵 BT94 . . . . . 69 C3
Cullamore 🔵
Augher BT77 . . . . 93 E1
Augher BT77 . . . . 109 E8
Cullatagh 🔵 BT92 . . . . 122 E7
Culleen 🔵 BT92 . . . . 124 C2
Cullen 🔵 BT93 . . . . 86 E3
Cullenbrone 🔵 BT77 . . . . . 94 B6
Cullenfad 🔵 BT70 . . . . 78 C5
Cullenfad Rd BT70 . . . . 78 C5
Cullenramer 🔵 BT70 . . . . . 78 B3
Cullenramer Rd BT70 . . . . 77 F5
Cullentra 🔵
Dungannon BT70 . . . . 77 D3
Fivemiletown BT75 . . . . . . 107 F7
Cullentragh 🔵 BT92 . . . . . 112 F5
Culliagh 🔵 BT74 . . . . 102 D3
Culligan 🔵 BT68 . . . . 111 B4
Cullion 🔵
Dungannon BT71 . . . . 61 F2
Enniskillen BT92 . . . . 126 C1
Enniskillen BT94 . . . . 89 C1
Londonderry BT47 . . . . 2 B4
Omagh BT79 . . . . 26 C1
Cullindoo 🔵 BT92 . . . . 125 E6
Cullion Rd
Cookstown BT80 . . . . 31 A5
Dungannon BT71 . . . . 61 F3
Cullnagor 🔵 BT71 . . . . 79 E6
Culmore 🔵 BT78 . . . . 136 A3
Culmore Gdns BT78 . . . . . 136 A3
Culmore Pk BT78 . . . . 136 A2
Culnagor 🔵 BT71 . . . . 79 E6
Culnagor Row BT71 . . . . . 137 F4
Culnagrew 🔵 BT71 . . . . 79 E6
Culnagrew Rd BT71 . . . . . . 79 F5
Culnaha 🔵 BT70 . . . . 75 E1
Culrevog 🔵 BT71 . . . . 97 F8
Culrevog Rd BT71 . . . . 97 F8
Cultiagh 🔵 BT74 . . . . 104 E2
Culvacullion 🔵 BT79 . . . . . 26 C8
Culvacullion Rd BT79 . . . . 15 A1
Cumber 🔵
Aughnacloy BT69 . . . . 96 A3
Omagh BT78 . . . . 73 A7
Cumber Rd BT69 . . . . 95 F2
Cunninghams La BT71 . . . 137 E4
Cup & Ring Marked Stones ★
BT74 . . . . 101 E2
Curglassan 🔵 BT71 . . . . . . 45 E2
Curglassan Cross Roads
BT71 . . . . 45 E2
Curlagh 🔵 BT69 . . . . 95 F1
Curlagh Rd BT69 . . . . 95 F1
Curleyhill Rd BT82 . . . . 5 F2
Curloan 🔵 BT80 . . . . 61 A7
Curly 🔵 BT78 . . . . 72 B8
Curly Rd BT78 . . . . 72 B8
Curr 🔵 BT79 . . . . 74 F8
Curragh 🔵
Enniskillen BT92 . . . . 113 D6
Enniskillen BT92 . . . . 125 E2
Curraghamulkin 🔵 BT78 . . 53 E5
Curraghanall 🔵 BT94 . . . . 117 C8
Curraghfad 🔵 BT75 . . . . . . 107 C1
Curragh Glebe 🔵 BT78 . . . 52 F7
Curraghinalt 🔵 BT79 . . . . . 27 F7
Curraghlare 🔵 BT94 . . . . . 104 E4
Curraghmacall 🔵 BT78 . . . 35 D3
Curraghmore 🔵 BT93 . . . . 50 C2
Curran 🔵
Dungannon BT71 . . . . 61 F1
Dungannon BT71 . . . . 97 C7
Currans Brae BT71 . . . . . . 80 A1
Currin 🔵
Enniskillen BT94 . . . . 88 C3
Enniskillen BT94 . . . . 105 F3
Currogs 🔵 BT92 . . . . 116 F2
Curr Rd BT79 . . . . 56 F1
Curryann 🔵 BT94 . . . . 116 F7
Curryfree 🔵 BT47 . . . . 2 D5
Curryfree Rd BT47 . . . . 2 D6
Cushwash 🔵 BT92 . . . . . . 117 D2
Cuslea 🔵 BT92 . . . . 126 E4
Cuttymanhill 🔵 1 A3
Dairies Big 🔵 BT93 . . . . . . 86 F1
Dairies Little 🔵 BT93 . . . . 86 F2

D

Daisy Pk Rd BT82 . . . . 12 D6
Dales The BT80 . . . . 135 E6

Dalriada Pk BT70 137 B7
Daly Pk BT93 65 A4
Dame St BT74 138 C5
Danny's Mill Rd BT74 138 A5
Darling St BT74 138 C5
Dartan Ree BT60 111 E3
Dartans BT81 22 C4
Davagh LowerⓉ BT79 30 A7
Davagh Pk BT79 29 F7
Davagh Rd
 Magherafelt BT45 18 F1
 Omagh BT79 28 E8
Davagh UpperⓉ BT79 29 F8
Davies Rd BT78 24 E8
Davis Cres ❺ BT78 25 A6
Davog Dr BT93 65 A4
Dean Brian Maguirc Coll BT79 41 E1
Deer ParkⓉ
 Enniskillen BT92 114 B2
 Enniskillen BT92 120 C3
 Enniskillen BT94 118 A8
Deer Park (Clarke)Ⓣ BT78 38 B1
Deer Park (McCormick)Ⓣ BT78 38 C1
Deerpark Rd BT78 24 C7
Deer Pk BT78 24 F6
Deers Leap Rd BT79 25 D2
Delaney Cres BT82 134 D3
DemesneⓉ
 Caledon BT68 111 D4
 Enniskillen BT94 89 F1
Denamona Crt BT78 73 C6
Denamona Prim Sch BT78 73 C6
Dennet View BT82 1 D1
Deramore View BT80 135 B6
DergaltⓉ BT82 5 B1
Dergalt Rd BT82 5 B1
Dergany (Neville)Ⓣ BT78 71 B4
DergbroughⓉ BT79 14 F2
Dergbrough Rd BT79 14 F3
DergenaghⓉ BT70 77 B2
Dergenagh Rd BT70 77 B4
Derg Fold ❻ BT81 22 E5
Dergmoney Ave BT78 136 D3
Dergmoney Ct BT78 136 D2
Dergmoney Hts BT78 136 D1
Dergmoney LowerⓉ BT78 136 D2
Dergmoney Pl BT79 136 D3
Dergmoney UpperⓉ BT79 136 E1
Derg Money View BT78 136 D1
Derg Rd BT82 24 B8
Dergvale BT81 22 D4
Dergview BT81 22 D5
Derg Villas ❹ BT82 134 D4
DernabackyⓉ BT92 119 B1
DernabaneⓉ BT69 94 F6
DernaboreyⓉ BT70 77 D1
Dernaborey Rd BT70 77 D2
DernaghⓉ BT71 62 D4
DernagillyⓉ BT78 71 C1
Dernaglebe Rd BT82 13 A4
Dernaglug and DrumaaⓉ BT92 127 A7
DernaglushⓉ 131 A3
DernagolaⓉ 94 D1
DernagoreⓉ BT92 130 A5
Dernalear Rd BT78 37 D6
DernalebeⓉ BT82 13 A5
DernanaughtⓉ BT70 60 A1
Dernanaught Rd BT70 60 A1
DernaseerⓉ BT70 60 B1
DernasellⓉ BT77 93 F4
DernasheskⓉ BT74 103 B5
Dernasigh Rd BT60 97 B1
Dernish IslandⓉ BT92 125 B3
Dernmore Cl BT71 62 D2
Dernmore Dr BT71 62 D2
Deroar Rd BT79 57 C6
DeroranⓉ BT79 57 A8
DerraghadoanⓉ BT71 61 C1
Derraghadoan Rd BT71 61 D1
Derramore Way BT80 135 B6
DerroaryⓉ 131 C4
Derreens EastⓉ BT74 114 D6
Derreens WestⓉ BT74 113 E6
DerriesⓉ BT77 93 D7
DerrinⓉ
 Enniskillen BT93 66 F8
 Enniskillen BT94 89 D2
DerrinleaghⓉ BT80 43 E8
Derrin Pk BT74 138 B6
Derrinraw Rd BT62 81 F5
Derrin Rd BT74 138 B6
DerrinsⓉ 133 F4
DerrintonyⓉ
 Enniskillen BT92 129 F8
 Enniskillen BT94 107 B4
DerroarⓉ BT79 57 C5
DerryⓉ
 Coalisland BT71 62 B3
 Enniskillen BT92 115 F1
 Omagh BT78 89 A7
DerryadⓉ BT92 125 B5
DerryaddⓉ BT71 81 C5
DerryaghnaⓉ BT74 114 E7
DerryallaghanⓉ 120 D7
DerryallenⓉ BT78 89 B6
Derryallen GlebeⓉ BT78 89 C6
Derryallen Rd BT78 89 A5
DerryalskeaⓉ BT70 60 C1
DerryaneⓉ BT71 81 B6
Derryane Rd BT71 81 B6
DerryanyⓉ BT92 125 D5
DerryardⓉ BT92 120 C3
Derryardry La BT71 81 A5
DerryargonⓉ BT74 103 F7
DerryarmushⓉ 131 C3
DerryarritⓉ 120 F6
DerryartⓉ BT92 130 A8
DerryartryⓉ 120 E4
DerryasnaⓉ BT92 116 E2
DerryaughⓉ BT62 81 D7
DerrybardⓉ BT78 73 E6
Derrybard Rd BT78 73 D6
DerrybegⓉ
 Clones 127 B1
 Enniskillen BT74 104 C1
Derry BegⓉ BT93 51 F2
Derrybeg EastⓉ BT92 131 E7
Derrybeg WestⓉ BT92 125 C2
DerrybrackⓉ BT92 132 F8
DerrybrickⓉ
 Enniskillen BT92 124 E4
 Enniskillen BT93 50 F3
DerrybruskⓉ BT74 116 A7
Derrybrusk Church★ BT74 116 A8
DerrycallaghanⓉ BT94 116 C4
DerrycanonⓉ
 Enniskillen BT92 124 F2
 Enniskillen BT92 125 D6
DerrycarkⓉ 131 B3
DerrycawⓉ
 Craigavon BT62 81 D5
 Dungannon BT71 80 D2
Derrycaw La BT62 81 C5
Derrycaw Rd BT71 80 C1
DerrychaanⓉ BT92 125 B7
DerrycharaⓉ BT74 138 D3
Derrychara Dr BT74 138 E4
Derrychara Ind Est BT74 138 D4
Derrychara Link BT74 138 D4
Derrychara Pk BT74 138 E4
Derrychara Rd BT74 138 E4
DerrychorranⓉ BT92 130 B8
DerrychreeⓉ BT92 124 F3
Derrychrin Prim Sch BT80 46 F8
DerrychullaⓉ BT92 117 B1
DerrychullooⓉ BT93 66 C8
DerrychurraⓉ BT92 114 F6
DerryclawanⓉ BT94 104 F3
DerryclayⓉ BT77 93 F6
DerryclegnaⓉ BT92 123 A6
DerrycloonyⓉ BT77 93 F3
Derrycloony Rd BT77 93 E4
DerrycooseⓉ BT62 81 B3
Derrycoose Rd BT62 81 A3
DerrycorⓉ BT62 81 C4
DerrycorbanⓉ BT92 125 C7
DerrycorbyⓉ BT92 126 A3
DerrycormickⓉ BT74 114 D8
Derrycor Rd BT62 81 C4
Derrycorry NorthⓉ BT62 81 A3
Derrycorry SouthⓉ BT71 80 F2
DerrycourtneyⓉ BT68 111 A8
Derrycourtney Rd BT69 95 E2
DerrycreeⓉ BT92 127 D6
DerrycreevyⓉ
 Aughnacloy BT69 94 E6
 Dungannon BT71 97 B5
Derrycreevy (Knox)Ⓣ BT71 79 E5
Derrycreevy La BT71 79 D5
Derrycreevy Rd BT71 79 E4
DERRYCRIN BT80 46 E8
Derrycrin (Conyngham)Ⓣ BT80 46 E7
Derrycrin Cotts BT80 46 F8
Derrycrin (Eglish)Ⓣ BT80 46 E8
Derrycrin Rd BT80 46 E7
DerrycrumⓉ BT75 107 D2
DerrycrummyⓉ BT80 31 F2
DerrycullionⓉ BT94 107 B3
DerrycushⓉ BT69 95 A6
Derrycush Pk BT69 95 A5
Derrycush Rd BT62 81 F5
DerrydoonⓉ BT92 131 D8
DerrydorraghⓉ BT60 97 B1
DerrydrummondⓉ BT76 93 D1
DerryelvinⓉ BT92 131 F6
DerryfubbleⓉ BT71 97 C8
Derryfubble Rd BT71 79 A3
DerrygallyⓉ BT71 80 D4
Derrygally DemesneⓉ BT71 80 C3
Derrygally Rd BT71 80 D3
Derrygally Way BT71 80 C3
DerryganardⓉ BT45 31 D7
DerrygannonⓉ BT92 120 A5
Derrygany (Maguire)Ⓣ BT78 71 C4
Derrygavad Rd BT62 81 B1
DerrygellyⓉ BT92 120 C5
DerrygennedyⓉ BT92 126 A3
DerrygiffⓉ BT92 114 E8
DerrygoasⓉ BT92 127 C1
DerrygoniganⓉ BT80 45 D6
Derrygonigan Rd BT80 45 D6
DerrygonnellyⓉ BT93 85 F5
DERRYGONNELLY (DOIRE ÓG CONAÍLE) BT93 85 F5
Derrygonnelly Prim Sch BT93 85 F5
Derrygonnelly Rd BT74 138 A6
DerrygoolyⓉ BT68 111 C8
DerrygoonⓉ BT81 23 C1
DerrygoonanⓉ BT71 97 B6
Derrygoonan Rd BT81 21 C3
DerrygoreⓉ BT74 138 B7
Derrygore Rd BT74 138 C8
Derrygore Terr BT74 138 C6
DerrygortaneaⓉ BT70 60 D7
DerrygortrevyⓉ BT70 78 F3
DerrygurdryⓉ BT92 124 A4
DerryharneyⓉ BT94 116 C5
DerryhashⓉ BT70 43 A1
DerryhawlaghⓉ BT92 115 C4
Derryhaw Rd BT60 111 F3
DerryheanlishⓉ BT92 120 D4
DerryheelyⓉ BT92 117 E5
Derryhelvin GlebeⓉ BT92 114 F1
DerryhennyⓉ BT92 115 C2
DerryhillaghⓉ BT74 104 C7
DerryhirkⓉ BT62 81 A3
Derryhirk Rd BT71 80 F2
DerryhoarⓉ BT70 78 B2
DerryhoneyⓉ BT94 105 C3
DerryhoolyⓉ BT92 130 A6
Derryhowlaght EastⓉ BT94 116 D5
Derryhowlaght WestⓉ BT92 114 E6
Derryhubbert EastⓉ BT71 81 A5
Derryhubbert NorthⓉ BT71 80 F5
Derryhubbert Rd BT71 81 B5
Derryhubbert SouthⓉ BT71 80 F4
DerryhurdinⓉ BT92 117 C4
DerryinchⓉ BT92 115 E5
DerrykeeghanⓉ BT74 104 B8
DerrykeevanⓉ BT62 81 F3
DerrykenyⓉ BT92 131 E8
DerrykerribⓉ BT92 131 E5
DerrykillewⓉ 65 B5
DerrykintoneⓉ BT68 111 C5
DerrylaneyⓉ BT92 130 A7
DerrylappenⓉ BT70 96 E6
Derrylappen Rd BT70 96 D5
DerrylardⓉ BT62 81 F7
Derrylard Rd BT62 81 F6
Derrylatinee Prim Sch BT70 78 C1
DerrylattineeⓉ BT70 78 C1
Derrylattinee Rd BT70 96 B8
DerryleaⓉ
 Enniskillen BT92 122 F6
 Enniskillen BT92 124 B2
 Enniskillen BT92 125 C5
 Knockatallan 120 E5
 Omagh BT78 89 E7
DerryleagueⓉ BT92 115 D3
DerryleckⓉ BT74 114 B8
DerryleeⓉ BT71 81 A7
DerryleediganⓉ 120 F4
Derrylee Rd BT71 80 F6
DerryleggonⓉ 128 E5
DerrylesterⓉ BT92 114 F2
DerrylileaghⓉ BT62 81 D7
Derrylileagh Rd BT62 81 C6
DerrylinⓉ BT94 70 D1
DERRYLIN (DOIRE LOINN) BT92 124 A4
Derrylin Rd BT92 103 E2
DerrylomanⓉ BT94 106 F4
DerrylooⓉ BT92 120 B5
Derryloran alias KirktownⓉ BT80 135 A3
Derryloran Ind Est BT80 135 A1
Derryloran Pl BT80 135 D3
DerryloughanⓉ BT71 63 C1
Derryloughan Ave BT71 63 C1
Derryloughan Rd BT71 81 A8
DerryloughterⓉ BT93 49 B2
DerrymacannaⓉ BT78 70 F2
DerrymacauseyⓉ BT92 124 E4
DerrymacrowⓉ BT92 125 D2
DerrymagowanⓉ BT71 80 D2
Derrymagowan Rd BT71 80 D2
DerrymakeenⓉ BT74 104 B3
DerrymeenⓉ
 Augher BT77 94 B6
 Dungannon BT71 80 B8
 Enniskillen BT92 126 F6
Derry MoreⓉ BT93 51 E2
DerrynacloyⓉ BT92 119 E1
DerrynacrannogⓉ BT93 65 E7
DerrynacrossⓉ BT93 64 D1
DerrynafaugherⓉ BT93 85 D3
DerrynahescoⓉ 120 B7
DerrynameeoⓉ BT93 82 E8
Derrynananta LowerⓉ 121 A1
DerrynannyⓉ BT94 87 F8
DerrynascobeⓉ BT77 93 D5
DerrynaseerⓉ
 Ballyshannon 82 B8
 Omagh BT78 53 F3
Derrynaseer Amenity Area★ 82 B7
Derrynaseer Rd BT78 53 E3
Derrynasell WestⓉ 120 C8
DerrynasheskⓉ BT93 51 A7
DerrynavogyⓉ BT75 107 B5
Derrynawilt Cross Roads BT92 119 D1
Derrynawilt EastⓉ BT92 120 C3
Derrynawilt WestⓉ BT92 119 C1
DerryneeseⓉ BT92 120 A5
DerryneeveⓉ BT93 51 C4
DerrynimⓉ BT74 114 A8
DerrynureⓉ BT92 132 E7
DerryoghillⓉ BT71 97 F6
Derryoghill Rd BT71 97 F6
Derryowen Pl ⓫ BT71 62 C2
DerryraghanⓉ
 Dungannon BT71 61 E8
Derryraghan *continued*
 Enniskillen BT94 88 F2
Derry Rd
 Coalisland BT71 62 B3
 Omagh BT78 136 A5
 Strabane BT82 134 E6
DerryrealtⓉ 122 C1
DerryreeⓉ BT92 117 C3
Derryrona GlebeⓉ BT93 65 F7
DerryscobeⓉ BT92 103 A1
DerryscollopⓉ BT71 98 D8
Derryscollop Rd BT71 98 D8
DerryshandraⓉ BT74 102 D1
DerrysteatonⓉ BT92 131 C6
DerrytreskⓉ BT71 80 D8
Derrytresk Rd BT71 62 F1
DerryvahonⓉ BT93 84 F6
Derryvale Ind Est BT71 62 A3
Derryvale Pk BT71 62 A3
Derryvale Rd BT71 62 A3
DerryvaranbegⓉ BT71 63 B2
Derryvaren Rd BT71 80 E8
Derryvar Rd BT62 81 F6
Derryvary BegⓉ BT93 86 B3
Derryvary MoreⓉ BT93 86 A3
DerryveenⓉ BT70 79 A5
Derryveen Ave BT70 78 F5
Derryveen Cres BT70 78 F5
DerryveoneⓉ BT94 70 B5
Derryvinney Rd BT62 81 D6
DerryvogueⓉ BT74 102 E3
DerryvolanⓉ BT92 120 D5
DerryvonyⓉ 131 B7
DerryvoreⓉ
 Enniskillen BT74 104 B2
 Enniskillen BT92 130 E8
DerryvraneⓉ BT92 123 E8
DerryvreeⓉ BT94 117 D7
DerryvullanⓉ BT74 104 C1
Derryvullan Rd BT74 104 D1
Derrywinnin GlebeⓉ BT71 62 B2
DervaghroyⓉ BT79 56 F3
Dervagh Roy BT79 57 B4
Dervaghroy Rd BT79 56 F4
DesertⓉ BT82 4 F6
DesertcreatⓉ BT80 44 E2
Desertcreat Rd BT80 44 E2
Desert Rd BT79 57 B1
DevenishⓉ
 Enniskillen BT74 103 D8
 Enniskillen BT74 103 E8
Devenish Coll BT74 138 D3
Devenish Cres BT74 103 D6
Devenish Island Mus★ BT74 103 E7
Deverney Pk ❷ BT79 39 B1
Deverney Rd BT79 39 B1
Devesky Rd BT79 41 E2
Diamond The
 Clones 127 F2
 ❶ Dungannon BT70 42 F1
 Lifford 134 C7
 ❹ Moy BT71 80 A1
DinnydoonⓉ BT74 102 F7
DirnanⓉ BT80 31 D5
Dirnan Rd BT80 31 E6
DisertownⓉ BT47 2 C7
Disertown Rd BT47 2 D6
DivinaghⓉ BT77 93 C8
DivinyⓉ BT93 52 C2
Doagh GlebeⓉ BT93 84 F4
Docherty's Glen Rd BT61 97 B3
Dock St BT82 134 D6
Dog BigⓉ BT93 84 C2
Dog LittleⓉ BT93 84 B3
DOIRE LOINN (DERRYLIN) BT92 124 A4
DOIRE ÓG CONAÍLE (DERRYGONNELLY) BT93 85 F5
DOMHNACH MÓR (DONAGHMORE) BT70 61 B3
DonacaveyⓉ BT78 73 C8
Donacavey Church★ BT78 73 C7
Donacavey Rd BT78 73 C7
DONAGH BT92 126 A7
DonaghⓉ BT92 126 B6
DonaghanieⓉ BT79 56 E6
Donaghanie Rd BT79 56 E6
Donaghedy Church★ BT82 2 F1
Donaghedy Rd BT82 1 E3
Donaghendry Rd BT71 62 B8
DonaghenryⓉ BT71 62 B8
DONAGHEY BT71 61 F8
Donaghey Prim Sch BT71 61 E8
DonaghmoreⓉ BT70 61 B2
DONAGHMORE (DOMHNACH MÓR) BT70 61 B3
Donaghmore Prim Sch BT70 61 B2
Donaghmore Rd BT70 137 B6
DonaghmoyneⓉ BT75 92 A4
DonaghriskⓉ BT80 44 F2
Donaghrisk Rd BT80 44 F2
DonegallⓉ BT74 102 F7
Donemana Prim Sch BT82 6 C8
Donnelly's Hill Rd BT71 97 B4
DonnydeadeⓉ BT71 79 D4
DonnygowenⓉ BT82 11 F6
DooardⓉ 82 F2
DooballyⓉ 64 D6
DoocharnⓉ BT92 117 F5
DoochrockⓉ BT93 52 B7
DoocrockⓉ BT78 70 E7
Doocrock Rd BT78 70 E7
DooedernyⓉ
 Enniskillen BT92 103 C1
 Fivemiletown BT75 107 A8
DoogaryⓉ
 Enniskillen BT94 70 B3
 Fivemiletown BT75 107 B4
 Omagh BT79 56 A6
Doogary Rd
 Armagh BT60 111 F1
 Omagh BT79 56 C4
DoohatⓉ BT92 125 F2
Doohatty GlebeⓉ BT92 122 D7
DooishⓉ BT78 53 E8
Dooish Rd BT78 53 F4
DoolargyⓉ BT69 77 B1
Doolargy Rd BT69 95 B8
DooletterⓉ BT74 101 E3
DoonⓉ
 Enniskillen BT92 123 E3
 Enniskillen BT94 105 E8
 Scotshouse 132 F2
DoonanⓉ BT94 69 B1
Doon and EshcleaghⓉ BT92 119 A5
Doon Ave BT71 63 B3
DooneenⓉ
 Enniskillen BT92 113 E1
 Enniskillen BT94 90 C6
Dooneen Rd BT94 90 D6
Doonroe Cairn★ BT79 28 E5
DoonsⓉ BT80 30 D1
Doons Rd BT80 30 D1
Dooraa NorthⓉ BT93 51 C2
Dooraa SouthⓉ BT93 51 C1
DooraghⓉ BT71 45 C1
DooratⓉ BT82 7 B1
DoorlessⓉ BT80 45 C5
DoorossⓉ BT92 125 D7
DorasⓉ BT71 61 F4
Dorney Bridge Rd BT94 88 C7
DornogaghⓉ BT93 113 C7
Dorothys Cross Roads 133 D6
DOUGLAS BRIDGE BT82 13 B2
Douglas Rd BT82 13 C2
Dovecote Way BT93 87 B2
DownsⓉ BT80 44 F1
Downs Rd BT80 44 F1
Down St BT74 138 D5
DraghⓉ BT92 124 B5
DrainⓉ BT82 6 E7
Drapersfield Rd BT80 45 B5
DraughtonⓉ BT78 73 D5
Dredge Bridge★ BT60 111 E5
DreemoreⓉ BT71 79 F4
Dreemore La BT71 79 F4
Dreemore Rd BT71 79 F4
DreenⓉ BT47 9 B4
DreenanⓉ
 Castlederg BT81 21 F5
 Enniskillen BT93 67 B7
Dreenan Rd
 Castlederg BT81 21 F6
 Omagh BT79 56 F8
DreighⓉ BT78 89 C7
DressogeⓉ
 Enniskillen BT94 117 D8
 Omagh BT78 37 D1
 Omagh BT78 53 F2
DresternanⓉ
 Enniskillen BT92 120 A1
 Enniskillen BT92 124 C3
 Enniskillen BT93 85 D7
Dresternan Castle★ BT92 124 E3
DringⓉ BT94 87 E6
Dristernan and DredoltⓉ BT70 78 A8
DroganⓉ BT94 87 B8
DroghillⓉ 130 C3
DROICHEAD MHIG UIDHIR (MAGUIRESBRIDGE) BT94 117 B7
DROIM CAOIN (DRUMQUIN) BT78 36 E3
DroitⓉ BT78 25 F8
Droit Rd BT78 25 F8
DrolesⓉ BT94 116 E5
DromoreⓉ
 Caledon BT68 96 A1
 Dromore BT78 71 E8
 Dungannon BT71 46 C2
 Enniskillen BT74 102 E7
 Enniskillen BT93 85 D5
 Enniskillen BT94 69 E2
DROMORE (AN DROIM MÓR) BT78 71 E7
Dromore BigⓉ BT93 51 B7
Dromore LittleⓉ BT93 51 B6
Dromore LowerⓉ BT76 73 F1
Dromore MiddleⓉ BT76 92 A8
Dromore Prim Sch BT78 71 F7
Dromore Rd
 Caledon BT68 96 B1
 Irvinestown BT94 70 A3
 Omagh BT78 72 D6
 Omagh BT78 136 B2
Dromore Rd Ret Pk BT78 136 B3
Dromore UpperⓉ BT76 92 B7
DroneⓉ BT69 94 F7
DrudgeonⓉ BT78 55 B5
Drudgeon Rd BT78 55 B5
Druhgalla Rd BT81 23 C1
Druid's Altar & Chambered Grave★ BT94 105 C5

Druid's Altar & Giant's Grave★ BT94 ....105 B4
Druids Stone★ BT75 ....107 D4
Drum
  Cookstown BT80 ....44 B6
  Omagh BT78 ....55 F3
Drumaa BT74 ....102 A7
Drumacrittin BT92 ...120 E1
Drumad
  Cookstown BT80 ....46 C5
  Enniskillen BT94 ......105 B1
Drumadagarve BT94 ...105 F2
Drumadarragh BT77 ... 94 A6
Drumadillar BT93 ....86 A4
Drumad La BT80 ....46 C6
Drumadown BT93 ....86 C5
Drumadraghy BT93 ....51 D1
Drumadravy BT94 .....69 C4
Drumadravy Rd BT94 ....69 C3
Drumad Rd BT80........46 C5
Drumady BT92 ......127 D6
Drumageever BT74 ...102 F2
Drumagore BT47 ....2 B6
Drumagullion BT71 ... 62 C7
Drumalee
  Belturbet 130 D3
  Belturbet 131 E2
Drumane
  Ballyconnell 129 B2
  Enniskillen BT92 ......115 E1
Drumannon Dr 7 BT78... 55 D8
Drumannon Gr 8 BT78 ...55 D8
Drumannon Mews BT78 .136 B1
Drumannon Rise 2
  BT78 ....136 A2
Drumannon View BT78..136 A2
Drumanphy BT62 .....81 E1
Drumanphy Rd BT62 .....81 E1
Drumanuey BT71 .....80 A2
Drumanure
  Enniskillen BT93 ......85 F2
  Rossinver 82 F2
Drumany
  Enniskillen BT92 ......117 B1
  Enniskillen BT92 ......123 E8
Drumany Beg BT92 ...124 F2
Drumany More BT92 ..130 A8
Drumaran
  Enniskillen BT74 ......113 E8
  Enniskillen BT94 ......69 A3
Drumaraw BT74 .....102 E6
Drumard
  Clones 127 E5
  Cookstown BT80 ....44 C6
  Dungannon BT71 ....61 F5
  Dungannon BT71 ....63 A7
  Enniskillen BT74 ......104 C2
  Enniskillen BT93 ......69 A6
Drumard Cross BT71 ...80 B5
Drumardcross Rd BT71...80 B5
Drumard Glebe BT71 ...80 B5
Drumardnagross BT78 .71 D3
Drumarky BT94 ....69 B3
Drumarn BT71........98 B6
Drumarraght BT92 ...117 D6
Drumart BT61 ....98 F4
Drumary
  Enniskillen BT93 ......85 F4
  Enniskillen BT93 ......85 F7
Drumash BT78 ....89 B8
Drumask or Ballycullen
  BT71 ....98 B6
Drumaslaghy BT70 .....94 D8
Drumaspil BT71........80 B6
Drumaspil Rd BT71 ......80 B6
Drumataffan BT93 .....65 D2
Drumaveel BT93 ......85 F1
Drumawill BT74.......103 D3
Drumawill Gdns BT74 ...103 D3
Drumawillin BT74......113 D7
Drumay BT71 ....97 D8
Drumbad BT92 ......117 C6
Drumbadbeg BT92 ...117 D5
Drumbadmeen BT93 ...66 C2
Drumbad More BT93 ..116 F7
Drumbadreevagh BT93 .65 B2
Drumbaghlin BT94 ....116 F7
Drumballyhugh BT70...61 A8
Drumballyhugh Rd BT70..60 F8
Drumbanaway BT71 ....45 E3
Drumbane BT93 ......69 C6
Drumbar 122 F2
Drumbaran BT93......51 F4
Drumbargy BT92......115 D5
Drumbarley BT78 .....37 C2
Drumbarley Rd BT78 .....37 B3
Drumbarlom 130 F2
Drumbarna BT93......68 F5
Drumbarry BT92 .....126 D6
Drumbawn BT74 ....138 E8
Drumbawn Cl BT74 .....138 E7
Drumbealimy BT92....127 B6
Drumbearn BT70......60 F2
Drumbee BT61........97 F1
Drumbeg BT74........138 E8
Drumbeggan BT74 .....86 B2
Drumbeggar BT93 .....85 E1
Drumberny BT93.......87 B1
Drumbinnion BT78 ....71 B3
Drumbinnis BT92 ....115 A1
Drumbinnisk BT92....127 A6
Drumbo BT94.........69 D1
Drumboarty BT93 .....52 B3
Drumbockany BT93 ...86 A7

Drumboghanagh
  Glebe 132 A4
Drumbominy BT92 ...124 F1
Drumboory
  Enniskillen BT74 ......103 B8
  Enniskillen BT92 ......130 C8
  Swanlinbar...........122 D1
Drumboy BT74.......102 D6
Drumbrick BT93 ......52 A4
Drumbrughas
  Belturbet 130 D1
  Enniskillen BT92 ......115 C4
  Enniskillen BT92 ......119 E1
  Enniskillen BT92 ......124 B7
  Enniskillen BT94 ......117 D7
  Swanlinbar...........122 F3
Drumbrughas East
  BT92 ....126 A1
Drumbrughas North
  BT92 ....117 B4
Drumbrughas South
  BT92 ....125 C6
Drumbrughas West
  BT92 ....125 F4
Drumbulan BT94......69 F5
Drumbulcan BT94......88 A7
Drumbulgan BT71.....45 F4
Drumbullog BT92 ....126 E5
Drumcahy BT93......52 C2
Drumcairne Rd BT71 .....63 A7
Drumcanon BT92 ....114 F1
Drumcard BT92 ......114 E2
Drumcask 122 C1
Drumcaw
  Enniskillen BT92 ......125 E6
  Enniskillen BT94 ......87 B7
  Killeevan 128 E3
Drumchorick BT93 ....51 E4
Drumclamph BT81 .....23 E4
Drumclamph Rd BT81 ....23 D5
Drumclay
  Enniskillen BT74 ......138 F7
  Enniskillen BT92 ......126 B3
Drumclay Cl 1 BT92 ....126 C3
Drumclay Ct BT74......138 E7
Drumclay Link BT74 ....138 F6
Drumclay Pk N BT74 ....138 F7
Drumclay Pk S BT74 ....138 F7
Drumcloona BT93.....51 A2
Drumclounish BT92 ..114 D2
Drumcole 130 E2
Drumcolgny BT74.....114 A7
Drumcon BT94........116 E3
Drumconan BT47 ......2 D8
Drumconlan East
  BT74 ....114 D8
Drumconlan West
  BT74 ....113 D7
Drumconnelly BT78...56 A3
Drumconnelly Rd BT78...56 B3
Drumconnis
  Dromore BT78.........71 F8
  Enniskillen BT94 ......88 A3
Drumconnor Rd BT70 ....61 C5
Drumconor
  Dungannon BT70 ....61 C6
  Enniskillen BT74 ......102 F5
  Enniskillen BT92 ......124 E1
Drumconvis BT80 .....46 C6
Drumconvis Rd BT80 ....46 C6
Drumcoo
  Dungannon BT70 ......137 C6
  Enniskillen BT74 ......103 F7
  Enniskillen BT93 ......112 F8
  Enniskillen BT94 ......116 E3
Drumcoo (Foster) ...109 E1
Drumcoo Gn BT71 ......137 C7
Drumcoo or Belview
  BT74 ....104 B1
Drumcoo Rd BT74 ......138 D8
Drumcor BT75........90 D2
Drumcorban BT74 ....86 E2
Drumcor Cross Roads
  BT75 ....90 D2
Drumcor Hill BT74 .....138 C6
Drumcorke BT70......94 C8
Drumcose
  Enniskillen BT92 ......52 C2
  Enniskillen BT93 ......87 A3
Drumcraig Rd BT47 ......2 B6
Drumcramph
  Enniskillen BT94 ......115 F5
  Enniskillen BT94 ......116 F5
Drumcraw BT80 ......45 B7
Drumcree BT80 ....135 C3
Drumcreen BT94......88 D5
Drumcrin
  Enniskillen BT74 ......104 C3
  Enniskillen BT92 ......117 A4
  Enniskillen BT93 ......132 A5
  Enniskillen BT93 ......50 D4
  Enniskillen BT93 ......69 B7
  Enniskillen BT94 ......69 D2
Drumcroohen BT93 ...86 A2
Drumcrooil BT94......115 F5
Drumcrow
  Dungannon BT71 ....80 C7
  Enniskillen BT74 ......104 D3
  Scotshouse 133 F5
Drumcrow East BT93 ..86 A8
Drumcrow West BT93 ..66 F2
Drumcru
  Anlore 128 B1
  Enniskillen BT92 ......117 D5
  Enniskillen BT92 ......126 B2
  Enniskillen BT92 ......127 D5
  Smithborough 128 E6
Drumcullen BT71 .....98 B3

Drumcullen Rd BT71 .....98 B4
Drumcullion
  Augher BT77 ....94 A8
  Enniskillen BT74 ......116 A8
  Enniskillen BT92 ......122 D5
  Enniskillen BT93 ......51 D4
  Enniskillen BT94 ......88 A3
Drumcullion La BT70 ....94 B8
Drumcully BT93.......100 A5
Drumcunny BT92 .....117 C4
Drumcurren BT93 .....51 B3
Drumderg
  Dungannon BT71 ....97 F5
  Enniskillen BT74 ......114 B7
  Enniskillen BT92 ......129 E6
  Enniskillen BT94 ......105 C5
Drumderg Glebe BT78 .72 E8
Drumdoney BT92 ....124 A3
Drumdran
  Enniskillen BT94 ......105 B1
  Omagh BT78 ....89 B7
Drumduff
  Dungannon BT71 ....97 E3
  Enniskillen BT92 ......114 E3
  Enniskillen BT93 ......51 E5
  Enniskillen BT93 ......70 A5
  Omagh BT79 ....57 D7
Drumduff La BT71 ....97 D3
Drumduff Prim Sch BT79. 57 C8
Drumduff Rd BT79 ......57 C6
Drumeagle BT82......12 C3
Drumeagle Rd BT82.....12 C3
Drumearn
  Aughnacloy BT69.......95 D4
  Cookstown BT80 ....31 B1
Drumearn Rd BT80 ......44 B8
Drumee BT94.........106 B1
Drumeen Rd BT79 ....56 F6
Drumeeshil BT92 ....124 D1
Drumelly BT93.......100 F1
Drumenagh BT71......80 B5
Drumenny Big BT82....1 C1
Drumenny (Conyngham)
  BT80 ....47 A6
Drumenny Little BT82. . 1 C2
Drumenny Rd BT71 ......46 F5
Drumenny (Stewart)
  BT80 ....46 F6
Drumeny Rd BT82........1 C1
Drumerheeve BT92 ..120 B3
Drumersee 123 A2
Drumerwinter BT92 ..119 F2
Drumess BT68 ....111 C7
Drumettagh BT92 ....130 B5
Drumey
  Dungannon BT71 ....61 E5
  Dungannon BT71 ....62 B7
Drumfad BT70 ....77 A3
Drumferrer 109 E7
Drumflugh BT71 ......97 C5
Drumflugh Rd BT71 .....97 B6
Drumgague BT92 ....114 F3
Drumgallan
  Enniskillen BT92 ......103 D2
  Enniskillen BT92 ......126 C6
  Omagh BT78 ....36 B8
Drumgallan Rd BT78 ....36 C8
Drumgallon BT92 ....138 A2
Drumgamph BT74......102 B5
Drumgane 99 A8
Drumgarrell BT80.....45 C7
Drumgarrel Rd BT80.....45 C7
Drumgarrow BT94 ....87 F6
Drumgarrow Ct 7 BT74 .104 B6
Drumgart
  Belturbet 130 C4
  Dungannon BT71 ....80 B2
Drumgauty BT82......1 C3
Drumgay BT74........104 A8
Drumgay Cl BT74 ....138 D7
Drumgaze 133 D2
Drumgivery BT93 .....70 B7
Drumglass High Sch
  BT71 ....137 C8
Drumglass Way BT71....137 C8
Drumgoast BT92 ....120 B2
Drumgoland BT92.....126 B3
Drumgold BT71.......79 E3
Drumgole BT92 ......126 A6
Drumgolliff BT60 ....111 F6
Drumgoon BT94 ......117 B6
Drumgormal
  Dungannon BT71 ....62 F6
  Dungannon BT71 ....137 B1
Drumgormal Rd BT71 ...137 B1
Drumgormly BT93 .....85 E3
Drumgorran BT94.....117 E8
Drumgose BT71.......97 D6
Drumgose Rd BT71 ......97 E6
Drumgowna BT94 ....105 E1
Drumgowna East BT93 .52 A5
Drumgowna West BT93 50 E5
Drumgramph BT92 ...132 C5
Drumgrannon BT71 ...80 A1
Drumgrannon Rd BT71...79 F2
Drumgrass BT80 ......31 E2
Drumgrass Rd BT80 .....31 F2
Drumgrenaghan BT93..68 A8
Drumgriar Fort★ BT94 ..104 C5
Drumgrone 133 E3
Drumguiff
  Enniskillen BT92 ......120 A3
  Enniskillen BT92 ......125 B6
Drumguiff Cross Roads
  BT92 ....125 C6
Drumguillagh BT92 ..126 C4
Drumhack
  Enniskillen BT92 ......115 A3

Drumhack continued
  Enniskillen BT94 ......116 F3
Drumharriff
  Dungannon BT71 ....137 F6
  Enniskillen BT74 ......113 F8
  Enniskillen BT92 ......122 F8
  Enniskillen BT92 ......127 B4
  Enniskillen BT94 ......116 D4
Drumharvey BT94.....70 B4
Drumhaw BT92 ......117 C3
Drumhaw Pk BT92 ......117 D3
Drumhervin BT92 ....123 D7
Drumhillagh BT92 ....132 F3
Drumhirk
  Augher BT77 ....93 A7
  Dungannon BT70 ....78 D6
  Enniskillen BT74 ......102 E4
  Enniskillen BT92 ......52 A5
  Enniskillen BT94 ......116 A5
  Fivemiletown BT75 .....90 E2
Drumhirk Glebe BT77..93 B7
Drumhirk Lower BT74.102 C6
Drumhirk Rd BT78 ......72 E2
Drumhirk Upper BT74.102 D6
Drumhoney
  Enniskillen BT93 ......69 B6
  Enniskillen BT94 ......69 B2
Drumhonish BT78.....36 F1
Drumhorrik BT71......80 B7
Drumhose BT92 ......125 D6
Drumhoy BT94........106 D3
Drumhubbart Rd BT71 ...63 A7
Drumhubbert BT71....63 C7
Drumierna BT93 ......51 F3
Drumillar BT93 ....65 C3
Druminisclin 131 D3
Druminishill
  Enniskillen BT92 ......115 A4
  Enniskillen BT92 ......124 E1
Druminshin Beg BT94..87 E7
Druminshin More BT94.87 D7
Drumkee BT71........80 B8
Drumkeen
  Ballinamallard BT94 ...88 C4
  Ederney BT93 ....52 A1
  Enniskillen BT92 ......103 E2
Drumkeenagh BT93 ..100 B4
Drumkeen Ct BT94......88 C5
Drumkeenragh BT94 ..105 E6
Drumkeen Rd BT92 .....103 E2
Drumkeeran BT93.....51 E3
Drumkern BT71.......63 A7
Drumkillen BT92 .....124 F2
Drumlagher BT78.....73 A3
Drumlaghy
  Enniskillen BT94 ......114 B7
  Enniskillen BT94 ......114 D4
Drumlaney 132 A3
Drumlar Pk BT74........138 F7
Drumlea BT79 ....27 C7
Drumlea Cres BT79 .....136 B7
Drumleages Big
  BT94 ....116 F4
Drumleages Little
  BT94 ....116 E7
Drumlea Pk BT80 ....135 B2
Drumlea Rd BT79 ....27 B7
Drumlee BT71........97 F6
Drumlee BT71........97 F5
Drumlegagh BT78.....36 F8
Drumlegagh Church Rd
  BT78 ....36 E5
Drumlegagh Prim Sch
  BT78 ....23 F1
Drumlegagh Rd N BT78..23 E1
Drumlegagh Rd S BT78...37 C8
Drumlester BT79......58 B7
Drumliff BT92.........117 B5
Drumlin Ct BT74 ....138 A2
Drumlin Glen BT74 .....138 B2
Drumlin Hts BT74 ......138 A2
Drumlisaleen BT93....65 A2
Drumlish
  Enniskillen BT93 ......86 A1
  Omagh BT78 ....54 B3
Drumlish Prim Sch BT78. 54 B3
Drumlish Rd BT78 ......53 C3
Drumlister Rd BT79 .....57 F5
Drumlone
  Enniskillen BT92 ......125 D4
  Enniskillen BT94 ......105 D3
Drumlongfield BT93...50 C5
Drumlught
  Enniskillen BT92 ......117 B3
  Enniskillen BT92 ......124 C2
Drumlyon BT74 ......103 D5
Drumlyon Dr BT74 ......103 D6
Drummacabranagher
  BT92 ....114 F4
Drummacahan BT93 ..51 E4
Drummacalara BT93 ..51 F1
Drummack BT94 .....116 F4
Drummackan BT94 ....90 A4
Drummackilowney
  BT94 ....87 D6
Drummacoorin BT74 ..102 C5
Drummahon BT81......35 B4
Drummal BT94.........69 A2
Drummallard BT78 ....72 A5
Drumman
  Enniskillen BT93 ......101 E1
  Strabane BT82.........6 B6
Drumman Beg BT61....98 F1
Drumman Ct BT82 .....134 C4
Drummanmore Rd BT61..98 F1

Drummannagapple
  BT82 ....124 D2
Drum Manor Forest Pk★
  BT80 ....43 F6
Drummans 120 F5
Drummans Glebe
  BT92 ....127 E7
Drummany 131 F2
Drummaw BT92 ......126 F4
Drummee
  Enniskillen BT93 ......103 C5
  Enniskillen BT94 ......116 B5
Drummeer BT94 .....116 F8
Drummenagh BT78 ...36 B6
Drummenagh Beg BT93 85 E8
Drummenagh More
  BT93 ....67 F1
Drummillard BT70 ....43 F1
Drummoan or Newtate
  BT92 ....114 C4
Drummoghan BT93 ...87 A1
Drummonaghan BT94..69 A3
Drummond
  Aughnacloy BT69.......95 C4
  Cookstown BT80 ....45 B5
  Dungannon BT70 ....60 F6
  Dungannon BT71 ....79 D2
  Omagh BT78 ....72 F7
Drummond Rd
  Cookstown BT80 ....45 B4
  Dungannon BT70 ....60 F7
  Omagh BT78 ....72 F7
Drummoney BT93 .....51 B4
Drummoyagh BT93....69 A5
Drummuck
  Dungannon BT71 ....79 F6
  Enniskillen BT92 ......114 E2
Drummullan 128 F2
DRUMMULLAN BT45 ....45 C7
Drummully
  Enniskillen BT92 ......124 E5
  Enniskillen BT92 ......132 C4
Drummurl Glebe BT92 125 E5
Drummurrer BT71 .....62 F2
Drummurrer La BT71.....62 F2
Drummurry BT94 ......88 B5
Drummurry Ct BT94......88 C5
Drummurry Gdns BT94 ..88 B5
Drummusky BT92 ....127 A4
Drumnabey BT81......23 B5
Drumnabey Pk BT81 .....23 A5
Drumnabey Prim Sch
  BT81 ....23 A5
Drumnabey Rd BT81 ....23 B5
Drumnaboy BT82 .....12 F7
Drumnacross BT93....69 C8
Drumnacross Lower
  BT80 ....44 A5
Drumnacross Rd BT80...44 B6
Drumnacross Upper
  BT80 ....43 F6
Drumnafern BT78 .....78 C5
Drumnafern Rd BT70.....78 C5
Drumnaforbe BT78 ....36 F2
Drumnagalliagh BT93 ..51 D5
Drumnaglogh BT80 ...30 F1
Drumnagreshial BT93..51 D5
Drumnagroagh 64 B4
Drumnahoe BT82 .....13 C3
DRUMNAKILLY BT79 .....40 B2
Drumnakilly Rd BT79 ....39 D2
Drumnamalra BT78 ...35 F2
Drumnamalragh BT94.102 E2
Drumnamalta
  Cookstown BT80 ....30 F1
  Dungannon BT70 ....75 E4
Drumnamalta Rd BT80 ..30 F2
Drumnameel BT75 ....91 A1
Drumnamoless BT70 ..78 D1
Drumnanane BT93 ....85 D5
Drumnarullagh BT93 ..51 C1
Drumnashaloge BT70..78 C2
Drumnashear 1 E8
Drumnaspar Rd BT79....15 E4
Drumnasper Rd BT79 ....15 D4
Drumnasreane BT93 ..82 D7
Drumnastrade BT71 ...79 B2
Drumnavahan BT93 ...52 A4
Drumod Glebe 122 F3
Drumoghill BT92 ....114 D4
Drumoris BT94 ......117 E7
Drumowen BT78......36 B2
Drumpeen BT94 ......69 B3
Drumquillia BT92 ....126 C2
Drumquin BT78 ......36 E3
DRUMQUIN (DROIM CAOIN)
  BT78 ....36 E3
Drumquin Rd BT81......22 F3
Drumragh Ave BT79.....136 C4
Drumragh (Caldwell)
  BT78 ....55 F6
Drumragh Church★ BT78 55 F6
Drumragh Intergrated Coll
  BT79 ....56 B8
Drumragh (J McCausland)
  BT78 ....55 F6
Drumragh Rd BT78.......55 F6
Drumragh View BT78 ...136 D1
Drumrainbane BT92...126 A5
Drumrainbane BT92...126 B4
Drumrainey Ave BT70....78 D8
Drumrainey Gdns BT70...78 D8
Drumrainy
  Ballinamallard BT94 ...88 C5
  Enniskillen BT74 ......116 B8
  Enniskillen BT92 ......114 F8
  Enniskillen BT92 ......127 D4
Drumralla BT92......126 E1

Drumraw⊕ BT80........ 44 E1
Drumrawn⊕ BT78........ 37 A3
Drumrawn Rd BT78.... 36 F2
Drum Rd
  Castlederg BT81 ...... 23 D4
  Cookstown BT80 ...... 43 C7
  Londonderry BT47...... .2 F6
  Omagh BT78 .... 55 F4
  Strabane BT82.......... 12 E7
Drumreagh Cres BT71... 61 F5
Drumreagh Etra⊕ BT71.. 62 A4
Drumreagh Otra⊕ BT71.. 61 F5
Drumreane⊕ BT94...... 69 C5
Drumreany⊕ BT70...... 78 D7
Drumreany Rd BT70.... 78 E8
Drumrearty⊕ BT92 .... 125 F4
Drumreask⊕ BT93 ...... 67 E1
Drumreenagh⊕
  Killeevan 133 F8
  Scotshouse 133 E5
Drumroo⊕ BT94 .... 116 F8
Drumroosk⊕
  Enniskillen BT92 ...... 117 B2
  Enniskillen BT92 ...... 123 C6
Drumrot Rd BT45 .... 45 C8
Drumrush⊕ BT93 .... 51 A1
Drumrusk⊕ BT61 .... 97 C2
Drumsallan Lower⊕
  BT61 .... 97 C1
Drumsara⊕ BT94 .... 69 E1
Drumsastry⊕ BT92 .... 126 A5
Drumsawna Beg⊕ BT93... 52 B1
Drumsawna More⊕ BT93. 52 D2
Drumscollop⊕ BT74 .... 86 C1
Drumscra⊕ BT78........ 36 E2
Drumscra Rd BT78...... 36 E2
Drumshanbo Glebe⊕
  BT80 .... 43 C7
Drumshancorick⊕ BT92. 120 A2
Drumshane⊕ BT94...... 69 C3
Drumshanly⊕ BT78...... 55 E6
Drumsheil⊕ BT78........ 54 C2
Drumshimuck⊕ BT92 .. 124 C1
Drumshinney BT79...... 57 E5
Drumsillagh⊕
  Enniskillen BT74 ...... 102 E1
  Enniskillen BT74 ...... 103 B7
  Enniskillen BT92 ...... 114 E2
Drumskea⊕ BT94...... 69 C1
Drumskew⊕ BT74 ...... 103 D5
Drumskimly⊕ BT93 .... 86 A5
Drumskinney Rd BT78.. 71 D7
Drumskinny⊕
  Dungannon BT70 ...... 96 E5
  Enniskillen BT93 ...... 51 D7
  Omagh BT78 .... 71 E6
Drumskool⊕ BT94...... 69 C5
Drumsloe⊕
  Enniskillen BT94 ...... 88 D4
  Scotshouse 132 D6
Drumsluice⊕ BT94...... 87 E5
Drumsna⊕ BT74........ 138 E1
Drumsonnus⊕ BT94 .... 88 E7
Drumsoo⊕ BT92........ 127 D7
Drumsroohil⊕
  Enniskillen BT92 ...... 103 B1
  Enniskillen BT94 ...... 114 E5
Drumswords⊕
  Enniskillen BT92 ...... 127 D8
  Scotshouse 133 E6
Drumullan Rd BT45 .... 45 E8
Drumully⊕ 128 F6
Drumummery⊕ 120 F2
Drumurcher⊕ 133 D2
Drumvale Ave BT80 .... 135 C3
Drumvale Pk BT80 ...... 135 B3
Drumwhinny⊕ BT93 .... 69 A7
Drumwhisker⊕ BT78.... 73 C8
Drumyarkin⊕ BT92 .... 120 B1
Drungan⊕ 82 D3
Drunlish⊕ BT92 .... 123 B8
Dryarch Rd BT79........ 56 E7
Dublin Pk Rd BT78...... 24 F5
Dublin Rd
  Enniskillen BT74 ...... 138 E3
  Omagh BT78 .... 136 C4
Dublin Rd Ind Est BT82. 134 D1
Dublin St BT78............ 25 A6
Duckfield⊕ 112 F2
Dufless⊕ BT71.......... 45 C4
Dufless Rd BT80........ 45 C5
Dullaghan⊕ BT78........ 53 C2
Dullaghan Rd BT78...... 70 E8
Dullerton⊕ BT82........ 1 F3
Dullerton Rd
  Londonderry BT47........ 2 A4
  Strabane BT82............ 1 F3
Dulrush⊕ BT93.......... 66 A4
Dumisk Fort ⭑ BT79.... 58 E7
Dunady⊕ BT47.......... .7 F7
Dunamoney Rd BT70.... 78 E3
Dunamony⊕ BT70...... 78 E3
Dunamore Rd BT80...... 29 D2
Dunardon Dr BT94...... 105 A2
Dunavon Hts BT71...... 137 D8
Dunavon Pk
  Dungannon BT71...... 137 C4
  Dungannon BT71...... 137 D8
Dunavon Rd BT78........ 36 E4
Dunbiggan⊕ BT78...... 74 D4
Dunbiggan Rd BT78...... 74 E4
Dunbreen⊕ BT79........ 25 F2
Dunbreen Cl BT79...... 136 A7
Dunbunrawer⊕ BT78.... 26 A6
Duncan Pk BT78 .... 73 B6
Duncastle Rd BT82........ 2 B2
Dunclare Pk BT71........ 137 C4

Dunclare Way BT71...... 137 B4
Dundee⊕ 1 A7
Dundivin Glebe⊕ BT78... 73 C2
Dundonagh⊕ 110 C2
Dundrumman⊕ 120 F6
Dunena Ave 3 BT94 .... 69 F3
Dungannon Bsns Pk
  BT71 .... 137 D8
DUNGANNON (DÙN
  GEANAINN) BT71...... 137 E6
Dungannon Ent Ctr BT71. 61 E1
Dungannon Leisure Ctr
  BT71 .... 137 D6
Dungannon Pk BT71 .... 62 B3
Dungannon Prim Sch
  BT71 .... 137 D7
Dungannon Rd
  Aughnacloy BT69........ 95 A5
  Cookstown BT80 ...... 44 E2
  Craigavon BT62........ 81 F4
  Dungannon BT70...... 76 E3
  Moy BT71............... 80 A1
Dungannon St 3 BT71... 80 A1
Dungate⊕ BT80 .... 29 D2
DÙN GEANAINN
  (DUNGANNON) BT71.... 137 E6
Dungogen⊕ BT94...... 106 A3
Dungoran⊕ BT78...... 73 B3
Dungorman Rd BT71...... 79 F4
Dungororan⊕ BT70...... 60 D6
Dungororan Rd BT70.... 60 D5
Dunleath Ave BT80...... 135 D3
Dunlea Vale BT71........ 137 D8
Dunlogan⊕ BT45........ 10 F2
Dunmacmay⊕ BT69...... 95 E1
Dunmacmay Rd BT69.... 95 D2
Dunmakeever⊕ 121 B4
Dunmore⊕ BT80........ 31 A6
Dunmore Cl BT80 ...... 135 D6
Dunmore Cres BT80.... 135 D6
Dunmore La BT80...... 31 B5
Dunmore Pk BT80...... 135 D7
Dunmoyle⊕ BT79...... 58 C1
Dunmullan⊕ BT79...... 38 E8
Dunmullan Prim Sch
  BT79 .... 38 E8
Dunmullan Rd BT79...... 25 E2
Dunnalong⊕ BT82...... 1 D7
Dunnalong Rd BT82...... 1 C4
DÙN NA MANACH
  (DUNNAMANAGH) BT82...6 B8
Dunnamanagh Castle ⭑
  BT82.................... 6 D8
DUNNAMANAGH (DÙN NA
  MANACH) BT82.........6 B8
Dunnamona⊕ BT78...... 55 B3
Dunnamona Glebe⊕
  BT78 .... 73 D6
Dunnamona Rd BT78.... 55 A2
Dunnamonna Rd BT78.. 55 A3
Dunnamore⊕ BT80...... 29 E2
Dunnaree⊕ BT78........ 36 D1
Dunne Cres BT79........ 15 A4
Dunnyboe⊕ BT82........ 6 D3
Dunnyboe Rd BT82...... 6 C6
Dunore Ave BT71........ 137 E1
Dunowen Pk............ 11 F7
Dunrevan⊕ BT81........ 22 F6
Dunrevan Rd BT81...... 22 F6
Dunroe Rd BT76........ 93 C3
Dunseark⊕ BT71........ 79 B3
Dunseark Rd BT71...... 79 B4
Dunteige⊕ BT78........ 37 D7
Dunteige Rd BT78...... 37 E7
Dunwish⊕ BT78........ 38 A4
Dunwish Rd BT78........ 37 F3
Durless Black⊕ BT77 .. 94 A3
Durless White⊕ BT77 .. 94 A4
Duross⊕ BT94.......... 68 E2
Dyan⊕ BT68............ 96 E2
Dyan Rd BT70.......... 96 F5
Eagralougher⊕ BT61 .. 98 F5
Eary Lower⊕ BT71...... 46 A1
Eary Upper⊕ BT71...... 46 A1

East Bridge Pl 7 BT74 . 138 D4
East Bridge St 2 BT74 . 138 D4
East Circular Rd BT80.. 135 E6
East Tullynadall⊕ BT93 . 86 B6
East Tyrone Coll of FE & HE
  BT71 .... 137 D8
East Tyrone Coll of F & H Ed
  BT80.................... 135 C5
Eastvale Ave BT71...... 137 E5
East W View Terr 3
  BT78 .... 136 B3
Eccles Gr BT78.......... 73 B5
Ecclesville Ctr BT78 .... 73 C5
Ecclesville Demesne⊕
  BT78 .... 73 C5
Ecclesville Rd BT78...... 73 B3
Ecclesville View BT78 .. 73 C5
Ecclesville Wy BT78.... 73 D5
Eden⊕
  Londonderry BT47........ 9 A7
  Rossinver............... 82 F2
  Strabane BT82.......... 1 E3
Edenaclogh⊕ BT93 .... 52 D3
Edenacrannon⊕ BT70.. 78 B6
Edenafogry⊕ BT78...... 55 C2
Edenaforan⊕ 128 C4
Edenagee⊕ BT93...... 70 C8
Edenageeragh⊕ BT69.. 95 D5
Edenagilhorn⊕ BT94.. 106 B8

Edenagon⊕ BT78........ 71 E4
Edenagore⊕ 64 D5
Edenamohill Black⊕
  BT93 .... 52 E1
Edenamohill Under⊕
  BT93 .... 52 C3
Edenasop⊕ BT81........ 35 B6
Edenasop East⊕ BT78.. 73 C5
Edenasop West⊕ BT78.. 73 C6
Edenatoodry⊕ BT78.... 73 C2
Edenbane⊕ BT93...... 52 B4
Eden Back⊕ BT79...... 15 D5
Edenbane⊕ BT78........ 90 D1
Edenbrack Rd BT79.... 136 E8
Edenclaw Great⊕ BT93.. 52 B1
Edenclaw Little⊕ BT93.. 52 B2
Edenderry⊕
  Dungannon BT71...... 97 D3
  Omagh BT79 .... 56 C6
Edenderry La BT71...... 97 E3
Edenderry Rd BT79...... 56 D7
Edendoit⊕ BT70........ 43 B2
Edendoit Rd BT70...... 43 A2
EDENDORK BT71........ 61 F2
Edendork Prim Sch BT71. 61 F2
Edendork Rd BT71...... 61 F1
Edenfel⊕ BT79.......... 136 E3
Edenfel Cotts BT79...... 136 F2
Edenfel Pk BT79........ 136 E3
Eden Fore⊕ BT79...... 15 C5
Eden Mill⊕ BT79........ 15 C4
Edenmore⊕
  Augher BT77........... 94 A4
  Enniskillen BT92 ...... 114 E4
  Enniskillen BT94 ...... 89 E1
Edenmore Cres 4 BT94.. 89 E1
Edenmore Hts BT94...... 89 E1
Edenmore Rd BT94...... 89 E1
Eden Pk BT81........... 22 E5
Edenreagh⊕ BT81...... 35 A7
Edenreagh Rd BT81...... 35 A7
Eden Rd BT47........... 8 F7
Edenreagh⊕ BT81...... 35 A7
Eden St BT74........... 138 C5
Eden Terr BT82......... 134 D5
Edenticromman⊕ BT93 . 51 C4
Edentiloan⊕ BT69...... 95 F8
Edenvale Pk BT78...... 136 A5
Ederdacurragh⊕ BT74.. 116 E6
Ederdaglass or Hollybank⊕
  BT94 .... 105 A1
Ederdamone⊕ 65 A5
Edergole⊕
  Enniskillen BT94 ...... 117 A6
  Omagh BT78 .... 91 B6
Edergool⊕ BT92........ 132 A5
Edergoole Ave BT78.... 55 D3
Edergoole Lower⊕ BT78.. 55 E3
Edergoole Rd BT78...... 73 C8
Edergoole Upper⊕ BT78. 55 E3
Edernagh⊕ BT71...... 45 F4
EDERNEY BT93.......... 52 A2
Edernish⊕ BT93 .... 51 F1
Edfield Way BT75...... 91 C1
Edinburgh Dr BT80.... 135 C6
Edinburgh Pk BT79 .... 136 F4
Edinburgh Villas BT79.. 136 F4
Ednagee Rd BT81...... 22 F2
Ednashanlaght⊕ BT78.. 36 B8
Edwards Cl BT81........ 22 E6
Edwards Prim Sch 13
  BT81.................... 22 E5
Edymore⊕ BT82........ 13 A7
Effernan Glebe⊕ BT78.. 89 C5
Effernan Rd BT78...... 89 C6
Eglish⊕ BT62.......... 81 D2
EGLISH BT71............ 79 A1
Eglish⊕ BT71.......... 97 D3
Eglish Pk BT62.......... 81 D3
Eglish (Portadown) Prim Sch
  BT62.................... 81 D3
Eglish Prim Sch BT71 .. 79 A1
Eglish Rd
  Craigavon BT62........ 81 D3
  Dungannon BT71...... 79 A3
Elagh⊕
  Dungannon BT71...... 46 C3
  Strabane BT82.......... 13 B4
Elagh Rd BT82.......... 13 B4
Ellinuro⊕ 133 E8
Elliott Pl BT74.......... 138 B4
Elmbrook Sch BT74.... 138 A6
Elm Rd BT82............ 6 B6
Elms The BT71.......... 79 E8
Ely Gdns BT74.......... 138 A4
Ely Island⊕ BT93...... 87 B4
Emerson Terr BT82...... 12 D5
Empire Ave BT71...... 137 D5
EMYVALE (SCRAIRB AN
  GCAORACH).......... 110 B4
Enagh⊕
  Armagh BT60........... 111 F3
  Caledon BT68.......... 111 D7
Enaghan⊕ BT93........ 86 F2
Ennish⊕ BT70.......... 78 A3
Enniskillen⊕
  Dungannon BT71...... 45 F5
  Enniskillen BT74 ...... 138 C4
Enniskillen Airport (St
  Angelo) BT74.......... 87 E2
Enniskillen Bsns Ctr
  BT74 .... 104 B6
ENNISKILLEN (INIS
  CEITHLEANN) BT74..... 138 C4
Enniskillen Intergrated Prim
  Sch BT74............... 138 C8
Enniskillen Model Prim Sch
  BT74 .... 138 F4
Enniskillen Rd BT94...... 70 A2

Ennismore Rd BT62 .... 81 D7
Envagh⊕ BT78........ 37 A7
Envagh Prim Sch BT78 . 37 B8
Envagh Rd BT78........ 37 A7
EOCHAIR (AUGHER) BT77.. 93 B7
Erdinagh⊕ BT75...... 107 D4
ERGANAGH BT81........ 23 A6
Erganagh Glebe⊕ BT79. 39 A6
Erganagh Prim Sch BT81. 23 A6
Erganagh Rd
  Castlederg BT81........ 23 A7
  Omagh BT79 .... 39 A6
Erin Rd BT82........... 13 B3
Erne Dr
  Enniskillen BT74 ...... 138 C6
  Enniskillen BT93 ...... 51 F1
Erne Hospl BT74........ 138 D6
Erne Intergrated Coll
  BT74.................... 138 C8
Erne Pk BT93.......... 68 F8
Erne Rd BT74.......... 138 D6
Erne Sch BT74.......... 138 A6
Erneside Sh Ctr BT74 . 138 D4
Erne Sq............... 127 E3
Erne Terr BT93........ 86 A4
Errasallagh⊕ BT92..... 119 C4
Errasallagh Cross Roads
  BT92 .... 119 C3
Errigal⊕ BT70........ 75 D2
Errigal Rd BT70........ 75 E3
Erveny⊕ BT92........ 122 E8
Ervey⊕
  Enniskillen BT92 ...... 119 D4
  Londonderry BT47...... 3 F8
Ervey Rd BT47......... 3 F7
Ervey Wood Country Pk ⭑
  BT47.................... 3 F7
Eshacorran⊕ BT94..... 118 B6
Eshacrin⊕ 109 C1
Eshanummmer⊕ BT92.. 118 A4
Eshbane⊕ BT92...... 118 C4
Eshbralley⊕ BT92 .... 118 B2
Eshcarcoge⊕ BT92 ... 118 C5
Eshcloghfin⊕ 109 E3
Eshekerin⊕ BT92...... 119 D5
Eshmeen⊕ BT92...... 118 D4
Eshmore Rd BT78...... 72 E1
Eshnadarragh⊕
  Enniskillen BT92 ...... 119 F6
  Enniskillen BT94 ...... 118 C8
Eshnadeelada⊕ BT92.. 118 F4
Eshnaglogh⊕ 109 A3
Eshnagorr⊕ BT92..... 118 B3
Eshnaheeda⊕ 109 D5
Eshnanumera⊕ BT94.. 118 D8
Eshnascreen⊕ BT92... 118 B4
Eshnasillog Beg⊕ BT75. 119 A8
Eshnasillog More⊕
  BT94 .... 118 E8
Eshthomas⊕ BT94..... 118 B4
Eshveragh⊕ 109 E5
Eshywulligan⊕ BT92... 119 C6
Esker⊕ BT78.......... 71 D6
Eskeradooey⊕ BT79 ... 25 F4
Eskeragh⊕ BT94...... 106 E4
Eskerboy⊕ BT79...... 58 C6
Esker Hill Rd BT70...... 59 D1
Eskermore⊕
  Augher BT77........... 75 B1
  Omagh BT79 .... 57 A5
Eskermore Rd BT79...... 57 A4
Eskernabrogue⊕ BT76.. 74 E1
Esker Rd
  Cookstown BT80 ...... 30 D1
  Omagh BT78 .... 71 D6
Eskragh⊕
  Dungannon BT70...... 77 D3
  Dungannon BT70...... 78 F6
  Omagh BT78 .... 74 D3
Eskragh Rd BT70...... 78 F6
Eskragh Terr BT70...... 78 F5
Eskra Rd BT78.......... 74 D4
Espey Pk 4 BT71........ 80 A6
Essan⊕ BT81.......... 33 C7
Essan Rd BT81......... 33 E8
Everglades BT74...... 104 B5
Evish⊕ BT82........... 42 A6
Evishacrancussy⊕ BT80. 42 C7
Evishanoran⊕ BT70.... 42 D6
Evishbrack⊕
  Cookstown BT80 ...... 29 F3
  Cookstown BT80 ...... 30 A3
Evish Gr BT82.......... 134 F4
Evish Prim Sch BT82 ... 5 C1
Evish Rd BT82.......... 134 F4

Faccary BT79........... 39 E4
Faccary⊕ BT79........ 39 F6
Factory La BT80........ 135 C6
Factory Rd BT74....... 138 D6
Fairfield BT71.......... 137 C4
Fairgreen BT70........ 76 C2
Fairgreen St
  Dungannon BT70...... 42 F1
  6 Irvinestown BT94.... 69 F3
Fairhill Cl BT80........ 135 C5
Fairhill Gr BT80........ 135 C4
Fairhill Rd BT80........ 135 B5
Fairmount Ave 9 BT78. 136 B3
Fairmount Cotts 4 BT78 136 B3
Fairmount Pk BT70...... 137 B5
Fairmount Rd 2 BT78... 136 B3
Fairmount Terr 8 BT78. 136 B3
Fair View BT70......... 137 B5

Fairview Ave 5 BT74... 138 D4
Fairview Gdns BT78...... 71 E8
Fairview La BT74........ 138 E4
Fairview or Mucklagh⊕
  BT60.................... 111 D3
Fairview Pk BT93........ 85 F5
Fallaghearn⊕
  Omagh BT78 .... 55 C1
  Omagh BT79 .... 76 A8
Fallaghearn Rd BT70.... 75 F7
Fallagh Lower⊕ BT79.. 27 C5
Fallagh Middle⊕ BT79... 27 C4
Fallagh Rd BT79....... 27 D3
Fallagh Upper⊕ BT79... 27 D4
Falls⊕ BT94........... 105 E4
Falskey Rd BT78........ 55 A8
Farburn Rd BT79....... 25 F2
Far Circular Rd BT71.... 79 D5
Fardross Demesne⊕
  BT76 .... 92 E2
Fardross Mountain⊕
  BT76 .... 108 D7
Fardross Rd BT76...... 92 D3
Fardrum⊕ BT93........ 87 A3
Fargrim⊕
  Enniskillen BT92 ...... 126 F4
  Enniskillen BT93 ...... 69 B6
Farlough⊕ BT71........ 61 F3
Farlough Rd
  Craigavon BT62........ 81 F5
  Dungannon BT71...... 61 F4
Farm⊕ BT92........... 132 A8
Farmhill Cl BT79........ 39 B2
Farmhill Mdws 13 BT79. 39 B2
Farmhill Rd BT79........ 39 B2
Farnacht⊕ BT74....... 116 C8
Farnaconnell⊕ BT74... 102 A6
Farnamullan⊕ BT94... 116 C8
Farnamullan Est BT94.. 105 A1
Farranaconaghy⊕ BT92. 117 E1
Farranacurky⊕ BT92... 125 C8
Farranasculloge⊕ BT92 117 D1
Farrancassidy⊕ BT93... 65 B1
Farrancassidy Cross Roads
  BT93 .... 65 A1
Farranetra⊕ BT76...... 93 B5
Farrest⊕ BT79......... 38 E8
Farriter⊕ BT70........ 77 D4
Farriter Rd BT70...... 77 C5
Farsnagh⊕ BT80...... 47 C3
Fartagh⊕
  Enniskillen BT74 ...... 102 E8
  Enniskillen BT93 ...... 52 B6
Fasglashagh⊕ BT70.... 77 D6
Fasglashagh Cl BT70... 77 D5
Fashglashagh Rd BT70.. 77 D6
Fassagh⊕ BT93........ 64 E1
Faughard⊕ BT94...... 105 A1
Faugher⊕
  Enniskillen BT74 ...... 102 A6
  Enniskillen BT74 ...... 102 F7
Faurkagh⊕ BT92...... 124 B7
Favor Royal Demesne⊕
  BT77 .... 94 B5
Favour Royal BT77...... 94 A6
Favour Royal Rd BT77... 93 E6
Fawney⊕ BT82......... .2 F2
Feagh⊕
  Dungannon BT71...... 46 B1
  Enniskillen BT92 ...... 119 F2
Featherbed Glade BT74. 138 A5
Feddan⊕
  Dungannon BT70...... 76 B1
  Enniskillen BT94 ...... 104 F7
Feddan Rd BT70...... 76 A1
Feddans⊕ BT93....... 51 B2
Fedian⊕ BT93......... 86 C5
Feegarran⊕ BT80...... 31 B3
Feegarran La BT80...... 31 B2
Feegarren Rd BT80..... 31 B2
Feegarren Rod BT80.... 31 D1
Feenan⊕ BT78......... 73 B7
Feeney's La BT70....... 137 C6
Feglish⊕ BT78........ 70 D4
Feglish Rd BT78....... 70 C3
Ferguson Cres 8 BT71.. 22 E5
Ferguy Hts BT71....... 135 D6
Fermanagh Coll Skills Ctr
  BT74.................... 138 F2
Fermanagh Cty Mus ⭑ 10
  BT74.................... 138 C5
Fermanagh St.......... 127 E3
Fernagh⊕ BT79........ 40 A4
Fernaghandrum⊕ BT78. 74 D5
Fernagh Rd BT79....... 39 F4
Fernamenagh⊕ BT70... 75 E2
Ferndale
  Clogher BT76.......... 93 A5
  Strabane BT82......... 134 C1
Ferney⊕
  Enniskillen BT94 ...... 88 C4
  Omagh BT78 .... 70 D5
Ferney Rd BT78........ 70 D4
Ferney Rise BT74...... 138 A5
Ferneyview BT94....... 88 C5
Fern Valley BT74....... 138 F4
Ferone Dr BT79........ 25 A6
Feroy⊕ BT70........... 61 D4
Ferry Rd BT71.......... 63 C2
Festival Pk
  Cookstown BT80 ...... 135 F4
  Omagh BT78 .... 136 C3
Feugh⊕ BT92......... 126 E1

Fifth Corgary or First
Croagh BT81 .... 20 B5
Finbarr Rd BT79 ..... 40 A2
Fincarn BT47 .... 9 E8
Findermore BT76 .... 92 D3
Findermore Rd BT76 ... 92 D4
Findrum BT70 .... 76 C3
Findrum Rd BT70 .... 76 C3
Finelly BT71 .... 79 D1
Fingerpost Rd BT78 ... 89 A6
Finglen
　Londonderry BT47 ...... 10 B5
　Londonderry BT47 ...... 18 E8
Finglush BT68 .... 111 A7
Finglush Rd BT68 ..... 111 B8
Fingrean Rd BT79 .... 40 E5
Finlane BT92 .... 114 B1
Finmill Rd BT79 ..... 58 B4
Finner BT93 .... 65 A4
Finnobar BT80 .... 46 B7
Finn Pk BT92 .... 120 C1
Finn Side Cl 134 A5
Finn Valley Enterprise Pk 134 A7
Finn View BT82 .... 134 B4
Fintona BT78 .... 73 C6
FINTONA (FIONNTAMHNACH) BT78 .... 73 C6
Fintona Golf Club BT78 .. 73 B5
Fintona Rd
　Clogher BT76 .... 92 E5
　Dromore BT78 .... 71 F7
Finulagh BT70 .... 78 B8
Finulagh Rd BT70 .... 60 B1
Finvey BT80 .... 61 C8
Finvey La BT80 .... 61 C8
FIONNTAMHNACH (FINTONA) BT78 .... 73 C6
Fireagh (Cochrane) BT78 .... 55 D7
Fireagh (Gardiner) BT78 .... 55 C6
Fireagh Rd BT78 ..... 55 D5
Fireagh (Thompson) BT78 .... 55 C7
Fir Gr Ct BT74 .... 104 B5
Firs BT93 .... 50 B3
First Corgary BT81 ..... 20 F4
Five Acres BT82 .... 134 C2
FIVE LOAN ENDS BT62 .... 81 C2
Fivemiletown BT75 .... 107 C8
FIVEMILETOWN (BAILE NA LORGAN) BT75 .... 107 C8
Fivemiletown High Sch BT75 .... 107 B8
Fivemiletown Ind Est BT75 .... 107 C8
Fivemiletown Mus ★ 7 BT75 .... 107 C8
Fivemiletown Prim Sch BT75 .... 91 C1
Flaxfield Pk BT74 ..... 138 F4
Flax Valley BT74 ..... 69 F3
Fleming Way BT82 .... 134 C2
Florance Rd BT78 ..... 74 F2
Floraville BT74 .... 138 E6
Flo Rd BT80 .... 43 D8
Florence Court Demesne BT92 .... 114 C3
Florence Ct ★ BT92 .... 114 C3
Florence Ct Prim Sch BT92 .... 114 E4
Flushtown BT82 .... 12 B8
Flushtown Rd BT79 .... 57 F4
Foalies 131 A6
Fogart BT76 .... 92 D8
Fogart Rd BT76 .... 92 D8
Foggyhill Rd BT81 ..... 22 B3
Foglish BT75 .... 107 C6
Folliard Rd BT82 .... 11 F1
Follum Big BT92 .... 119 D3
Follum Little BT92 ..... 119 D2
Foreglen Rd BT47 ...... 3 F6
Foremass
　Enniskillen BT92 ...... 125 E8
　Omagh BT79 .... 58 A3
Foremass Lower BT79 .. 58 A3
Foremass Rd BT79 .... 58 C2
Foremass Upper BT79.. 58 B2
Forest Cres BT78 ...... 24 A4
Forestry Sch BT70 .... 43 A1
Forest View BT79 ..... 40 C7
Forfey BT92 .... 117 E4
Forge Rd BT47 .... 2 F7
Forglen Rd BT47 ...... 3 F6
Formil
　Enniskillen BT92 ...... 130 D7
　Enniskillen BT93 ..... 51 A5
　Omagh BT79 .... 28 E3
Forsters Rd BT81 ..... 23 F4
Forth Glen BT80 ..... 135 A6
Forthill BT94 .... 69 F3
Forthill Dr BT80 ..... 135 B4
Forthill Pk BT78 ..... 24 F6
Forthill Rd BT74 ..... 138 D5
Forthill Rise BT80 ... 135 B4
Forthill St BT74 ..... 138 D5
Fortified House ★ 132 C2
Fort Rd
　Castlederg BT81 ...... 21 F2
　Strabane BT82 .... 12 B7
Fort-Town BT82 .... 12 B7
Fortview Pk
　Enniskillen BT94 ..... 105 A2

Fortview Pk continued
　Kesh BT93 .... 68 F8
Forum View BT74 .... 138 D3
Foundary Ln BT78..... 136 C4
Fountain Cl BT80 .... 135 D4
Fountain Ct BT80 .... 135 E4
Fountain La
　5 Omagh BT78..... 136 B4
　Omagh BT79 .... 57 B5
Fountain Pk BT82 .... 134 F3
Fountain Rd BT80 .... 135 D4
Fountain St BT82 .... 134 F4
Four Oaks The BT94.... 87 E3
Foxborough BT70 .... 137 A7
Foxhill Cl BT74 ..... 138 D7
Fox Pk BT79 .... 40 A1
Foyarr BT60 .... 111 F7
Foyarr Rd BT60 ..... 111 F6
Foydragh BT94 ..... 106 A4
Foyfin BT81 .... 11 D6
Foygh BT70 .... 60 E1
Foygh Rd BT70 .... 60 F1
Foylevale BT82 ..... 134 D6
Foyleview Cres BT82 .... 5 A6
Frenchmans La BT70 .. 78 C7
Freuglough BT81 ..... 22 D7
Freuglough Rd BT81 .. 22 E7
Freughmore
　Clogher BT76 .... 92 E3
　Omagh BT78 .... 56 A4
　Omagh BT78 .... 73 F7
Freughmore Rd BT78 .. 73 E7
Frevagh BT93 .... 99 D7
Friars Way BT74 .... 103 D5
Friary Rd BT70 ..... 96 C8
Friths Pass BT74 .... 138 E4
Furnaceland BT82 ... 122 D3
Furnish BT75 .... 91 A2
Fyagh BT74 .... 116 A3
Fyfin
　Strabane BT82 .... 5 F4
　Strabane BT82 .... 23 C7
Fyfin Rd BT82 .... 23 C7
Fyfin Rd Link BT82 ... 12 D3
Fymore Moutray BT77.. 93 F5
Fymore Todd BT77 ... 93 F5
Gadalough BT93 ..... 65 D5

G

Gaelscoil Ui Dhocartaigh BT82 .... 134 E3
Gaelscoil Ui Neill BT71 ... 62 D3
Galbally
　Dungannon BT70 .... 60 B2
　Enniskillen BT92 ... 127 D6
　Omagh BT78 .... 71 D4
　Omagh BT79 .... 56 B7
Galbally Rd BT78 .... 71 E5
Galcussagh BT70 .... 43 F2
Gallagh
　Augher BT77 .... 94 A6
　Enniskillen BT92 ... 114 E2
Gallanagh BT80 ..... 44 E3
Gallanbridge Rd BT78 .. 13 F1
Gallan Lower BT78 ... 13 F1
Gallan Rd
　Omagh BT78 .... 25 A8
　Strabane BT82 .... 13 E4
Gallan Upper BT78 ... 13 F3
Gallany BT82 .... 12 C7
Galliagh Pk BT74 ... 138 A5
Galliagh Shore BT74 .. 138 A5
Galliagh Terr BT74 .. 138 C6
Galloon BT92 .... 131 C7
Galloon Gdns BT92.... 126 C3
Gallows Hill BT70 ... 137 B6
Gallrock BT62 .... 81 D4
Gallrock Rd BT62 .... 81 D4
Galvally or Stevensons Dowery BT71....... 62 C8
Gamble Pk BT81 ..... 23 B6
Gammy BT78 .... 55 D5
Ganard La BT80 ..... 31 E6
Gannon's Cross 131 F1
Gan Snál 134 A6
Ganvaghan Hemphill BT81 .... 22 B2
Ganvaghan Kyle BT81 .. 22 B3
Ganvaghan Rd BT81.... 22 C4
Ganvaghan Semple BT81 .... 22 C3
Gaol Sq BT74 .... 138 E4
Gap Rd BT79 .... 40 D1
Gardenhill BT93 .... 101 D2
Garden Mews BT80 ... 135 C6
Garden Rd BT82 ..... 12 D5
Garden Terr 11 BT82 .. 12 D6
Gardenville Ave BT79 .. 136 C5
Gardiners Cross Rd BT94 .... 117 B7
Gardiner's Cross Roads BT94 .... 105 F3
Gardrum
　Dromore BT78 .... 71 F8
　Enniskillen BT74 ... 102 F1
Gargadis BT78 .... 70 F2
Gargadis Rd BT78 .... 71 B2
Gargrim
　Enniskillen BT93 .... 70 A8
　Omagh BT78 .... 73 E5
Gargrim Rd BT78 .... 73 E5
Garlaw BT75 .... 91 F3
Garlaw Rd
　Clogher BT76 .... 92 B3
　Fivemiletown BT75 .. 91 F3

Garnet Cl 3 BT81 .... 22 E5
Garranbane Stone ★ BT94 .... 105 D7
Garraroosky BT92.... 125 F5
Garrifly BT92 .... 114 C1
Garrison BT93 .... 83 A4
GARRISON BT93 .... 83 A5
Garrison Glebe BT78 .. 52 E6
Garrison Pl BT71.... 98 B8
Garryowen Rd BT79 .... 41 F7
Gartagher BT78 .... 36 E2
Gartan Ave BT82 .... 134 D3
Garvagh
　Castlederg BT81 ..... 21 E6
　Dungannon BT70 .... 61 B3
　Omagh BT78 .... 54 F4
　Omagh BT79 .... 15 F1
　Omagh BT79 .... 17 A7
Garvagh Blane BT81 .. 21 D6
Garvagh Blane Rd BT81.. 21 D6
Garvagh Pullans BT81.. 21 D7
Garvaghullion BT78 .. 37 C5
Garvaghy
　Dungannon BT70 .... 75 B4
　Dungannon BT71 .... 97 B8
　Enniskillen BT92 ... 125 B8
　Enniskillen BT94 ... 70 C3
　Omagh BT79 .... 56 D7
Garvaghy Brdige Rd BT70 75 E4
Garvaghyhill Rd BT70 .. 75 D5
Garvaghy Rd BT70 .... 75 B4
Garvallagh BT78 ..... 74 A6
Garvallagh Rd BT78 .. 73 F3
Garvan Pk BT82 ..... 12 C6
Garvan Rd BT82 ..... 12 C6
Garvary
　Enniskillen BT74 ... 104 D6
　Enniskillen BT92 ... 103 C1
　Enniskillen BT92 ... 129 F7
　Enniskillen BT93 .... 66 B7
GARVETAGH BT81 ..... 22 E2
Garvetagh Lower BT81.. 22 E2
Garvetagh Rd BT81 ... 22 E2
Garvetagh Upper BT81.. 22 E1
Garvey BT69 .... 94 D6
Garvoghill BT92..... 117 A5
Garvros BT93 .... 82 F6
Gas La 127 F2
Geaglum BT92 ..... 125 A3
Georges St
　Dungannon BT70 .... 137 C5
　7 Omagh BT78..... 136 B4
Genedra BT47 .... 10 D4
Genedra Rd BT47...... 9 F8
Geraghtys La BT70 ... 137 C6
Gibson Prim Sch BT79 .. 136 D5
Gillygooley Prim Sch BT78 .... 38 A3
Gillygooley Rd BT78 ... 37 E2
Gillygooly BT78 .... 38 A3
Gillyholme (Ely) BT74 .. 102 F8
Gillyholme (L'estrange) BT74 .... 86 E1
Giltagh
　Enniskillen BT93 .... 86 B3
　Enniskillen BT94 ... 105 E3
Glack
　Aughnacloy BT69 .... 95 B6
　Buckode 82 A4
Glasdrumman
　Enniskillen BT92 ... 117 F2
　Enniskillen BT92 ... 123 B5
　Enniskillen BT93 .... 50 E7
　Enniskillen BT94 ... 105 B7
Glasdrummond BT69.. 95 F4
Glasdrummond Rd BT69.. 95 F8
Glashygolgan BT78 ... 14 E3
GLASLOCH (GLASLOUGH) BT70 .. 110 F2
GLASLOUGH (GLASLOUGH) BT70 .. 110 F2
Glasmullagh
　Dungannon BT70 .... 43 F3
　Dungannon BT70 .... 78 E7
　Enniskillen BT74 ... 102 D3
　Enniskillen BT74 ... 104 C2
　Enniskillen BT92 ... 130 C7
　Enniskillen BT93 .... 52 A1
　Enniskillen BT93 .... 52 C5
　Omagh BT78 .... 37 E8
Glasmullagh North BT78 .... 71 E2
Glasmullagh Rd BT78 .. 37 E8
Glasmullagh South BT78 .... 89 A6
Glassdrummond Rd BT70.. 78 B1
Glear BT82 .... 128 B3
Glebe
　Castlederg BT81 ..... 21 F1
　Omagh BT78 .... 37 B2
　Sion Mills BT82 ... 12 C6
　Strabane BT82 .... 5 C6
Glebe (Artrea) BT71.. 45 D5
Glebe (Ballyclog) BT71.. 45 E3
Glebe Ct BT70 .... 79 A8
Glebe (Derryloran) BT70
　Cookstown BT80 .... 135 B2
　Dungannon BT71 .... 62 C8
Glebe Farm BT71 .... 62 E5
Glebe Gdns BT82..... 12 C6
Glebe Lissagorry BT92 126 B7
Glebe Mews BT70.... 79 A8
Glebe (Old) BT82 .... 12 C6
Glebe Pk
　Dungannon BT70 .... 79 A8
　10 Enniskillen BT74.. 104 B6
　Strabane BT82 .... 12 C5

Glebe Rd
　Dungannon BT70 .... 79 A8
　Omagh BT78 .... 89 B6
Glen
　Belturbet 130 D3
　Enniskillen BT94 ... 89 D4
Glenadush BT70 ..... 78 F7
Glenagoorland Rd BT82 ..2 F3
Glenalt BT94 .... 69 D1
Glenalt Rd BT78 ..... 75 A3
Glenaness Rd BT79 ... 57 F1
Glenarb BT68 .... 111 E8
Glenard Gdns 2 BT78.. 38 D1
Glenard Rd 4 BT78 ... 38 D1
Glenarn BT93 .... 53 B4
Glenarn Cl BT93 ..... 52 F3
Glenarn Rd BT93 ..... 53 B4
Glenarny BT80 .... 44 A4
Glenarny Rd BT80 .... 44 A5
Glenavon Gdns BT80 .. 135 C3
Glenavon Pk BT80 ... 135 C3
Glenbane Rd BT78 .... 36 B2
Glenbeg BT70 .... 60 B3
Glenburrisk BT70 .... 60 C3
Glencam BT79 ..... 136 D8
Glencash BT82....... 4 C6
Glenchiel BT79 ..... 16 C7
Glenchiel Rd BT79 ... 16 D6
Glenchuil BT70 ..... 75 F3
Glencon BT71 .... 61 E6
Glencon Rd BT71 .... 61 D5
Glencoonra BT94 .... 88 A6
Glencoppagh Rd BT82.. 14 E7
Glencoppogagh BT79 .. 15 A5
Glencordial BT79 .... 39 C6
Glencordial Rd BT79 .. 136 E8
Glencosh BT82....... 6 A8
Glencosh Rd BT82 .... 6 A8
Glencovet Glebe BT75.. 90 F3
Glencree BT80 ..... 135 D3
Glencrew BT69 .... 95 C5
Glencrew Rd BT69 ... 95 D4
Glencull BT69....... 95 C6
Glencullin Rd BT79 ... 27 E8
Glencunny BT74 ..... 103 B2
Glencurry Rd BT79 ... 39 D3
Glendavagh BT69 .... 95 E3
Glendavagh Rd BT69 .. 95 D3
Glenderg BT79 .... 39 A5
Glendore Pk 5 BT79 .. 39 B2
Glendore Wood 6 BT79.. 39 B2
Glen East BT93 .... 83 F4
Glenedra BT47 .... 10 D4
Glenedra Rd BT47...... 9 F8
GLENEENY BT79 .... 58 D5
Gleneeny BT79 .... 58 E5
Gleneeny Rd BT79 .... 58 F5
Glenelly Gdns BT79 .. 136 B6
Glenelly Rd
　Omagh BT79 .... 15 D4
　Plumbridge BT79 ... 15 A4
Glenelly View BT79 ... 15 A4
Glenerin BT79 .... 9 F1
Glenevish Hill BT82 .. 134 F6
Glenfern Rd BT78 .... 55 A6
Glenfinn Pk BT82 ... 134 A4
Glenforan Rd BT79 ... 15 D1
Glenga BT79 .... 15 B6
Glengarrow BT47 ..... 7 E1
Glengawna BT79 ..... 39 C8
Glengeen BT78 ..... 72 B2
Glengeen Rd BT78 ... 72 B1
Glengesh BT94....... 90 D7
Glenglush BT82....... 23 D8
Glengomma BT45 ..... 18 F7
Glengrainne Pk 2 BT47.. 8 E7
Glenhordial Rd BT78 .. 39 B4
Glenhoy BT77....... 75 C1
Glenhoy Rd BT77..... 75 A1
GLENHULL BT79 .... 28 C6
Glenhull Wlk BT79 .. 136 B7
Glenkeel
　Enniskillen BT93 ... 101 B8
　Kiltyclogher 99 B3
Glenkeen
　Aughnacloy BT69 .... 95 E2
　Enniskillen BT93 .... 69 B5
Glenknock or Cloghogle BT78 .... 25 A8
Glenlark BT79 .... 16 F2
Glenlee Ave BT79 ... 136 E5
Glenlevan BT93 ..... 86 A5
Glenlough BT47....... 3 E3
Glenmacoffer BT79 ... 27 A4
Glenmacoffer Rd BT79 .. 27 C5
Glenmont Pk BT71.... 137 C4
Glenmornan Prim Sch (St Josephs) BT82....... 5 E3
Glenmornan Rd BT82 ...5 E3
Glennagarran BT93 ... 50 F4
Glennageeragh BT77.. 75 C2
Glennagoorland Glebe BT82 .... 2 F4
Glennan BT78 .... 54 F2
Glennan Brae 10 BT79.. 39 B2
Glennan Cl 12 BT79 .. 39 B2
Glennan Gr 11 BT79 .. 39 B2
Glennan Pk BT79 .... 39 B2
Glennan Rd BT79 .... 54 F3
Glennasheevar BT93 .. 84 D6
Glennoo BT76 ..... 108 C4
Glenpark Rd BT79.... 26 B2
Glen Pk BT71 .... 62 B4
Glenrandal Rd BT47.... 8 A7
Glen Rd
　Castlederg BT81 ..... 35 A8
　Enniskillen BT94 ... 89 D4
　Omagh BT78 .... 52 E6

Glen Rd continued
　Strabane BT82....... 134 F6
Glenree Ave BT71 ... 137 E8
Glenroan BT79 .... 16 A5
Glenroe BT69 .... 94 F7
Glenross BT94 .... 68 F1
Glenshane Rd BT47 .... 3 D8
Glenside
　Omagh BT79 .... 136 F6
　Strabane BT82..... 134 F8
Glenside Specl Sch BT82 134 F7
Glentimon BT82 ..... 12 C4
Glentown BT82 .... 12 A5
Glen Upper BT79..... 40 D5
Glenvannan BT93 .... 51 C8
Glen View 1 BT94.... 89 F1
Glenview Cotts 7 BT78 .. 136 B3
Glenview Pk BT82.... 134 F5
Glenviggan BT45..... 18 D1
Glenviggan Rd BT45... 18 F2
Glen West BT93 ..... 83 E4
Glenwinny BT93 ..... 86 B6
Glenwood Cres BT80 .. 135 D2
Glenwood Gdns BT74 .. 138 A2
Gloudstown BT82 ...... 1 F1
Gobnascale BT82....... 6 A7
Gola
　Enniskillen BT94 ... 106 C1
　Enniskillen BT94 ... 116 C7
Goladoo BT93 .... 70 B8
Goladuff BT92 ..... 131 D6
Golan
　Dungannon BT70 .... 77 A2
　Enniskillen BT92 ... 126 E2
　Omagh BT78 .... 54 B2
　Omagh BT79 .... 25 E1
Golan Adams BT81 ... 22 F4
Goland BT70 .... 76 F1
Golanduff BT80..... 133 D8
Golandun Dolan BT81 .. 34 B6
Golandun Mc Hugh BT81 .... 34 B4
Golan Glebe BT78.... 89 D6
Golan (Hunter) BT81 .. 23 A4
Golan Rd
　Castlederg BT81 ..... 22 F3
　Omagh BT79 .... 25 D1
Golan Sproul BT81 ... 22 F3
Gole BT92 .... 125 A1
Goles BT79 .... 18 C8
Goles Rd BT79 .... 18 B8
Golfcourse Rd BT78 .. 24 D5
Golf View BT80 ..... 135 E3
Goorland Rd BT82 ..... 2 F3
Gorestown BT71 ..... 79 F1
Gorestown La BT71 ... 97 F8
Gorestown Rd BT71 ... 79 E1
Gorey BT70 .... 77 F6
Gorey Rd BT70 .... 77 F6
Gorgesh BT92 ..... 123 C2
Gorse Rd BT82....... 5 F8
Gort
　Dungannon BT70 .... 75 D3
　Dungannon BT70 .... 96 D7
Gortacar BT93 .... 50 D2
Gortacar (Doris) BT80.. 44 C3
Gortacar (Glassy) BT80.. 44 A4
Gortacarn BT92..... 122 E8
Gortacar Rd BT80 .... 44 C3
Gortacashel 122 E4
Gortacharn BT92..... 117 D3
Gortaclady BT70 .... 42 F5
Gortaclare
　Omagh BT79 .... 56 F1
　Strabane BT82....... 6 F7
Gortaclare Rd BT82 .... 6 D6
Gortacloghan BT71 ... 62 B8
Gortadrehid BT74 ... 103 A3
Gortadrehid Big BT92.. 138 D1
Gortadrehid Little BT92 .... 138 B1
Gortagammon BT80.... 45 A1
Gortagammon Rd BT80.. 45 A2
Gortagowan BT80..... 61 E8
Gortahurk BT92..... 129 C7
Gortahurk East BT74 .. 103 A1
Gortahurk West BT74 .. 102 B1
Gortaloughan BT74 ... 88 A1
Gortalowry BT80..... 135 C3
Gortalowry Pk BT80 .. 135 D2
Gortalughany BT92.... 122 B6
Gortaquill BT92 ..... 112 A7
Gortaree
　Enniskillen BT92 ... 113 A4
　Enniskillen BT92 ... 129 D8
Gortatole
　Enniskillen BT74 ... 102 A1
　Enniskillen BT92 ... 113 C5
Gortatole Outdoor Ed Ctr ★ BT92 .... 113 C5
Gortatray BT71 ..... 62 E7
Gortatray Bog BT71 ... 62 D6
Gortavale BT70 ..... 60 E7
Gortavale Rd BT70 ... 60 F7
Gortavea BT82....... 1 C5
Gortavilly BT80 ..... 44 B2
Gortavoy BT70 .... 60 C5
Gortawee or Scotchtown 129 C5
Gortbrannan BT92 .. 126 E4
Gortdonaghy BT92 .. 115 C6
Gorteen
　Enniskillen BT92 ... 113 E5
　Enniskillen BT92 ... 119 D3
　Enniskillen BT93 ... 123 F3
　Enniskillen BT93 .... 68 F6
　Enniskillen BT93 .... 83 C3
　Enniskillen BT93 ... 112 F8

Gorteen continued
Enniskillen BT94 . . . . 106 B6
Swanlinbar. 122 D2
Gortermoan❶ BT92 . . . . 113 F5
Gortevin Terr ⑩ BT71 . . . 62 C2
Gortfad❶ BT80 . . . . 44 B3
Gortfad Glebe❶ BT80 . . . 61 B7
Gortfad La BT80 . . . . 61 A7
Gortfin❶ BT79. . . . . 58 C6
Gortfinbar❶ BT79 . . . . . . 58 F3
Gortgall❶ BT74. . . . . 102 B3
Gortgarran❶ BT92 . . . . . 117 A3
Gortgarvan❶ BT92 . . . . . 127 B3
Gortgeran❶ BT93. . . . . . . 51 D1
Gortgommon❶ BT92 . . . 126 D3
Gortgonis❶ BT71 . . . . 62 C3
Gortgonis Pk BT71. . . . . . . 62 D2
Gortgonis Rd BT71. . . . . . . 62 C2
Gortgonnell❶ BT74 . . . . 104 B3
Gortgor❶ BT93 . . . . 85 D2
Gortgoran Cross Roads
BT92 . . . . 124 E1
Gortgorgan❶ BT92 . . . . . 124 E1
Gortgranagh❶
Enniskillen BT92 . . . . 125 C5
Omagh BT78 . . . . 24 F3
Gortgranagh Rd BT78 . . . 25 A3
Gortgullenan❶ BT92 . . . 113 F4
Gorticashel BT79 . . . . 28 F3
Gorticashel Lower❶
BT79 . . . . 16 A1
Gorticashel Rd BT79 . . . . 26 F7
Gorticashel Upper❶
BT79 . . . . 16 C1
Gorticrum Irish❶ BT82 . . . .5 E5
Gorticrum Rd BT82. . . . . . . .5 E3
Gorticrum Scotch❶ BT82 . .5 E4
Gortigal❶ BT71 . . . . 46 A2
Gortileck❶ BT82 . . . . .5 F6
Gortileck Rd BT82. . . . . .5 F5
Gortin❶
Cookstown BT80 . . . . 44 B8
Dungannon BT71. . . . . 62 A2
GORTIN BT79. . . . . 26 D6
Gortin❶
Londonderry BT47. . . . . 2 B8
Omagh BT79 . . . . 26 D5
Gortinagin❶ BT78 . . . . . . 25 A1
Gortin Cres BT71 . . . . 62 A2
Gortindarragh❶
Dungannon BT70 . . . . 43 B1
Dungannon BT70. . . . . 60 C4
Enniskillen BT92 . . . . 127 F8
Gortindarragh Rd BT70. . 60 C3
Gortineddan❶ BT92 . . . 129 E6
Gortin Fort★ BT80 . . . . . 44 C8
Gortin Hts BT71. . . . . 62 A2
Gortin Manor BT47. . . . . . . 2 B8
Gortin Prim Sch BT79 . . . 26 D7
Gortinure❶ BT71 . . . . . . 127 B5
Gortinure Pk BT92 . . . . . 127 B4
Gortinure Rd BT47 . . . . 2 C8
Gortlaunaght❶ 122 F1
Gortleet❶ BT92 . . . . 126 C6
Gortlenaghan and
Derrykeel❶ BT70. . . . . . 77 F7
Gortlenaghan Rd BT70 . . 60 B1
Gortlogher❶ BT82 . . . . . . 12 B3
Gortmaconnell❶ BT92 . . 121 E7
Gortmalegg❶ BT60 . . . . 111 E5
Gortmellan❶ BT47 . . . . 2 C3
Gortmellon Rd BT47 . . . . . 2 B3
Gortmerron❶
Dungannon BT70 . . . . 96 E7
Dungannon BT71. . . . . . . 137 E4
Gortmerron Ave BT71 . . . 137 D4
Gortmerron Hts BT71 . . . 137 F3
Gortmerron Link Rd
BT71 . . . . 137 F4
Gortmerron Mews BT71. 137 F4
Gortmessan❶
Enniskillen BT74 . . . . 104 C7
Strabane BT82. . . . . 1 C4
Gortmessan La BT74 . . . 104 B7
Gortmonly❶ BT82 . . . . .1 F4
Gortmonly Rd
Londonderry BT47. . . . . 2 A4
Strabane BT82. . . . . 1 B8
Gortmore❶
Fivemiletown BT75 . . . . . . 91 E1
Omagh BT78 . . . . 136 A5
Gortmore Dr BT78 . . . . . 136 A5
Gortmore Gdns BT78 . . . 136 A5
Gortmore Pk BT78 . . . . . 136 A4
Gortmourne Pl BT82 . . . 134 E1
Gortmullan❶ BT92 . . . . 129 D7
Gortnacally❶ BT92 . . . . 132 C5
Gortnacarrow❶ BT92 . . 132 C5
Gortnacreagh❶ BT78 . . . 38 A7
Gortnacreagh Rd BT78 . . 38 A8
Gortnaderg❶ BT93 . . . . 113 B8
Gortnaderry❶ 99 B6
Gortnaderrylea❶ 122 E2
Gortnagarn❶ BT79 . . . . . 59 E8
Gortnagarn Prim Sch
BT79 . . . . 38 F6
Gortnagarn Rd BT78 . . . . 38 D6
Gortnaglogh❶ BT71 . . . 63 A6
Gortnaglough Rd BT71 . . 63 B6
Gortnaglush❶ BT71. . . . . 61 E3
Gortnaglush Rd BT71. . . . 61 E3
Gortnagola❶ BT70. . . . . . 60 D2
Gortnagola Rd BT70. . . . . 60 C2
Gortnagriffin❶ BT92 . . . 114 A4
Gortnagross❶
Castlederg BT81 . . . . 34 C8
Cookstown BT80. . . . . 44 C7

Gortnagross Rd BT80. . . . 44 B7
Gortnagullion❶ BT93 . . . 51 B5
Gortnagwyg❶ BT71. . . . . 63 B6
Gortnalee❶ BT93 . . . . . . 83 C8
Gortnaleg❶ 112 D4
Gortnana❶ 133 C6
Gortnaran Rd BT47. . . . . . . 3 F4
Gortnaree❶ BT93 . . . . . . 34 C1
Gortnasaor❶ BT71. . . . . 137 E4
Gortnaskea❶
Coalisland BT71. . . . . 62 D3
Dungannon BT71. . . . . 45 F2
Gortnaskea Rd BT71 . . . . 45 F3
Gortnaskey❶ BT47. . . . . . . 3 D2
Gortnasoal Glebe❶ BT78 . 52 D7
Gortnawinny❶ 127 F4
Gortoorlan❶ 129 C4
Gortoral❶ BT92 . . . . 122 F4
Gortowen Ct ⑫ BT71. . . . 62 C2
Gortraw❶ BT71 . . . . 126 E3
Gort Rd
Cookstown BT80 . . . . 46 F7
Dungannon BT70. . . . . 78 C1
Gortrea❶ BT71 . . . . 80 C3
Gortreagh❶
Cookstown BT80 . . . . 43 D5
Cookstown BT80. . . . . 44 C8
Gortrush❶ BT78 . . . . 38 D2
Gortrush Dr BT78 . . . . . . 136 A4
Gortrush Ind Est BT78 . . . 38 D2
Gortscraheen Rd BT70 . . 42 E3
Gortscreagan❶ BT47 . . . . 8 C7
Gortscreagan Rd BT47 . . . 8 B6
Gortshalgan❶ BT71. . . . . 79 E8
Gort View BT71. . . . . 62 C2
Gortwell BT79 . . . . 136 C7
Gosheden❶ BT47. . . . . 3 C6
Gosheden❶ BT47. . . . . 3 D7
Gosheden Rd BT47. . . . . . . 3 D6
Gowny❶ BT92 . . . . 127 A4
Gowshill❶ BT80 . . . . 45 B2
Graan❶ BT74. . . . . 103 C7
Graffy❶
Belleek BT93 . . . . 65 A3
Enniskillen BT92 . . . . 123 C8
Grahamstown Rd BT81 . . 23 B7
Granagh❶ BT71 . . . . 41 D5
Grange❶
Ballygawley BT70 . . . . 76 D2
Cookstown BT80. . . . . 45 B4
Dungannon BT71. . . . . 79 F3
Omagh BT78 . . . . 25 A5
GRANGE BLUNDEL BT61 . 98 D3
Grange Blundel Rd BT61 . 98 D4
Grange Foyle❶ BT82. . . . . 1 C3
Grangefoyle Rd BT82. . . . . 1 C1
Grange Pk
Ballygawley BT70 . . . . 76 C2
❸ Newtownstewart BT78 . 25 A6
Grange Rd
Ballygawley BT70 . . . . 76 C2
Cookstown BT80. . . . . 45 A4
Dungannon BT71. . . . . 79 F3
Omagh BT78 . . . . 25 A5
Strabane BT82. . . . . 1 C3
Grangewood BT82 . . . . . 134 F4
Gransha Beg❶ 128 D4
Granshagh Big❶ BT92 . . 115 A8
Granshagh Little❶ BT92. 115 A8
Gransha More❶ 128 D4
GRANVILLE BT70. . . . . . . 78 F5
Granville Ind Est BT70 . . . 78 F6
Granville Prim Sch BT70 . 78 F6
Granville Rd BT70. . . . . . . 78 E4
Granville Terr BT70 . . . . . 78 F5
Granville Terr Rd BT70 . . 78 F5
Grattan❶ BT92 . . . . 124 D4
Greagh❶
Carrickroe 93 F1
Enniskillen BT94 . . . . 117 F6
Greaghacapple❶ BT92 . 119 E2
Greaghacholea❶ BT92 . 119 D3
Greaghaphort❶ BT93 . . 100 C3
Greaghatirrive❶ BT92 . . 118 B2
Greaghaverrin❶ BT92. . 119 F5
Greaghavockan❶ BT92. 122 D5
Greaghawarren❶ BT92 . 120 B5
Greaghcashel❶ BT92 . . 118 D2
Greaghmore❶
Enniskillen BT92 . . . . 124 B2
Enniskillen BT93 . . . . 50 E6
Enniskillen BT93 . . . . 85 D3
Greaghnafine❶ BT82 . . 123 A3
Greaghnagleragh❶
BT93 . . . . 100 E3
Greaghnagore❶ BT92 . . 119 F4
Greaghnamoyle❶ BT92 . 120 A4
Greaghrawer❶ BT94 . . . 105 D8
Greathill❶ 131 A6
Great Northern Link
BT82 . . . . 134 B3
Great Northern Rd BT78. 136 A5
Great Northern Ret Pk
BT78 . . . . 136 A4
Green Acres BT80. . . . . . 135 C3
Greenan❶
Armagh BT61. . . . . 98 F3
Enniskillen BT92 . . . . 122 B5
Omagh BT78 . . . . 53 D4
Omagh BT78 . . . . 89 F7
Omagh BT79 . . . . 28 A8
Greenan Rd BT78 . . . . . . 89 E8
Greenbrae❶ BT82 . . . . . 134 E6
Greenbrae Pk BT82 . . . . 134 D6
GREENCASTLE BT79. . . . 28 B3
Greencastle Rd BT79 . . . 27 E2
Greenfield BT75 . . . . 91 C1
Greenhill❶ BT94. . . . . . . 106 B4

Green Hill Demesne❶
BT80 . . . . 76 B4
Greenhill Rd BT70 . . . . . . 76 B5
Greenisland Rd BT62. . . . 81 F7
Greenlaw❶ BT82 . . . . 5 A7
Greenlaw Dr BT82 . . . . 5 A6
Greenlaw Pk BT82 . . . . 5 A6
Greenlaw Rd BT82 . . . . 5 A7
Greenmount Rd BT78 . . . 74 A6
Green Rd BT82. . . . . .6 F2
Greenvale Commercial Pk
BT80 . . . . 135 B3
Greenvale Dr BT80 . . . . . 135 C4
Greenville Rd
Castlederg BT81 . . . . 23 E6
Omagh BT78 . . . . 24 A7
Greenwoodhill❶ BT74 . . 113 D7
Greerstown or Cloghore❶
BT47 . . . . 2 C8
Greeves Pk BT82. . . . . . . 134 B2
Grey Printers Mus★
BT82. . . . . 134 D5
Greystone❶ BT71 . . . . . 103 C4
Greystone Ave BT81. . . . . 22 D5
Grilly❶ 131 C3
Grogey❶ BT75. . . . . 107 C2
Grouse Pk Rd BT78 . . . . . 25 A4
Grove Pk BT93 . . . . 52 A1
Grove Rd BT81 . . . . 23 A8
Grove Way BT71 . . . . 137 E1
Grubbaroe❶ BT93 . . . . . . 68 D6
Guardhill❶ 128 E1
Gubb❶ BT92 . . . . 128 E1
Gubbacrock❶ BT92 . . . 113 F4
Gubbakip❶ BT93 . . . . 68 A8
Gubdoo❶ BT92 . . . . 132 B4
Gublusk❶ BT94. . . . . 87 C5
Gubnafarna❶ 122 C2
Gubnaguinie❶ BT93 . . . . 49 F2
Gubrimmaddera❶ 122 C3
Gubrusdinna❶ BT94. . . . 115 E4
Gulladoo❶ BT78. . . . . . . 72 E4
Gunnell❶ BT76. . . . . 92 B3
Gushedy Beg❶ BT93 . . . 51 F7
Gushedy More❶ BT93. . . 51 F6
Guystown❶. 4 A5
Hackincon❶ BT78 . . . . . . 70 E2
Halftown❶ BT77 . . . . 94 A7

H

Halftown Rd BT77. . . . . . . 94 A7
Hallaghan Rd BT79. . . . . . 57 E3
Hall's La BT74 . . . . 138 C5
Hall Stevenson Pk BT82 . . 5 C6
Hanging Rock Nature
Reserve★ BT92 . . . . . . 113 B5
Hanover Sq BT80 . . . . 46 B7
Harmony Hts BT78 . . . . . 136 A4
Harpur Pk BT81. . . . . 22 E6
Harpur Rd BT78. . . . . 54 D4
Harry Avery's Castle★
BT78 . . . . 24 F6
Harryville BT74 . . . . 117 B7
Hawkes Cres BT79. . . . . . 39 D3
Hawthorne Cres BT70 . . 137 B7
Hawthorne Manor BT45 . 45 E7
Hawthorne Rd BT79 . . . . 39 C2
Hawthorn Gr
Dungannon BT71. . . . . 79 E8
Omagh BT78 . . . . 136 D5
Hawthorn Pk BT81. . . . . . 22 E5
Hawthorns The ⑦ BT82 . 12 D6
Hazelbrook BT71. . . . . . . 62 C4
Hazeldene BT82 . . . . 134 E6
Hazelhill Rd BT79 . . . . . . 41 D1
Hazelwood
Irvinestown BT94 . . . . . . 70 A3
❶ Omagh BT79. . . . . 39 B1
Hazelwood Dr. 134 A8
Head St BT74. . . . . 138 C5
Head Stone The★ BT78. . 36 B4
Healy Pk (GAA Football Gnd)
BT79. . . . . 136 C7
Heatherbank Specl Sch ⑥
BT79. . . . . 39 C1
Henderson Pk BT71 . . . . . 62 D7
Henry's La
Cookstown BT80 . . . . 30 E1
Dungannon BT70. . . . . 43 D2
Henry St BT74 . . . . 138 B5
Henrystughan❶ BT92 . . 117 D5
Heritage Ctr ⑦ BT74 . . 138 C5
Heritage Ctr The★ BT70 . 61 A2
Hermitage❶ BT92 . . . . . 132 D4
High Cross❶ BT80 . . . . . 45 A1
Highcross Rd BT80. . . . . . 62 A8
High Gr BT92 . . . . 117 D1
Highland Rd BT79. . . . . . . 75 B8
High Rd BT82 . . . . 12 C5
High St
❻ Enniskillen BT74. . . . . 138 D5
Newtownbutler BT92. . . . 126 C3
Omagh BT78 . . . . 136 C4
Hillcrest
Aughnacloy BT69. . . . . . . 95 A5
Strabane BT82. . . . . 134 E6
Hillcrest Dr BT94. . . . . . . 69 F3
Hillcrest Pk BT71 . . . . . . 137 E1
Hillcroft BT71. . . . . 137 E8
Hillfoot Rd BT79 . . . . 39 E2
Hill Head❶ BT78. . . . . . . 36 B2
Hillhead Rd
Dungannon BT71. . . . . 62 D2
Strabane BT82. . . . . 12 B5
Hillmount Gr BT82 . . . . . 134 F5
Hill Rd BT78 . . . . 23 F7

Hillside BT80 . . . . 44 C1
Hillside Cres ⑮ BT71. . . . 80 A1
Hillview❶ BT81. . . . . 22 E6
Hillview Ave BT70. . . . . . . 61 A2
Hillview Pk
Enniskillen BT74 . . . . 138 D7
Omagh BT78 . . . . 24 B8
Hillview Pl BT71 . . . . 80 A1
Hillview Rd BT71. . . . . 80 A1
Hillview Rd Mews BT74. 138 D7
Hilton Demesne❶ 133 B5
Holliefields BT71 . . . . . . 137 B2
Hollow La BT71. . . . . 137 B2
Hollowbank BT71 . . . . . . 117 D1
Hollows The ⑧ BT71. . . . 80 A1
Hollybank BT92 . . . . 117 E2
Hollybrook❶ BT92 . . . . . 117 E2
Holly-Hill❶ BT82 . . . . 5 C3
Hollyhill Cres BT74. . . . . 138 E5
Hollyhill La BT74. . . . . . . 138 E5
Hollyhill Link BT74. . . . . 138 E5
Hollyhill Rd
Cookstown BT80 . . . . 31 C1
Enniskillen BT74 . . . . 138 E5
Strabane BT82. . . . . 5 B3
Hollyhill View BT74. . . . . 138 E5
Hollymount❶ BT94 . . . . 105 F1
Hollywell Pk (Páirc Na
Dabhcha) BT93. . . . . . . 112 F7
Holme Rd BT78 . . . . 53 E4
Holmview Ave BT79 . . . . 136 D4
Holmview Hts ④ BT78. . . 25 A6
Holy Cross Coll BT82. . . 134 C3
Holy Trinity Coll BT80 . . 135 C4
Holy Trinity Prim Sch
BT80 . . . . 135 C4
Holy Trinity Prim Sch The
BT74 . . . . 138 C6
Honeyford La BT78. . . . . . 24 F5
Horna Rd BT82. . . . . 6 C4
Hospital Rd
Castlederg BT81 . . . . 22 E6
Omagh BT79 . . . . 136 E4
Howard Prim Sch BT71. . 137 F2
Hudson Hts ❶ BT94. . . . . 69 F3
Humes Villas BT94 . . . . . . 70 A4
Hunters Cres BT78 . . . . . 136 A6
Hunterstown❶ BT82 . . . 11 F6
HUNTS CORNER BT62 . . . 81 C5

I

Illanmean Rd BT78 . . . . . 54 A4
Imeroo❶ BT94. . . . . 90 B3
Imeroo Cross Roads BT94 90 C3
Inchenny❶ BT82. . . . . 12 B8
Inchenny Rd BT82. . . . . . . 12 C8
Inchenny Upper❶ BT82 . . 12 B7
Ingleside Dr BT82. . . . . . 134 E6
INIS CEITHLEANN
(ENNISKILLEN) BT74 . . 138 C4
Inisclan❶
Dungannon BT79 . . . . 40 D8
Strabane BT82. . . . . 11 F2
Inisclin❶ BT93. . . . . 50 D6
Inishammon❶ 128 F8
Inishative❶ BT79 . . . . . . 59 A6
Inishative Rd BT79 . . . . . 58 F6
Inishcollan❶ BT92 . . . . 124 F8
Inishcreenry❶ BT94 . . . 116 D2
Inishcrevan❶ BT92 . . . . 124 E6
Inisherk❶ BT92 . . . . 125 C1
Inishfendra❶ BT92. . . . . 131 B8
Inishkeen❶ BT74 . . . . . . 104 A1
Inishkeen❶ BT71 . . . . . . 137 C3
Inishleague❶ BT92 . . . . 116 A1
Inishmacsaint❶ BT93 . . 86 E7
Inishmagh❶ BT70 . . . . . . 76 F4
Inishmore Pk ㉚ BT71. . . 62 C3
Inishrook❶ BT92 . . . . . . 116 E1
Iniswar❶ BT93 . . . . 86 E5
Innevall❶ BT80. . . . . 45 C1
Innisclan Rd BT79 . . . . . . 40 C7
Innisfree Gdns BT82. . . . 134 F4
Innishmore Pk ㉙ BT71. . 62 C3
Inniskeen Cl BT74. . . . . . 138 C6
Inniskeen Pk BT74 . . . . . 138 C5
Inniskillings Regimental
Mus★ ⑥ BT74. . . . . . . 138 C5
Integrated Coll Dungannon
BT71 . . . . 137 F3
Inver❶ BT92. . . . . 128 B8
Inver Cl BT92 . . . . 120 C1
Iona Villas BT82 . . . . 134 E3
Irish St
Augher BT77 . . . . 93 C6
Dungannon BT70. . . . . . . 137 C5
Irishtown Rd BT79 . . . . . 136 D3
Irvines Cres BT74 . . . . . . 104 B6
IRVINESTOWN (BAILE AN
IRBHINIGH) BT94 . . . . . 69 E3
Irvinestown Prim Sch
BT94 . . . . 69 F3
Irvinestown Rd
Enniskillen BT93 . . . . 69 B7
Enniskillen BT94 . . . . 103 F8
Irwin's Hill Rd BT71. . . . . 98 D6
Islands❶ 109 B1
Island Spa❶ BT60. . . . . . 111 E1
I'town Rd BT74 . . . . 138 E5
Ivy Ave BT82. . . . . 134 F4
Ivybank Pk BT70 . . . . 61 B2
Ivy Hill❶ 94 F3
Ivy Terr❶ BT70 . . . . 61 B2

J

Jacksonville Rd BT71 . . . 137 E1
James St
Cookstown BT80 . . . . 135 D5
Omagh BT78 . . . . 136 B3
Jefferson Ct BT81 . . . . . . 134 B4
Jockey La ❼ BT71 . . . . . . 80 A1
John St
⑫ Castlederg BT81 . . . . . . 22 E5
Dungannon BT70. . . . . . . 137 B5
Omagh BT78 . . . . 136 B4
Johnston Pk BT78. . . . . . 136 C3
John Wesley St BT82. . . . 134 D5
Jones Meml Prim Sch
BT92 . . . . 138 A1
Jubilee Hill BT94. . . . . 87 F2
Jubilee Pk BT80 . . . . 135 D3
Jubilee Rd. 127 F3

K

Kalendra Ct BT71 . . . . . . 137 E6
Kalendra Pk BT71 . . . . . . 137 E5
Kanes Rampart Rd BT71. 63 B1
Keadew❶ BT93 . . . . 85 D4
Keady❶
Augher BT77 . . . . 75 F1
Enniskillen BT92 . . . . 125 E2
Keady Rd BT79. . . . . 58 C1
Kedew❶ BT68. . . . . 96 E1
Kedew Rd BT68 . . . . 96 F1
Keelaghan❶ BT93 . . . . . . 86 F1
Keelagho❶ BT93 . . . . . . 113 C8
Keelaghy❶ BT92. . . . . . . 132 F6
Keelpark Glebe❶ BT92. . 115 A1
Keel Rd BT78 . . . . 90 E7
Keemore Hts BT80 . . . . . . 29 E2
Keenaghan❶
Cookstown BT80 . . . . 43 C4
Dungannon BT71. . . . . 79 F8
Dungannon BT71. . . . . 98 B7
Enniskillen BT92 . . . . 122 F7
Enniskillen BT93 . . . . 65 C4
Strabane BT82. . . . . 5 D2
Keenaghan Rd
Cookstown BT80 . . . . 43 C4
Strabane BT82. . . . . 5 D3
Keenaghy❶ BT92 . . . . . . 117 F3
Keenogue❶ BT78. . . . . . 71 B2
Keenogue Rd BT78 . . . . . 71 C2
Keeran❶
Enniskillen BT93 . . . . 52 E1
Enniskillen BT94 . . . . 70 A6
Keerin❶ BT79 . . . . 28 F7
Keerin Rd BT79 . . . . 29 A8
Keery Pk BT47 . . . . 1 F7
Keery Rd BT47 . . . . .1 F6
Kell Rd BT75. . . . . 92 B1
Kennedies❶ BT60. . . . . . 111 F4
Kennedies Rd BT60 . . . . 111 F4
Kennedy St ❷ BT82. . . . . 134 E5
Kennystown❶ BT82. . . . . 12 B6
Kerran Beg❶ BT92 . . . . 126 D7
Kerran More❶ BT92 . . . 126 C7
Kerrib❶ BT70. . . . . 60 D5
Kerr Villas BT79 . . . . 57 E4
KESH (AN CHEIS) BT93 . 68 F8
Kesh Prim Sch BT93 . . . 68 F8
Kesh Rd BT94. . . . . 69 E4
Kettle La BT71. . . . . 62 B3
Kevenagh❶ BT92 . . . . . . 131 D8
Kevlin Ave BT78 . . . . 136 C4
Kevlin Gdns BT78 . . . . . . 136 C2
Kevlin Glen BT78. . . . . . . 136 C2
Kevlin Gr BT78. . . . . 136 C2
Kevlin Hts BT78. . . . . . . 136 C1
Kevlin Rd BT78 . . . . 136 C2
K'hevlin Demesne BT74 . 138 F1
Kilbarron National Sch . 64 A6
Kilcam❶ BT79. . . . . 57 E3
Kilcam Rd BT79. . . . . 57 D3
Kilcarn❶ BT60. . . . . 96 F3
Kilcatten Rd BT47. . . . . . . .3 F4
Kilclay❶ BT77. . . . . 93 D6
Kilclean❶ BT81. . . . . 22 C8
Kilclean Rd BT81. . . . . . . 22 D7
KILCONNY 130 F2
Kilcoole Dr BT71. . . . . . . 137 E5
Kilcoony❶ BT71 . . . . 62 F7
Kilcootry❶ BT78. . . . . . . 73 D7
Kilcootry Rd BT78 . . . . . . 73 D7
Kilcreen❶ BT47 . . . . .9 B6
Kilcreen Rd BT47 . . . . .9 B7
Kilcroagh❶ BT81. . . . . . . 22 D6
Kilcroagh Rd BT81 . . . . . 22 C5
Kilcroagh❶ BT80. . . . . . . 44 D4
Kilcronagh Rd
Cookstown BT80 . . . . 44 C5
Cookstown BT80. . . . . . . 135 A1
Kilcurragh Pk BT81 . . . . . 22 D5
Kildoag❶ BT47. . . . . 3 C4
Kildoag Rd BT47. . . . . 3 D4
Kildress Church★ BT80. . 44 A7
Kildress Lower❶ BT80. . . 44 B7
Kildress Upper❶ BT80. . . 44 A7
Kildrum❶ BT78. . . . . 72 A8
Kildrum Rd BT78. . . . . . . 54 B2
Kilduff❶ BT93 . . . . 85 E4
Kileen Rd BT82 . . . . 23 F8

Kilgarrett⊕ BT92 . . . . 126 D2
Kilgarrow⊕
  Enniskillen BT92 . . . . . . 131 F7
  Enniskillen BT93 . . . . 85 B4
Kilgarrow Glebe⊕ BT92 . 122 F8
Kilgort⊕
  Londonderry BT47 . . . . 8 C5
  Omagh BT78 . . . . 73 E8
Kilgortnaleague⊕ BT94 . . 88 A4
Kilgort Rd
  Londonderry BT47 . . . . 8 C5
  Omagh BT78 . . . . 73 E7
Kilgowney⊕ BT68 . . . . . . 111 C6
Kilgreen Lower⊕ BT77 . . . 75 D2
Kilgreen Upper⊕ BT77 . . . 75 D1
Kilknock⊕ BT78 . . . . 90 A7
Kill⊕ BT76 . . . . 108 B7
KILLADEAS BT94 . . . . 87 D6
Killadroy⊕ BT79 . . . . 74 E7
Killadroy Rd BT78 . . . . . . 74 E5
Killafinta⊕ BT92 . . . . . . 115 E2
Killaghaduff⊕ 122 E2
Killaghy⊕ BT92 . . . . 126 D3
Killaloo⊕ BT47 . . . . 3 F6
Killaney Lower⊕ BT76 . . . 92 D7
Killaney Upper⊕ BT76 . . . 92 B8
Killaragrange BT71 . . . . . . 97 D2
Killarbran⊕ BT75 . . . . . . 106 F4
Killard⊕ BT92 . . . . 125 D3
Killark⊕ 132 F2
Killartry⊕ BT94 . . . . 106 B1
Killary Glebe⊕ BT71 . . . . 62 E5
Killary La BT71 . . . . 62 E5
Killashanbally⊕ BT94 . . 117 B8
Killaspeenan⊕ BT92 . . . 126 B5
Killaveney⊕ BT77 . . . . . . 93 F4
Killcoo Cross Roads BT93 83 C1
Killea⊕ 99 A4
Killee⊕
  Enniskillen BT94 . . . . 88 F3
  Enniskillen BT94 . . . . . . 105 C6
Killeen⊕ 64 B4
KILLEEN BT71 . . . . 62 F4
Killeen⊕ BT82 . . . . 23 F8
Killeenan⊕ BT80 . . . . 43 A7
Killeeshill⊕ BT70 . . . . 77 C4
Killeeshill Rd BT70 . . . . . . 77 A4
KILLEEVAN 128 E2
KILLEN BT81 . . . . 22 B1
Killen⊕ BT78 . . . . 36 D3
Killen Ent Ctr BT81 . . . . . 22 D3
Killen Far BT81 . . . . 35 B8
Killen Near⊕ BT81 . . . . . . 22 B1
Killenny⊕ BT82 . . . . 6 C6
Killen Pk BT81 . . . . 22 C1
Killen Prim Sch BT81 . . . . 22 C1
Killernam⊕ BT92 . . . . . . 113 D5
Killesher⊕ BT92 . . . . 113 D4
Killeter⊕ BT81 . . . . 34 E8
Killeter Nature Reserve★
  BT81 . . . . 19 E3
Killeter Rd BT81 . . . . 22 D5
Killey⊕ BT70 . . . . 60 A7
Killins⊕ BT79 . . . . 40 A7
Killins Rd BT79 . . . . 40 A6
Killinure⊕ BT78 . . . . 38 C7
Killinure Rd BT78 . . . . . . 38 B8
Killnahusogue Rd BT78 . . 73 D3
Killoan⊕ BT78 . . . . 36 A5
Killoon⊕ BT71 . . . . 45 F2
Killowen BT71 . . . . 62 B3
Killucan⊕ BT80 . . . . 42 E8
Killucan Rd BT80 . . . . 42 E8
Killybane⊕ BT80 . . . . . . 107 D8
Killybasky⊕ BT80 . . . . 31 F3
Killybearn⊕ BT80 . . . . . . 45 C6
Killybearn Rd BT45 . . . . . 45 D7
Killy Beg⊕ BT93 . . . . 83 D7
Killybern⊕ 109 F8
Killyberry⊕ BT78 . . . . 73 A3
Killyblane⊕ BT92 . . . . . . 114 D1
Killyblunick Glebe⊕ BT78 89 F6
Killybrack⊕
  Omagh BT79 . . . . 39 A4
  Omagh BT79 . . . . 136 F8
Killybracken⊕
  Dungannon BT70 . . . . 78 F4
  Enniskillen BT93 . . . . 83 A7
Killybracken Rd BT70 . . . 79 A5
Killybrack Mews BT79 . . 136 D7
Killybrack Rd BT79 . . . . . 136 D7
Killybracky⊕ BT71 . . . . . . 61 E1
Killybreagy⊕ BT94 . . . . . 118 A7
Killybreed⊕ BT74 . . . . . . 103 D4
Killyburn Rd BT79 . . . . . . 40 A3
Killycanavan Lower⊕
  BT71 . . . . 47 B2
Killycanavan Rd BT71 . . . 47 A2
Killycanavan Upper⊕
  BT71 . . . . 47 A2
Killycappy⊕ BT93 . . . . . . 52 C2
Killycarnan⊕ BT92 . . . . . 132 B8
Killycarney⊕ 112 B5
Killycat⊕ BT74 . . . . 102 F5
Killycavan Manor BT71 . . 80 A6
Killycawna★ BT75 . . . . . 108 B3
Killycloghan⊕ BT79 . . . . . 39 B3
Killyclogher Rd BT79 . . . . 39 C2
Killycloghy⊕ BT94 . . . . . 105 D2
Killyclooney⊕ BT82 . . . . . .5 E8

Killyclooney Rd BT82 . . . . . .5 F8
Killyclowny⊕ 92 F5
Killyclowny⊕ BT92 . . . . . 125 E3
Killycolp⊕ BT80 . . . . 44 E3
Killycolp Cl BT80 . . . . 44 F3
Killycolp Rd BT80 . . . . 44 F3
Killycolpy⊕ BT71 . . . . 63 D8
Killycolpy Rd BT71 . . . . . . 46 D1
Killycopely Rd BT71 . . . . . 63 D8
Killycorran⊕ BT76 . . . . . . 92 B3
Killycramph⊕
  Enniskillen BT92 . . . . . . 117 D6
  Enniskillen BT92 . . . . . . 130 D5
Killycurragh⊕
  Cookstown BT80 . . . . 30 E3
  Omagh BT79 . . . . 39 E2
Killycurragh Rd
  Cookstown BT80 . . . . 30 F2
  Omagh BT79 . . . . 39 E3
Killycurry⊕ BT82 . . . . 5 D8
Killycurry Rd BT82 . . . . . . .5 E8
Killydart⊕ BT78 . . . . 24 E4
Killydart Rd BT78 . . . . . . 24 E4
Killydrum⊕ BT93 . . . . . . 101 E8
Killyfaddy⊕ BT76 . . . . . . 92 E6
Killyfana⊕ 132 A1
Killyfole⊕ BT92 . . . . 127 B8
Killyfuddy⊕
  Killeevan 128 F3
  Omagh BT78 . . . . 71 F1
Killyfuddy Rd BT78 . . . . . 71 F2
Killygarry⊕ BT93 . . . . 51 F3
Killygarudn⊕ BT80 . . . . . 44 F1
Killygarvan⊕ BT71 . . . . . . 61 F8
Killygarvan Rd BT80 . . . . 61 E8
Killygavanagh⊕ BT70 . . . 61 C3
Killygone⊕ 128 D1
Killygonlan⊕ BT71 . . . . . . 46 F4
Killygoonagh⊕ 128 D3
Killygordon⊕ BT78 . . . . . 91 A5
Killygowan Island⊕
  BT94 . . . . 116 A3
Killygrania⊕ BT74 . . . . . 104 D2
Killygreagh⊕ BT92 . . . . . 124 B4
Killygullan⊕ BT92 . . . . . . 117 D2
Killygullan⊕ BT92 . . . . . . 117 D2
Killyharry Glebe⊕ BT70 . . 60 E1
Killyharry Rd BT70 . . . . . 60 E1
Killyhevlin⊕ BT74 . . . . . . 138 E2
Killyhevlin Ind Est BT74 . 138 F2
Killyhevlin Pk BT74 . . . . 104 B3
Killyhommon⊕ BT74 . . . . 102 A7
Killyhommon Prim Sch
  BT74 . . . . 102 B7
Killykeeghan⊕ BT92 . . . . 113 B1
Killykeeghan Nature
  Reserve★ BT92 . . . . . . 113 B3
Killykeeran⊕ BT94 . . . . . 117 E8
Killylack Glebe⊕ BT71 . . . 61 E1
Killylacky⊕ BT92 . . . . . . 127 B7
Killylea⊕
  Belturbet 131 C5
  Enniskillen BT93 . . . . 69 A8
Killylea Rd BT60 . . . . . . 111 F5
Killylevin⊕ BT70 . . . . 78 A6
Killylifferbane Glebe⊕
  BT92 . . . . 127 E8
Killylifferdoo⊕ BT92 . . . . 127 E8
Killyliss⊕
  Dungannon BT70 . . . . 78 D5
  Fivemiletown BT75 . . . . . 90 D1
  Omagh BT78 . . . . 72 F5
Killyliss Rd
  Dungannon BT70 . . . . 78 E5
  Omagh BT78 . . . . 72 E5
Killylyn⊕ BT61 . . . . 98 C2
Killymackan⊕ BT92 . . . . 130 C6
Killymaddy⊕ BT60 . . . . . . 97 B2
Killymaddy (Evans)⊕
  BT70 . . . . 77 F5
Killymaddy (Knox)⊕
  BT70 . . . . 137 A4
Killymallaght⊕ BT47 . . . . . 2 C5
Killymallaght Rd BT47 . . . . 2 B4
Killymam⊕ BT80 . . . . 135 A7
Killyman Prim Sch 2
  BT71 . . . . 80 A5
Killyman Rd BT71 . . . . . . 137 E5
Killyman St BT71 . . . . 80 B1
Killymeal⊕ BT71 . . . . 137 E6
Killymeal Pk BT71 . . . . . . 137 D7
Killymeal Rd BT71 . . . . . . 137 E7
Killymenagh⊕ BT71 . . . . . 46 D3
Killymendon⊕ BT94 . . . . . 88 C7
Killymerron Pk BT71 . . . . 137 E5
Killymittan⊕ BT94 . . . . . . 88 E5
Killymoonan⊕ BT78 . . . . . 55 D1
Killymoonan Rd BT78 . . . 73 A8
Killymoon Cres BT80 . . . 135 D2
Killymoon Demesne⊕
  BT80 . . . . 135 F1
Killymoon Golf Club The
  BT80 . . . . 135 F3
Killymoon Rd BT80 . . . . . 135 E3
Killymoon St BT80 . . . . . 135 D3
Killymore⊕
  Enniskillen BT93 . . . . 83 C7
  Omagh BT78 . . . . 25 D6
Killy More⊕ BT93 . . . . 83 D6
Killymore Rd
  Dungannon BT70 . . . . 78 A4
  Omagh BT78 . . . . 25 C8
Killymore Wood BT74 . . 104 C6

Killymorgan⊕ BT70 . . . . . 76 C4
Killymorgan Rd BT70 . . . . 76 D4
Killymoyle⊕ BT70 . . . . . . 78 B4
Killymuck Rd BT80 . . . . . 47 G2
Killymurphy⊕ BT71 . . . . . 45 D1
Killymurry⊕ 110 C7
Killynacran⊕ BT92 . . . . . 125 F3
Killynaght⊕ BT82 . . . . .5 E6
Killynaght Rd BT82 . . . . . . .5 C6
Killynamph⊕ BT92 . . . . . 117 C1
Killynaul⊕ BT68 . . . . 96 D2
Killynaul Rd BT68 . . . . . . 96 B1
Killyneedan⊕ BT80 . . . . . 44 C1
Killyneedan Rd BT80 . . . . 61 B8
Killyneery⊕ BT69 . . . . 95 A8
Killyneill⊕ BT71 . . . . 79 D6
Killyneill Ct BT71 . . . . . . 137 F4
Killyneill Rd BT71 . . . . . . 79 E7
Killynenagh⊕ 133 F1
Killynick⊕ BT92 . . . . 130 E5
Killynoogan⊕ BT93 . . . . . 50 B3
Killynubber⊕ BT92 . . . . . 125 F1
Killynure⊕ BT77 . . . . 104 B4
Killynure Cres BT74 . . . . 138 F4
Killynure Gdns BT74 . . . . 138 F4
Killynure Gn BT74 . . . . . 138 F4
Killynure Pk BT74 . . . . . . 138 F4
Killypaddy⊕ BT92 . . . . . . 117 C2
Killypaddy Rd BT92 . . . . . 117 C2
Killyphort⊕ BT93 . . . . . . 100 D2
Killyquin⊕ BT71 . . . . 97 D2
Killyquinn⊕ BT71 . . . . 79 B4
Killyraw⊕ BT92 . . . . 131 D8
Killyreagh⊕ BT74 . . . . . . 104 D3
Killyreagh Rd BT74 . . . . 104 D2
Killyroo⊕ BT92 . . . . 126 C4
Killyrover⊕ BT94 . . . . . . 116 F5
Killyslavan⊕ 94 D2
Killytaggart⊕ BT74 . . . . . 102 B6
Killyvannan⊕ BT74 . . . . . 104 E1
Killyveagh Glebe⊕ BT74 . 86 D2
Killyveen Pk BT70 . . . . . . 78 F5
Killyvilly⊕ BT74 . . . . 104 C5
Killyvilly⊕ BT74 . . . . 104 C6
Killyvilly⊕ BT92 . . . . 120 E2
Killywilling⊕ BT92 . . . . . 115 D7
Killywoolaghan⊕ BT71 . . . 46 E1
Killywoolaghan Rd BT71 . . 46 E1
Kilmacbrack⊕ BT92 . . . . 126 C6
Kilmacormick⊕ BT74 . . . 138 D7
Kilmacormick Ave (Ascaill
  Chill Mich Cormaic)
  BT74 . . . . 138 D7
Kilmacormick Cl (Clós Chill
  Mhic Cormaic) BT74 . . 138 D7
Kilmacormick Dr (Céide Chill
  Mhic Cormaic) BT74 . . 138 D7
Kilmacormick Rd
  Enniskillen BT74 . . . . . . 138 D7
  Enniskillen BT74 . . . . . . 138 D7
Kilmacrannel 4 BT92 . . 117 D2
Kilmakardle⊕ BT70 . . . . . 60 D4
Kilmakardle Rd BT70 . . . . 60 D4
Kilmalanophy⊕ BT74 . . . 104 B1
Kilmascally⊕ BT71 . . . . . 47 B3
Kilmascally Rd BT71 . . . . 47 A3
Kilmatroy⊕ BT61 . . . . 97 D1
Kilmore⊕
  Dungannon BT70 . . . . 60 D3
  Dungannon BT70 . . . . 96 D4
  Dungannon BT71 . . . . 98 C4
  Enniskillen BT74 . . . . . . 102 E6
  Enniskillen BT93 . . . . 50 B3
  Omagh BT78 . . . . 37 F4
Kilmore Gn BT92 . . . . . . 117 D2
Kilmore Irvine⊕ BT78 . . . 36 E7
Kilmore North⊕ BT94 . . . 105 D1
Kilmore Rd BT78 . . . . 36 C6
Kilmore Robinson⊕ BT78 36 C7
Kilmore South⊕ BT92 . . 125 B8
Kilnabrack⊕ BT92 . . . . . 130 D8
Kilnacart⊕ BT70 . . . . 78 E2
Kilnacart Rd BT70 . . . . . . 78 F2
Kilnacran⊕ BT92 . . . . . . 126 D5
Kilnagrew⊕ BT71 . . . . 97 C6
Kilnaheery⊕ BT79 . . . . . . 74 F6
Kilnahusogue⊕ BT78 . . . . 92 B8
Kilnahusogue Rd BT76 . . 92 C8
Kilnakelly⊕ BT92 . . . . . . 124 C5
Kilnakirk⊕ BT92 . . . . 126 C5
Kilnaloo⊕ BT74 . . . . 103 A7
Kilnamaddoo⊕ BT74 . . . 102 C5
Kilnamaddy⊕
  Enniskillen BT74 . . . . . . 104 D3
  Killeevan 128 F3
Kilnambrahar⊕ BT94 . . . 105 F6
Kilnameel⊕ BT92 . . . . . . 113 A3
Kilnarainy⊕ BT92 . . . . . . 124 D5
Kilnaslee⊕ BT70 . . . . 60 E2
Kilnaslee Rd BT70 . . . . . . 60 D3
Kiln St BT71 . . . . 73 C6
Kilpie Terr 6 BT71 . . . . . 62 C2
Kilready⊕ BT92 . . . . 126 E2
Kilready Dr BT92 . . . . . . 126 D3
Kilreal Lower⊕ BT81 . . . . 23 B2
Kilreal Upper⊕ BT81 . . . . 23 A2
Kilriddy⊕ BT92 . . . . 127 C6
Kilronan⊕ BT92 . . . . 118 A1
Kilrooskagh⊕ BT93 . . . . . 112 D8
Kilroosky⊕ BT92 . . . . . . 127 E4
Kilruddan⊕ BT76 . . . . 93 C4
Kilsallagh⊕ BT94 . . . . . . 104 E2
Kilsally⊕ BT71 . . . . 46 B4
Kilsampson⊕ BT68 . . . . . 111 D5
Kilsannagh⊕ BT70 . . . . . . 96 C5
Kilshannagh La BT70 . . . . 96 D4

Kilshannagh Rd BT70 . . . . 96 E4
Kilskeery Glebe⊕ BT78 . . 89 A7
Kilskeery Rd BT78 . . . . . . 88 F7
Kilsmullan⊕ BT93 . . . . . . 52 E2
Kilstrule⊕ BT78 . . . . 23 F6
Kilstrule Rd BT81 . . . . . . 23 F5
Kiltaglassan⊕ 112 D5
Kilteen Glebe⊕ BT92 . . . 115 B3
Kiltenamullagh⊕ BT94 . . 116 D7
Kiltermon⊕ BT75 . . . . . . 91 F1
Kiltierney⊕ BT93 . . . . 69 D7
Kiltober⊕ BT92 . . . . 132 A7
Kilturk North⊕ BT92 . . . 126 C8
Kilturk South⊕ BT92 . . . 127 A2
Kilturk West⊕ BT92 . . . . 125 E3
Kiltyclay⊕ BT70 . . . . 44 A1
Kiltyclay Rd BT80 . . . . . . 44 B2
Kiltyclogher⊕
  Cookstown BT80 . . . . 44 B2
  Kiltyclogher 99 E3
KILTYCLOGHER (COILTE
  CLOCHAIR) 99 D6
Kiltyclogher Rd BT80 . . . . 44 A4
Kiltycrose⊕ BT92 . . . . . . 129 F6
Kiltyfelan⊕ BT93 . . . . . . 113 B7
Kimran⊕ BT92 . . . . 119 A4
Kinagha More⊕ 131 C1
Kinarla⊕ BT74 . . . . 103 C6
Kinarla Rd BT74 . . . . 103 D6
KINAWLEY (CILL NÁILE)
  BT92 . . . . 123 B8
Kincorragh⊕ 128 E8
Kindrum BT71 . . . . 137 E8
Kinego⊕ BT71 . . . . 80 A5
Kingarrow⊕ BT79 . . . . . . 38 F3
Kingarrow North⊕ BT92 124 B6
Kingarrow Rd BT79 . . . . . 38 F8
Kingarrow South⊕
  BT92 . . . . 125 A1
Kingarve⊕ BT71 . . . . 137 F8
Kingarve Ct BT71 . . . . . . 137 E8
Kingarve Rd BT71 . . . . . . 137 F8
Kinglass⊕ BT92 . . . . 115 C1
Kingspark BT80 . . . . 45 A2
King St BT78 . . . . 73 B6
Kingstown⊕ BT92 . . . . . . 117 F3
Kinine⊕ BT78 . . . . 70 E3
Kinkit⊕ BT71 . . . . 70 E3
Kinmeen Notrh⊕ BT92 . . 124 D4
Kinmeen South⊕ BT92 . . 125 A4
Kinmore⊕ BT92 . . . . 116 F1
Kinnabo⊕ 112 E5
Kinnagillan Rd BT80 . . . . 29 A2
Kinnagillian⊕ BT79 . . . . . 29 B1
Kinnegoe⊕ BT61 . . . . 98 D5
Kinnegoe Rd BT61 . . . . . . 98 D5
Kinnine Rd BT78 . . . . 70 E2
Kinoughtragh⊕ BT92 . . . 130 B8
Kinrush⊕
  Cookstown BT80 . . . . 47 A5
  Enniskillen BT92 . . . . . . 130 E6
Kinrush Rd BT71 . . . . 44 A7
Kinturk⊕ BT80 . . . . 47 B8
Kinturk Cultural Ctr★
  BT80 . . . . 47 B7
Kinturk Rd BT80 . . . . 47 B8
Kirlish⊕ BT78 . . . . 36 D5
Kirlish Rd BT78 . . . . 36 C5
Kishaboy⊕ BT71 . . . . 98 B8
Kivin⊕ BT78 . . . . 55 F7
Kivvy⊕ 132 E1
Knader⊕ 64 C7
Knappagh⊕ BT72 . . . . . . 127 E7
Knockaconey⊕ BT61 . . . . 98 D3
Knockaconey Rd BT61 . . . 98 D3
Knockaconny⊕ BT80 . . . . 44 D4
Knockacullion⊕ 120 F8
Knockadoois⊕ BT92 . . . . 129 E5
Knockadoo Rd BT80 . . . . . 31 F5
Knockadore 2 BT82 . . . . 126 C3
Knockadreen⊕ BT69 . . . . 95 B5
Knockageehan⊕ BT92 . . 113 D4
Knockaginny Rd BT68 . . 110 F7
Knockaleery⊕ BT80 . . . . . 43 D6
Knockaleery Rd BT80 . . . . 43 C5
Knockalough⊕ BT74 . . . . 138 F7
Knockanbrack⊕ BT82 . . . . .5 F3
Knockanearla⊕ 109 C4
Knockanroe⊕ BT71 . . . . . 45 C4
Knockanroe Rd BT80 . . . . 45 B3
Knockaraven⊕ BT78 . . . . 54 A1
Knockarevan⊕
  Enniskillen BT92 . . . . . . 130 C8
  Enniskillen BT93 . . . . 83 B5
Knockarogan Glebe⊕
  BT70 . . . . 96 F4
KNOCKATALLAN 120 E7
Knockateggal⊕ BT92 . . . 129 C7
Knockavaddy⊕ BT70 . . . . 43 E1
Knockavaddy Rd BT70 . . . 43 D2
Knockavea⊕ BT92 . . . . . . 120 B2
Knockavoe Cres BT82 . . 134 D4
Knockawaddy⊕ BT92 . . . 126 F6
Knockballyroney⊕ 109 E3
Knock Beg⊕ BT93 . . . . . . 85 A2
Knockbodarra⊕ BT92 . . . 122 D6
Knockboy⊕ BT92 . . . . . . 126 B8
Knockbrack⊕ BT78 . . . . . 23 A4
Knockbrack⊕
  Castlederg BT81 . . . . 23 A5
  Dungannon BT70 . . . . 75 E4
  Londonderry BT47 . . . . 3 B6
Knockbrack Rd BT47 . . . . . .3 B5
Knockbrackcravagh Gr BT79 136 F6
Knock Cres BT70 . . . . 76 C2
Knockennis⊕ BT94 . . . . . 90 B7
Knockgreenan Ave BT79 136 F3

Knockgreenan Cl BT79 . 136 F3
Knockgreenan Pk BT79 . 136 F3
Knockiniller⊕ BT82 . . . . . 13 C4
Knockiniller Rd BT82 . . . . 13 D5
Knock Island⊕ BT94 . . . 115 F7
Knocklnarvoer⊕ BT82 . . . . .6 B3
Knockmacaroony Glebe⊕
  BT92 . . . . 119 D2
Knockmackegan⊕ BT92 . 125 D4
Knockmacmanus⊕ BT94 106 F1
Knockmaddaroe⊕ BT92 . 126 A5
Knockmanoul⊕ BT94 . . . 88 C3
Knockmany⊕ BT77 . . . . . 93 B8
Knockmany Rd
  Augher BT77 . . . . 93 A7
  Clogher BT76 . . . . 74 D1
Knock More⊕ BT93 . . . . . 85 C3
Knockmore Dr BT71 . . . . 137 C7
Knockmore Pk BT93 . . . . 85 F4
Knockmore Rd BT93 . . . . 85 F4
Knockmoyle⊕ BT80 . . . . . 135 E3
Knockmoyle⊕ BT79 . . . . . 38 D7
Knockmoyle Dr BT79 . . . . 38 E7
Knockmoyle Gr BT79 . . . 136 B6
Knockmoyle Rd BT79 . . . . 38 E7
Knockmoy Pk 8 BT71 . . . 62 C2
Knockmoy Terr 9 BT71 . . 62 C2
Knocknabrass⊕ BT74 . . . 125 D1
Knocknabrattoge or
  Greentown⊕ BT92 . . . 114 A3
Knocknacarney⊕ BT75 . . 92 B5
Knocknaclogha⊕ BT70 . . 59 D4
Knocknacloy⊕ BT70 . . . . 97 A5
Knocknageeha⊕ 109 A1
Knocknagor Prim Sch
  BT78 . . . . 70 E5
Knocknahorn⊕ BT78 . . . . 53 B1
Knocknahorn⊕ BT82 . . . . . .5 D1
Knocknahorn Rd BT78 . . . 53 C1
Knocknahunshin⊕ BT93 101 E7
Knocknalear⊕ BT92 . . . . 120 A6
Knocknalosset⊕ BT92 . . 118 F3
Knocknalun⊕ 109 C1
Knocknamoe Pk Rd 10
  BT79 . . . . 39 B2
Knocknamoe Rd BT79 . . 136 F5
Knocknarney⊕ BT69 . . . . 95 D8
Knocknaroy⊕ BT70 . . . . . 96 B8
Knocknashangan⊕ BT93 . 83 C2
Knocknastackan⊕ BT75 . . 90 F1
Knockninny⊕ BT92 . . . . . 124 A8
Knockonny⊕ BT70 . . . . . . 76 C4
Knockonny Rd BT70 . . . . . 76 B5
Knockranny⊕ 122 B2
Knock Rd BT82 . . . . 13 B4
Knockroe⊕
  Enniskillen BT93 . . . . 52 C4
  Strabane BT82 . . . . 13 A2
  Swanlinbar 122 A1
Knockroe Archdall⊕
  BT94 . . . . 69 E3
Knockroe Irvine⊕ BT94 . . 69 E2
Knockroe Rd BT82 . . . . . 134 A1
Knockronaghan⊕ 110 A1
Knocks⊕
  Enniskillen BT93 . . . . . . 118 B4
  Enniskillen BT92 . . . . . . 127 A5
Knocks East⊕ 133 B1
Knockshee Pk BT79 . . . . 136 E6
Knocksilla Pk BT79 . . . . . 136 E3
Knocksilla Rise BT79 . . . . 136 E4
Knocks West⊕ 133 A2
Koram Rd BT82 . . . . .5 E2
Koram Sq BT82 . . . . 134 C4
Kylemore Ct BT79 . . . . . 136 E5
Kylemore Dr BT79 . . . . . 136 E5
Kylemore Gdns BT79 . . . 136 E5

L

Labby Dermot Chambered
  Grave★ BT79 . . . . 41 B5
Lack⊕ BT93 . . . . 52 F3
LACK BT93 . . . . 52 F3
Lackaboy View 13 BT74 . 104 B6
Lackagh⊕
  Londonderry BT47 . . . . 3 B3
  Omagh BT78 . . . . 36 C3
  Omagh BT78 . . . . 73 D2
Lackaghboy⊕ BT74 . . . . 104 C6
Lackaghboy Ind Est
  BT74 . . . . 104 C6
Lackagh Rd BT47 . . . . .3 B2
Lack Prim Sch BT93 . . . . . 52 F3
Lack Rd BT94 . . . . 69 F3
Lacky⊕ BT92 . . . . 127 E5
Ladiesview Trail BT79 . . . 26 C2
Lagan⊕ 130 D3
Lagan Terr 4 BT71 . . . . . 62 C2
Lagavadder⊕ BT82 . . . . . . .6 B3
Lagavittal⊕ BT82 . . . . .6 A3
Laghel Rd BT81 . . . . 22 C2
LAGHEY CORNER BT71 . . 80 A6
Laghey Prim Sch 1 BT71 80 A6
Laght⊕ BT78 . . . . 37 D4
Laghtfoggy⊕ BT81 . . . . . . 21 B5
Laghtfoggy Rd BT81 . . . . 21 C5
Laghtmorris⊕ BT81 . . . . . 21 C5
Laghtmorris Rd BT81 . . . . 21 C5
Laght Rd
  Castlederg BT81 . . . . 21 D5
  Omagh BT78 . . . . 37 D4
Laghty Barr⊕ 99 F2
Lagnagalloglagh⊕ BT82 . . 5 F5
Lairakean⊕ BT68 . . . . . . 111 D8
Lakeland Forum★ BT74 . 138 C4

Lakemount Rd BT78 72 A5
Lakeside Ave BT74 138 E7
Lakeside Ctr★ 64 B6
Lakeside Gdns BT71 137 B2
Lakeside Terr BT71 137 B2
Lakeview BT77 93 C6
LAKEVIEW BT71 137 C3
Lakeview Cotts BT71 46 F4
Lakeview Pk
Dungannon BT71 62 F4
Enniskillen BT74 138 C3
Lakeview Rise
Enniskillen BT92 115 D7
1 Lisnaskea BT92 117 D2
Lambfields BT71 137 D8
Lambrook Cl BT78 55 D8
Lambrook Gdns 6 BT78 55 D8
Lambrook Hts 3 BT78 55 D8
Lambrook Mdws 4 BT78 55 D8
Lambrook Rd BT78 55 D8
Lambrook Way 5 BT78 55 D8
LammyⓉ
Cookstown BT80 61 C7
Enniskillen BT92 126 E6
Omagh BT78 55 D8
Lammy Cres 17 BT78 38 D1
Lammy Dr 3 BT78 38 D1
Lammy Rd BT80 61 C7
Lammy Wlk 1 BT78 38 D1
Lampton Ct BT82 134 C5
LanaghranⓉ BT74 102 E1
LanaglugⓉ BT80 46 D8
Landahussy Rd BT79 15 A3
Landahussy UpperⓉ
BT79 15 D3
LandbrockⓉ BT92 131 F8
Landbrook Cross Roads
BT92 131 E8
Langfield Cres BT78 36 E3
Langfield Prim Sch BT78 36 E3
LankillⓉ BT92 103 D1
LanlissⓉ 112 F5
LanmoreⓉ BT92 113 F3
LannaghtⓉ BT92 120 A4
Lansdowne Pk BT82 134 D4
LaraghⓉ
Enniskillen BT92 103 E1
Enniskillen BT92 123 D8
Enniskillen BT94 87 F3
Laragh BT94 87 F3
LaraghⓉ
Omagh BT78 24 E6
Omagh BT79 57 A3
Laragh Rd BT79 57 B3
LaraghshankillⓉ BT71 97 D2
Laragh View BT79 57 B4
Larch Dr BT82 12 D6
LargalinnyⓉ BT93 85 B6
LarganacarranⓉ BT92 122 D7
LargandoyⓉ BT94 90 A4
LarganhughⓉ 82 C1
LargyⓉ
Clones 127 F3
Enniskillen BT93 52 F2
Enniskillen BT94 104 F2
Enniskillen BT94 117 F8
LargybegⓉ BT78 24 B5
Largy Coll 127 F2
LarkhillⓉ BT93 66 B8
LarmoreⓉ BT93 50 E4
Laste's La BT82 134 C5
LatbegⓉ BT76 92 F8
Latbeg Rd BT76 74 F1
LatgallanⓉ 128 D5
LattacappleⓉ 133 D1
LattacrossanⓉ 133 B2
LattonaghⓉ BT93 101 D8
LattoneⓉ
Enniskillen BT93 100 B6
Kiltyclogher 99 B7
LaughillⓉ BT93 64 C2
Laure Hill BT47 8 E6
Laurelbank Rd BT78 55 D4
Laurel Dr BT82 134 D1
Laurel Hill Cross Rds 132 D3
Laurel Rd
Omagh BT78 55 A7
Strabane BT82 5 C6
Laurels The BT79 136 E4
Laurelvale Ct BT74 138 B2
Laurelview BT71 137 F4
LavaranⓉ BT93 69 B7
Lawnakilla Pk BT74 138 D8
Lawnakilla Way BT74 138 E8
Lawson Pk BT82 5 A6
LeaghanⓉ
Enniskillen BT93 69 C7
Omagh BT79 28 C1
Leaghan Rd BT79 28 D1
LeaghsⓉ BT79 18 C5
LeamⓉ BT94 90 C1
Leam BegⓉ BT74 102 F3
LeambresienⓉ BT94 104 F2
Leam MoreⓉ BT74 102 F3
LeamnamoyleⓉ BT92 113 D5
LeanyⓉ BT70 77 D2
Leany Rd BT70 77 E1
Leaplane Rd BT79 56 D7
LearⓉ BT47 8 D4
Learden LowerⓉ BT79 14 E1
Learden Rd BT79 14 E1
Learden UpperⓉ BT79 14 F1
LearmoreⓉ BT81 22 D3
Learmore Rd BT81 22 D3
Learmount Rd BT47 8 D7
LeatⓉ BT82 6 B7
Leatham Cres BT93 52 A2
LeballyⓉ BT94 105 C1
LecharrownahoneⓉ 129 B2
LeckⓉ BT71 45 E3
LeckinⓉ BT79 28 A8
LeckpatrickⓉ BT82 5 A7
Leckpatrick Gdns BT82 5 C6
Leckpatrick Rd BT82 5 B7
Leck Rd BT71 45 D2
LedergⓉ BT71 79 F7
LeeffaⓉ BT92 113 E3
Leenagrenagh BT74 138 F5
LegacurryⓉ
Cookstown BT80 44 C1
Enniskillen BT92 120 A2
Omagh BT78 25 A3
Omagh BT79 74 C8
Legacurry Rd BT79 74 D8
LegaduffⓉ BT92 122 D6
LegaghoryⓉ BT47 3 D6
LegaloughⓉ 112 F3
LegamagheryⓉ BT78 91 D8
Legamaghery Rd BT78 73 D2
LeganeⓉ BT69 96 B7
Legane Rd BT69 96 B7
LeganvyⓉ BT78 37 A3
Legar Hill La BT71 98 A8
LegaroeⓉ BT70 76 E5
Legaroe Rd BT70 76 E5
LegatiggleⓉ BT78 72 E6
Legatiggle Rd BT78 72 F6
LegatillidaⓉ BT75 119 B8
LegatoneganⓉ BT81 21 E4
Legatonegan Rd BT81 21 F4
LegcloghfinⓉ BT79 16 F7
Legcloghfin Rd BT79 16 F5
LegeelanⓉ 112 D3
LeggⓉ
Enniskillen BT92 121 D8
Enniskillen BT93 67 A2
LeggsⓉ BT93 66 A5
LeggykellyⓉ 132 A2
LegillyⓉ BT70 78 D3
Legilly Rd BT70 78 D3
LeginnⓉ BT92 124 C4
LeglandⓉ
Enniskillen BT93 85 B2
Omagh BT78 37 B8
Leglands Rd BT78 37 C6
LeglehidⓉ BT93 83 C4
LegmacaffryⓉ BT92 126 F2
LegmurnⓉ BT71 62 F8
Legmurn Rd BT71 45 E1
LegnabraidⓉ BT78 25 E5
Legnabraid Rd BT78 25 D5
LegnabrockyⓉ BT92 121 C8
LegnacashⓉ BT80 43 F6
Legnacash Rd BT80 43 E6
LegnaderkⓉ 121 D1
LegnagappogeⓉ BT47 8 A1
Legnagay BegⓉ BT74 101 C5
Legnagay MoreⓉ BT74 102 A5
LegnahornaⓉ BT92 113 E3
LegnakellyⓉ 128 B4
LegnaveaⓉ BT92 122 D8
LegphressyⓉ BT78 54 A7
LehillⓉ BT74 104 A1
LehinchⓉ BT92 126 A3
LeifearⓉ 134 B7
LEIFEAR (LIFFORD) 134 A6
LeighanⓉ BT93 86 C3
LeitrimⓉ
Castlederg BT81 35 A8
Enniskillen BT74 101 F8
Enniskillen BT92 132 C8
Strabane BT82 3 A1
LemnagoreⓉ BT60 111 D4
LenadremnaghⓉ BT71 63 B6
LenaghⓉ
Emyvale 110 A6
Omagh BT79 27 B3
LenaghanⓉ
Enniskillen BT74 103 C5
Enniskillen BT93 85 D8
Lenagh Rd BT79 27 C3
LenamoreⓉ BT79 26 E5
Lenamore Rd BT79 26 E5
Leonards IslandⓉ 128 A4
LerawⓉ BT92 117 D4
LerganⓉ BT93 65 E1
LeskyⓉ BT74 102 A4
LetfernⓉ BT78 74 B7
Letfern Ave BT78 55 F2
Letfern Rd BT78 56 A1
LettanⓉ BT94 105 F7
LetterⓉ
Enniskillen BT93 49 E1
Enniskillen BT93 67 A1
LetteranⓉ BT45 31 E8
Letteran Rd BT80 31 E6
LetterbaileyⓉ BT94 90 A5
LetterbinⓉ BT78 24 A3
Letterbin Rd BT78 23 F3
LetterboyⓉ BT93 51 E1
LetterbratⓉ BT79 14 F4
Letterbrat Rd BT79 14 E3
LetterbreenⓉ BT74 102 F1
LettercarnⓉ BT81 35 D6
Lettercarn Rd BT81 35 C6
LettercloryⓉ BT71 62 E7
LettergashⓉ BT78 70 F7
Lettergesh Rd BT78 70 F7
LettergreenⓉ BT92 126 C5
LetterkeenⓉ BT93 51 B1
LettermoneyⓉ BT94 87 F7
LetteryⓉ
Dungannon BT70 76 B2
Omagh BT78 53 B2
Lettery Rd
Dungannon BT70 76 B2
Lettery Rd *continued*
Omagh BT78 53 B2
Lettice St BT69 95 A4
LevaghyⓉ BT74 104 A7
Levally LowerⓉ BT93 87 B1
Levally UpperⓉ BT93 87 A1
Levercaw Rd BT78 26 A6
LiffordⓉ BT78 90 A8
Lifford & Clonleigh Resource Ctr 134 A7
LIFFORD (LEIFEAR) 134 A6
Lifford Rd BT82 134 C6
Lifford Stadium 134 B7
LigatraghtⓉ
Omagh BT79 17 C1
Omagh BT79 28 E8
Ligford Rd BT82 13 B8
Ligfordrum or DouglasⓉ
BT82 13 E6
LiggartownⓉ BT82 12 E5
LigginsⓉ BT79 17 B1
Liggins Rd BT79 17 B1
LignameeltogeⓉ BT94 68 F1
Lilac Ave BT82 6 C7
Lime HillⓉ BT70 42 E3
Limehill Rd BT70 42 F2
Limekiln La BT80 135 D6
Limes The BT74 138 A6
Lindsayville Rd BT80 44 F2
Lineside 4 BT71 62 C3
Lineside Rd 5 BT71 62 C3
Linfield St BT71 137 B5
Linkside Gr BT82 134 E3
Linkside Pk BT82 134 E3
LinnyglassⓉ BT71 45 F1
LÍOS BÉAL ÁTHA (LISBELLAW) BT94 105 A1
LIOS NA NDARÓG (LISNARICK) BT94 69 C3
LIOS NA SCÉITHE (LISNASKEA) BT92 117 D2
LisabuckⓉ 133 C7
LisaclareⓉ BT71 62 F5
Lisaclare Rd BT71 62 F6
LisadavilⓉ BT69 95 B5
Lisadavil Pk BT69 95 A5
LisadearnyⓉ BT94 117 C5
LisahoppinⓉ BT79 56 D7
LisanellyⓉ BT79 136 C6
Lisanelly Ave BT79 136 C5
Lisanelly Hts BT79 136 C6
Lisanelly Pk BT79 136 D6
LisarearkeⓉ 133 D4
LisavaddyⓉ BT78 73 C4
LisbancarneyⓉ BT71 97 B7
LisbaneⓉ BT76 93 B3
LisbanlemneighⓉ BT71 97 D7
LisbegⓉ BT70 76 D1
Lisbeg Rd BT70 76 D1
LISBELLAW (LÍOS BÉAL ÁTHA) BT94 105 A1
Lisbellaw Prim Sch BT94 104 F1
LisblakeⓉ BT92 114 B5
LisbofinⓉ BT74 102 F1
Lisbofin Rd BT71 98 B5
LisboyⓉ
Clogher BT76 92 D4
Dungannon BT70 61 C4
Dungannon BT71 45 D4
Enniskillen BT94 106 D7
Omagh BT79 56 E7
Lisboy Rd
Dungannon BT71 45 D3
Omagh BT79 56 E6
LisbunnyⓉ BT47 7 D8
Lisbunny Rd BT82 7 C8
LiscabbleⓉ BT78 25 E6
Liscabble Rd BT78 25 E6
LiscausyⓉ BT71 45 E4
LISCLOON BT82 6 F8
Liscloon LowerⓉ BT82 3 B1
Liscloon UpperⓉ BT82 7 A8
LisconduffⓉ BT69 95 D6
Lisconduff Rd BT69 95 E6
LisconreaⓉ BT78 72 D2
Liscoole BT80 135 C7
LiscoskerⓉ BT94 117 E8
Liscreevaghan or Clady -
SproulⓉ BT82 12 F3
LiscreevinⓉ BT94 69 C2
LiscurryⓉ BT82 5 C6
Liscurry Gdns BT82 5 C6
Liscurry Pk BT82 5 C6
Lisdarragh BT71 98 A5
LisdeadⓉ BT93 85 E2
LisderganⓉ BT78 73 C5
Lisdergan Rd BT78 73 B5
LisdermotⓉ BT71 79 D3
LisderryⓉ BT92 114 B5
Lisdillion Rd BT82 3 A4
LisdillonⓉ BT47 3 A7
Lisdillon Rd BT47 3 A6
Lisdivin LowerⓉ BT82 1 E1
Lisdivin Rd BT82 1 D1
Lisdivin UpperⓉ BT82 1 E2
LisdivrickⓉ BT92 114 A3
LisdoartⓉ BT70 94 C8
Lisdoart Rd BT70 94 C7
LisdonwillyⓉ BT61 98 D1
Lisdonwilly Rd BT61 98 C1
LisdooⓉ
Omagh BT78 70 E5
Strabane BT82 6 A4
Strabane BT82 11 F4
LisdoodanⓉ BT93 85 F1
Lisdoo Rd BT82 11 F2
LisdrumⓉ BT94 117 C7
LisduffⓉ
Dungannon BT71 97 D6
Maguiresbridge BT94 117 C8
Lisduff La BT71 97 D5
LiseggertonⓉ 127 E3
LisfeartyⓉ BT70 77 E3
Lisfearty Prim Sch BT70 77 E3
LisgallⓉ 128 F6
LisgallonⓉ BT70 78 A3
Lisgallon Rd BT70 78 A3
LisgallyⓉ BT92 114 A3
Lisgarty Rd BT78 54 D2
LisginnyⓉ BT69 94 D7
Lisginny Rd BT69 94 E7
LisglassⓉ BT47 2 E8
Lisglass Rd BT47 2 E7
LisgobbanⓉ BT71 97 D7
Lisgobban Rd BT71 97 D6
LisgonnellⓉ BT70 76 C3
LisgooleⓉ BT92 103 F2
Lisgoole BT92 138 A2
Lisgoole Abbey★ BT92 103 F2
Lisgoole Pk BT92 103 D3
LisgorranⓉ BT76 93 D2
LisingleⓉ BT93 68 F7
LiskeabrickⓉ 120 F3
Liskey Brae BT78 73 B6
LiskillyⓉ BT92 120 B1
LiskinbweeⓉ BT82 4 F2
LiskinconⓉ BT79 57 E4
LiskittleⓉ BT71 62 B6
Liskittle Rd BT71 62 B6
LiskyⓉ
Fintona BT78 73 B6
Strabane BT82 12 F3
Lisky GlebeⓉ BT78 36 D3
Lisky Rd BT82 12 E7
LislafertyⓉ BT78 24 B5
Lislafferty Rd BT78 24 A5
LislairdⓉ BT81 21 F3
Lislaird Rd BT81 22 B4
LislaneⓉ BT75 91 F6
LislannanⓉ 128 D6
Lislap EastⓉ BT79 26 C3
Lislap WestⓉ BT78 25 B4
LislarrisⓉ BT92 126 F2
LislaslyⓉ BT61 98 D6
Lislasly Rd BT71 98 C5
LisleaⓉ
Enniskillen BT92 127 D3
Enniskillen BT94 105 E1
Omagh BT78 74 C3
Omagh BT79 56 C6
LisleeⓉ BT71 45 D2
LisleenⓉ BT81 22 C1
Lisleen Rd BT81 22 C1
LislimnaghanⓉ BT78 38 C4
LislongfieldⓉ 133 F5
LisloonyⓉ BT60 111 F3
LismacsheelaⓉ BT92 120 D3
LismaloreⓉ BT94 106 D1
LismonaghanⓉ BT92 123 B7
LismoneyⓉ BT45 45 A8
Lismoney Rd BT45 45 A8
LismoonlyⓉ BT92 114 C1
LismoreⓉ
Aughnacloy BT69 94 C6
Clogher BT76 92 E3
Lismore Dr BT70 61 A2
Lismore Gr 10 BT82 12 D6
Lismore La BT78 136 A3
Lismore Pk
Omagh BT78 136 A2
9 Sion Mills BT82 12 D6
Lismore Rd BT70 94 C7
Lismourne Pl BT82 134 D1
LismulladownⓉ BT68 96 B2
LismulrevyⓉ BT71 79 C3
LisnabaneⓉ BT94 106 C6
LisnabulreveyⓉ BT78 73 B4
LisnabunnyⓉ BT70 94 C7
LisnaclinⓉ BT71 137 F5
Lisnaclin Ct BT71 137 F4
LisnacloonⓉ BT81 22 A4
Lisnacloon Rd BT81 21 F5
LisnacreaghtⓉ
Omagh BT78 37 F7
Omagh BT79 15 B3
Lisnacreaght Rd BT78 37 E6
LisnacreeveⓉ BT78 73 D4
LisnacroyⓉ BT71 97 C6
LisnadurkⓉ BT92 132 E4
Lisnadurk Glebe North
Middle GlebeⓉ BT92 132 E5
Lisnadurk Glebe SouthⓉ
BT92 132 E4
LisnafeedyⓉ BT60 97 B1
Lisnafeedy Rd BT60 97 A2
LisnafinⓉ BT78 13 D2
Lisnafin Pk BT82 134 C4
Lisnafin Rd BT78 13 D1
LisnagardyⓉ BT78 73 C5
LisnagirrⓉ BT78 38 B5
Lisnagirr Rd BT78 38 B6
LisnagleerⓉ BT70 61 C5
Lisnagleer Rd BT70 61 C5
LisnagoleⓉ BT92 117 B5
Lisnagole Rd BT92 117 B5
Lisnagort Ct BT79 136 C6
LisnagowanⓉ BT71 61 D4
Lisnagowan Rd BT70 61 C4
LisnahallⓉ BT71 45 E5
Lisnahall Rd BT71 45 E5
LisnahannaⓉ BT78 70 E1
Lisnahanna Rd BT78 70 F1
LisnaharneyⓉ BT79 26 A4
Lisnaharney Rd BT79 25 F3
LisnahoyⓉ BT71 79 F6
LisnahullⓉ BT70 137 A7
Lisnahull Gdns BT70 137 A6
Lisnahull Pk BT70 137 A7
Lisnahull Rd BT70 137 A6
LisnaknockⓉ BT92 126 B4
LisnaleeⓉ 133 C4
LisnamagheryⓉ BT76 93 B5
LisnamallardⓉ
Enniskillen BT92 126 E7
Omagh BT79 136 C5
LisnamonaghanⓉ BT70 78 D7
Lisnamonaghan Rd BT70 78 D7
LisnananeⓉ BT80 61 D8
Lisnanane La BT80 61 D8
LisnarableⓉ BT78 74 D5
Lisnarable Rd BT78 74 D5
Lisnaragh IrishⓉ BT82 6 E5
Lisnaragh Rd BT82 6 F5
Lisnaragh ScotchⓉ BT82 6 E6
LISNARICK (LIOS NA NDARÓG) BT94 69 C3
Lisnarick Rd BT94 69 D3
Lisnaroe FarⓉ 127 D3
Lisnaroe NearⓉ 127 D3
LisnashillidaⓉ BT92 126 E4
Lisnaskea Bsns Ctr BT92 117 C4
Lisnaskea High Sch
BT92 117 D2
LISNASKEA (LIOS NA SCÉITHE) BT92 117 D2
LisnastraneⓉ BT71 62 D4
Lisnastrane Ct BT71 62 C4
Lisnastrane Hts BT71 62 C4
Lisnastrane Pk BT71 62 C4
Lisnastrane Rd BT71 62 D4
Lisnatunny GlebeⓉ BT78 24 E8
LisnavoeⓉ BT92 128 B8
LisnaweryⓉ BT77 94 A7
Lisnawery Rd BT77 93 E7
LisnawesnaghⓉ BT92 120 D2
LisneightⓉ BT71 62 E8
LisoartyⓉ 128 C6
LisolvanⓉ BT94 106 C1
Lisolvin Pk BT94 106 C1
LisoneillⓉ BT92 117 D3
LisraceⓉ BT92 127 D6
LisreaghⓉ BT94 104 F3
Lisreagh Fort★ BT94 104 F3
LisroanⓉ BT71 80 A2
LisroddyⓉ BT92 103 C1
LisroonⓉ BT92 128 A7
LissachollyⓉ 64 C3
LissanⓉ
Cookstown BT80 31 D3
Dungannon BT71 79 B4
Enniskillen BT74 104 D8
Omagh BT78 55 F7
Lissan Cl BT80 135 C7
Lissan Ct BT78 136 D1
Lissan DemesneⓉ BT80 31 D3
Lissan Dr
Cookstown BT80 135 C6
Omagh BT78 136 D1
LissanedenⓉ BT78 72 B5
Lissan Mews BT78 136 D1
Lissan Prim Sch BT80 31 E3
Lissan Rd BT78 56 A7
Lissan View BT78 136 D2
LissinagroaghⓉ 99 A2
LissiniskaⓉ 82 B2
ListamletⓉ BT71 80 B3
Listamlet Rd BT71 80 B4
ListymoreⓉ BT81 23 A8
Listymore Pk BT81 23 B6
Listymore Rd BT82 11 F1
LittleⓉ BT74 103 B4
Littlebridge Rd BT45 45 F7
LittlehillⓉ BT94 116 F5
LittlemountⓉ BT94 106 A1
Little Scotch St BT70 137 C5
Loane Dr BT74 104 B6
Lockard BigⓉ BT74 103 A5
Lockard LittleⓉ BT74 103 A5
Lodge Cross Roads BT70 59 D5
Lomond Hts BT80 135 D3
LongfieldⓉ
Clones 128 B5
Fivemiletown BT75 107 E7
LonghillⓉ BT78 53 F2
Longhill Rd BT78 71 B4
Longland Rd BT82 7 A8
LongridgeⓉ BT77 75 D1
LongrobⓉ BT93 86 B4
Lonsdale Gr 2 BT79 136 F4
Loran Way BT80 135 D3
Loreto Convent Prim Sch
BT78 136 A4
Loreto Gram Sch 1
BT78 136 B4
LossetⓉ BT75 91 E3
LoughachorkⓉ BT93 84 E8
LoughanⓉ 112 C7
Loughan Rd BT82 6 E7
LoughansⓉ BT70 77 A1
Loughans Rd BT70 77 B1
Loughaphonta BarrⓉ 99 D2
LoughashⓉ BT82 7 C6
Loughash Prim Sch BT82 7 B6
Loughash Rd BT82 7 A5
LoughdoolyⓉ 131 A4
Loughdoo Rd BT80 42 E7
Loughermore GlebeⓉ
BT75 108 A8
Lougher Rd BT82 12 B3
Lougherush Rd BT78 70 E1

M

Lough Fea Rd BT80 . . . . . . 31 C3
Loughgall Rd BT61. . . . . . . 98 E1
Loughgare⊕ BT92 . . . . . . 127 B7
Lough Hill⊕ BT92. . . . . . . 118 A3
Loughkillygreen⊕ BT92. 127 A1
LOUGHMACRORY BT79 . . . . 40 F4
Loughmacrory⊕ BT79. . . . 41 A6
Loughmacrory Pk BT79. . . 40 F4
Loughmacrory Rd BT79. . . 40 D4
Loughmallon Rd BT79. . . . 42 A5
Loughmuck (Alcorn)⊕
  BT78 . . . . 55 D6
Loughmuck Rd
  Omagh BT78 . . . . 55 D6
  Omagh BT78 . . . . 73 B7
Loughmuck (Wallace)⊕
  BT78 . . . . 55 C5
Lough Naman Bog Nature
  Reserve★ BT93 . . . . . . 84 C5
Loughnamarve Rd BT70 . . 42 E3
Loughneas⊕ BT82 . . . . 1 D1
Loughneas Rd BT82 . . . . . . 1 D1
Lough Rd BT78 . . . . 36 F7
Loughrey Terr BT78 . . . . . 36 F3
Loughry⊕ BT80. . . . . 44 F3
Loughry College(Lindsay
  Hall) BT80. . . . . 44 F3
Loughshore Rd BT74 . . . . 103 D6
Lough Shore Rd
  Enniskillen BT74 . . . . . . 103 C8
  Enniskillen BT93 . . . . . . 65 C2
Loughterush⊕ BT78 . . . . . 70 F1
Loughtilube⊕ BT47 . . . . . . .8 E8
Loughultan⊕ 49 B6
Loughview Cl BT71. . . . . . 62 D7
Loughview Dr (Céide
  Radharc An Locha)
  Enniskillen BT74 . . . . . . 138 C7
  Enniskillen BT93 . . . . . . 112 F7
Loughview Gdns ⑪ BT71. 62 C3
Loughview Rd BT71. . . . . . 62 C2
Lough Yoan Rd BT74 . . . . 138 F3
Lovers La BT74 . . . . 138 A6
Low Cross⊕ BT80. . . . . . . 45 A2
Lower Barnes⊕ BT79 . . . . 16 A3
Lower B'arton Rd BT47. . . . .3 F4
Lower Celtic Pk BT74 . . . 138 E4
Lower Chanterhill Rd
  BT74 . . . . 138 F7
Lower Drumnaspar⊕
  BT79 . . . . 15 E3
Lower Grange Rd BT80 . . . 45 B3
Lower Kildress BT80 . . . . . 44 B7
Lower Landahussy⊕
  BT79 . . . . 15 C3
Lower Mill St BT74. . . . . . 138 D5
Lower Mullan⊕ BT80 . . . . 47 H1
Lower or Old Deer Park⊕
  BT78 . . . . 24 E7
Lower Parklands BT71 . . . 137 C4
Lower Rusky⊕ BT80 . . . . . 46 B8
Lower Strabane Rd BT81 . . 23 A6
Lowertown⊕ BT71. . . . . . . 79 E7
Lowertown Rd
  Dungannon BT71. . . . . . . 79 E7
  Strabane BT82. . . . . 5 C8
Lower Tully⊕ BT47 . . . . 2 A8
Lowery⊕ BT93. . . . . 50 A2
Lowerybane⊕ BT93. . . . . . 65 F4
Lowry's La BT82 . . . . .5 B8
Loy⊕ BT80. . . . . 135 D5
Loy St BT80. . . . . 135 D4
Lucy St BT70. . . . . 42 F1
Lugasnaghta⊕ 99 B4
Lugmore⊕ BT93 . . . . 51 D7
Lungs⊕ BT76. . . . . 92 C4
Lupin Ave BT82 . . . . .6 C8
Lurgaboy La BT71. . . . . . 137 E8
Lurgacullion⊕ BT70 . . . . . 77 A4
Lurgan⊕
  Brookeborough BT94. . . 106 C1
  Enniskillen BT93 . . . . . . 112 F8
Lurganaglare⊕ BT78. . . . . 74 A4
Lurganbane⊕ BT94 . . . . . 106 D5
Lurganboy⊕
  Castlederg BT81 . . . . 22 E8
  Cookstown BT80 . . . . 45 C4
  Dungannon BT71. . . . . . . 61 E1
  Enniskillen BT93 . . . . . . 50 C5
  Enniskillen BT93 . . . . . . 70 B8
  Newtownbutler BT92. . . 126 D2
  Omagh BT78 . . . . 25 B3
  Omagh BT78 . . . . 72 D2
  Omagh BT79 . . . . 58 D1
  Scotshouse 133 E4
Lurganboy Pk BT92 . . . . . 126 D2
Lurganboy Rd BT81 . . . . . . 11 D1
Lurgan Buoy Rd BT81 . . . . 22 E7
Lurganclabby⊕ BT75 . . . . . 90 F2
Lurganclabby BT75 . . . . . . 90 F3
Lurgandarragh⊕ BT74 . . 103 B4
Lurganeden⊕ BT70 . . . . . . 60 C7
Lurganeden Rd BT70 . . . . . 59 F8
Lurganmore Rd BT70. . . . . 76 D7
Lurgaoin⊕ BT71. . . . . . . 137 E8
Lurgy⊕ BT71 . . . . 62 A7
Lurgylea⊕ BT70 . . . . 59 F3
Lurgylea Rd BT70 . . . . 59 D5
Lurgy Rd BT71. . . . . 61 F8
Lurgyroe⊕ BT71. . . . . 47 B3
Lusty Beg⊕ BT94. . . . . . . 115 F2
Lusty Beg Island⊕ BT93 . 67 E7
Lusty More⊕ BT94. . . . . . 115 F2
Lusty More Island⊕ BT93. 67 E6

Mccay Ct ① BT81 . . . . 22 E5
Mcclay Gr ③ BT79 . . . . . 136 F4
Mcclay Pk BT79. . . . . 136 F4
Mccleerys Rd BT82. . . . . . . 23 B8
Mcclintock Prim Sch
  BT78. . . . . 74 A8
Mac Crackens⊕ BT82 . . . . .5 D7
MCCREADY'S CORNER
  BT61 . . . . 98 C2
Mccrea Pk
  Clogher BT76. . . . . 93 A5
  Omagh BT78 . . . . 36 E1
Mccullaghstown Rd BT79. 15 A5
Mcgeagh's Well★ BT80. 135 B7
Mcgovern Dr BT80 . . . . . 135 C4
**MACHAIRE MHÍLIE
  (MAGHERAVEELY)**
  BT92 . . . . 127 B4
Mcivor Villas ⑭ BT79 . . . 39 B2
MACKAN BT92. . . . . 115 C3
Mackan Glebe⊕ BT92. . . 115 C3
Mackenny⊕ BT80. . . . . . . 44 B7
Mackenny Rd BT80. . . . . . 44 A7
Mckeone Villas BT79 . . . . 41 D1
Mckinney Pk BT80 . . . . . 135 A6
Macknagh⊕ BT92. . . . . . 117 E1
Mcnally Pk BT81. . . . . 21 F2
Macnean Pk (PÁirc Mhic
  Nein) BT93 . . . . 112 F7
Mcnulty Pk BT79. . . . . 27 D6
Mcquaid Villas BT94 . . . . . 88 C5
Magaraty⊕ BT62. . . . . 81 D1
Magharenny⊕ BT78. . . . . 54 B8
Magherabrack Rd
  Londonderry BT47. . . . . . .9 B8
  Omagh BT78 . . . . 13 F1
  Omagh BT79 . . . . 16 A1
Magheracoltan⊕ BT78 . . . 24 C6
Magheracoltan Rd BT78. . 24 D6
Magheracreggan⊕ BT81. 23 C3
Magheracreggan Rd BT81 23 C3
Magheracross⊕ BT94. . . . 88 E6
Magheradunbar⊕ BT74 . 103 C7
Magheragannon⊕ BT74. 103 A8
Magheragar⊕ BT82. . . . . . 12 B4
Magheragart⊕ BT78 . . . . 72 A6
Magheragart (Donnell)⊕
  BT78 . . . . 71 F6
Magheragart or Sessiaghs⊕
  BT78 . . . . 72 A6
Magheragart Rd BT78. . . . 71 F6
Magheraglass⊕ BT80 . . . . 43 D5
Magheraglass Rd BT80. . . 43 D6
Magherahar⊕ BT93. . . . . . 86 E4
Magherakeel⊕ BT81. . . . . 34 B7
Magherakeel Rd BT81. . . . 34 C8
Magheralamfield⊕ BT71. 63 B5
Magheralegh Rd BT81. . . . 23 D2
Magheralough⊕
  Castlederg BT81 . . . . 23 C3
  Omagh BT78 . . . . 89 B8
Magheralough Prim Sch
  BT78. . . . . 71 A1
Magheralough Rd BT78 . . 71 A1
MAGHERAMASON BT47. . . .1 E7
Magheramenagh⊕ BT93. 65 E3
**Magheramenagh Castle (in
  ruins)★** BT93 . . . . 65 D4
Magheramore⊕ BT92. . . 127 B4
Magheramulkenny⊕
  BT71 . . . . 62 E3
Magheranageeragh⊕
  Castlederg BT81 . . . . 21 E2
  Enniskillen BT74 . . . . . . 102 F8
Magheranageeragh Rd
  BT81 . . . . 21 D2
Magheranure⊕ 128 A6
Magherareagh⊕
  Enniskillen BT92 . . . . . . 127 B4
  Strabane BT82. . . . . 1 D2
**MAGHERAVEELY (MACHAIRE
  MHÍLIE)⊕** BT92. . . . . 127 B4
Magherenny Rd
  Castlederg BT81 . . . . 22 A7
  Omagh BT78 . . . . 37 B1
Magherintemple⊕ BT79. 133 D1
Magherliss Rd BT79. . . . . 27 A6
Maghery⊕ 120 F1
MAGHERY BT71. . . . . 81 B8
Maghery Ct BT47 . . . . .1 F7
Maghery Rd BT62. . . . . . . 81 D7
Maghery Rural Enterprise Ctr
  BT71. . . . . 81 C8
Magho⊕ BT93. . . . . 67 B3
Maginn Rd BT79 . . . . 58 D6
Magirr⊕ BT82. . . . . 134 C4
Magirr Pk BT82 . . . . 134 D4
Magonragh⊕ BT94 . . . . . 105 C4
**MAGUIRESBRIDGE
  (DROICHEAD MHIG UIDHIR)**
  BT94 . . . . 117 B7
Maguiresbridge Prim Sch
  BT94 . . . . 117 B7
Maine⊕ BT79. . . . . 39 E4
Maine Rd BT79. . . . . 39 E3
Main Rd BT71. . . . . 137 E1
Main St Sh Ctr BT78 . . . 136 C4
Main St
  Armagh BT60. . . . . 111 E3
  Augher BT77 . . . . 93 C6
  Aughnacloy BT69. . . . . . 95 D7
  Ballygawley BT70 . . . . . . 76 D2
  Caledon BT68 . . . . 111 D6
  Carrickmore BT79 . . . . . 41 C1
  Castlederg BT81 . . . . 21 E1

Main St continued
  Clogher BT76. . . . . 92 F4
  ③ Coalisland BT71. . . . . 62 C3
  Cookstown BT80 . . . . 45 A2
  Cookstown BT80 . . . . 46 B7
  Dromore BT78 . . . . 71 F7
  Drumquin BT78 . . . . 36 E3
  Dungannon BT70 . . . . . . 42 F1
  Dungannon BT70 . . . . . . 61 A2
  Dungannon BT71 . . . . . . 97 D5
  Enniskillen BT93 . . . . . . 112 F7
  Fintona BT78 . . . . 73 C6
  Fivemiletown BT75 . . . . . 91 C1
  Gortin BT79 . . . . 26 D6
  Lifford 134 B6
  Mountfield BT79 . . . . 40 B6
  Newtownstewart BT78 . . 25 A6
  Omagh BT78 . . . . 89 D8
  Omagh BT79 . . . . 14 F4
  Plumbridge BT79 . . . . . . 15 A4
  Sion Mills BT82 . . . . 12 D6
  Six Mile Cross BT79 . . . . 57 F4
  Strabane BT82. . . . . 134 D5
  Ballinamallard BT94 . . . . 88 C5
  Brookeborough BT94. . . 106 C1
  Enniskillen BT93 . . . . . . 52 E3
  Enniskillen BT93 . . . . . . 85 F5
  Enniskillen BT94 . . . . . . 117 B6
  ⑧ Irvinestown BT94. . . . 69 F3
  Newtownbutler BT92. . . 126 C3
  Enniskillen BT92 . . . . . . 124 A4
Major La BT71 . . . . 79 F2
Makenny⊕ BT94 . . . . 88 B8
Makenny Cres ② BT94 . . . 88 C6
Mallabeny⊕ BT76. . . . . . . 92 C7
Mallabeny Rd BT76 . . . . . 92 B6
Mallard Hts BT92 . . . . . . 115 C7
Mallybreen⊕ BT93. . . . . . 48 D2
Maloon⊕ BT80. . . . . 135 B6
Maloon Ct BT80. . . . . 135 B6
Maloon Dr BT80 . . . . 135 B6
Maloon Hill BT80 . . . . . . 135 B6
Maloon Hts BT80. . . . . . . 135 B6
Maloon Manor BT80 . . . . 135 B6
Maloon Pk BT80. . . . . . . 135 A6
Maloon Pl BT80 . . . . 135 B6
Maloon Rd BT80 . . . . 135 A6
Maloon View BT80. . . . . 135 B6
Maloon Way BT80. . . . . . 135 B6
Manger⊕ BT93 . . . . 64 B2
Manoo⊕ BT93. . . . . 69 B7
Manoo Rd BT93 . . . . 69 C7
Manor View
  ③ Enniskillen BT94. . . . . 89 F1
  Enniskillen BT79 . . . . . . 105 E8
Manor Water House⊕
  BT92 . . . . 125 E8
Manragh Lower⊕ 112 E2
Manragh Upper⊕ 112 F3
Manse Rd
  Dungannon BT71. . . . . . 137 B4
  Omagh BT78 . . . . 36 F4
Mantlin⊕ BT93 . . . . 69 A8
Mantlin Rd BT93. . . . . 69 B8
Maplebrook Ct ㉒ BT71. . 62 C3
Maplebrook Gn ㉕ BT71. . 62 C3
Maplebrook Gr ㉔ BT71 . . 62 C3
Maplebrook Hill ⑳ BT71. 62 C3
Maplebrook Rise ㉑ BT71. 62 C3
Maplebrook Way ㉘ BT71. 62 C3
Maple Rd BT82 . . . . .5 A6
Marble Arch Caves★
  BT92 . . . . 113 D3
**Marble Arch Nature
  Reserve★** BT92 . . . . . 113 D3
Marhill Rd BT78. . . . . 56 B1
Marian Pk BT82. . . . . 134 F4
Marion Ave BT71. . . . . 81 C8
Market Ct ⑤ BT74 . . . . . 104 B5
Market Rd BT79. . . . . 136 D4
Market Sq ④ BT70 . . . . . 137 C5
Market St
  Ederney BT93 . . . . 52 A1
  ① Enniskillen BT74. . . . 138 C5
  Omagh BT78 . . . . 136 C4
  Strabane BT82. . . . . 134 E5
Mark St BT71. . . . . 137 C4
Marlbank⊕ BT92 . . . . 113 A4
Marrassit or College Hall⊕
  BT60 . . . . 111 E5
Marshalls Row BT82 . . . . . 12 D6
Martray⊕ BT70 . . . . 76 E3
Martray House★ BT70. . 76 E3
Martray Rd BT70 . . . . 76 D4
Maryville Pk BT79. . . . . . . 28 B3
Mason Rd BT47 . . . . .1 F6
Mass Rock★ 133 D7
Mautiagh⊕ 82 A2
Mavis Rd BT47. . . . . 3 D8
Maydown⊕ BT71 . . . . 97 D4
Maydown Rd BT71. . . . . . . 97 D2
May Hill⊕ 132 A3
Meadow Bank BT71. . . . . 137 A5
Meadow Brook
  ② Enniskillen BT94. . . . . 89 F1
  Fintona BT78 . . . . 73 C6
Meadow Cres ⑥ BT82. . . . 12 D6
Meadowcroft BT78. . . . . . 71 F8
Meadow Farm BT74. . . . . 104 C6
Meadow La BT74. . . . . . . 138 A2
Meadows The
  Dungannon BT71. . . . . . . 80 A5
  Irvinestown BT94 . . . . . . 70 A3
Meadowvale
  Dungannon BT71 . . . . . . 137 D7
  Enniskillen BT74 . . . . . . 104 E1
Meadowvale Pk BT79 . . . 136 E6

Meadowview BT71 . . . . . . 80 B1
Meadowviewdrive BT62. . 81 A2
Meadowviewlodge BT62. . 81 A2
Meadowview Pk BT62. . . . 81 A2
Meaghy⊕ BT81. . . . . 23 F5
Meaghy Rd BT81. . . . . 23 E5
Meelmore Dr BT79 . . . . . 136 B6
Meeltogues⊕ BT78 . . . . . 70 E5
**Meenablagh or Fourth
  Corgary** RT81 . . . . . . 20 D5
Meenablagh Rd BT81 . . . . 20 D4
Meenacloyabane⊕ BT93. 84 A6
Meenacloy Rd BT81 . . . . . 34 F2
Meenacrane⊕ BT79. . . . . . 16 B5
Meenadoan⊕ BT78 . . . . . 52 C8
**Meenadoan Nature
  Reserve★** BT78 . . . . . 52 C8
Meenadoo⊕ BT79. . . . . . . 26 F8
Meenadoo Rd BT79 . . . . . 15 C1
Meenafergus⊕ BT81. . . . . 33 A7
Meenagarragh⊕ BT79 . . . 14 E5
Meenagar Rd BT78. . . . . . 72 C3
Meenagh⊕
  Dungannon BT71 . . . . . . 62 E2
  Kiltyclogher 100 B2
Meenagh Hill⊕ BT82. . . . . .1 E6
Meenagh Pk BT71. . . . . . . 62 C3
Meenagh Rd BT82 . . . . 1 E6
Meenagleragh⊕ BT93. . . . 84 D4
Meenagorp⊕ BT79. . . . . . 14 D5
Meenagorp Rd BT82 . . . . . 14 D6
Meenagowan⊕ BT78. . . . . 71 B6
Meenagrogan⊕ BT81 . . . . 20 E1
Meenaheery Glebe⊕
  BT78 . . . . 52 F6
Meenakeeran⊕ BT81. . . . . 20 A3
Meenamullan⊕ BT81. . . . . 34 C5
Meenamullin Rd BT81. . . . 34 D7
Meenanea⊕ BT80. . . . . . . 29 E3
Meenanea Rd BT80 . . . . . 29 E4
Meenapergus Rd BT81 . . . 33 B7
Meenarainy⊕ BT93 . . . . . 100 C6
Meenarodda⊕ BT79 . . . . . 17 D4
Meenascallagh⊕ BT80. . . 29 C2
Meenashesk Pl BT82. . . . 134 C4
Meenatully⊕ BT93. . . . . . . 48 B2
Meenawargy⊕ BT93 . . . . 100 E2
Meenbog⊕
  Ballybofey 19 F8
  ˙Castlederg BT81 . . . . . . 35 B1
Meencargagh⊕ BT81. . . . . 36 A7
Meencargagh Rd BT81. . . 36 A7
Meencarriga⊕ BT81. . . . . 35 B5
Meenclogher⊕ BT81. . . . . 34 E3
Meendamph⊕ BT82. . . . . . .6 E1
Meendamph Rd BT82. . . . . 6 D2
Meenmore⊕ BT93 . . . . . . 52 F1
Meenmore Rd BT79 . . . . . 56 E1
Meenmossogue Glebe⊕
  BT78 . . . . 52 D7
Meentullyclogh⊕ BT93. . . 51 E8
Meetinghousehill⊕
  BT78 . . . . 136 B3
Meetinghouse La ⑤ BT81 22 E5
Meetinghouse Rd BT79. . . 57 E5
Meetinghouse St BT82 . . 134 E4
Melissa Terr ⑤ BT71. . . . . 62 C2
Mellon Pk Rd BT78. . . . . . 38 C3
Mellon Rd BT78. . . . . 25 C1
Melmount Gdns BT82 . . 134 C3
Melmount Mews BT82. . . 134 C2
Melmount Pk BT82. . . . . 134 C2
Melmount Rd BT82. . . . . 134 D3
Melmount Villas ⑤
  BT82 . . . . 134 D4
Melvin Hall BT82. . . . . . 134 D4
Melvin Pk Sports Complex
  BT82. . . . . 134 E4
Melvin Rd BT82. . . . . 134 D4
Melvin View BT82. . . . . . 134 D4
Menapian Way BT74 . . . . 138 E3
Merchantstown Glebe⊕
  BT79 . . . . 40 D3
Merchantstown Rd BT79. 40 D3
Methodist La ② BT78 . . . 25 A6
Mews The
  ④ Castlederg BT81 . . . . 22 E5
  Fintona BT78 . . . . 73 B6
Middle Deer Park⊕ BT78. 24 F7
Middleton St ② BT74 . . . 138 C5
Middletown⊕ BT93 . . . . . 68 B8
Midhill⊕ BT92. . . . . 126 A8
Milburn Ave BT80 . . . . . . 135 B6
Milburn Cl BT80. . . . . . . 135 C6
Milburn Pk BT80 . . . . 135 C6
Milestone Ctr BT79 . . . . 58 D8
Milestone The BT70. . . . . 79 A8
Mill Ave BT82. . . . . 12 E6
Millbank Cl BT79. . . . . . . 136 D6
Millbank Ct BT79 . . . . . . 136 D6
Millbank La BT79 . . . . . . 136 D6
Millberry⊕ BT80. . . . . . . 111 C5
Millbrae Rd T BT78. . . . . . 38 A3
Millbridge Rd BT78 . . . . . 73 F8
Millbrook Gdns BT81. . . . 22 D5
Millbrook La BT78 . . . . . . 24 F6
Millbrook Rd BT82 . . . . . . 24 C8
Mill Cross Roads The
  BT70 . . . . 61 A5
Millgreen BT93 . . . . 85 F5
Millhaven BT82 . . . . 12 D6
Milligan⊕ 120 E6
Milligans⊕ BT92. . . . . . . 120 D2
Millix⊕ BT70 . . . . 76 D6
Millix Rd BT70 . . . . 76 C6

Mill Rd
  Aughnacloy BT69. . . . . . 95 A5
  Cookstown BT80 . . . . . . 29 E1
Millside Cres ① BT47 . . . .8 E7
Mill St
  Aughnacloy BT69. . . . . . 95 A4
  Caledon BT68 . . . . 111 D6
  Enniskillen BT74 . . . . . . 138 E5
  Fintona BT78 . . . . 73 C6
  Irvinestown BT94 . . . . . . 69 F3
  ⑦ Newtownstewart BT78 . 25 A6
  ⑧ Strabane BT82. . . . . . 134 E5
Milltate⊕
  Enniskillen BT74 . . . . . . 104 E3
  Enniskillen BT92 . . . . . . 125 E7
  Irvinestown BT94 . . . . . . 70 A2
MILLTOWN
  Craigavon BT62. . . . . . . 81 D8
  Dungannon BT71. . . . . . 97 C4
Milltown⊕
  Enniskillen BT92 . . . . . . 124 B2
  Omagh BT78 . . . . 24 B7
MILLTOWN BT78. . . . . 36 F1
Milltown⊕
  Strabane BT82. . . . . 5 B5
  Strabane BT82. . . . . 134 F3
Milltown Blaney⊕ BT93 . 86 D5
MILLTOWN BURNDENNET
  BT82 . . . . 1 F1
Milltown Ct BT92 . . . . . . 126 D3
Milltown La BT62 . . . . 81 D8
Milltown Pk BT82 . . . . 1 F1
Milltown Rd
  Dungannon BT71. . . . . . . 97 C3
  Dungannon BT71. . . . . . 137 C5
  Omagh BT78 . . . . 24 B6
  Strabane BT82. . . . . 134 F3
Millview Pk BT82 . . . . .5 C5
Millwood⊕ BT94. . . . . . . 105 B1
Minadinna Rd BT79 . . . . . 41 A1
Minaradan BT70 . . . . 137 B5
Mineveigh⊕ BT71. . . . . . . 61 E4
Mineveigh Rd BT71 . . . . . 61 E4
Minran⊕ BT93. . . . . 85 E7
MINTERBURN BT68 . . . . . . 96 B3
Minterburn Prim Sch
  BT68. . . . . 96 B3
Minterburn Rd BT68 . . . . . 96 A4
Moat La BT92 . . . . 117 D3
Moat Prim Sch BT92 . . . 117 D2
Moboy⊕ BT70. . . . . 43 A4
Moboy Rd BT70. . . . . 43 A5
Mobuy⊕ BT45 . . . . 31 C7
Mobuy La BT70. . . . . 31 C7
Mobuy Rd BT80. . . . . 31 B7
Mockbeggar⊕ BT92 . . . . 126 D3
Modagh Rd BT79. . . . . 57 C2
Modeenagh⊕ BT94 . . . . . 105 F5
Moghan⊕ BT70. . . . . 78 A8
Moghan Rd BT70. . . . . 78 A7
Moher⊕ 129 A4
Moheranea⊕ BT92. . . . . 122 C5
Moher (Killesher)⊕
  BT92 . . . . 122 D8
Moher (Kinawley)⊕
  BT92 . . . . 123 A7
Moleena⊕ BT92. . . . . 132 F7
Molesworth Ct BT80 . . . . 135 C5
Molesworth Rd BT80. . . . 135 D5
Molesworth St BT80. . . . . 135 D5
Molly⊕ BT92 . . . . 123 A4
Mollynadinta⊕ 82 C3
Monadore Rd BT47. . . . . . .8 F7
Monaghan⊕ BT74 . . . . . . 102 D8
Monaghan St 127 F2
Monalla⊕ BT94. . . . . 87 F4
Monanaclova⊕ BT92. . . . 118 B3
Monanameal⊕ BT79 . . . . 28 C5
Monavreece⊕ BT93. . . . . 52 A3
Monawilkin⊕ BT93 . . . . . 85 C5
MONEA BT93. . . . . 86 E2
Monea Castle (in ruins)★
  BT93 . . . . 86 E2
Moneen⊕ BT92. . . . . 113 E5
Moneenbane⊕ BT92. . . . 122 C6
Moneendogue⊕ BT93. . . . 64 F2
Moneycannon Rd BT82. . . .7 B7
Moneycanon⊕ 7 B8
Moneyconey⊕ BT79. . . . . 18 F4
Moneyconey Rd BT45. . . . 18 F3
Moneycree⊕ BT61. . . . . . 98 E3
Moneygal Rd BT81 . . . . . . 11 H1
Moneygar⊕ BT78. . . . . . . 89 E8
Moneygaragh⊕ BT70 . . . . 43 D1
Moneygaragh Rd BT70 . . 43 D1
Moneygar Rd BT78. . . . . . 71 E1
Moneygashel⊕ 112 D2
Moneyhaw Rd BT45. . . . . . 45 E8
Moneyhoghan⊕ BT47 . . . . .9 B7
Moneykee⊕ BT94. . . . . . . 69 F4
Moneymakin⊕ BT92 . . . . 117 B3
Moneymore Rd BT80. . . . 135 E7
Moneyneany Rd BT47 . . . . 10 F4
Moneyneddy⊕ BT94. . . . . 106 E5
**Moneynoe Glebe or
  Chanterhill⊕** BT74 . . 104 E6
Moneynoe Pk ④ BT74 . . 104 B6
Moneyouragan⊕ BT74 . . 102 A1
Mongavlin⊕ 1 A3
Mongibbaghan⊕ BT94. . 106 D4
Monmurry⊕ BT94 . . . . . . 106 C3
Monrush⊕ BT80. . . . . . . 135 D7
Montiaghroe⊕ BT93 . . . . 51 C6
**Monydoo or
  Tonycrom⊕** 122 B4
Moor Cl BT71. . . . . 62 D3
Moore Island Rd BT61. . . 98 D4

Moore St BT69 .... 95 A5
Moorfield BT78 .... 70 F3
Moorfield Rd BT78 ..... 70 E5
Moorlands BT71 .... 62 D2
Moorlough BT92 ...... 126 A7
Moorlough Rd
  Lisnaskea BT92 .... 117 E1
  Strabane BT82 .... 5 D4
Moor Rd BT71 .... 62 D2
MOORTOWN BT80 ..... 47 B6
Moorville BT71 .... 45 E5
Moree BT70 .... 60 E8
Morgan Cl BT80 ...... 135 B6
Morgan Dr BT80 ...... 135 B6
Morgan Pk BT78 ...... 71 F7
Morgans Hill Rd BT80 .. 135 B6
Morrisons La BT61 ..... 98 F7
Morris Rd BT79 .... 28 F5
Morrow Pk BT75 .... 90 F3
Mossband Rd BT80 .... 46 C7
Mossfield Rd BT94 ..... 88 A3
Mossmore BT71 .... 79 B1
Moss Rd
  Cookstown BT80 ..... 46 E7
  Craigavon BT62 ...... 81 B2
Moughley BT92 ...... 125 E8
Mountain Rd BT93 ..... 53 A4
Mountain View BT78 ... 123 C8
Mount Anketell 110 A8
Mount Bernard BT81 ... 22 F5
Mount Bernard Dr BT81 .. 22 F5
Mount Carmel Hts BT82 . 134 F4
Mountcastle BT82 .... 2 B2
Mount Castle ★ BT82 ..... 2 B2
Mount Darby BT80 .... 127 A8
Mountdrum BT94 ..... 105 A4
MOUNTFIELD BT79 ..... 40 C7
Mounthall BT62 .... 81 D5
MOUNT HAMILTON OR
  SPERRIN BT79 .... 17 C7
MOUNTJOY
  Dungannon BT71 .... 63 C5
  Omagh BT78 .... 38 B7
Mountjoy Ave BT78 ..... 63 C5
Mountjoy Castle ★ BT71 . 63 B5
Mountjoy Forest East
  Division BT79 .... 38 F5
Mountjoy Forest West
  Division BT78 .... 38 D5
Mountjoy Rd
  Dungannon BT71 .... 63 A4
  Omagh BT78 .... 136 C4
Mount Lourdes Gram Sch 1
  BT74 .... 138 D6
Mount Pleasant BT82 .....5 B6
Mount Prospect or
  Tullyoran BT92 ..... 124 D3
Mount Sion BT82 ..... 134 D3
Mount Stewart BT78 ... 73 D1
Mountstewart Rd BT78 .. 73 D2
Mourne Ave
  Coalisland BT71 .... 62 C3
  Strabane BT82 .... 134 D4
Mourne Beg BT81 ...... 22 B4
Mournebeg Rd BT81 ... 22 B4
Mourne Cres 8 BT71 ... 62 C3
Mourne Pk BT78 ...... 24 F6
Mourne Pl BT82 ...... 134 D4
Mourne St BT82 ...... 134 E4
Mourneview BT82 ...... 12 F3
Mourne Wlk BT78 ...... 24 F6
Mousetown BT71 ...... 62 C5
Mousetown Rd BT71 ... 62 B5
Movarran BT93 .... 34 C1
Moveagh BT80 .... 44 C4
Moveagh Rd BT80 ..... 44 C4
Moy BT71 .... 80 A1
Moyagh Rd BT47 .... 2 A3
Moyallen Terr 13 BT71 .. 62 C3
MOY (AN MAIGH) BT71 ... 80 A1
Moyard
  Dungannon BT71 .... 97 E4
  Omagh BT79 .... 18 D3
Moyard Rd BT45 ...... 18 E2
Moybane BT74 .... 102 F4
Moybrone BT74 .... 103 A4
MOYGASHEL BT71 .... 137 D1
Moygashel BT71 ...... 137 F1
Moygashel La BT71 ... 137 E1
Moygashel Pk BT71 ... 79 C4
Moygashel Row BT71 .. 137 E1
Moyglass BT74 .... 103 A7
Moykeel BT74 .... 102 E3
Moylagh BT79 .... 56 D1
Moylagh Rd BT79 ..... 57 B2
Moyle Glebe BT78 ..... 25 B6
Moylehid BT74 .... 102 C3
Moyle Rd BT78 .... 25 A6
Moyletra Gdns BT74 ... 138 C7
Moymore BT70 .... 43 A3
Moynagh BT80 .... 61 B8
Moynaghan North BT94 69 C5
Moynaghan South
  BT94 .... 87 C8
Moy Rd
  Armagh BT61 .... 98 C2
  Dungannon BT71 ..... 137 E3
Moy Regional Prim Sch 1
  BT71 .... 80 A1
Moysnaght BT75 ...... 90 F5
Muckenagh
  Enniskillen BT74 ..... 102 A8
  Enniskillen BT93 ...... 82 D7
Mucklagh BT 129 D5
Muckros BT93 .... 51 A1
Muff Rd BT80 .... 31 F3
Muggalnagrow BT93 ... 83 C6

MUILEANN AN TSIÁIN (SION
  MILLS) BT82 .... 12 E6
Mulboy BT70 .... 79 A5
Muldoon Pk BT78 ..... 71 E8
Mullabryan BT 110 A8
Mullagh BT81 .... 23 F3
Mullaghadrolly BT71 .. 137 B2
Mullaghadun BT71 ..... 137 E7
Mullaghadun La BT71 .. 137 E8
Mullaghahy BT 112 B7
Mullaghalevin BT74 .. 103 C3
Mullaghanagh BT71 .... 137 C3
Mullaghanagh La BT71 .. 137 C3
Mullagharn BT78 ...... 38 A3
Mullagharn Rd BT78 ... 38 B3
Mullagharn (Young)
  BT78 .... 38 A3
Mullaghbane
  Dungannon BT70 ...... 76 F3
  Dungannon BT70 ..... 78 B4
  Enniskillen BT92 ..... 112 F6
  Omagh BT78 .... 54 D2
Mullaghbane Rd
  Dungannon BT70 ..... 78 B5
  Omagh BT79 .... 16 A3
Mullaghblaney BT92 .. 126 D4
Mullaghboy
  Blacklion 112 D1
  Dungannon BT71 ...... 97 F7
  Enniskillen BT92 ..... 125 F5
  Scotshouse 133 D6
Mullaghbrady BT92 .. 120 D2
Mullaghbreedin BT92 . 126 D4
Mullaghcapple BT92 .. 126 B8
Mullaghcapple Glebe
  BT92 .... 126 B8
Mullaghconnelly BT92. 120 C2
Mullaghconor Glebe
  BT70 .... 78 F8
Mullaghcreevy BT70 ... 78 E8
Mullaghcreevy Rd BT70 . 61 A1
Mullaghdaly BT71 ..... 79 A4
Mullaghduff BT 129 E2
Mullaghdun BT74 ..... 113 F8
Mullaghfad BT75 ...... 108 C1
Mullaghfurtherland
  BT70 .... 60 E3
Mullaghfutherland BT70.. 60 E3
Mullaghgare BT92 .... 132 A7
Mullaghgarrow BT92 .. 123 C8
Mullaghglass
  Dungannon BT71 ...... 46 A3
  Enniskillen BT92 ..... 120 B1
Mullaghinshogagh
  BT92 .... 130 A8
Mullaghkeel or
  Ballymackilroy BT92 .. 117 F3
Mullaghkippin BT94 ... 116 D6
Mullaghlehan BT92 ... 126 D6
Mullaghlongfield BT70.. 78 F1
Mullaghmaddy BT74 .. 113 E6
Mullaghmakervy BT94.. 116 E6
Mullaghmarget BT71 ... 62 A1
Mullaghmarget Rd BT71.. 62 A1
Mullaghmeen BT94 ... 88 B2
Mullaghmenagh Ave 2
  BT78 .... 38 D2
Mullaghmenagh Lower
  BT78 .... 38 C2
Mullaghmenagh Mdws 1
  BT78 .... 38 C2
Mullaghmenagh Upper
  BT78 .... 38 D2
Mullaghmena Pk Rd BT78 38 D2
Mullaghmena Rd BT78 .. 38 C2
Mullaghmore
  Armagh BT61 .... 98 E6
  Augher BT77 .... 93 D7
  Dungannon BT70 ...... 61 C1
  Enniskillen BT74 ..... 102 C4
  Enniskillen BT93 ...... 51 D1
  Fivemiletown BT75 .... 92 A2
  Maguiresbridge BT94 . 117 B8
  Omagh BT78 .... 55 C5
  Omagh BT78 .... 56 B1
  Omagh BT79 .... 136 F5
Mullaghmore Dr BT79.. 136 E6
Mullaghmore East
  BT68 .... 96 D1
Mullaghmore Glebe
  BT70 .... 60 F1
Mullaghmore Pk BT70.. 137 A6
Mullaghmore Rd BT70 . 137 A7
Mullaghmore West
  BT69 .... 95 C5
Mullaghmossagh
  BT68 .... 111 B6
Mullaghmossog Glebe
  BT71 .... 97 E8
Mullaghmoyle BT71 ... 62 C6
Mullaghmoyle Rd BT71.. 62 C6
Mullaghnese BT70 .... 77 E1
Mullaghpeak BT 110 C1
Mullagh Rd
  Castlederg BT81 ...... 23 D2
  Omagh BT78 .... 71 C3
Mullaghree BT74 .... 103 C4
Mullaghroddan BT70.. 61 B4
Mullaghroddan Rd BT70.. 61 B3
Mullagh- shantullagh
  BT80 .... 44 C2
Mullaghsillogagh BT75. 91 A3
Mullaghslin Glebe BT79 40 F1
Mullaghslin Rd BT79 .. 40 F1
Mullaghteige BT71 .... 62 A1
Mullaghteige Rd BT71.. 62 A1
Mullaghtironey BT80 ... 46 A6
Mullaghwinny Rd BT78.. 55 A1

Mullaghwortragh BT80.. 46 E6
Mullaghy BT92 .... 103 C1
Mullaliss BT 110 F4
Mullan
  Armagh BT60 .... 111 E1
  Enniskillen BT92 ..... 122 E6
  Enniskillen BT92 ..... 130 B6
  Enniskillen BT93 ..... 100 E1
Mullanabreen BT81 ... 21 E3
Mullanacaw BT74 ..... 103 D5
Mullanacloy BT 128 C5
Mullanaffrin BT 130 C2
Mullanahinch BT92 ... 128 B8
Mullanahoe BT71 ..... 46 F3
Mullanahoe Rd BT71 .. 46 E2
Mullanamoy BT 127 E2
Mullanary BT71 .... 98 B5
Mullanary Rd BT71 .... 98 B5
Mullanasaggart BT93 .. 69 C8
Mullanaskea BT94 .... 104 E6
Mullanatoomog BT78 .. 37 E5
Mullanatoomog Rd BT78. 37 F5
Mullanavehy BT92 ... 114 F5
Mullanawinna BT93 .. 100 D3
Mullanbeg BT79 ...... 41 D2
Mullanboy
  Omagh BT78 .... 54 B1
  Omagh BT78 .... 73 B8
Mullanbreen Rd BT81... 21 E3
Mullandavagh BT 120 F1
Mullanmeen Middle
  BT93 .... 51 A8
Mullanmeen Under
  BT93 .... 50 F8
Mullanmeen Upper
  BT93 .... 51 B8
Mullanmore BT 41 C3
Mullanmore Rd BT79... 41 B3
Mullan or Bumper Lodge
  BT92 .... 114 E3
Mullan Pk BT79 .... 40 B6
Mullan Rd
  Armagh BT60 .... 111 E2
  Cookstown BT80 ..... 46 F8
Mullanrody BT93 ...... 70 B7
Mullans
  Augher BT77 .... 93 C5
  Ballyshannon 64 D5
  Enniskillen BT92 ..... 127 F8
  Enniskillen BT93 ...... 67 C7
  Omagh BT78 .... 73 A6
Mullanshellistragh
  BT93 .... 100 C3
Mullans (Killyfaddy)
  BT76 .... 92 D8
Mullantain BT71 ...... 62 D6
Mullantur BT61 .... 97 D1
Mullan Upper BT80 ... 47 A8
Mullanvaum BT92 ..... 119 B6
Mullasiloga BT78 ..... 72 F3
Mullavea Glebe BT92.. 119 D1
Mullawinny BT78 ..... 54 F1
Mullenakill North BT71. 80 F7
Mullenakill Pk BT71 .... 80 E6
Mullenakill South BT71. 80 F5
Mullenakill West BT71 . 80 E6
Mullies
  Enniskillen BT92 ..... 124 C5
  Enniskillen BT94 ..... 68 F2
Mullintill Rd BT47 ......7 E5
Mullintor BT68 .... 96 D3
Mullyard BT93 .... 101 B1
Mullyardlougher BT74. 102 C1
Mullybrack BT94 ...... 69 B2
Mullybrannon BT71 ... 79 C4
Mullybrannon Rd BT71.. 79 C2
Mullybreslen BT94 .... 70 A2
Mullybritt BT74 .... 104 F1
Mullycar BT70 .... 78 B2
Mullycarnan
  Caledon BT68 .... 96 B4
  Dungannon BT71 ...... 79 B3
Mullycar Rd BT70 .... 78 C1
Mullycavan BT92 ...... 128 A7
Mullycovet BT93 ..... 113 C8
Mullycrunnet BT70 .... 61 A4
Mullydinnity BT92 .... 126 C5
Mullydoo Rd BT79 .... 28 C4
Mullyduff BT92 .... 126 F7
Mullyfabeg BT81 ...... 20 C1
Mullyfamore Rd BT81.. 20 D2
Mullyfarmore BT81 ... 20 B1
Mullygarry BT74 ...... 102 E5
Mullygruen BT70 ...... 61 A2
Mullykivet BT93 .... 86 B5
Mullyknock or Topped
  Mountain BT94 .... 105 B7
Mullyleggan BT71 ..... 98 A4
Mullylogan BT92 ...... 138 A1
Mullyloughan BT71 ... 97 E2
Mullylun BT92 .... 124 E2
Mullylusty BT93 ...... 101 C2
Mullymesker BT92 ... 115 A7
Mullynaburtlan BT92.. 118 B3
Mullynacoagh BT92... 130 F7
Mullynagowan BT92.. 126 D3
Mullynaherb BT92 .... 123 E4
Mullynahunshin BT92. 113 F4
Mullynalughoge BT71 . 127 C7
Mullynascarty BT92... 114 A4
Mullynaskeagh BT93 .. 85 A5
Mullynavale BT75 ..... 108 E3
Mullynavannoge BT92. 127 C3
Mullynaveagh BT68... 96 D1
Mullyned BT92 .... 126 B5
Mullyneeny BT92 ..... 124 A4
Mullyneill BT68 .... 96 C3

Mullyneill Rd BT68 ..... 96 C3
Mullynure BT70 .... 43 D2
Mullyroddan BT70 .... 78 A2
Mullysilly BT70 .... 77 B6
Mulmona Rd BT78 .... 55 D3
Mulnadoran BT94 ..... 118 B7
Mulnafye BT70 .... 40 C6
Mulnafye Rd BT79 .... 40 C5
Mulnagoagh BT78 ..... 71 F6
Mulnagore BT70 ...... 61 A5
Mulnagore La BT80 ... 61 B6
Mulnagore Rd BT80 ... 61 A6
Mulnagork BT94 ..... 88 F6
Mulnahorn
  Aughnacloy BT69 ...... 95 B3
  Enniskillen BT92 ..... 126 C4
Mulnahunch BT70 ..... 77 F5
Mulnanarragh BT 132 E2
Mulrod BT74 .... 104 E1
Mulvin BT82 .... 12 F3
Mulvin Rd BT82 .... 12 F2
Munderrydoe BT70 .... 60 C7
Munie BT81 .... 22 D2
Munie Rd BT81 .... 22 D1
Muntober BT80 ...... 30 E2
Muntober Rd BT80 .... 30 E2
Munville BT92 .... 117 D4
Murley Cross Roads BT75 91 C3
Murley Rd BT78 .... 91 B5
Murnells BT70 .... 42 E5
Murnells Rd BT70 ..... 42 D5
Murrins Nature Reserve
  The ★ BT79 .... 40 E7
Mweelbane BT93 ..... 52 E4
Myrtle Hts BT77 .... 93 C6
Myrtle Rd BT82 .... 12 F3
Naan Island West
  BT92 .... 124 C8
NA CORACHA BEAGA
  (ORRITOR) BT80 ..... 44 B8
NA CORACHA MÓRA (SIX
  MILE CROSS) BT79 .... 57 E5

N

Nancys La BT91 .... 134 E6
Napple Rd BT82 .... 6 C1
Nart BT 120 F1
Ned BT92 .... 124 C6
Nedsherry BT93 .... 70 C8
Nelson Pk 1 BT75 .... 107 C8
Neville Dr BT71 .... 137 E1
New Bldgs Ind Est BT47 ... 2 B8
New Bridge Rd 5 BT92 . 117 D2
New Buildings BT80.... 135 F5
Newell Rd BT70 .... 137 B6
New Line Rd BT80 ..... 42 F7
New Rd BT80 .... 30 E1
Newrow BT 4 D7
Newry BT75 .... 92 A3
New St Link BT82 ..... 12 D5
New St
  Clady BT82 .... 11 F7
  Ederney BT93 .... 52 A2
  Enniskillen BT74 ..... 138 D4
  Sion Mills BT82 ...... 12 D5
Newtown
  Enniskillen BT93 ..... 86 A3
  Swanlinbar 122 F1
NEWTOWNBUTLER (AN
  BAILE NUA) BT92 ..... 126 C2
Newtownbutler Prim Sch
  BT92 .... 126 C3
Newtownbutler Rd 127 D2
NEWTOWNHAMILTON 1 D8
Newtown Kennedy St
  BT82 .... 134 E4
Newtown Pl BT82 ..... 134 E5
NEWTOWNSAVILLE BT78.. 74 E4
Newtownsaville Rd
  Dungannon BT70 ...... 75 A3
  Omagh BT78 .... 74 C6
Newtown St BT82 ..... 134 E5
Newtown Stewart BT78 24 F5
NEWTOWNSTEWART (AN
  BAILE NUA) BT78 .... 25 A6
Newtownstewart Golf Club
  BT78 .... 24 D5
Newtownstewart Model Prim
  Sch BT78 .... 24 F6
Noghan BT 131 A3
North and South Lislea
  BT79 .... 14 D2
Northland Gdns BT80.. 135 D7
Northland Row BT71 .. 137 D5
Northland Terr 2 BT71. 137 C5
Northland Village 137 E4
Northland Way BT71 .. 137 E1
North St Pk BT71 ...... 62 D7
North St
  Dungannon BT70 ...... 42 F1
  Dungannon BT71 ...... 62 D7
North West Inst of F & H Ed
  BT82 .... 134 E6
Nurchossy BT76 ...... 92 D2
Nurchossy Irish BT76... 92 C2
Nurchossy Scotch BT76 92 C2
Nutfield BT94 .... 117 E6

Nutfield Cross Roads
  BT94 .... 117 E6
Oaghmonicroy BT79 .. 28 D8

O

Oakburn BT78 .... 24 F6
Oakfield BT92 .... 103 B1
Oakfield Dr BT71 ...... 80 B1
Oakland Ave BT79 ..... 136 F6
Oakland Ct BT79 ..... 136 E5
Oakland Dr BT81 ...... 23 A6
Oakland Hts BT81 .... 23 B6
Oakland Pk BT82 ...... 134 D4
Oakland Rd BT79 .... 136 F6
Oaklands BT80 .... 44 A6
Oaklands Rd BT80 ..... 44 A5
Oakland Villas BT79 .. 136 F5
Oak Rd BT82 .... 5 A5
Oak Rise BT 136 D1
Oaks Ctr The BT71 .... 137 D7
Oaks Rd BT71 .... 137 D7
Oakview BT71 .... 137 E7
Oakwood Manor 3 BT71. 80 A6
Obre Ave BT62 .... 81 E3
O Brien Pk BT78 ...... 54 F4
O'connor's Stronghold The ★
  BT71 .... 63 F1
Oggal BT 112 B3
Ogham Stone ★ BT79 ... 28 D4
Oghill
  Dungannon BT71 ...... 63 B8
  Enniskillen BT92 ..... 117 B4
  Enniskillen BT93 ...... 52 A3
  Enniskillen BT94 ...... 87 D7
Oghillicartan BT93 .... 52 E5
OILEÁN AN GHUAIL
  (COALISLAND) BT71 ... 62 B3
O Kane Pk BT78 .... 136 A2
O'kane Rd BT82 .... 134 C2
Old Barr BT93 .... 85 C1
Old Bridge Rd BT82 ... 24 C8
Oldcastle Rd BT78 .... 24 E5
Old Caulfield Rd BT70.. 78 F7
Old Chapel Rd BT69 .... 94 F6
Old Coagh Mill BT80 .. 135 E6
Old Coagh Rd BT80 .... 135 E6
Old Dungannon Rd BT70. 76 D2
Old Eglish Rd BT71 .... 137 B1
Oldford Rd BT78 ...... 56 A2
Old Henry St BT74 ..... 138 B5
Old Junction Rd BT94 .. 88 E8
Old Loughry Rd BT80.. 44 F3
Old Market Pl BT78 ... 136 C4
Old Mill Ct BT94 ...... 105 A1
Old Monaghan Rd BT76. 93 B2
Old Mountfield Rd BT79. 136 E5
Old Moy Rd BT71 ..... 79 E4
Old Omagh Rd BT70 .... 76 B2
Old Rectory Cl BT80 ... 135 C2
Old Rectory Cres BT80. 135 C2
Old Rectory Ct BT80 ... 135 C2
Old Rectory Glen BT80. 135 C2
Old Rectory Hts BT80.. 135 C1
Old Rectory Mdws BT80. 135 C2
Old Rectory Pk BT80 ... 135 C2
Old Rossorry BT74 .... 138 B3
Old Rossorry Cres BT74. 138 C3
Old Rossorry Pk BT74.. 138 B3
Old Rossorry Rd BT74.. 138 A2
Old Station Pk BT94 .... 88 C5
Old Tempo Rd BT74 .... 104 B5
Oldtown St BT80 ...... 135 C6
Olympic Dr BT82 ...... 134 D3
Omagh BT78 .... 136 C4
Omagh Acad BT78 .... 136 C5
OMAGH (AN OMAIGH)
  BT78 .... 136 D5
Omagh Bsns Complex
  BT78 .... 38 D2
Omagh Coll of Further & H
  Ed BT79 .... 136 C4
Omagh Ctr BT79 ..... 39 B1
Omagh Cty Prim Sch
  BT79 .... 136 D1
Omagh Golf Club BT78. 136 D6
Omagh High Sch BT79. 136 D6
Omagh Integrated Prim Sch
  BT78 .... 136 D1
Omagh Leisure Complex
  BT79 .... 136 D5
Omagh Rd
  Dromore BT78 .... 71 F8
  Omagh BT78 .... 37 A1
  Omagh BT78 .... 54 C1
Oneill Pk BT80 .... 45 A2
O'nolan Pk BT82 ...... 134 D5
Ora Beg BT93 .... 101 C3
Oranbeg Dr BT71 ..... 63 B4
Oranbeg Hts BT71 ..... 63 B4
Orangefield Pk 4 BT79. 136 F3
Orchard Ct BT69 ...... 95 B5
Orchard Dr BT69 ...... 95 B5
Orchard Rd BT82 ...... 12 A3
Orchard Rd Ind Est BT82 134 B1
Orchard St BT82 ...... 134 E4
Orchard Terr BT78 .... 136 C4
Orchard The BT82 ..... 134 C1
Orpheus Dr BT71 ..... 137 D6
Orritor BT80 .... 44 A8
Orritor Cres BT80 .... 135 C5
Orritor La BT80 .... 135 C6
ORRITOR (NA CORACHA
  BEAGA) BT80 .... 44 B8

Orritor Prim Sch BT80 . . 44 A8
Orritor Rd BT80. . . . . . . 43 F8
Orritor St BT80. . . . . . . 135 C6
Orr Pk BT78 . . . . 24 F6
Oughtagh Rd BT47. . . . . . .3 F6
Oughtboy⊕ BT79 . . . . . . 16 E8
Oughtdoorish⊕ BT79. . . 16 C7
Oughterard⊕
 Dungannon BT70. . . . . . 43 F1
 Omagh BT78 . . . . 53 E1
Oughterard Rd
 Dungannon BT70. . . . . . 60 E8
 Omagh BT78 . . . . 53 D1
Oughterdrum⊕ BT93. . . 65 F4
Oughtmame⊕ BT79. . . . 17 B8
Oughtnamwella⊕ BT79. . 17 D8
Outlands of Galvally⊕
 BT71 . . . . 62 C8
Owenbreeding⊕ BT94. . 117 F8
Owenreagh⊕ BT82 . . . . . . .5 F1
Owenreagh Dr BT82. . . . 134 C4
Owenreagh Pass BT82 . 134 C4
Owenreagh Rd BT79 . . . . 53 F1
Owenskerry⊕ BT75 . . . 107 A4
Oweyanirvore Chambered
 Grave★ BT79 . . . . 40 C4
Oxtown⊕ BT79 . . . . 40 C5

P

Paget La BT74 . . . . 138 C5
Paget Sq 5 BT74 . . . . . . 138 C5
Páirc Mhic Nein Macnean Pk
 BT93 . . . . 112 F7
Páirc Na Dabhcha (Hollywell
 Pk) BT93 . . . . 112 F7
PARK BT47. . . . . .8 E7
Parkanaur Rd BT70 . . . . . 78 C6
Park Ave
 Cookstown BT80 . . . . . 135 C5
 Dungannon BT71 . . . . . 137 B2
Parker's Farm⊕ BT71. . . 62 D7
Parkhill⊕
 64 A8
 Enniskillen BT93 . . . . . . 69 F7
Park Hill BT94 . . . . 117 C2
Park La BT71 . . . . 137 D4
Parkland View BT82. . . . 134 C4
Parkmore BT79 . . . . 58 E6
Parkmount BT80 . . . . . . 135 C5
Park Rd
 Castlederg BT81 . . . . . . 21 D1
 Dungannon BT71 . . . . . 137 C5
 Strabane BT82. . . . . .4 F5
Parkside Gdns BT82. . . . 12 D5
Parkview BT74. . . . . 138 F4
Park View
 Dungannon BT71 . . . . . . 62 D7
 Dungannon BT71 . . . . . 137 C2
Parkview Ct BT81 . . . . . . 22 E5
Parkview Dr BT70 . . . . . . 42 E1
Parkwood Ct BT71 . . . . . 137 E5
Parkwood Manor BT71 . 137 E5
Parson's Green Glebe⊕
 BT92 . . . . 132 A7
Patrician Villas BT82. . . 134 F3
Patrick Rd BT79 . . . . 57 C5
Patrick St BT82 . . . . 134 E5
Pattens Rd BT82. . . . . 5 A1
Patterson Pk
 Fintona BT78 . . . . 73 C5
 Strabane BT82. . . . . . . 134 B2
Peacockbank⊕ BT82. . . 12 B4
Peacock Rd BT82 . . . . . . 12 C5
Pearse Gdns BT82 . . . . . 134 D4
Perry St BT71. . . . . 137 C5
PETTIGOE 50 A3
Pettigoe Rd
 Enniskillen BT93 . . . . . . 50 B3
 Kesh BT93 . . . . 68 F8
Phoenix Manor BT93. . . 64 F3
Pine Bank Pk 3 BT71. . . 62 C2
Pinefield Ave 4 BT79 . . . 39 B3
Pinefield Ct 9 BT79 . . . . 39 B2
Pinefield Dr BT79 . . . . . . 39 B3
Pinefield Gdns 2 BT79. . 39 B2
Pinefield Gr 2 BT79 . . . . 39 B2
Pinefield Mdws BT79. . . 39 B3
Pinefield Mews BT79. . . 39 B3
Pinefield Rise 4 BT79 . . . 39 B2
Pinefield Wlk 3 BT79. . . 39 B2
Pinefield Wood
 1 Omagh BT79. . . . . 39 B2
 1 Omagh BT79. . . . . 39 B3
Pine Rd BT82 . . . . .5 B5
Pines The BT80 . . . . 135 B4
Pinewood Ave BT79 . . . 136 F3
Pinewood Cl 4 BT79 . . . 136 F4
Pinewood Manor BT70 . . 76 C2
Pipers Hill BT92 . . . . . . 126 B4
Plaister⊕ BT71 . . . . 95 C7
Plantation Rd BT47. . . . . . 8 D5
Platers Hill BT71. . . . . . . 62 C3
PLUMBRIDGE BT79. . . . . 14 F4
Plumbridge Rd BT78 . . . 25 C8
Point⊕ BT74 . . . . 113 E7
Polfore⊕ BT78 . . . . 72 B7
Pollagininver⊕ BT79. . . 50 D1
Pollanroe Bridge Rd BT79 27 F3
Polliniska⊕ 122 B5
Pollnoranny⊕ 48 A6
Pollockstown⊕ BT82. . . .5 B7
POMEROY BT70. . . . . 42 F1
Pomeroy⊕ BT70 . . . . . . 43 A1

Pomeroy Rd
 Cookstown BT80 . . . . . . 44 B5
 Dungannon BT70 . . . . . . 60 B7
Poplar Hill Rd BT80 . . . . 45 A3
Portbeg⊕ BT92. . . . . . . 115 E3
PORTHALL. 4 E8
Portinaghy⊕ 110 D4
Portinode⊕ BT93 . . . . . . 50 E1
Portmush BT74. . . . . . . 103 B5
Portnablahy⊕ BT93. . . . 49 D1
Portnacloyaduff⊕ BT93. 67 E2
Portnasnow Glebe⊕
 BT74 . . . . 104 B2
Portora⊕ BT74 . . . . 138 A6
Portora Castle★ BT74. . 138 A7
Portora Royal Sch BT74. 138 B6
Portreagh⊕ BT92. . . . . 115 D3
Portruan⊕ 131 B4
Ports⊕ BT92 . . . . 125 C3
Pottiagh⊕ BT92 . . . . . . 120 D1
Pound Hill 127 E3
Pound Loanan BT71. . . . 98 C6
Pound St 7 BT94 . . . . . . 69 F3
President Wilson's House★
 BT82 . . . . 5 B1
Priestsessagh⊕ BT81 . . 22 F8
Priestsessagh Rd BT81. . 22 E8
Priests La BT81 . . . . 22 E5
Prieststown Rd BT78 . . . 54 A1
Priest's Well★ BT80. . . . 30 F2
Primate Dixon Prim Sch
 BT71 . . . . 82 B4
Primrosehill BT81. . . . . . 93 A5
Primrose Pk Rd BT82. . . 12 D6
Prince Andrew Cres BT71 79 C4
Prince Andrew Terr BT93. 85 F1
Princess Ave BT80 . . . . 135 C7
Procklis⊕ BT93. . . . . 50 E5
Prolusk⊕ BT76 . . . . 92 C6
Prospect⊕ BT82 . . . . . . 12 B6
Prospect Rd T BT82 . . . . 12 B6
Prughlish⊕ BT78 . . . . . . 36 A1
Pubble⊕
 Enniskillen BT94 . . . . . 105 D7
 Omagh BT78 . . . . 24 F8
Pullans Rd BT81 . . . . 21 F8
Pullateebee⊕ BT82. . . . . 6 C3
Pullyernan⊕ BT81 . . . . . 22 B8
Pullyernan Rd BT81. . . . 11 H1
Pullytean Rd BT81 . . . . . 33 F6

Q

Quarry La BT70 . . . . 137 B7
Quarry Rd BT79. . . . . 41 C1
Quay La 3 BT74 . . . . 138 D4
Quay Mount BT71. . . . . . 98 A5
Quay Pass 4 BT74 . . . . . 138 D4
Quays The BT71. . . . . 98 B8
Queen Elizabeth II Prim Sch
 4 Dungannon BT71 . . . . 42 F1
 Omagh BT78 . . . . 89 A8
Queen Elizabeth Rd
 BT74 . . . . 138 D5
Queens Ave BT80 . . . . . 135 C6
Queens Par BT71 . . . . . 136 F4
Queens Pk
 Enniskillen BT94 . . . . . 105 A2
 Fivemiletown BT75 . . . 107 C8
Queen St BT74. . . . . 138 C5
Quiggy⊕ BT79 . . . . 17 B5
Quintanmanus Rd BT71. 61 E2
Quintinmanus⊕ BT71 . . 61 E4
Quivvy⊕ 131 C5
Rabbit Island⊕ BT92. . . 132 E8
Rabron⊕ BT93. . . . . 87 A1
Rabstown⊕ BT82 . . . . . 12 B5

R

Rabstown Rd BT82. . . . . 12 A6
Racaulfield⊕ 133 D7
Racolpa⊕ BT79. . . . . 39 F3
Racolpa Rd BT79. . . . . . . 39 F3
Raconnell⊕ 131 F3
Racrane⊕ BT78 . . . . 73 B6
Racrane Crt BT78 . . . . . . 73 B6
Radeerpark⊕ 133 F7
Radergan⊕ BT79 . . . . . . 57 D2
Radergan Rd
 Dungannon BT70 . . . . . . 75 C5
 Omagh BT79 . . . . 57 D2
Rafian⊕ 130 D1
Rafintan⊕ BT75 . . . . . . 106 E7
Rahack Glebe⊕ BT75 . . 108 B8
Rahall⊕ BT94 . . . . 69 E5
Rahallan⊕ BT74. . . . . . . 102 C1
Rahalton⊕ BT93 . . . . . . 86 B6
Raheelan⊕ 130 F4
Raheelin⊕ 99 A6
Raheen⊕ 64 B5
Rahony⊕ BT78 . . . . 72 B4
Rahony Rd BT78 . . . . 72 C2
Rahoran⊕ BT75 . . . . 91 C3
Railway Cres BT92 . . . . 126 D3
Railway Junc Ret Pk
 BT74 . . . . 138 C5
Railway Pk BT93 . . . . 69 A8
Railway Rd
 Dungannon BT71 . . . . . 137 B5
 Enniskillen BT93 . . . . . 112 F7
Rakeelan Glebe⊕ BT74. 104 A8
Rakeeragh⊕ BT78 . . . . . 55 C5
Rakeeranbeg⊕ BT78. . . 72 C5
Rakeernan Rd BT78 . . . . 72 B5

Rakelly⊕ BT78. . . . . 24 E5
Ralaghan⊕ 110 D8
Rallagh Rd BT47. . . . . . . 10 A8
Ramackan⊕ BT79. . . . . . 57 E6
Ramackan Rd BT79 . . . . 57 F6
Ramaket⊕ BT68. . . . . . . 111 B7
Ramaley⊕ BT75 . . . . 90 D4
Ramaley⊕ BT75 . . . . 90 F3
Rameen⊕ BT70. . . . . 76 C2
Ramper Rd BT80 . . . . . . 30 F4
Ramult⊕ BT75 . . . . 106 F7
Ranaghan⊕ BT79 . . . . . 137 B8
Ranaghan Rd BT71. . . . . 137 C7
Randall Dr BT78 . . . . . . 136 A4
Randalshough⊕ BT93. . . 86 D3
Raneese⊕ BT78 . . . . 73 F5
Raneese Rd BT78 . . . . . . 73 E4
Ranelly⊕ BT79 . . . . 56 D4
Ranenly⊕ BT75 . . . . 91 F1
Ranfurly Ave BT71 . . . . . 137 F3
Ranfurly Cres BT71 . . . . 137 F2
Ranfurly Hts BT71 . . . . . 137 F3
Ranfurly Pk BT71 . . . . . . 137 D4
Ranfurly Rd BT71 . . . . . . 137 D5
Rarogan⊕ BT70 . . . . 75 C3
Rarogan Rd BT70. . . . . . . 75 C3
Rarone⊕ BT79. . . . . 56 D2
Rarone Rd BT79 . . . . 56 D2
Rash Rd BT78. . . . . 38 C5
Raspberry Hill⊕ BT47. . . .3 B2
Rateen⊕ BT92 . . . . 126 F7
Rathbeg BT80 . . . . 135 C4
Ratheen Ave BT80 . . . . . 135 C4
Rathfort Cres BT93. . . . . 65 A4
Rathfraggan⊕ BT78. . . . 56 A1
Rathfure⊕ BT92 . . . . . . 124 E4
Rathkeelan⊕ BT94. . . . . 106 A2
Rathkeevan⊕ BT92 . . . . 128 C7
Rathlands 4 BT94 . . . . . 69 F3
Rathmoran⊕ BT92 . . . . 126 E7
Rathmore BT93 . . . . 65 A3
Rathmore BT80 . . . . 135 C3
Rathmore Ct BT80 . . . . . 135 C4
Rathmullan BT71 . . . . . . 137 D7
Rathowen BT92. . . . . . . 117 B4
Rathview BT74. . . . . 138 A2
Rathwarren⊕ BT78 . . . . 73 A5
Ratoal⊕ BT92 . . . . 126 F5
Ratona⊕ BT78 . . . . 103 B6
Ratoran⊕ BT94 . . . . 105 C8
Ratory⊕ BT76 . . . . 92 C5
Ratyn⊕ BT81 . . . . 23 D3
Ratyn Rd BT81. . . . . 23 D3
Raughan Castle★ BT71. . 62 A5
Raveagh⊕ BT78 . . . . 74 C5
Raveagh Rd BT78 . . . . . . 74 C5
Ravella Rd BT69 . . . . 94 F4
Ravellea⊕ BT69 . . . . 94 F5
Raw⊕
 Enniskillen BT94 . . . . . . 70 B6
 Enniskillen BT94 . . . . . 107 A3
 Omagh BT79 . . . . 56 E2
Reaghan⊕ BT79 . . . . 25 E3
Reaghan Rd BT79 . . . . . . 25 E4
Realtons⊕ BT78 . . . . 89 B4
Realtons Rd BT78 . . . . . . 89 C5
Reaskcor⊕ BT70. . . . . . . 78 D6
Reaskmore⊕ BT70. . . . . 78 C4
Reaskmore Rd BT70. . . . 78 D3
Reaskor⊕ BT70. . . . . 78 C6
Recarson⊕ BT79. . . . . . . 56 E8
Recarson Prim Sch BT79 39 D1
Reclaim⊕ BT70 . . . . 60 A1
Reclaim Rd BT70 . . . . . . 59 E2
Rectory Ave BT79 . . . . . 57 A4
Rectory Rd BT80 . . . . . . 43 E7
Red Bridge Rd BT45. . . . 45 D8
Redford Pk BT71. . . . . . . 79 E3
REDHILLS (AN CROC
 RUA) 132 C1
Reenaderry Rd BT71 . . . 80 E8
Regal Pass 1 BT74 . . . . 138 D4
Regents Ct 2 BT71 . . . . 62 C2
Rehaghy⊕ BT79 . . . . 95 F5
Rehaghy Rd BT69 . . . . . . 95 C5
Reihill Pk 11 BT94. . . . . . 69 F3
Reilly⊕ BT92 . . . . 125 A2
Reilly and Gole Wood Nature
 Reserve★ BT92 . . . . . . 125 A2
Relagh⊕
 Enniskillen BT94 . . . . . 104 B8
 Enniskillen BT94 . . . . . . 88 D2
 Omagh BT78 . . . . 89 B7
Relaghdooey⊕ BT78. . . 55 E5
Relagh Guinness⊕ BT94. 88 C8
Relagh Rd BT78. . . . . 89 B7
Relessy⊕ BT75. . . . . . . 108 B7
Relicknalanic★ BT79. . . 41 D1
Relicknaman★ BT79. . . . 41 C1
Relicknapain★ BT77 . . . 93 E4
Rellan⊕ BT92 . . . . 120 E3
Reloagh⊕ BT70. . . . . 61 A3
Renogher Glebe⊕ BT92. 132 E5
Reskatirriff⊕ BT70. . . . . 78 A1
Retreat Ave BT79 . . . . . 136 F5
Retreat Cl BT79 . . . . 136 F4
Retreat Hts BT79. . . . . . . 39 B2
Retreat Manor BT79. . . 136 F5
Retreat View 17 BT79 . . . 39 B2
Reyfad⊕ BT74. . . . . 101 B7
Rhone Rd BT71. . . . . 79 D1
Richmond⊕ BT70 . . . . . 76 B2
Richmond Dr BT76. . . . . 93 A5
Richmond La BT76 . . . . . 76 C2
Richmond Pk
 Ballygawley BT70 . . . . . 76 D2
 Omagh BT79 . . . . 39 B2
Ridgewood Ave BT71. . . 79 F1

Rigg⊕ BT74 . . . . 103 B4
Ring⊕
 Enniskillen BT74 . . . . . 103 F8
 Enniskillen BT74 . . . . . 115 D8
 Enniskillen BT74 . . . . . 116 A7
Ringvilla⊕ BT92. . . . . . . 127 A3
Ringville⊕ BT71 . . . . 80 D6
Riverdale BT71. . . . . 80 D6
Riverdale Dr BT80. . . . . . 44 F4
Riverdale Rd BT80 . . . . . 44 F4
River Rd BT81 . . . . 23 E6
River Row BT78 . . . . 136 B4
Riversdale Leisure Ctr
 BT82. . . . . 134 B5
Riversdale Rd BT78 . . . . 53 E8
Riverside BT74. . . . . 138 C6
Riverside Dr BT80 . . . . . 135 B2
Riverside Pk BT94. . . . . . 88 C5
Riverside Rd
 Enniskillen BT93 . . . . . . 51 A1
 Kesh BT93 . . . . 68 F8
Riverstown⊕ BT78. . . . . 55 A4
Riverview BT77 . . . . 93 C6
Riverview⊕ BT92 . . . . . . 39 B1
Riverview Gall★ BT74. . 138 B5
Riverview Pk 5 BT79 . . . 136 F4
Riverview
 Castlederg BT81 . . . . . . 22 A2
 Omagh BT79 . . . . 39 B1
ROAN BT70. . . . . 79 A1
Roan Pk BT70. . . . . 78 F1
Roan Prim Sch BT71 . . . 79 A1
ROBINSONS TOWN BT62. . 31 C6
Rocheville BT80 . . . . . . 135 D4
Rockdale⊕ BT80 . . . . . . 44 B1
Rockdale Cl BT70 . . . . . . 43 F1
Rockdale Rd BT70 . . . . . 44 A1
Rockfield⊕
 Enniskillen BT92 . . . . . 126 B7
 Enniskillen BT74 . . . . . . 87 D6
Rockfield Gdns BT93. . . 65 A4
Rockfield Pk BT93 . . . . . 65 A4
Rockfield Sch. 64 E4
Rockhead⊕ BT80 . . . . . . 44 F4
Rocklea Rd BT81. . . . . . . 23 C5
Rockmore Rd BT78. . . . . 74 F5
Rock Rd
 Omagh BT79 . . . . 28 E2
 Omagh BT79 . . . . 56 F2
Rocksavage Rd BT61. . . 98 D4
Rockstown Rd
 Carrickmore BT79 . . . . . 41 E1
 Omagh BT79 . . . . 42 B1
Rocorn⊕ BT93. . . . . 64 F3
Rodgers Rd BT78 . . . . . . 55 A6
Rodgers Villas BT79. . . . 136 E4
Roeglen Rd BT78 . . . . . . 57 D8
Ronan Rd BT78 . . . . 74 A4
Rookery Dr BT71. . . . . . . 97 D5
Rooskagh North⊕ BT92. 115 B1
Rooskagh South⊕ BT92. 122 C6
Roosky⊕
 Buckode. 82 B5
 Enniskillen BT93 . . . . . . 86 B5
 Enniskillen BT93 . . . . . . 87 A2
 Killeevan 128 F4
Roranna⊕ 132 C7
Rosaleen Rd BT78. . . . . . 74 B7
Roscavey⊕
 Omagh BT79 . . . . 57 B1
 Omagh BT79 . . . . 74 F8
Roscavey Prim Sch BT79. 75 A7
Roscavey Rd BT79 . . . . . 75 A7
Roscor⊕ BT78 . . . . 88 E8
Rosedene Rd BT81. . . . . 23 A8
Rosemary Rd
 Londonderry BT47. . . . . . 3 E4
 Omagh BT78 . . . . 38 C2
Rosemeilan⊕ BT75 . . . . 91 C2
Rosevale 8 BT92 . . . . . . 12 D6
Roskeen Rd BT71 . . . . . 137 E1
Roslea BT47 . . . . .2 E1
Roslea Golf Ctr BT92. . . 120 E3
ROS LIATH (ROSSLEA)
 BT92. . . . . 120 C1
Rosnamuck⊕ BT79 . . . . 38 F8
Ross⊕
 Dungannon BT71 . . . . . . 62 B7
 Enniskillen BT74 . . . . . 102 C7
 Enniskillen BT92 . . . . . 115 B5
 Enniskillen BT93 . . . . . . 99 E6
Rossaa⊕ BT92. . . . . 113 B5
Rossaa Forest Nature
 Reserve★ BT92 . . . . . . 113 B5
Rossachrin⊕ BT94. . . . . 68 F3
Rossahilly⊕ BT94. . . . . . 87 E2
Rossarrell⊕ 110 D1
Rossavally⊕ BT92 . . . . . 115 D6
Rossbeg⊕
 Enniskillen BT92 . . . . . 117 B2
 Enniskillen BT93 . . . . . . 66 B5
Ross Beg⊕ BT71. . . . . . . 61 D2
Rossbrick Glebe⊕ BT92. 127 A6
Rossca⊕ BT93. . . . . 68 F8
Rosscarn⊕ BT92 . . . . . . 103 F1
Ross Cl BT74 . . . . 138 C2
Rossclare⊕ BT94 . . . . . . 87 B7
Rosscolban⊕ BT93 . . . . 69 A8
Rosscolban Ave BT93 . . 69 A8
Rosscolban Pk BT93 . . . 69 A8
Rosscoltan⊕ BT74 . . . . 102 D7
Rosscor⊕ BT93 . . . . 65 E2
Rosscrennagh⊕ BT93. . 66 F7
Rossculban Ct BT93 . . . 69 A8
Rossculban Mdws BT93. 69 A8
Rossdagamph or St
 Catherines⊕ BT93. . . . 86 C7
Rossdanean⊕ BT92. . . . 114 F2
Rossdoney⊕ BT92 . . . . 115 D4
Rossfad⊕ BT94. . . . . 87 E5
Rossgad⊕ BT92 . . . . . . 125 C8

ROSSGEIR 4 C5
Rossgole⊕ BT93. . . . . . . 50 B1
Rossgweer⊕ BT94 . . . . . 87 A8
Rossharbour⊕ BT93 . . . 66 D7
Rossharbour Old⊕ BT93. 66 E7
Rossigh⊕ BT94 . . . . 86 F8
Rossinnan⊕ BT74 . . . . . 87 A7
Ross Inner⊕ BT93 . . . . . 87 C3
Rossinure Beg⊕ BT93. . 84 E3
Rossinure More⊕ BT93 . 84 F2
ROSSINVER 82 E1
ROSSLEA (ROS LIATH)
 BT92. . . . . 120 C1
Rosslea St. 120 C1
Ross Lough Nature Reserve★
 BT74 . . . . 102 C7
Rossmacaffry⊕ BT92 . . 117 B2
Rossmacall⊕ BT92. . . . 125 B8
Rossmacawinny⊕ BT92. 114 A6
Rossmacole⊕ BT92 . . . 116 F1
Rossmore⊕
 Cookstown BT80 . . . . . . 31 E3
 Enniskillen BT93 . . . . . . 66 C4
 Enniskillen BT94 . . . . . . 68 D3
Ross More⊕ BT71 . . . . . 61 D1
Rossmore Rd BT71. . . . . 61 D1
Rossnafarsan⊕ BT93. . . 87 A3
Rossnagalliagh⊕ BT47. . 2 A8
Rossnareen⊕ BT78 . . . . 89 F6
Rossnareen Rd BT78 . . . 89 D6
Rossole⊕ BT74 . . . . 138 A3
Rossole Pk BT74 . . . . . . 138 B3
Rossole Rd BT74. . . . . . 138 C3
Rossorry⊕ BT74 . . . . . . 138 B2
Rossorry Church Rd
 BT74 . . . . 103 D5
Rossorry Quay BT74 . . . 138 C4
Ross Outer⊕ BT93. . . . . 87 C1
Rosspoint or Cosbystown
 East⊕ BT93 . . . . 86 E6
Rossview 3 BT92 . . . . . . 117 D2
Rossyvullan⊕ BT74. . . . 104 C4
Roughan⊕
 Augher BT77 . . . . 93 F8
 Craigavon BT62. . . . . . . 81 F1
 Dungannon BT71. . . . . . 62 A5
 Omagh BT78 . . . . 73 A5
Roughan Cl BT71 . . . . . . 62 B4
Roughan Rd BT71 . . . . . 61 F5
Rough Hill⊕
 Augher BT77 . . . . 93 F7
 Knockatallan. 120 E4
Roundhill⊕ BT82 . . . . . . .4 F4
Round 'O' The BT74. . . . 138 B5
Rousky⊕
 Aughnacloy BT69. . . . . . 95 B8
 Dungannon BT71. . . . . . 62 A8
 Omagh BT79 . . . . 27 D6
 Strabane BT82. . . . . 6 D5
Rousky Rd BT82 . . . . .6 E4
Rouskyro⊕ BT71. . . . . . . 62 C8
Routingburn Rd BT79 . . 74 F6
Rowantreehill⊕ 64 D3
Roxborough Hts 13 BT71. 80 A1
Roxborough Pk 10 BT71. 80 A1
Roy⊕ BT77. . . . . 93 C7
Royal Arms Mews BT78. 136 C4
Royal Sch Dungannon The
 BT71 . . . . 137 D5
Rushall Rd BT47 . . . . .2 E7
Rushill Rd BT79. . . . . 39 F3
Rushin⊕
 Enniskillen BT92 . . . . . 115 B8
 Enniskillen BT93 . . . . . 112 E8
Rushinbane⊕ BT93 . . . . 34 B1
Rushindoo⊕ BT93. . . . . 51 A8
Ruskey Rd BT80. . . . . . . 46 B8
Rusky Upper⊕ BT80. . . . 46 B8
Rylagh⊕ BT79 . . . . 39 B7
Rylagh Rd BT79 . . . . 39 A7
Rylands⊕
 Omagh BT78 . . . . 55 D7
 Omagh BT79 . . . . 26 B5

S

Sacred Heart Coll BT78 . 136 B2
Sacred Heart Prim Sch. . 127 F3
Sacred Heart Prim Sch
 (Rock) BT70 . . . . 43 F1
St Aidens High Sch BT92 124 B4
St Anne's Prim Sch 5
 BT82. . . . . 134 C4
St Brigids Prim Sch
 Mountfield BT79 . . . . . . 40 B7
 Omagh BT79 . . . . 16 F5
 Omagh BT79 . . . . 58 B1
St Brigid's Prim Sch BT71 63 C5
St Cairealls Prim Sch
 BT81. . . . . 21 D3
St Ciarans High Sch BT70 76 C1
St Colmans Dr BT82. . . . 134 C4
St Colmcille's Prim Sch
 Armagh BT61. . . . . 98 D3
 Omagh BT78 . . . . 136 B4
St Columbans Prim Sch
 BT93. . . . . 101 A1
St Columba's Prim Sch
 Omagh BT78 . . . . 72 C8
 Strabane BT82. . . . . 11 F6
St Columba's Terr 6
 BT78 . . . . 136 B3
St Columbkilles Prim Sch
 BT79. . . . . 41 D1
St Comghalls High Sch
 BT92. . . . . 117 C4
St Conor's Prim Sch BT78 38 D1

St Davogs Prim Sch BT93 .. 65 A4
St Davogs Prim Sch
  (Scraghey) BT81 .... 34 E2
St Dympnas Gaa BT78 .... 71 F8
St Dympnas Prim Sch 4
  BT78 .... 71 F8
St Dympnas Rd BT78 .... 70 F8
St Dympna's Rd BT78 .... 71 D8
St Endas Gac BT79 ..... 136 C7
St Eugenes Prim Sch
  BT79 .... 26 A2
St Eugenes Coll BT92 .. 120 C1
St Eugenes High Sch
  BT81 .... 22 D5
St Eugenes Prim Sch
  BT92 .... 118 C4
St Eugene's Prim Sch
  BT82 .... 12 F3
St Eugenes St 8 BT82 .. 25 A6
St Fanchea's Coll BT74.. 138 D5
St Jarlath's Prim Sch
  BT71 .... 98 A5
St Jeans Cotts BT80..... 135 B5
St Johns High Sch BT78.. 71 F7
St Johns Pl BT82........ 134 F4
St John's Prim Sch
  Dungannon BT71 .... 63 B1
  2 Moy BT71............. 80 A1
SAINT JOHNSTOWN 1 B6
St John the Baptist Prim Sch
  BT93 .... 65 D2
St Joseph's Coll
  Coalisland BT71........ 62 B3
  Enniskillen BT74 .... 138 F6
St Josephs Gram Sch
  BT70 .... 61 A2
St Joseph's High Sch
  BT79 .... 14 F4
St Josephs Prim Sch
  Cookstown BT80 .... 43 C7
  Drumquin BT78 .... 36 F2
  Dungannon BT70........ 60 B3
St Joseph's Prim Sch
  Caledon BT68 .... 111 D5
  Ederney BT93 .... 52 A1
  Enniskillen BT92 ...... 126 B7
St Julian's Brae BT79 .. 136 D6
Saint Julian's Cotts
  BT79 .... 136 D6
Saint Julian's Ct 1 BT79 136 E6
Saint Julian's Down 3
  BT79 .... 136 E6
St Julian's Rd BT79 .... 136 D6
Saint Julian's Rd 4
  BT79 .... 136 E6
Saint Julian's Rise 2
  BT79 .... 136 E6
Saint Julian's Way BT79. 136 E6
St Lawrence's Prim Sch
  BT78 .... 73 B6
St Macartan's (Cathedral)
  BT76 .... 93 A4
St Macartans Convent Prim
  Sch BT76 .... 92 F4
St Macartan's Prim Sch
  BT78 .... 53 C2
St Macartins Cath BT74. 138 C5
St Malachy's Pk BT80 ... 47 C6
St Malachys Prim Sch
  BT70 .... 76 A4
St Malachy's Prim Sch
  BT45 .... 45 A7
St Martins Prim Sch BT93 83 A5
St Mary's Abbey★ BT74. 103 E7
St Mary's Altinure Prim Sch
  BT47 .... 8 E7
St Mary's Boys Prim Sch
  BT82 .... 134 D3
St Marys Cloughcor Prim Sch
  BT82 .... 5 B8
St Marys Coll BT94...... 69 F3
St Marys Ct
  3 Omagh BT79......... 39 B3
  Omagh BT79 .... 136 F6
St Marys Dr BT82....... 134 D3
St Marys Girls Sch BT82 134 D4
St Marys High Sch BT93.. 65 A1
St Marys Pl BT82....... 134 D4
St Marys Prim Sch
  Aughnacloy BT69........ 95 A4
  Ballygawley BT70 ...... 76 D2
  Cookstown BT80 .... 29 E1
  Dungannon BT71....... 62 D7
  Enniskillen BT94 ...... 106 D2
  Maguiresbridge BT94 .. 117 C6
St Mary's Prim Sch
  Dungannon BT70....... 42 F1
  Dungannon BT70....... 61 C4
  Dungannon BT70....... 77 E5
  Dungannon BT71....... 81 C8
  Enniskillen BT92 ...... 114 F2
  Enniskillen BT92 ..... 130 B7
  Enniskillen BT94 ...... 89 F1
  Fivemiletown BT75 .... 107 C8
  Newtownbutler BT92... 126 D2
  19 Omagh BT79........ 39 B2
St Mary's Prim Sch (Laght)
  BT78 .... 37 C4
St Mary's Rd BT79 ..... 136 F7
St Matthews Prim Sch
  BT70 .... 75 B5
St Michael's Coll BT74.. 138 F6
St Molaise's Church★
  BT74 .... 103 E8
St Molaise's Well★ BT94 . 87 E4
St Ninnidhs Prim Sch
  BT92 .... 124 A4

St Oliver Plunkett Prim Sch
  BT79 .... 57 B3
St Patrick's Acad BT71.. 137 E6
St Patrick's Coll BT70... 137 B6
St Patrick's Cross★ 32 E2
St Patricks Pk BT82..... 120 D1
St Patricks Prim Sch
  Augher BT77 .... 93 E2
  Castlederg BT81 .... 22 D6
  Enniskillen BT93 ...... 85 F5
  Gortin BT79 .... 26 E6
  Newtownstewart BT78 .. 24 F6
  Omagh BT78 .... 74 D4
  Omagh BT79 .... 41 E7
St Patrick's Prim Sch
  Dungannon BT71 .... 46 F3
  Dungannon BT71....... 62 E2
  Dungannon BT71....... 137 D5
  Omagh BT78 .... 73 F4
  Strabane BT82.......... 6 C7
Saint Patricks St 5
  BT78 .... 136 B3
Saint Patricks Terr 1
  BT78 .... 136 B3
St Patrick's Well & Chair★
  BT77 .... 93 F2
St Paul's Prim Sch BT94.. 69 E3
St Peter's Prim Sch
  Cookstown BT80 .... 47 B5
  Dungannon BT71....... 98 C8
  Plumbridge BT79 ...... 14 F4
St Ronans Prim Sch
  BT92 .... 117 D3
St Scires Prim Sch BT78 . 89 D8
St Teresas Prim Sch BT79 40 F4
St Theresa's Prim Sch
  Enniskillen BT74 ...... 138 D5
  Strabane BT82......... 12 C6
St Tierneys Prim Sch
  BT92 .... 120 C2
Sallaghy❶ BT92 .... 125 F6
Salloon❶ BT94 .... 88 C6
Salloon Terr BT94....... 88 C6
Sallowilly❶ BT47....... 7 F8
Sallowilly Rd
  Londonderry BT47........ 7 F8
  Strabane BT82.......... 7 D6
Sallysgrove❶ BT92 .... 113 F3
Sallyswood BT94........ 69 F2
Salmon Leap La BT71 ... 97 D4
Saloon Gdns BT94 ...... 88 C6
Salry❶ BT94........... 88 B4
Salters Grange❶ BT61.. 98 E1
Salters Grange Rd BT61 . 98 D3
Salter's Grange Rd BT61 . 98 E1
Samsonagh❶ BT74 .... 102 D5
Sanaghanroe❶ BT71.... 79 A2
Sandhill❶ BT93......... 85 E5
Sandhills❶ 132 E4
SANDHOLES BT80........ 44 D1
Sandholes❶ BT82...... 126 C1
Sandholes Rd BT80 .... 135 B1
Sandville❶ BT82......... 1 E2
Sandy Row 1 BT71 ..... 62 B3
Savings Bank St BT70.. 137 B5
Sawelabeg❶ BT79 ..... 17 E6
Scaffog❶ BT74........ 103 D3
Scaffog Ave BT74 ..... 103 D3
Scaffog Pk BT74 ...... 138 A2
Scallen❶ BT94......... 70 B2
Scallen Rd BT94........ 70 D2
Scandally❶ BT93 ...... 86 B4
Scardans Lower❶ BT93 . 66 A8
Scardans Upper❶ BT93 . 48 C1
Scarffes Entry BT78.... 136 C4
Scarvagherin❶ BT81.... 23 C5
Scarvagherin Rd BT81... 23 B5
Scarvy❶ 133 D8
School Gdns BT71 ...... 62 D2
School La BT71 .... 62 B4
School Rd BT78......... 74 F3
School Terr BT82........ 12 C6
Scotch St Ctr BT70..... 137 C5
Scotch St BT70 .... 137 C5
Scotchtown❶ BT80..... 135 E3
Scotchtown La BT80 .... 46 F8
SCOTSHOUSE (TEACH AN
  SCOTAIGH) 133 B4
Scotstown❶ B182..... 12 A6
Scotstown Rd BT82 .... 11 F6
Scraghy❶ BT81......... 35 A3
Scraghy Rd BT81....... 35 A6
SCRAIRB AN GCAORACH
  (EMYVALE)............ 110 B4
Scralea❶ BT81 .... 34 F8
Screeby❶
  Fivemiletown BT75 .... 91 F2
  Omagh BT78 .... 89 A5
Screeby Rd
  Fivemiletown BT75 .... 91 E1
  Omagh BT78 .... 89 A6
Screevagh❶ BT92 .... 125 F7
Screggagh❶ BT78 ..... 73 B2
Scribbagh❶ BT93....... 99 E8
Scribby❶ BT92........ 128 D7
Seagrave Terr 2 BT71 .. 62 B3
Seagully Rd BT78 ...... 53 F8
Searkin❶ 133 F6
Seavagh❶ BT92 ...... 125 F7
Seavadog Mountain❶ .. 32 D1
Second Corgary❶ BT81 . 20 F4
Sedan Ave BT78 .... 136 B4
Sedennan❶ BT78 ..... 136 B1
Seegronan❶ BT81...... 34 D6
Seegronan Rd BT81..... 34 E7
Seein❶ BT82.......... 12 D5
Seein Pk BT82......... 12 D5
Seein Rd BT82......... 12 C4
Segully❶ BT78........ 53 F8

Segully Rd BT78 .... 36 F1
SEISCEANN ODHAR
  (SESKINORE) BT78 .... 74 B8
Sentry Rd BT82.......... 5 B5
Seskinore❶ BT78 ...... 74 A8
Seskinore Ct BT78 ..... 74 A8
Seskinore Rd BT78..... 56 B3
SESKINORE (SEISCEANN
  ODHAR) BT78......... 74 B8
Sess❶
  Augher BT77 .... 75 F1
  Fivemiletown BT75 .... 91 C2
Sessagh of Gallan❶ BT78 13 E2
Sessagh Rd BT78 ...... 25 A8
Sessia❶
  Augher BT77 .... 93 C5
  Cookstown BT80 .... 45 B3
  Cookstown BT80 ...... 46 B7
  Cookstown BT80 ...... 47 C5
  Dungannon BT71....... 61 F4
Sessiadonaghy❶ BT70 .. 59 E2
Sessiadonaghy Rd BT70.. 59 F2
Sessiagh❶
  Dungannon BT71....... 62 A8
  Omagh BT78 .... 55 E1
Sessiagh East❶ BT94 .. 116 A3
Sessiagh Rd BT80....... 45 B3
Sessiaghs❶ BT94 ..... 70 A1
Sessiagh (Scott)❶ BT70.. 43 E1
Sessiagh Scott Rd BT70 . 43 D1
Sessiagh West❶ BT92.. 115 A6
Sessiamagaroll❶ BT71.. 97 D6
Sess Killgreen❶ BT70... 76 A3
Sess Rd BT77 .... 93 E8
Seylorain❶ BT71....... 80 A4
Seyloran La BT71 ...... 80 A3
Shagrim Pk BT79 ..... 136 C7
Shallany❶ BT94........ 69 B4
Shambles La 3 BT70.. 137 C5
Shanaghy❶
  Castlederg BT81 .... 34 A6
  Enniskillen BT92 ..... 125 A6
  Enniskillen BT92 ..... 127 E7
Shanalurg❶ BT69...... 95 D6
Shanco❶
  Clogher BT76.......... 93 A2
  Enniskillen BT94 ..... 105 D4
Shanco Rd BT76 .... 93 A2
Shandon Pk
  11 Omagh BT78........ 38 D1
  Omagh BT78........... 136 A3
Shane Rd BT79 .... 58 C2
Shankey❶ BT71........ 45 B1
Shankey Rd BT71....... 45 B1
Shankill❶
  Enniskillen BT74 ..... 104 C7
  Enniskillen BT93 ...... 86 D4
  Smithborough 128 F7
Shanliss Lower❶ BT71 .. 62 D5
Shanliss Rd BT71 ...... 62 D5
Shanliss Upper❶ BT71.. 62 D5
Shanly Rd BT78 .... 55 F6
Shanmaghery Rd BT70 .. 59 F5
Shanmaghry❶ BT70 .... 60 B5
Shanmaghry Rd BT70 ... 60 B5
Shanmoy❶
  Dungannon BT70....... 78 F1
  Omagh BT78 .... 96 F8
Shanmullagh❶
  Enniskillen BT74 ..... 102 D1
  Enniskillen BT93 ...... 70 A8
  Enniskillen BT94 ...... 87 E4
Shanmullagh East❶ BT78 71 C3
Shanmullagh Glebe❶
  BT78 .... 71 E7
Shanmullagh or
  Ballycullen❶
  BT71 .... 98 A6
Shanmullagh Prim Sch
  BT94 .... 87 F4
Shanmullagh Rd BT78... 37 E5
Shanmullagh South❶ .. 128 C6
Shanmullagh West❶
  BT78 .... 70 C4
Shannagh Rd BT79...... 40 D1
Shannaghy Rd BT81..... 34 A6
Shannaragh❶ BT78 .... 54 E1
Shannaragh Rd BT78.... 54 D1
Shannock❶ BT92 ...... 127 C6
Shannock Green❶ BT92. 127 E6
Shanoch BT71 .... 62 B4
Shanog❶ BT81........ 35 C8
Shanog Rd BT81....... 35 C8
Shanonny East❶ BT78 .. 14 A2
Shanonny West❶ BT82.. 13 B1
Shanraa❶ BT92....... 123 B8
Shanrelick★ BT70...... 43 C3
Shanroy Pk BT70....... 42 E1
Shantavny❶ BT69...... 94 E5
Shantavny Irish❶ BT70.. 75 E6
Shantavny Rd BT70 .... 75 D6
Shantavny Scotch❶ BT70 75 E5
Shantonagh❶ BT75..... 91 E6
Shantonagh Rd BT75.... 91 E6
Shanvally❶ BT92 ..... 123 A7
Shasgar❶ 82 B4
Shean❶ BT93.......... 67 C2
Sheehinny❶ BT92 .... 124 A7
Sheelbeg❶ BT92....... 117 E2
Sheelin Lace Mus★
  BT92................... 115 C7
Sheenmuldoon❶ BT93 .. 70 C8
Sheeny❶ BT92........ 126 C3
Sheepwalk❶ BT92 .... 132 F7
Sheers Pl BT70 .... 77 D5
Sheetrim❶ BT92...... 124 A5
Shelahs Rd BT92........ 3 B1
Shergrim Glen BT79.... 136 B7

Sheridan❶ BT94........ 88 D8
Sheridan Rd BT94....... 88 D6
Sheridan's La BT61 ..... 97 F1
Sherrigrim❶ BT71...... 61 F7
Sherrigrim Rd BT71..... 61 E7
Sherwood Cl BT78 ..... 73 B6
Sheskinshule❶ BT78 ... 73 C6
Sheskinshule❶ BT71 ... 28 C3
Sheskinshule View BT79 . 28 A3
Shillanmore❶ BT94.... 105 F7
Shilling Crt BT78........ 73 C6
Shivey❶ BT80.......... 44 B3
Shivey Rd BT80......... 43 F2
Showgrounds Ret Pk
  BT79 .... 136 C5
Sidaire❶ BT94.......... 88 A5
Sigerson Pl BT82....... 134 D4
Sigersons Gaa BT82 ... 134 E3
Silverbrook Mills★ BT82.. 6 C6
Silverhill❶
  Enniskillen BT74 ...... 103 D7
  Enniskillen BT92 .... 5 D3
Silverhill Pk BT74 ...... 103 D7
Silverhill Rd
  Castlederg BT81 .... 22 D3
  Enniskillen BT74 ...... 103 C6
  Enniskillen BT92 .... 5 D2
Silverhill Rd T BT82..... 13 E8
Silverstream Ct 2 BT74 . 104 B6
Simpson Pk BT82....... 22 F2
Sinton Ct BT80......... 135 B5
SION MILLS (MUILEANN AN
  TSIÁIN) BT82.......... 12 E6
Sion Mills Prim Sch BT82 12 D5
Sion Terr Rd 4 BT82.... 12 D6
Six Mile Cross❶ BT79 .. 57 E5
Sixth Corgary or Second
  Croagh❶ BT81......... 19 F6
Sixtowns Rd BT79 ...... 29 C8
Skaghlea Cairn★ BT93 .. 84 B3
Skea❶
  Dungannon BT70....... 60 F3
  Enniskillen BT92 ..... 114 F7
  Enniskillen BT93 ...... 51 B8
Skeachorn❶ 128 A1
Skeagh❶
  Blacklion 112 F1
  Enniskillen BT94 ..... 105 F2
Skeboy❶ BT79......... 41 A3
Skeboy Rd BT79 .... 41 A3
Skelgagh❶
  Clogher BT76.......... 92 B6
  Omagh BT78 .... 72 E5
Skelgagh Rd BT76 ..... 92 B6
Skenahergny❶ BT70 ... 43 D3
Skenarget❶ BT80...... 44 C2
Skeoge❶ BT94........ 106 D2
Skeogue❶ BT78 .... 71 F2
Skerrick West❶ 133 A2
Skerryglass❶ BT82 .... 11 F5
Skey❶ BT69........... 94 F8
Skinboy❶ BT82........ 13 B3
Skinboy Mountain❶
  BT82 .... 13 C5
Skinboy Rd T BT82..... 13 C4
Skreen❶
  Enniskillen BT74 ..... 103 A2
  Enniskillen BT92 ..... 113 D3
  Omagh BT78 .... 55 A2
Skreen Rd BT78........ 54 F2
Skrinny❶ BT93........ 51 D3
Slaghtfreeden❶ BT79 .. 30 D7
Slaght Rd BT80......... 30 D6
Slapragh❶ BT93...... 100 E5
Slash La BT61.......... 98 D6
Slash Rd BT71 .... 98 D6
Slatbeg❶ BT76 .... 108 D8
Slate Quarry Rd BT70 .. 43 B1
Slatmore❶ BT92 ...... 92 C1
Slatmore Rd BT76...... 108 C8
Slattinagh❶ BT93...... 99 C8
Slawin❶ BT93......... 66 A2
Slee❶
  Enniskillen BT74 ..... 104 A1
  Enniskillen BT94 ..... 116 A4
Slieveard Gr 7 BT79 ... 39 B2
Slieveard Mews 8 BT79.. 39 B2
Slievecard Rd BT79..... 39 C2
Slieveard Rise BT79 .... 39 B2
Slievebane❶ BT94 ..... 69 F7
Slievebane Rd BT79..... 40 E4
Slievebeg Rd BT79..... 15 A2
Slieveboy Pk BT47...... 8 D8
Slievebrickan❶ 129 D1
Slievebuoy Rd BT47..... 8 F8
Slievecoole Pk 5 BT79.. 136 E6
Slievedoo❶ BT81...... 19 E1
Slieve View BT92 ..... 130 A7
Sligo Rd
  Enniskillen BT74 ..... 138 A3
  Enniskillen BT92 ..... 103 A1
Slisgarrow❶ BT93 ..... 84 A4
Sloans St BT70........ 137 C5
Slougham❶ BT78 ..... 35 F3
Sloughan Rd BT78 ..... 35 E3
Sluggan❶ BT79........ 59 B7
Sluggan Rd BT70....... 59 C7
Slush Hill❶ BT92 ..... 117 F4
Snowhill❶ BT94 ...... 105 C2
Snugborough❶ 129 B5
Soarn❶ BT71.......... 45 C3
Soarn Rd BT71......... 45 D3
Sollus❶ BT82.......... 1 D4
Somerville Rd BT82..... 12 B6
Somervilles-town❶ BT82 12 B6
South Tyrone Hospl
  BT70 .... 137 C7

SPAMOUNT BT81........ 23 B5
Spawell Rd BT80........ 30 F7
Spear Pk BT81.......... 22 C2
Speerholme❶ BT81..... 21 E1
Speerholme Rd BT81.... 21 D1
Sperrin Cl BT78 ...... 136 A2
Sperrin Ct BT80........ 135 D6
Sperrin Dr BT78 ...... 136 A3
Sperrin Her Ctr★ BT79 .. 17 A6
Sperrin Mews BT80 .... 135 E5
Sperrin Pk BT78 ...... 136 A3
Sperrin Rd
  Londonderry BT47........ 9 D3
  Omagh BT79 .... 17 D8
Sperrin View
  Cookstown BT80 ..... 135 A6
  Newtownstewart BT78 .. 24 F6
  Omagh BT78 .... 136 A3
  Sion Mills BT82 .... 12 D6
Sperrinview Specl Sch
  BT71 .... 137 D8
Spires The BT80 ...... 135 D4
Spout Gdns 6 BT75.. 107 C8
Spout Rd
  Fivemiletown BT75 ... 107 C8
  Strabane BT82.......... 5 A1
Springdale BT70 ...... 137 B6
Springfield Cres BT70... 137 A8
Springfield La BT70 ... 137 A8
Springfield Pk BT70.... 137 A8
Spring Grove❶ BT92 .. 128 C8
Springhill Pk BT82 .... 134 F4
Springhill Rd
  Magherafelt BT45...... 46 A8
  Omagh BT78 .... 74 F5
Spring Rd
  Castlederg BT81 .... 23 E4
  Mountfield BT79 ...... 40 B6
  Strabane BT82......... 23 D7
Springtown❶
  Augher BT77 .... 93 C4
  Enniskillen BT93 ..... 123 A5
  Enniskillen BT93 ...... 50 B2
Springtown Rd BT77 ... 93 E3
Springvale BT74 ...... 138 A5
Springwell Dr BT79 .... 57 C4
Sproul Rd BT81......... 23 A3
Spruce Hill BT74 ...... 70 A3
Spruce Rd BT82.......... 4 F5
Square The 6 BT71.... 62 C3
Sraduffy❶ 99 D4
Sraghcumber❶ BT81... 33 D8
Sraharory❶ BT92 .... 118 B3
Srahenny❶ BT94 ...... 87 D3
Sralahan❶ 122 A1
Srananny❶ 110 E1
Sraniff❶ BT93......... 85 C4
Sraud❶ 82 E2
Sruhanure❶ BT93 ..... 66 D2
Sruveel❶ 120 E6
Staghall❶ 130 F1
Stakernagh❶ BT70 .... 78 C6
Stangmore (Knox)❶
  BT71 .... 79 D5
Stangmore (Magee)❶
  BT71 .... 97 F6
Starraghan❶ BT92 .... 131 F7
Starrs Cres BT78...... 136 B3
Station Brae BT94...... 88 C5
Station Rd
  Clogher BT76.......... 93 A5
  Coalisland BT71........ 62 B3
  Dungannon BT70....... 59 F8
  Kesh BT93 .... 69 A8
  Strabane BT82.......... 5 B6
Station Sq Ret Pk BT80.. 135 D5
Stephenstown❶ BT82... 12 A7
Stevenson Ave BT71 .. 137 E1
Stewart Ave BT80 .... 135 D3
STEWARTSTOWN (AN
  CHRAOBH) BT71 ...... 62 C7
Stewartstown Harps Gaa
  BT71 .... 62 C6
Stewartstown Prim Sch
  BT71 .... 62 D7
Stewartstown Rd BT71 . 62 C4
Stiloga❶
  Dungannon BT71....... 79 B1
  Dungannon BT71....... 97 A8
Stiloga Rd BT71......... 79 A1
Stonefort❶ BT93 ...... 66 F7
Stoneleigh Rd BT79 .... 40 C1
Stonepark❶ BT92..... 123 F5
Stone Rd BT82......... 12 D1
Stonewalls❶ BT82 .... 12 D2
Stoneyfalls❶ BT82....... 6 C7
Stoneyfalls Pk BT82...... 6 C7
Stoney Hts BT81 ...... 22 D6
Stonyfalls❶ BT82...... 12 C2
Stonypath❶ BT82....... 5 B7
Strabane❶ BT78...... 72 D3
STRABANE (AN SRATH BÁN)
  BT82 .... 134 B5
Strabane Enterprise Agency
  BT82 .... 134 B1
Strabane Golf Course
  BT82 .... 134 C2
Strabane Gram Sch
  BT82 .... 134 F3
Strabane High Sch BT82 134 F7
Strabane Prim Sch BT82 134 E7
Strabane Rd BT78....... 24 F6
Strabane Reading Ctr
  BT82 .... 134 E8
Straclevan❶ 120 D8

Stradowan BT79 ... 27 A1
Straduff Ⓣ BT78 ... 54 A3
Straduff Rd BT78 ... 53 F4
Stragolan Ⓣ BT78 ... 50 E3
Stragole BT94 ... 90 B2
Stragowna Ⓣ BT92 ... 123 C7
Stragrane Ⓣ BT68 ... 96 F2
Stragullin Ⓣ BT82 ... 12 E7
Strahans Rd BT82 ... 134 B2
Strahull BT79 ... 17 C5
Strahulter Ⓣ BT78 ... 25 C7
Strahulter Rd BT78 ... 25 C7
Straid Rd BT47 ... 8 F8
Stralahan Ⓣ BT74 ... 101 D5
Straletterdallan BT78 ... 25 D8
Stralongford Ⓣ BT78 ... 70 E5
Stralongford Rd BT78 ... 70 E4
Stralustrin Ⓣ BT92 ... 127 D5
Stramackilroy ... 108 F1
Stramatt Ⓣ BT92 ... 123 C3
Stranabrosny Ⓣ BT82 ... 2 B1
Stranacally Ⓣ BT93 ... 84 B1
Stranadarriff Ⓣ BT93 ... 52 E4
Stranadarriff Rd BT93 ... 52 E4
Stranafeley Ⓣ BT94 ... 117 F7
Stranagalwilly BT47 ... 8 A3
Stranagummer Ⓣ BT78 ... 70 F1
Stranahone Ⓣ BT93 ... 52 F4
Stranahone Rd BT93 ... 53 A5
Stranamart Ⓣ ... 112 A1
Strananerriagh Ⓣ BT92 ... 119 A2
Strangemore Terr BT71 ... 137 F2
Stranisk Ⓣ
  Omagh BT78 ... 73 A1
  Strabane BT82 ... 5 E4
Strathall Ⓣ BT47 ... 3 D8
Strathmourne Pl BT82 ... 134 D1
Strathroy Pk BT79 ... 136 A8
Strathroy Rd BT79 ... 136 A7
Stratigore Ⓣ BT78 ... 73 B4
Stratonagher Ⓣ BT93 ... 85 A5
Stratore Ⓣ BT93 ... 85 F4
Straughroy Ⓣ BT79 ... 136 A8
Streefe Glebe Ⓣ BT79 ... 40 C3
Streefe Rd BT79 ... 40 C3
Strews Ⓣ BT70 ... 44 A3
Strews Rd BT70 ... 44 A3
Strifehill Ⓣ BT80 ... 44 A4
Strifehill Rd BT80 ... 135 C1
Stripe Ⓣ
  Fivemiletown BT75 ... 107 F1
  Fivemiletown BT75 ... 119 B8
Stroanbrack Ⓣ BT82 ... 7 D1
Stroancarbadagh Ⓣ BT78 ... 55 D3
Strule Pk BT78 ... 136 A4
STS Bsns Pk BT82 ... 134 D3
Stuart Hall Ⓣ BT71 ... 46 B1
Stughan Ⓣ BT71 ... 61 E6
Stumpys Hill Ⓣ BT92 ... 122 E5
Sullenboy Ⓣ BT80 ... 135 B4
Sullenboy Pk BT80 ... 135 C4
Sultan Ⓣ BT79 ... 42 B5
Sultan Rd BT79 ... 41 F7
Summerfield Ct BT78 ... 136 A3
Summerhill BT94 ... 88 C4
Summerhill Ⓣ BT92 ... 127 D5
Summerhill Ct BT82 ... 134 B3
Summerhill Pk [6] BT79 ... 136 F4
Summer Island Rd BT61 ... 98 E7
Sunningdale BT78 ... 136 B2
Sunnycrest Gdns BT79 ... 136 D5
Sunnyside BT82 ... 24 A8
Sunnyside Ct [3] BT74 ... 104 B6
Sunnyside Rd BT80 ... 46 D4
SWANLINBAR ... 122 D4
Swanlinbar Rd
  Enniskillen BT92 ... 114 E1
  Enniskillen BT92 ... 114 E5
Sweep Rd BT80 ... 135 D2
Swinging Bars Rdbt BT79 ... 136 D4
Sycamore Ave BT82 ... 12 D5
Sycamore Dr BT74 ... 104 B6
Sycamore Dr Loop [1] BT74 ... 104 B6
Sycamore Hts [3] BT47 ... 8 E7
Sydney Cres BT69 ... 95 A5
Sydney La BT69 ... 95 A5
Sydney St BT69 ... 95 A5
Syerla Ⓣ BT79 ... 79 D2
Syerla Rd BT71 ... 79 D4
Sylvan Hill BT92 ... 117 C3
Syonee Ⓣ BT78 ... 72 F4
Syonee Rd BT78 ... 73 A4
Syonfin Ⓣ BT78 ... 73 C4
Syunshin Ⓣ BT75 ... 91 F5
Tabagh Ⓣ BT93 ... 86 C5
Taboe Glebe Ⓣ BT82 ... 2 E4

T

Taboe Rd BT82 ... 2 E2
TA Ctr & Cadet Adventure
  Training Centre BT74 ... 138 B6
Tagharina Ⓣ BT47 ... 2 A7
Tagharina Rd BT47 ... 2 A7
Tallbridge Rd BT62 ... 81 C1
Tamlagh Rd BT80 ... 135 E8
Tamlaght Ⓣ BT80 ... 44 A8
TAMLAGHT BT74 ... 104 D1
Tamlaght Ⓣ
  Magherafelt BT45 ... 46 A7
  Omagh BT78 ... 55 B8
  Omagh BT78 ... 74 F4

Tamlaghtmore Ⓣ
  Cookstown BT80 ... 31 F1
  Dungannon BT71 ... 46 B2
  Dungannon BT71 ... 80 D6
Tamlaghtmore Rd
  Cookstown BT80 ... 31 F1
  Dungannon BT71 ... 46 B2
Tamlaght Pk BT74 ... 104 E2
Tamlaght Rd
  Magherafelt BT45 ... 46 A7
  Omagh BT78 ... 136 A3
Tamnabrady Ⓣ BT82 ... 1 D5
Tamnabrady Rd BT82 ... 1 D5
Tamnabryan Ⓣ BT82 ... 1 E3
Tamnaclare Ⓣ BT82 ... 1 D6
Tamnagh Ⓣ
  Londonderry BT47 ... 8 F3
  Omagh BT78 ... 24 A2
Tamnagh Rd BT47 ... 8 F3
Tamnakeery Ⓣ BT82 ... 1 E5
TAMNAMORE BT71 ... 80 D6
Tamnamore Cl BT71 ... 80 D5
Tamnamore Prim Sch
  BT71 ... 80 D6
Tamnamore Rd BT71 ... 80 B6
Tamnaskeeny Ⓣ BT80 ... 43 F4
Tamnaskeeny Rd BT80 ... 43 F4
Tamnavally Ⓣ BT71 ... 46 E2
Tamnawood Ⓣ ... 4 A5
Tamnyagan Ⓣ BT47 ... 9 E8
Tamnyhagan Ⓣ BT80 ... 31 C3
Tamnylennan Ⓣ BT71 ... 62 D8
Tamnymore Ⓣ BT47 ... 3 E8
Tanderagee Ⓣ
  Dungannon BT70 ... 60 B8
  Killeevan ... 128 C3
  Omagh BT78 ... 58 D4
Tanderagee Rd
  [3] Dungannon BT70 ... 42 F1
  Dungannon BT70 ... 60 C8
Tannagh Ⓣ BT69 ... 96 B5
Tannaghlane Ⓣ BT68 ... 96 C1
Tannaghlane Rd BT68 ... 111 C8
Tantramurry Ⓣ BT79 ... 38 D7
Tantybulk Ⓣ BT92 ... 127 A3
Tarlum Ⓣ BT78 ... 37 E3
Tarlum Rd BT78 ... 37 E3
Tarmon Brae BT74 ... 138 C2
Tartaraghan Rd BT62 ... 81 E3
Tarthlogue Ⓣ BT62 ... 81 D2
Tarthlogue Rd BT62 ... 81 E2
Tartlaghan Ⓣ BT71 ... 79 F8
Tartlaghan Rd BT71 ... 79 F8
Tatnadaveny Ⓣ BT76 ... 74 B2
Tatnagilta Ⓣ BT80 ... 31 D2
Tattanamallaght Ⓣ BT71 ... 104 F1
Tattanafinnell Ⓣ BT78 ... 91 B5
Tattanellan Ⓣ BT75 ... 107 F8
Tatteevagh Ⓣ BT92 ... 117 A3
Tattenabuddagh Ⓣ BT75 ... 107 E4
Tattenaheglish Ⓣ BT75 ... 107 B5
Tattenalee Ⓣ BT75 ... 106 E6
Tattenamona Ⓣ
  Enniskillen BT92 ... 114 D5
  Enniskillen BT94 ... 106 A3
Tattendillur Ⓣ BT94 ... 106 D2
Tattinbarr Ⓣ
  Enniskillen BT92 ... 120 C1
  Enniskillen BT94 ... 118 A6
Tattinderry Ⓣ BT78 ... 117 C7
Tattinderry Hts BT94 ... 117 C7
Tattinfree Ⓣ BT94 ... 106 D6
Tattintonegan Ⓣ BT92 ... 127 F7
Tattinweer Ⓣ BT94 ... 90 A2
Tattraconnaghty Ⓣ BT78 ... 38 D6
Tattycam Ⓣ BT92 ... 126 E8
Tattycor Ⓣ BT78 ... 72 D7
Tattygare Ⓣ
  Enniskillen BT92 ... 125 F8
  Enniskillen BT94 ... 105 A3
Tattygare Glebe Ⓣ BT74 ... 103 B3
Tattygare Hts BT94 ... 105 A2
Tattygare Pk BT94 ... 105 A2
Tattygare Prim Sch
  BT94 ... 105 A2
Tattygormican Ⓣ BT92 ... 128 A8
Tattykeel Ⓣ
  Cookstown BT80 ... 43 E6
  Omagh BT78 ... 56 C5
Tattykeel (Buchannan) Ⓣ
  BT78 ... 54 F6
Tattykeel Cotts BT79 ... 56 B5
Tattykeel Lower Ⓣ BT93 ... 69 B8
Tattykeel Rd BT78 ... 54 F6
Tattykeel Rd E BT78 ... 55 A6
Tattykeel (Rogers) Ⓣ
  BT78 ... 54 F6
Tattykeel Upper Ⓣ BT93 ... 69 C7
Tattykeeran Ⓣ
  Enniskillen BT94 ... 106 B7
  Omagh BT79 ... 57 A6
Tattymacall Ⓣ BT94 ... 105 A3
Tattymore Ⓣ BT92 ... 33 B3
Tattymorris Ⓣ BT92 ... 127 F6
Tattymoyle Lower Ⓣ BT78 ... 72 F1
Tattymoyle Middle Ⓣ
  BT78 ... 90 F8
Tattymoyle Rd BT78 ... 72 E2
Tattymoyle Upper Ⓣ BT78 ... 90 E8
Tattymulmona Ⓣ BT78 ... 55 C3
Tattynacunnian Ⓣ BT92 ... 127 E8
Tattynaveeragh Ⓣ BT92 ... 127 D7
Tattynagolan Ⓣ BT92 ... 127 D7
Tattynagole Ⓣ BT79 ... 38 D8
Tattynagole Rd BT79 ... 38 D7
Tattynuckle Ⓣ BT75 ... 107 A6
Tattynure Ⓣ BT79 ... 25 D1
Tattynure Rd BT79 ... 25 D1

Tattyreagh Ⓣ BT75 ... 107 B6
Tattyreagh Glebe Ⓣ BT78 ... 56 A2
Tattyreagh Rd BT78 ... 73 C7
Tattysallagh Ⓣ BT78 ... 54 F5
Tattysallagh Rd BT78 ... 53 F5
Tawlaght Ⓣ ... 50 A8
Tawnaghgorm Ⓣ BT93 ... 66 C6
Tawnaleck Ⓣ ... 82 C2
Tawnawanny Ⓣ BT93 ... 67 A8
Tawnydorragh Ⓣ BT93 ... 34 D2
Tawnylust Barr Ⓣ ... 99 A2
Tawnylust Barr Upper Ⓣ ... 99 D1
Tawnymakelly Ⓣ ... 112 E3
Tawnymore Ⓣ BT77 ... 93 E4
Tawnynoran Ⓣ BT93 ... 65 E4
Tawnyreagh Ⓣ BT74 ... 116 B7
Tawnyunshinagh Ⓣ ... 99 A1
TEACH AN SCOTAIGH
  (SCOTSHOUSE) ... 133 B4
Teagy Ⓣ BT62 ... 81 C2
Teagy Rd BT62 ... 81 C2
Technology Ed Ctr BT79 ... 136 D4
Tedd Ⓣ BT94 ... 70 C6
Tedd Cross Roads BT94 ... 70 C6
Tedd Rd BT93 ... 53 A2
Teebane Ⓣ
  Cookstown BT80 ... 29 C1
  Enniskillen BT93 ... 100 C7
Teebane East Ⓣ BT79 ... 28 D2
Teebane Rd BT80 ... 29 D1
Teebane West Ⓣ BT79 ... 27 F5
Teehill Ⓣ ... 127 E2
TEEMORE BT92 ... 130 B7
Teemore Bsns Complex
  BT92 ... 130 B7
Teer Ⓣ BT92 ... 132 D5
Teeraw Rd BT61 ... 98 A1
Teesnaghtan Ⓣ BT92 ... 122 D7
Tempanroe Ⓣ BT71 ... 79 F6
Templemoyle Ⓣ BT47 ... 10 A7
Templenafrrin Ⓣ BT93 ... 113 A8
Templenew Ⓣ ... 64 D4
Templereagh Ⓣ BT71 ... 45 D1
Templereagh Rd BT71 ... 45 D2
Templerushin ★ BT93 ... 112 E8
TEMPO (AN TLOMPÚ
  DEISEAL) BT94 ... 89 F1
Tempo Controlled Prim Sch
  BT94 ... 89 F1
Tempo Rd BT74 ... 138 F5
Tents Ⓣ BT74 ... 102 D1
Termon Ⓣ ... 112 C5
Termon Bsns Pk The
  BT79 ... 58 D8
Termon Cres BT79 ... 41 D1
Termon Rd BT79 ... 41 D1
Terraskane Rd BT61 ... 98 A1
Terrenew Ⓣ BT79 ... 78 B7
Terrenew Rd BT70 ... 78 B7
Terressan Ⓣ BT80 ... 45 B6
Terryglassog Ⓣ BT70 ... 96 F7
Terryglassog Rd BT70 ... 96 F7
Terryscallop Rd BT71 ... 97 A6
Terryscollop Ⓣ BT71 ... 97 B7
Terrywhinny La BT80 ... 43 F6
Terrywinny Ⓣ BT80 ... 43 F5
THE BATTERY BT80 ... 47 C6
The Bonn Ⓣ BT70 ... 60 B7
THE BUSH BT71 ... 79 E8
Thecurran Ⓣ BT94 ... 69 C4
THE DIAMOND BT71 ... 46 F4
The Gort alias Eglish Ⓣ
  BT80 ... 47 A7
The Meadows BT62 ... 81 A2
THE ROCK BT70 ... 43 F1
Thgortreagh Rd BT70 ... 43 D3
Third Corgary Ⓣ BT81 ... 20 C5
Third Corgary Rd BT81 ... 20 E4
Thloughbracken Rd BT70 ... 43 A3
Thomas St
  Castlederg BT81 ... 22 D5
  Dungannon BT70 ... 137 C6
Thomastown Ⓣ BT74 ... 104 C3
Thorn Hill Ⓣ BT82 ... 1 C6
Thornhill Glebe Ⓣ
  Dungannon BT70 ... 61 B5
  Enniskillen BT94 ... 87 F1
Thornhill or
  Mullandreena Ⓣ ... 112 A6
Thornhill Rd BT70 ... 60 E6
Thornlea Ⓣ BT79 ... 136 E3
Thornville Pk BT78 ... 136 A4
Thpomeroy Rd BT80 ... 43 F3
Tibberedoge Glebe Ⓣ
  BT92 ... 119 F3
Tievaveeny Ⓣ BT93 ... 34 D1
Tievealough Ⓣ BT93 ... 65 D4
Tievebrack Ⓣ BT79 ... 17 F3
Tievebunnan Ⓣ BT93 ... 100 D7
Tievecloghoge Ⓣ ... 20 D8
Tieveeny Rd BT82 ... 23 D7
Tievegarrow Ⓣ BT92 ... 132 F7
Tievemore Ⓣ ... 33 B3
Tievemore Rd BT78 ... 71 A1
Tievenagh Ⓣ BT71 ... 45 D4
Tievenameena Ⓣ BT79 ... 17 D2
Tievenameenta Ⓣ BT81 ... 33 F4
Tievenavarnog Ⓣ BT93 ... 51 D6
Tievenny Ⓣ BT82 ... 23 E7
Tievetooey Ⓣ ... 32 E5
Timpany Ⓣ BT76 ... 92 A2
Timulkenny Ⓣ BT62 ... 81 E1
Tintagh Ⓣ BT45 ... 31 E8
Tiraffy Ⓣ BT92 ... 125 E5
Tiraltan Ⓣ BT94 ... 105 C6
Tiranagher Beg Ⓣ BT93 ... 66 C2
Tiranagher More Ⓣ BT93 ... 66 B1

Tiraroe Ⓣ BT92 ... 124 D6
Tiravally Glebe Ⓣ BT92 ... 115 B2
Tiravree Glebe Ⓣ BT92 ... 122 F8
Tircahan Ⓣ ... 122 F1
Tircar Ⓣ BT75 ... 108 A8
Tirconnell Ⓣ BT74 ... 103 B7
Tirconnelly Ⓣ BT82 ... 6 E8
Tircooney Ⓣ ... 128 E5
Tircur Ⓣ BT92 ... 26 B1
Tircur Rd BT79 ... 25 F1
Tireaghty Ⓣ BT71 ... 98 A3
Tireeghan Ⓣ BT75 ... 107 E7
Tireenan Ⓣ BT78 ... 72 E3
Tireevil Ⓣ BT92 ... 127 A7
Tiregirter Ⓣ BT47 ... 8 E6
Tireighter Cotts BT47 ... 8 E7
Tireighter Rd BT47 ... 8 E5
Tirelugan Ⓣ BT69 ... 77 C1
Tirenny Ⓣ BT94 ... 106 C5
Tireugan Rd BT69 ... 95 C8
Tirgarve Ⓣ BT61 ... 98 B3
Tirgormly Ⓣ ... 130 B3
Tirieghter Rd BT47 ... 8 E5
Tirkeeveny Ⓣ BT47 ... 8 E5
Tirkernaghan Ⓣ BT82 ... 6 C4
Tirk Rd BT82 ... 6 B4
Tirmacrannon Ⓣ BT61 ... 98 C5
Tirmacrannon Rd BT61 ... 98 B5
Tirmacshane Ⓣ BT80 ... 30 F1
Tirmacspird Ⓣ BT93 ... 52 D6
Tirmegan Ⓣ BT82 ... 24 D8
Tirmegan Rd BT82 ... 13 B1
Tirmonen Ⓣ BT92 ... 123 A5
Tirmonel Ⓣ BT79 ... 26 B2
Tirmurty Ⓣ BT79 ... 26 B2
Tirmurty Rd BT79 ... 26 A2
Tirnahinch Far Ⓣ ... 127 F5
Tirnahinch Near Ⓣ ... 127 F4
Tirnanog BT80 ... 47 B6
Tirnaskea Ⓣ
  Dungannon BT70 ... 43 D1
  Dungannon BT70 ... 76 D5
Tirnaskea (Bayly) Ⓣ BT80 ... 44 B4
Tirnaskea Rd BT70 ... 43 C1
Tiroogan Ⓣ BT92 ... 123 B8
Tirooney Rd
  Omagh BT78 ... 58 C6
  Six Mile Cross BT79 ... 57 F5
Tiroony Ⓣ BT79 ... 58 D7
Tirowen Ct [14] BT71 ... 62 C2
Tirquin Ⓣ BT79 ... 39 D4
Tirquin Rd BT79 ... 39 C3
Tirwinny Ⓣ BT93 ... 52 C4
Tobarnasuil ★ BT93 ... 85 D6
Tober Ⓣ BT93 ... 101 E8
Toberanna ★ BT79 ... 15 F3
Tober Davagh ★ BT81 ... 33 E7
Toberlane Ⓣ ... 44 C8
Toberlane Rd BT80 ... 44 C7
Tobermesson Glebe Ⓣ
  BT71 ... 97 E7
Tobermesson Rd BT71 ... 97 D8
Tobermore Pk BT74 ... 138 F5
Tobernasool Ⓣ BT79 ... 69 D7
Tober Ninny ★ BT93 ... 65 E1
Toberpatrick ★
  Castlederg BT81 ... 34 B8
  Enniskillen BT93 ... 83 E5
Tobin Pk BT80 ... 47 B6
Tobradan Ⓣ BT74 ... 102 C6
Todds Leap Rd BT70 ... 76 A6
Todds Rd
  Omagh BT78 ... 38 C4
  Omagh BT79 ... 75 F8
Togherdoo Rd BT78 ... 71 F5
Tolvin Ⓣ BT70 ... 61 A8
Tomassan Ⓣ ... 130 B2
Tomkinroad Ⓣ ... 130 B2
Tonagh Glebe Ⓣ BT92 ... 115 A2
Tonanoran Ⓣ BT93 ... 85 A5
Tonardrum Ⓣ BT94 ... 102 A1
Tonavally Ⓣ BT92 ... 117 D6
Toneduff Ⓣ BT47 ... 3 E5
Toneel North Ⓣ BT74 ... 101 F8
Toneel South Ⓣ BT74 ... 102 B4
Tonegan Ⓣ BT79 ... 58 C7
Toney Ⓣ BT92 ... 117 E3
Tonity Bog Ⓣ BT92 ... 127 F7
Tonitygorman Ⓣ BT92 ... 127 B6
Tonlisderritt Ⓣ BT74 ... 102 C4
Tonnaboy Ⓣ BT92 ... 117 F1
Tonnacroob Ⓣ BT92 ... 124 C6
Tonnaghbane Ⓣ BT78 ... 73 B5
Tonnagh-Beg Ⓣ BT78 ... 72 F4
Tonnagh-More Ⓣ BT78 ... 72 F4
Tonnagh Rd BT78 ... 71 F3
Tonnore Ⓣ BT93 ... 52 A7
Tonyclea Ⓣ ... 109 F3
Tonydrummallard Ⓣ
  BT92 ... 119 F2
Tonyglaskan Ⓣ BT94 ... 90 B5
Tonyloman Ⓣ BT92 ... 115 D7
Tonymalloe Ⓣ BT94 ... 115 F5
Tonymore Ⓣ
  Enniskillen BT92 ... 129 B8
  Enniskillen BT92 ... 130 C5
Tonynelt Ⓣ BT92 ... 123 E4
Tonyquin Ⓣ ... 122 F2
Tonyrevan Ⓣ ... 129 A1
Tonystackan Ⓣ ... 109 E1
Tonystick Ⓣ BT74 ... 138 E5
Tonystick Mews BT74 ... 138 F5
Tonyteige Ⓣ BT92 ... 115 D6
Tonyvarnog Ⓣ BT92 ... 123 E5
Tonywall Ⓣ BT92 ... 123 F6

Toolinn Ⓣ BT92 ... 117 C5
Toomog Ⓣ BT70 ... 60 D1
Toomog Rd BT70 ... 60 D1
Toppan Ⓣ BT93 ... 100 F3
Toralt Ⓣ BT92 ... 130 E7
Tormore Rd BT79 ... 56 D8
Tornoge Rd BT82 ... 7 C3
Tower Beg Ⓣ BT93 ... 83 E2
Tower More Ⓣ BT93 ... 83 E1
Townagh Ⓣ BT76 ... 92 C5
Towncastle Rd BT82 ... 5 A3
Townhall St
  Enniskillen BT74 ... 138 D5
  [6] Newtownstewart BT78 ... 25 A6
Townhill Ⓣ BT94 ... 69 F3
Townhill Pk [2] BT82 ... 69 F3
Town Parks BT82 ... 134 E6
Town Parks BT82 ... 134 F8
Town Parks of Strabane Ⓣ
  BT82 ... 134 E5
Townsend St BT82 ... 134 E4
Townview Ave BT78 ... 136 C3
Townview Ave N BT78 ... 136 C3
Townview Ave S BT78 ... 136 C3
Trainors Terrrace BT70 ... 42 F1
Trannish Ⓣ BT92 ... 124 F6
Trasna Ⓣ BT94 ... 105 F5
Trasna Island Ⓣ BT92 ... 124 F4
Trasna Pk BT74 ... 138 A5
Trasna Way [6] BT92 ... 117 D2
Treel Ⓣ BT74 ... 102 A3
Tremoge Ⓣ BT79 ... 42 B1
Tremoge Rd BT70 ... 42 C1
Trench Rd BT47 ... 2 C7
Trew Ⓣ BT71 ... 80 B4
Trewmount Rd BT71 ... 80 A5
Trickvallen Ⓣ BT71 ... 46 E4
Trickwallen Rd BT71 ... 46 E4
Trien Ⓣ BT92 ... 114 A1
Trienamongan Ⓣ BT81 ... 21 D3
Trienamongan Rd BT81 ... 21 D3
TRILEAC (TRILLICK) BT78 ... 71 C1
Trillick Ⓣ ... 114 B8
Trillick Controlled Prim Sch
  BT78 ... 71 D1
TRILLICK (TRILEAC) BT78 ... 71 C1
Trinamadam Rd BT79 ... 15 C1
Trinamadan Ⓣ BT79 ... 26 E8
Trinamadan Rd BT79 ... 26 D7
Tristan Rd BT82 ... 5 C1
Tromogagh Ⓣ BT92 ... 121 B8
Trory Ⓣ BT94 ... 87 F1
Trustan Ⓣ BT94 ... 118 C3
Trustan Glebe Ⓣ BT92 ... 115 B3
Tuam Ⓣ ... 112 D7
Tubbrid Ⓣ BT93 ... 51 C3
Tudor Ct BT74 ... 104 F1
Tudor Gr BT78 ... 136 C1
Tudor Pk BT75 ... 91 C1
Tulacorr Dr BT82 ... 134 F8
Tulacorr Gdns BT82 ... 134 F8
Tulacorr Hts BT82 ... 134 F8
TULAIGH AN LÚIR
  (CHURCHTOWN) BT80 ... 31 E3
Tullagh Ⓣ BT80 ... 135 B4
Tullaghalost Ⓣ ... 133 C2
Tullagh Beg Ⓣ BT71 ... 62 B5
Tullaghbeg Rd BT71 ... 62 A5
Tullaghboy Rd BT45 ... 45 C8
Tullagh Dr BT80 ... 135 B5
Tullagherin Ⓣ BT78 ... 14 A3
Tullagherin Rd BT79 ... 14 A4
Tullaghmore Ⓣ BT71 ... 62 B5
Tullagh More Rd BT71 ... 62 B6
TULLAGHOGE BT80 ... 45 B2
Tullagh Rd BT80 ... 135 A5
Tullagh View BT80 ... 135 A4
Tullanafoile Ⓣ BT70 ... 75 A4
Tullanafoile Rd BT70 ... 75 B2
Tullanaginn Ⓣ BT93 ... 70 A4
Tullanaglare Ⓣ BT94 ... 69 E6
Tullanaglug Ⓣ BT93 ... 69 C7
Tullanaguiggy Ⓣ BT94 ... 69 D6
Tullanavert Ⓣ BT76 ... 92 C4
Tullanisken Hts BT71 ... 61 F4
Tullaville Ⓣ BT80 ... 135 A4
Tulleevin Pk BT74 ... 138 F6
Tullintaggart Ⓣ ... 99 D3
Tullinteskin Ⓣ BT93 ... 100 C7
Tullintloy Ⓣ ... 99 F5
Tullinwonny Ⓣ BT93 ... 100 F8
Tully Ⓣ
  Augher BT77 ... 93 C7
  Aughnacloy BT69 ... 95 A4
  Cookstown BT80 ... 44 C1
  Enniskillen BT92 ... 114 D3
  Enniskillen BT92 ... 115 D8
  Enniskillen BT92 ... 118 E2
  Enniskillen BT92 ... 123 C3
  Enniskillen BT93 ... 68 A1
  Enniskillen BT94 ... 87 D7
  Enniskillen BT94 ... 115 F6
  Omagh BT78 ... 38 B5
  Omagh BT78 ... 52 E8
Tullyallen Ⓣ BT70 ... 78 A5
Tullyaran Ⓣ BT70 ... 60 F4
Tullyaran Rd BT70 ... 60 F5
Tullyard Ⓣ
  Cookstown BT80 ... 44 D2
  Omagh BT78 ... 36 C5
  Strabane BT82 ... 5 A4
  Strabane BT82 ... 6 B8
Tullyard Rd
  Cookstown BT80 ... 44 D1
  Omagh BT78 ... 36 B5
Tullyavey Ⓣ BT94 ... 87 F3
Tullybaradair Ⓣ ... 65 A5
Tullybellina Ⓣ BT93 ... 100 B4

Tullybletty Rd BT69 95 F5
Tullyblety Ⓣ BT69 95 F4
Tullybrack or Ora More Ⓣ BT93 101 A3
Tullybrick Etra or Bondville Ⓣ BT60 111 C1
Tullybroom Ⓣ BT76 92 F6
Tullybroom Rd BT76 92 F6
Tullybryan Ⓣ BT70 76 B1
Tullybryan Rd BT70 76 C1
Tullycall Ⓣ BT80 31 C1
Tullycall Rd BT80 31 B1
Tullycallrick Ⓣ BT93 69 C7
Tullycar Ⓣ BT81 20 D3
Tullycarbry Ⓣ BT93 85 F3
Tullycar Rd BT81 19 E1
Tully Castle & Gdn ★ BT93 67 F1
Tullychurry Ⓣ BT93 48 F1
Tullyclea Ⓣ BT94 87 F5
Tullyclunagh Ⓣ BT78 72 C5
Tullyconnell Ⓣ BT80 45 C3
Tullycorker Ⓣ BT76 74 E1
Tullycorker Rd
Augher BT77 75 A2
Omagh BT78 74 D3
Tullycreevy Ⓣ BT74 86 D2
Tullycullion Ⓣ BT70 61 C2
Tullycullion Rd BT70 61 C2
Tullycunney Rd BT78 55 D3
Tullycunny Ⓣ BT78 55 C4
Tullycunny Rd BT78 55 E2
Tullydevenish Ⓣ BT74 103 D7
Tullydoortans Ⓣ BT82 12 A1
Tullydowey Ⓣ BT71 97 F4
Tullydowey Rd BT71 97 E5
Tullydraw Ⓣ BT70 61 B2
Tullydraw Rd BT70 61 B4
Tullyfad Ⓣ BT93 66 D7
Tullyfaughan Ⓣ BT80 45 B2
Tullygare Ⓣ BT80 135 F6
Tullygarran Ⓣ BT61 98 B2
Tullygarron Rd BT61 97 F1
Tullygerravra Ⓣ BT93 100 A8
Tullygiven Ⓣ BT70 96 F5
Tullyglush Ⓣ BT70 76 B6
Tullyglush Rd BT70 75 F4
Tullygoney Ⓣ BT71 97 E6
Tullygoonigan Ⓣ BT61 98 C2
Tullygoonigan Ind Est BT61 98 C3
Tullygun Ⓣ BT70 61 C2
Tullyharney Ⓣ BT74 104 D2
Tullyheeran Ⓣ BT79 56 D3
Tullyholvin Lower Ⓣ BT74 102 B5
Tullyholvin Upper Ⓣ BT74 102 A5
Tullyhommon Ⓣ BT93 50 B4
Tullyhorky Ⓣ 64 C8
Tullyhurken Ⓣ BT71 45 D4
Tullykelter Ⓣ BT74 86 D1
Tullykenneye Ⓣ BT75 107 A5
Tullykevan Ⓣ BT71 98 A6
Tullylagan Ⓣ BT80 44 D1
Tullylagan Rd BT80 44 C1
Tullylammy Ⓣ BT94 69 C1
Tullylearn Ⓣ BT71 97 F4
Tullyleek Ⓣ BT70 60 F2
Tullyleek Rd BT70 60 F3
Tullylig Ⓣ BT71 62 C6
Tullylinton Ⓣ BT70 76 B3
Tullylinton Rd BT70 76 A3
Tullylone Ⓣ BT94 87 F5
Tullylough Ⓣ BT93 66 E8
Tullyloughdaugh Ⓣ BT93 84 B5
Tullymagough Ⓣ BT78 71 B5
Tullymargy Ⓣ BT74 86 E1
Tullyminister Ⓣ 121 A3
Tullymoan Ⓣ BT82 12 A4
Tullymoan Rd BT82 11 F5
Tullymore Ⓣ BT93 82 E7
Tullymore Agowan Ⓣ BT71 97 F3
Tullymore Agowan La BT71 97 E3
Tullymore Etra Ⓣ BT71 97 B4
Tullymore La BT71 97 B3
Tullymore Otra Ⓣ BT71 97 B4
Tullymore Sch La BT60 97 B3
Tullymuck Ⓣ BT78 37 C7
Tullynabohoge Ⓣ BT93 66 D8
Tullynacor Ⓣ BT93 100 E2
Tullynadall Ⓣ BT79 14 C3
Tullynadall Rd BT78 14 C2
Tullynadall West Ⓣ BT93 86 A6
Tullynagarn Ⓣ BT94 69 E3
Tullynageeran Cemy ★ BT75 107 A7
Tullynaglug Ⓣ BT94 105 F8
Tullynagowan Ⓣ
Enniskillen BT93 85 F7
Enniskillen BT94 106 C4
Tullynahunshin Ⓣ 122 A5
Tullynaloob Ⓣ BT93 50 F7
Tullynample Ⓣ 133 F3
Tullynashammer Ⓣ BT93 51 D8
Tullynashane Ⓣ BT68 111 D7
Tullynasiddagh Ⓣ 48 A2
Tullynasrahan Ⓣ BT93 84 E1
Tullyneagh Rd BT61 97 E1
Tullyneevin Ⓣ BT92 117 E3
Tullyneevin Cross Roads BT92 117 E3
Tullyneil Rd BT79 40 E1
Tullynichol Ⓣ BT61 97 F2
Tullynicholl La BT61 97 F2
Tullynincrin Ⓣ BT78 70 D5
Tully North Ⓣ BT94 105 E1
Tullynure Ⓣ
Cookstown BT80 31 D4
Dungannon BT70 61 A1
Tullynure Rd
Cookstown BT80 31 D4
Cookstown BT80 44 D1
Tullyodonnell Ⓣ
Dungannon BT70 43 F2
Dungannon BT71 61 D2
Tullyodonnell Rd BT70 43 F2
Tullyowen Ⓣ 1 A5
Tullyquin Glebe Ⓣ BT75 91 F5
Tullyrain Ⓣ BT94 88 F6
Tullyraw Ⓣ BT80 45 D5
Tully Rd BT78 38 C5
Tullyreagh Ⓣ BT94 106 B5
Tullyreas Ⓣ 133 E8
Tullyreavy Ⓣ BT70 43 E3
Tullyreavy Rd BT70 43 D2
Tullyremon Ⓣ BT68 96 F3
Tullyroan Ⓣ BT80 44 A4
TULLYROAN CORNER BT71 80 F1
Tullyroan Prim Sch BT71 80 E1
Tullyroan Rd BT71 80 F1
Tullyrossmearan Ⓣ BT93 100 B5
Tullyrush Ⓣ
Omagh BT78 56 C3
Omagh BT78 73 B4
Tullyrush Rd BT78 56 C2
Tullysaran Ⓣ BT61 97 E1
Tullysaran Rd BT61 97 F1
Tully South Ⓣ BT92 125 C7
Tullysranadeega Ⓣ BT93 84 A2
Tullytrasna Ⓣ BT93 66 C7
Tullyullagh Ⓣ BT75 90 C2
Tully Upper Ⓣ BT47 2 A7
Tullyvallen Rd BT70 77 F5
Tullyvally Ⓣ BT78 56 A1
Tullyvally Rd BT78 73 E8
Tullyvannon Ⓣ BT70 77 B5
Tullyvar Ⓣ BT70 94 D8
Tullyvar Rd BT70 76 D1
Tullyvarrid Ⓣ BT93 66 F8
Tullyveagh Ⓣ BT71 45 C5
Tullyveagh Rd BT80 45 C5
Tullyvernan Ⓣ BT76 92 E7
Tullyvocady Ⓣ BT93 49 B1
Tullyvogy Ⓣ BT93 48 E2
Tullywee Ⓣ BT78 71 B5
Tullyweel Ⓣ BT75 106 F8
Tullyweery Ⓣ BT71 45 D5
Tullywhisker Ⓣ BT82 12 B2
Tullywiggan Ⓣ BT80 44 F4
Tullywiggan Rd BT80 44 F4
Tullywinny Ⓣ BT70 94 D8
Tullywinny Rd BT70 94 D8
Tullywolly Ⓣ BT78 70 C3
Tulnacross Ⓣ BT80 43 B8
Tulnacross Rd
Cookstown BT80 30 B1
Cookstown BT80 43 C8
Tulnagall Ⓣ BT70 61 A4
Tulnagall Rd BT70 61 A4
Tulnashane Ⓣ BT81 33 A5
Tulnashane Rd BT81 33 B5
Tulnavern Ⓣ BT70 76 D8
Tulnavern Rd BT70 76 E6
Tummery Ⓣ BT78 71 A5
Tummery Cotts BT78 70 F6
Tummery Prim Sch BT78 71 A5
Tummery Rd BT78 70 D5
Tumpher Ⓣ BT71 62 C5
Tumpher Rd BT71 62 C4
Tunker Ⓣ 131 D3
Ture Ⓣ 112 E6
Turleenan Ⓣ BT71 80 B3
Turnabarson Ⓣ BT70 59 E7
Turnabarson Rd BT70 59 E8
Turnaface Rd BT80 31 F4
Turnberry Manor [1] BT82 134 C1
Turrasaglin Well ★ BT47 8 D7
Turry Ⓣ BT60 111 F8
Tursallagh Ⓣ BT79 58 C5
Tursallagh Rd BT79 58 C5
Tycanny Ⓣ BT70 75 B3
Tycanny Rd BT70 75 B2
TYNAN BT60 111 E3
Tynure BT80 31 E3
Tyrone Cty Hospl BT79 136 E4
Tyrone Irish Crystal ★ BT71 137 E7

U

Ulster Cotts BT82 12 C6
Ummer Ⓣ BT94 89 C1
Ummera Ⓣ BT92 129 E7
Umrycam Rd BT47 8 F8
Unagh Ⓣ BT80 31 D1
Unagh Rd BT80 31 D1
Underwood Pk [12] BT74 104 B6
Unicks Ⓣ BT71 62 D6
Union Pl
Cookstown BT80 135 D5
Dungannon BT70 137 C6
Union St BT80 135 D5
Unshinagh Ⓣ BT78 54 B8
Unshogagh Ⓣ 112 C4
Upper Alla Ⓣ BT47 3 F1
Upper Barnes Ⓣ BT79 16 C3
Upper Barratitoppy Ⓣ 109 B3
Upper Celtic Pk BT74 138 F4
Upper Cranlome Rd BT70 77 A8
Upper Drumnaspar Ⓣ BT79 15 F3
Upper Kildress Rd BT80 44 A6
Upper Main St BT82 134 D5
Upper or New Deer Park Ⓣ BT78 24 E6
Upper Parklands BT71 137 C3
Upper Strabane Rd BT81 22 E5
Upperthird Ⓣ BT81 22 F2
Upper Tully Rd BT47 1 F7
Uragh Ⓣ 122 F4
Urbal Ⓣ BT80 46 B6
Urbal La BT80 46 C6
Urbal or Mossfield Ⓣ BT94 87 F3
Urbal Rd
Cookstown BT80 46 B7
Cookstown BT80 46 B7
Urbalreagh Ⓣ
Dungannon BT71 45 D1
Strabane BT82 12 F1
Urbalreagh Rd BT82 12 F2
Urbalshinny Rd BT79 56 F3
Urney Ⓣ BT82 12 A7
Urney Glebe Ⓣ BT82 12 A8
Urney Rd BT82 4 C1
Urros Ⓣ BT93 86 B6
U S Grant Ancestral Home ★ BT70 77 C3
Usnagh Ⓣ BT79 57 D3
Uttony Ⓣ BT92 127 B4

V

Vale Gr BT71 62 A3
Vale The BT71 62 A3
Vaughan Holm Sports Complex BT78 25 B7
Verner Pk BT81 22 C1
VICTORIA BRIDGE BT82 12 E3
Victoria Rd
Dungannon BT71 137 C5
Londonderry BT47 2 A8
Strabane BT82 5 B8
Victoria Way BT71 137 C5
Viewfort BT71 137 E7
Villa Terr BT93 52 A1
Vine Rd BT82 1 E3

W

Walker Meml Prim Sch BT70 78 D8
Wallace Hts BT47 1 F7
Warren Rd BT82 2 F3
Washing Bay Rd
Coalisland BT71 62 C3
Dungannon BT71 63 A3
Washingford Row BT71 137 C4
Waterloo Pl BT71 137 D4
Water St
Enniskillen BT74 138 D5
Lisnaskea BT92 117 D3
Water Wall BT82 134 D5
Waterworks Rd BT79 39 B4
Watson Pk BT78 38 D3
Watts Pk BT71 80 A5
Weavers La BT94 105 A3
Wellbourne Cres BT80 46 B7
Wellbrook Ave BT70 137 A6
Wellbrook Beetling Mill ★ BT80 43 E8
Wellbrook Manor BT70 137 A7
Wellbrook Rd BT80 43 F8
Wellington Pl
Dungannon BT71 137 D4
[3] Enniskillen BT74 138 C5
Wellington Rd BT74 138 C4
Wesley St BT74 138 C5
Westbury Cl BT80 135 B3
Westbury Cres BT80 135 B3
Westbury Dr BT80 135 B3
Westbury Gdns BT80 135 B3
Westbury Way BT80 135 B3
West Island Ⓣ BT94 116 B3
Westland Cres BT80 135 B5
Westland Ct BT80 135 C3
Westland Dr BT80 135 B5
Westland Pk BT80 135 B5
Westland Rd BT80 135 B5
Westland Rd S BT80 135 B4
West Rd BT78 25 B4
West St BT71 62 D7
Weststreetdrive BT71 62 D7
West Tullyhona Ⓣ BT92 114 A3
Westview Terr BT82 12 D5
West View Terr BT82 12 D5
Westville BT74 138 E5
Westway BT82 12 D5
Whaley Terr BT74 138 B5
Wheathill Ⓣ BT92 113 E4
Wheathill Glebe Ⓣ BT93 85 F7
Whilliter Ⓣ BT94 115 E4
Whinnigan Glebe Ⓣ BT74 116 B8
Whinn View BT82 134 C2
Whin Rd BT82 1 E1
Whisker Rd BT82 12 C2
Whitebridge Rd
Dungannon BT70 76 C6
Omagh BT79 58 E4
White Fort Cashel ★ BT82 5 D7
Whitehall St 127 F2
Whitehill Ⓣ BT74 102 F6
Whitehill North Ⓣ BT94 69 C3
Whitehill Rd BT78 37 A7
Whitehill South Ⓣ BT94 87 F5
Whitehouse Ⓣ
Carrigans 1 D8
Castlederg BT81 23 C4
Whitehouse Rd BT81 23 C3
Whitelough Rd BT69 95 E4
Whiterock Pk BT81 22 D5
Whiterocks Ⓣ BT93 67 B1
Whites Rd BT70 77 D6
Whitetown Ⓣ BT71 61 F6
Whitetown Rd BT71 61 F6
Wickham Pl BT74 138 E4
Willand Cres [8] BT75 107 C8
Williams St BT70 137 B5
William St
[13] Castlederg BT81 22 E5
Cookstown BT80 135 D5
Willmount Ⓣ BT78 36 A4
Willmount Rd BT78 36 A4
Willoughby Ct BT74 138 A6
Willoughby Pl BT74 138 B6
Willow Cl BT70 79 A8
Willow Cres BT70 79 A8
Willowcrest BT81 22 E6
Willow Dr BT70 79 A8
Willow Gdns BT70 79 A8
Willowmount Ave BT79 136 D7
Willowmount Cl BT79 136 D6
Willowmount Pk BT79 136 D6
Willow Rd BT82 1 D2
Willows The
Dungannon BT70 137 A7
Enniskillen BT74 138 F5
Sion Mills BT82 12 E5
Willow Vale [6] BT74 104 B6
Wilson's Hill Rd BT60 111 F6
Wilsontown Rd BT60 97 B2
Windmill Ct BT71 137 B5
Windmill Dr
Dungannon BT71 137 B5
Enniskillen BT74 138 A5
Windmill Hill Ⓣ BT74 138 B5
Windmill Hill Rd BT71 137 B4
Windmill Hts
Dungannon BT71 137 E4
Enniskillen BT74 138 B5
Windmill Integrated Prim Sch BT71 137 C4
Windmill Rd BT74 138 A5
Windsor Cres BT80 135 E5
Windsor Pl BT80 46 B7
Windsor Terr BT80 46 B7
Windsor Villas BT80 46 B7
Windyhaw Rd BT78 24 F8
Windyhill Ⓣ BT82 5 E7
Windyhill Rd BT82 5 E7
Windy Ridge BT74 86 D2
Winters Ct [1] BT79 136 F3
Winters Gdns BT79 136 F3
Winters Gr BT79 136 E3
Winters La BT79 136 E3
Woaghternerry BT74 104 B7
Woaghternerry Ⓣ BT74 104 B7
Wolfe Tones GAC BT78 36 F2
Woodbank Rd BT79 56 C8
Woodbrook Ⓣ BT78 25 F6
Woodburn Cres BT71 137 B5
Woodbury Hts BT82 5 A5
Woodend Ⓣ BT82 5 A5
Woodend Pk BT82 134 F8
Woodend Rd BT82 5 A5
Woodglen Cres BT80 135 B7
Woodhill Ⓣ
Dungannon BT71 61 E5
Enniskillen BT93 66 F8
Woodhouse Rd BT71 46 E1
Wood Island Ⓣ 134 C8
Woodland Dr BT80 135 E5
Woodland Rd BT79 26 C6
Woodlawn Dr BT70 137 C6
Woodlawn Pk BT70 137 C6
Woodlough Rd BT70 78 D5
Wood Rd The BT71 81 C7
Woodside Ⓣ BT81 21 F1
Woodside Ave BT79 136 C5
Woodside Rd BT81 21 F2
Woodvale Ave BT79 136 E4
Woodvale Pk BT71 137 E4
Woodview BT74 138 F6
Woodview Cres BT78 71 D1

Y

Yellow Ford La BT61 98 D3
Yoan Rd BT74 138 C7
Young Cres BT81 22 E5

Name and Address	Telephone	Page	Grid reference

PHILIP'S MAPS

the Gold Standard for drivers

◆ **Philip's street atlases cover all of England, Wales, Northern Ireland and much of Scotland**

◆ Every named street is shown, including alleys, lanes and walkways

◆ Thousands of additional features marked: stations, public buildings, car parks, places of interest

◆ Route-planning maps to get you close to your destination

◆ Postcodes on the maps and in the index

◆ Widely used by the emergency services, transport companies and local authorities

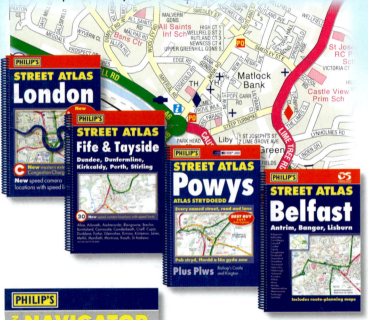

For national mapping, choose **Philip's Navigator Britain** the most detailed road atlas available of England, Wales and Scotland. Hailed by Auto Express as 'the ultimate road atlas', the atlas shows every road and lane in Britain.

'The ultimate in UK mapping'
The Sunday Times

Street atlases currently available

England

Bedfordshire and Luton	Surrey
Berkshire	East Sussex
Birmingham and West Midlands	West Sussex
	Tyne and Wear
Bristol and Bath	Warwickshire and Coventry
Buckinghamshire and Milton Keynes	Wiltshire and Swindon
	Worcestershire
Cambridgeshire and Peterborough	East Yorkshire Northern Lincolnshire
Cheshire	North Yorkshire
Cornwall	South Yorkshire
Cumbria	West Yorkshire
Derbyshire	
Devon	**Wales**
Dorset	Anglesey, Conwy and Gwynedd
County Durham and Teesside	Cardiff, Swansea and The Valleys
Essex	Carmarthenshire, Pembrokeshire and Swansea
North Essex	
South Essex	
Gloucestershire and Bristol	Ceredigion and South Gwynedd
Hampshire	Denbighshire, Flintshire, Wrexham
North Hampshire	
South Hampshire	Herefordshire Monmouthshire
Herefordshire Monmouthshire	Powys
Hertfordshire	
Isle of Wight	**Scotland**
Kent	Aberdeenshire
East Kent	Ayrshire
West Kent	Dumfries and Galloway
Lancashire	Edinburgh and East Central Scotland
Leicestershire and Rutland	Fife and Tayside
Lincolnshire	Glasgow and West Central Scotland
Liverpool and Merseyside	Inverness and Moray
London	Lanarkshire
Greater Manchester	Scottish Borders
Norfolk	
Northamptonshire	**Northern Ireland**
Northumberland	County Antrim and County Londonderry
Nottinghamshire	County Armagh and County Down
Oxfordshire	
Shropshire	Belfast
Somerset	County Tyrone and County Fermanagh
Staffordshire	
Suffolk	

How to order

Philip's maps and atlases are available from bookshops, motorway services and petrol stations. You can order direct from the publisher by phoning **0207 531 8473** or online at **www.philips-maps.co.uk**
For bulk orders only, e-mail philips@philips-maps.co.uk